MICROSOFT CERTIFIED SYSTEMS ENGINEER

# MCSE Certification

# Test Yourself™

# Practice Exams

Syngress Media, Inc.

Osborne McGraw-Hill

Berkeley  New York  St. Louis  San Francisco  Auckland  Bogotá  Hamburg  London  Madrid  Mexico City
Milan  Montreal  New Delhi  Panama City  Paris  São Paulo  Singapore  Sydney  Tokyo  Toronto

Osborne McGraw-Hill
2600 Tenth Street
Berkeley, California 94710
U.S.A.

For information on translations or book distributors outside the U.S.A.,
or to arrange bulk purchase discounts for sales promotions, premiums, or
fund-raisers, please contact Osborne/**McGraw-Hill** at the above address.

MCSE Certification Test Yourself™ Practice Exams

4567890  AGM AGM  019876543210

ISBN 0-07-211854-7

| | | |
|---|---|---|
| **Publisher** | **Copy Editor** | **Illustrators** |
| Brandon A. Nordin | Kathleen Faughnan | Lance Ravella |
| | | Brian Wells |
| **Editor-in-Chief** | **Proofreader** | |
| Scott Rogers | Carroll Proffitt | **Series Design** |
| | | Roberta Steele |
| **Acquisitions Editor** | **Computer Designers** | Arlette Crosland |
| Gareth Hancock | Ann Sellers | |
| | Mickey Galicia | **Cover Design** |
| **Project Editor** | Roberta Steele | Regan Honda |
| Cynthia Douglas | | |
| | | **Editorial Management** |
| **Technical Editor** | | Syngress Media, Inc. |
| D. Lynn White | | |

# FOREWORD

## From Global Knowledge Network

At Global Knowledge Network we strive to support the multiplicity of learning styles required by our students to achieve success as technical professionals. In this series of books, it is our intention to offer the reader a valuable tool for successful completion of the MCSE Certification Exam.

As the world's largest IT training company, Global Knowledge Network is uniquely positioned to offer these books. The expertise gained each year from providing instructor-led training to hundreds of thousands of students worldwide has been captured in book form to enhance your learning experience. We hope that the quality of these books demonstrates our commitment to your lifelong learning success. Whether you choose to learn through the written word, computer-based training, Web delivery, or instructor-led training, Global Knowledge Network is committed to providing you the very best in each of those categories. For those of you who know Global Knowledge Network, or those of you who have just found us for the first time, our goal is to be your lifelong competency partner.

Thank you for the opportunity to serve you. We look forward to serving your needs again in the future.

Warmest regards,

Duncan Anderson
Chief Operating Officer, Global Knowledge Network

## ABOUT SYNGRESS MEDIA

**Syngress Media** creates books and software for Information Technology professionals seeking skill enhancement and career advancement. Its products are designed to comply with vendor and industry standard course curricula, and are optimized for certification exam preparation. Visit the Syngress Web site at www.syngress.com.

## ABOUT THE CONTRIBUTORS

**Stace Cunningham** is a Systems Engineer with SDC Consulting in Biloxi, MS. SDC Consulting specializes in the design, engineering, and installation of networks. Stace received his MCSE in October 1996, and is also certified as an IBM Certified LAN Server Engineer, IBM Certified OS/2 Engineer, IBM Certified LAN Server Administrator, Microsoft Certified Product Specialist, IBM Certified LAN Server Instructor, and IBM Certified OS/2 Instructor.

Stace has participated as a Technical Contributor for the IIS 3.0 exam, SMS 1.2 exam, Proxy Server 1.0 exam, Exchange Server 5.0 exam, Exchange Server 5.5 exam, Proxy Server 2.0 exam, IIS 4.0 exam, IEAK exam, and the revised Windows 95 exam. He recently was an instrumental force in the design and engineering of a 1,700-node Windows NT network that is located in more than 20 buildings at Keesler Air Force Base in Mississippi. Among his current projects is assisting in the design and implementation of a 10,000-node Windows NT network, also located at Keesler Air Force Base.

His wife Martha and daughter Marissa are very supportive of the time he spends on the computers located throughout his house.

**Mike Swisher** (MCSE) is a 1st Lieutenant in the United States Air Force. He is a communications officer serving at Keesler Air Force Base in Mississippi. His current duties have him designing a networking infrastructure with NT as the primary network operating system for the entire base (over 10,000 users). He has received numerous awards in his three short years in the military. Two years in a row he was selected as the 81st Training Support Squadron Company Grade Officer of the Year. He also distinguished himself by graduating top in his class at the Air Force's Basic Communications Officer Course. He enjoys water skiing and—of course—computers. His hometown is Rock Hill, SC.

**Michael Cross** is an MCSE, MCP Specialist: Internet, Computer Programmer, Network Support Specialist, and an Instructor at private colleges. He is the owner of KnightWare; a company that provides consulting, programming, network support, web page design, computer training, and various other services. In his spare time, he has been a freelance writer for several years, in genres of fiction and non-fiction. He currently lives in London, Ontario Canada.

**Harry Flowers** (MCSE, MCPS) has been a Systems Administrator for over fifteen years. He has a B.S. degree in Mathematics/Computer Science from Rhodes College, and currently works as one of a small group of systems administrators responsible for central computing systems at the University of Memphis in Memphis, Tennessee. He supports several Windows NT servers for both academic and administrative systems as well as other Microsoft BackOffice products, such as Exchange and Systems Management Server. Harry is also a Windows NT consultant and trainer for Open Road Technologies.

## Technical Review by:

**D. Lynn White** (MCPS, MCSE, MCT) is president of Independent Network Consultants, Inc. She is a technical author, editor, trainer, and consultant in the field of networking and computer-related technologies. She has been delivering mainframe, Microsoft-official curriculum and other networking courses across the country for over eleven years.

# ACKNOWLEDGMENTS

We would like to thank the following people:

- Richard Kristof of Global Knowledge Network for championing the series and providing us access to some great people and information. And to Patrick Von Schlag, Robin Yunker, David Mantica, Stacey Cannon, and Kevin Murray for all their cooperation.

- To all the incredibly hard-working folks at Osborne/McGraw-Hill: Brandon Nordin, Scott Rogers, and Gareth Hancock for their help in launching a great series and being solid team players. In addition, Cynthia Douglas, Steve Emry, Anne Ellingsen, and Bernadette Jurich for their help in fine-tuning the book.

# CONTENTS

## 2   Windows NT Server 4.0

## 3   Networking Essentials

## 4    Windows NT Server 4.0 in the Enterprise

## 5 Test Yourself: Practice Exams

We built this book for a specific reason. Every time we asked MCSEs and MCSE candidates what they wanted in their study materials, they answered "More questions!" Based on that resounding request, we built a book full of questions on the core exams so you can test yourself to your heart's desire.

# In This Book

This book is organized in parts, by exam. We cover each of the four core exams in its own module, and we also have a fifth part—the Test Yourself module.

## The Q&A Modules

You will find one Q&A module for Workstation 4.0, Server 4.0, Networking Essentials and Server 4.0 in the Enterprise. Each module has 300 original questions, followed by an answer section that has full explanations of the correct choices.

Each module is divided into categories, so you will cover every topic tested by Microsoft. Each topic is a heading within the chapter, so you can study by topic if you like. Should you find you need further review on any particular topic, you will find that the topic headings correspond to the chapters of individual books within Osborne/McGraw-Hill's Certification Press series (*MCSE Windows NT Workstation 4.0 Study Guide, MCSE Windows NT Server 4.0 Study Guide,* etc.) Want to simulate an actual exam? The section "The Test Yourself Modules" explains how.

In addition, throughout the Q&A modules, we have sprinkled helpful notes in the form of Exam Watches and Q&A scenarios:

■ **Exam Watch** notes call attention to information about, and potential pitfalls in, the exam. These helpful hints are written by MCSEs who have taken the exams and have received their certification—who better to tell you what to worry about? They know what you're about to go through!

■ **Q&A** sections lay out problems and solutions in a quick-read format.

## QUESTIONS AND ANSWERS

| | |
|---|---|
| I am installing NT and I have HPFS… | Convert it before you upgrade. NT 4 does not like HPFS. |
| I do not require the capability to assign permissions or use compression… | Use FAT. Dead giveaway. |
| My hard disk is 120MB… | Use FAT. NTFS is not as efficient for a drive that size. |

## The Test Yourself Modules

If you have had your fill of exam questions, answers, and explanations, the time has come to test your knowledge. Or maybe you want to start with one of the Test Yourself modules to see where your strengths and weaknesses are, and then review only certain topics. Either way, turn to the final part of the book, the Test Yourself section. In this section we actually simulate the exams. We have given you two practice tests per exam, with the number of randomly ordered questions corresponding to the actual exam. Lock yourself in your office or clear the kitchen table, set a timer, and jump in.

# MCSE Certification

Although you've obviously picked up this book to assess your skills or to prepare for taking the core MCSE exams, we'd like to spend some time covering what you need to complete in order to attain MCSE status. Because this information can be found on the Microsoft web site, www.microsoft.com/train_cert, we've repeated only some of the more important information. You should review the train_cert site and check out Microsoft's information, along with their list of reasons to become an MCSE, including job advancement.

As you probably know, to attain MCSE status, you must pass a total of six exams—four requirements and two electives. One required exam is on networking basics, one on NT Server, one on NT Server in the Enterprise, and one on a client (either Windows NT Workstation or Windows 95). There are several electives from which to choose—and many of these electives also count toward Microsoft's new MCSE+Internet (MCSE+I) certification. Indeed, the most popular electives now include the Internet Information Server 4 exam, which counts toward both certifications. The following table lists the exam names, their corresponding course numbers, and whether they are required or an elective. We're showing you the NT 4.0 track and not the NT 3.51 track (which is still offered).

| Exam Number | Exam Name | Required or Elective |
|---|---|---|
| 70-58 | Networking Essentials | Required |
| 70-63 | Implementing and Supporting Microsoft Windows 95 | Required (either 70-63 or 70-73) |
| 70-67 | Implementing and Supporting Microsoft Windows NT Server 4.0 | Required |
| 70-68 | Implementing and Supporting Microsoft Windows NT Server 4.0 in the Enterprise | Required |
| 70-73 | Implementing and Supporting Microsoft Windows NT Workstation 4.0 | Required (either 70-73 or 70-63) |
| 70-14 | Supporting Microsoft System Management Server 1.2 | Elective |
| 70-59 | Internetworking with Microsoft TCP/IP on Windows NT 4.0 | Elective |
| 70-81 | Implementing and Supporting Microsoft Exchange Server 5.5 | Elective |
| 70-85 | Implementing and Supporting Microsoft SNA Server 4.0 | Elective |
| 70-87 | Implementing and Supporting Microsoft Internet Information Server 4.0 | Elective |

| Exam Number | Exam Name | Required or Elective |
|---|---|---|
| 70-88 | Implementing and Supporting Microsoft Proxy Server 2.0 | Elective |
| 70-28 | System Administration for Microsoft SQL Server 7.0 | Elective |
| 70-29 | Implementing a Database Design on SQL Server 7.0 | Elective |

## The Global Knowledge Network Web Site

Global Knowledge Network invites you to become an active member of the Access Global web site. This site is an online mall and an information repository that you'll find invaluable. You can access many types of products to assist you in your preparation for the exams, and you'll be able to participate in forums, on-line discussions, and threaded discussions. No other book brings you unlimited access to such a resource. You'll find more information about this site in Appendix A.

# How to Take a Microsoft Certification Examination

**by John C. Phillips, Vice President of Test Development, Self Test Software**
**(Self Test's PEP is the official Microsoft practice test.)**

## Good News and Bad News

If you are new to Microsoft certification, we have some good news and some bad news. The good news, of course, is that Microsoft certification is one of the most valuable credentials you can earn. It sets you apart from the crowd, and marks you as a valuable asset to your employer. You will gain the respect of your peers, and Microsoft certification can have a wonderful effect on your income.

The bad news is that Microsoft certification tests are not easy. You may think you will read through some study material, memorize a few facts, and pass the Microsoft examinations. After all, these certification exams are just computer-based, multiple-choice tests, so they must be easy. If you believe this, you are wrong. Unlike many "multiple guess" tests you have been exposed to in school, the questions on Microsoft certification examinations go beyond simple factual knowledge.

The purpose of this introduction is to teach you how to take a Microsoft certification examination. To be successful, you need to know something about the purpose and structure of these tests. We will also look at the latest innovations in Microsoft testing. Using *simulations* and *adaptive testing*, Microsoft is enhancing both the validity and security of the certification process. These factors have some important effects on how you should prepare for an exam, as well as your approach to each question during the test.

We will begin by looking at the purpose, focus, and structure of Microsoft certification tests, and examine the effect these factors have on the kinds of questions you will face on your certification exams. We will define the structure of examination questions and investigate some common formats. Next, we will present a strategy for answering these questions. Finally, we will give some specific guidelines on what you should do on the day of your test.

# Why Vendor Certification?

The Microsoft Certified Professional program, like the certification programs from Lotus, Novell, Oracle, and other software vendors, is maintained for the ultimate purpose of increasing the corporation's profits. A successful vendor certification program accomplishes this goal by helping to create a pool of experts in a company's software, and by "branding" these experts so that companies using the software can identify them.

We know that vendor certification has become increasingly popular in the last few years because it helps employers find qualified workers, and because it helps software vendors like Microsoft sell their products. But why vendor certification rather than a more traditional approach like a college degree in computer science? A college education is a broadening and enriching experience, but a degree in computer science does not prepare students for most jobs in the IT industry.

A common truism in our business states, "If you are out of the IT industry for three years and want to return, you have to start over." The problem, of course, is *timeliness*; if a first-year student learns about a specific computer program, it probably will no longer be in wide use when he or she graduates. Although some colleges are trying to integrate Microsoft certification into their curriculum, the problem is not really a flaw in higher education, but a characteristic of the IT industry. Computer software is changing so rapidly that a four-year college just can't keep up.

A marked characteristic of the Microsoft certification program is an emphasis on performing specific job tasks rather than merely gathering knowledge. It may come as a shock, but most potential employers do not care how much you know about the theory of operating systems, networking, or database design. As one IT manager put it, "I don't really care what my employees know about the theory of our network. We don't need someone to sit at a desk and think about it. We need people who can actually do something to make it work better."

You should not think that this attitude is some kind of anti-intellectual revolt against "book learning." Knowledge is a necessary prerequisite, but it is not enough. More than one company has hired a computer science graduate as a network administrator, only to learn that the new employee has no idea how to add users, assign permissions, or perform the other day-to-day tasks necessary to maintain a network. This brings us to the second major characteristic of Microsoft certification that affects the questions you must be prepared to answer. In addition to timeliness, Microsoft certification is also job task oriented.

The timeliness of Microsoft's certification program is obvious, and is inherent in the fact that you will be tested on current versions of software in wide use today. The job task orientation of Microsoft certification is almost as obvious, but testing real-world job skills using a computer-based test is not easy.

## Computerized Testing

Considering the popularity of Microsoft certification, and the fact that certification candidates are spread around the world, the only practical way to administer tests for the certification program is through Sylvan Prometric testing centers. Sylvan Prometric provides proctored testing services for Microsoft, Oracle, Novell, Lotus, and the A+ computer technician certification. Although the IT industry accounts for much of Sylvan's revenue, the company provides services for a number of other businesses and organizations, such as FAA pre-flight pilot tests. In fact, most companies that need secure test delivery over a wide geographic area use the services of Sylvan Prometric. In addition to delivery, Sylvan Prometric also scores the tests and provides statistical feedback on the performance of each test question to the companies and organizations that use their services.

Typically, several hundred questions are developed for a new Microsoft certification examination. The questions are first reviewed by a number of subject matter experts for technical accuracy, and then are presented in a beta test. The beta test may last for several hours, due to the large number of questions. After a few weeks, Microsoft Certification uses the statistical feedback from Sylvan to check the performance of the beta questions.

Questions are discarded if most test takers get them right (too easy) or wrong (too difficult), and a number of other statistical measures are taken of each question. Although the scope of our discussion precludes a rigorous treatment of question analysis, you should be aware that Microsoft and other vendors spend a great deal of time and effort making sure their examination questions are valid. In addition to the obvious desire for quality, the fairness of a vendor's certification program must be legally defensible.

The questions that survive statistical analysis form the pool of questions for the final certification examination.

# Test Structure

The kind of test we are most familiar with is known as a *form* test. For Microsoft certification, a form usually consists of 50–70 questions and takes 60–90 minutes to complete. If there are 240 questions in the final pool for an examination, then four forms can be created. Thus, candidates who retake the test probably will not see the same questions.

Other variations are possible. From the same pool of 240 questions, *five* forms can be created, each containing 40 unique questions (200 questions) and 20 questions selected at random from the remaining 40.

The questions in a Microsoft form test are equally weighted. This means they all count the same when the test is scored. An interesting and useful characteristic of a form test is that you can mark a question you have doubts about as you take the test. Assuming you have time left when you finish all the questions, you can return and spend more time on the questions you have marked as doubtful.

Microsoft may soon implement *adaptive* testing. To use this interactive technique, a form test is first created and administered to several thousand certification candidates. The statistics generated are used to assign a weight, or difficulty level, for each question. For example, the questions in a form might be divided into levels one through five, with level one questions being the easiest and level five the hardest.

When an adaptive test begins, the candidate is first given a level three question. If it is answered correctly, a question from the next higher level is presented, and an incorrect response results in a question from the next lower level. When 15–20 questions have been answered in this manner, the scoring algorithm is able to predict, with a high degree of statistical certainty, whether the candidate would pass or fail if all the questions in the form were answered. When the required degree of certainty is attained, the test ends and the candidate receives a pass/fail grade.

Adaptive testing has some definite advantages for everyone involved in the certification process. Adaptive tests allow Sylvan Prometric to deliver more tests with the same resources, as certification candidates often are in and out in 30 minutes or less. For Microsoft, adaptive testing means that fewer test questions are exposed to each candidate, and this can enhance the security, and therefore the validity, of certification tests.

One possible problem you may have with adaptive testing is that you are not allowed to mark and revisit questions. Since the adaptive algorithm is interactive, and all questions but the first are selected on the basis of your response to the previous question, it is not possible to skip a particular question or change an answer.

# Question Types

Computerized test questions can be presented in a number of ways. Some of the possible formats are used on Microsoft certification examinations, and some are not.

### True/False

We are all familiar with True/False questions, but because of the inherent 50 percent chance of guessing the correct answer, you will not see questions of this type on Microsoft certification exams.

### Multiple Choice

The majority of Microsoft certification questions are in the multiple-choice format, with either a single correct answer or multiple correct answers. One interesting variation on multiple-choice questions with multiple correct answers is whether or not the candidate is told how many answers are correct.

EXAMPLE:

Which two files can be altered to configure the MS-DOS environment? (Choose two.)

Or

Which files can be altered to configure the MS-DOS environment? (Choose all that apply.)

You may see both variations on Microsoft certification examinations, but the trend seems to be toward the first type, where candidates are told explicitly how many answers are correct. Questions of the "choose all that apply" variety are more difficult, and can be merely confusing.

### Graphical Questions

One or more graphical elements are sometimes used as exhibits to help present or clarify an exam question. These elements may take the form of a network diagram, pictures of networking components, or screen shots from the software on which you are being tested. It is often easier to present the concepts required for a complex performance-based scenario with a graphic than with words.

Test questions known as *hotspots* actually incorporate graphics as part of the answer. These questions ask the certification candidate to click on a location or graphical element to answer the question. As an example, you might be shown the diagram of a network and asked to click on an appropriate location for a router. The answer is correct if the candidate clicks within the *hotspot* that defines the correct location.

### Free Response Questions

Another kind of question you sometimes see on Microsoft certification examinations requires a *free response* or type-in answer. An example of this type of question might present a TCP/IP network scenario and ask the candidate to calculate and enter the correct subnet mask in dotted decimal notation.

## Knowledge-Based and Performance-Based Questions

Microsoft Certification develops a blueprint for each Microsoft certification examination with input from subject matter experts. This blueprint defines the content areas and objectives for each test, and each test question is created to test a specific objective. The basic information from the examination blueprint can be found on Microsoft's web site in the Exam Prep Guide for each test.

Psychometricians (psychologists who specialize in designing and analyzing tests) categorize test questions as knowledge-based or performance-based. As the names imply, knowledge-based questions are designed to test knowledge, while performance-based questions are designed to test performance.

Some objectives demand a knowledge-based question. For example, objectives that use verbs like *list* and *identify* tend to test only what you know, not what you can do.

EXAMPLE:
Objective: Identify the MS-DOS configuration files.
Which two files can be altered to configure the MS-DOS environment? (Choose two.)

    A. COMMAND.COM

    B. AUTOEXEC.BAT

    C. IO.SYS

    D. CONFIG.SYS
    Correct answers: B,D

Other objectives use action verbs like *install, configure,* and *troubleshoot* to define job tasks. These objectives can often be tested with either a knowledge-based question or a performance-based question.

EXAMPLE:
Objective:  Configure an MS-DOS installation appropriately using the PATH statement in AUTOEXEX.BAT.
Knowledge-based question:
What is the correct syntax to set a path to the D:\APP directory in AUTOEXEC.BAT?

    A. SET PATH EQUAL TO D:\APP

    B. PATH D:\APP

XXVI MCSE Certification Test Yourself Practice Exams

C. SETPATH D:\APP

D. D:\APP EQUALS PATH

**Correct answer: B**

Performance-based question:

Your company uses several DOS accounting applications that access a group of common utility programs. What is the best strategy for configuring the computers in the accounting department so that the accounting applications will always be able to access the utility programs?

A. Store all the utilities on a single floppy disk, and make a copy of the disk for each computer in the accounting department.

B. Copy all the utilities to a directory on the C: drive of each computer in the accounting department, and add a PATH statement pointing to this directory in the AUTOEXEC.BAT files.

C. Copy all the utilities to all application directories on each computer in the accounting department.

D. Place all the utilities in the C:\DOS directory on each computer, because the C:\DOS directory is automatically included in the PATH statement when AUTOEXEC.BAT is executed.

**Correct answer: B**

Even in this simple example, the superiority of the performance-based question is obvious. Whereas the knowledge-based question asks for a single fact, the performance-based question presents a real-life situation and requires that you make a decision based on this scenario. Thus, performance-based questions give more bang (validity) for the test author's buck (individual question).

# Testing Job Performance

We have said that Microsoft certification focuses on timeliness and the ability to perform job tasks. We have also introduced the concept of performance-based questions, but even performance-based multiple-choice questions do not really measure performance. Another strategy is needed to test job skills.

Given unlimited resources, it is not difficult to test job skills. In an ideal world, Microsoft would fly MCP candidates to Redmond, place them in a controlled environment with a team of experts, and ask them to plan, install, maintain, and troubleshoot a Windows network. In a few days at most, the experts could reach a valid decision as to whether each candidate should or should not be granted MCSE status. Needless to say, this is not likely to happen.

Closer to reality, another way to test performance is by using the actual software, and creating a testing program to present tasks and automatically grade a candidate's performance when the tasks are completed. This *cooperative* approach would be practical in some testing situations, but the same test that is presented to MCP candidates in Boston must also be available in Bahrain and Botswana. Many Sylvan Prometric testing locations around the world cannot run 32-bit applications, much less provide the complex networked solutions required by cooperative testing applications.

The most workable solution for measuring performance in today's testing environment is a *simulation* program. When the program is launched during a test, the candidate sees a simulation of the actual software that looks, and behaves, just like the real thing. When the testing software presents a task, the simulation program is launched and the candidate performs the required task. The testing software then grades the candidate's performance on the required task and moves to the next question. In this way, a 16-bit simulation program can mimic the look and feel of 32-bit operating systems, a complicated network, or even the entire Internet.

Microsoft has introduced simulation questions on the certification examination for Internet Information Server 4.0. Simulation questions provide many advantages over other testing methodologies, and simulations are expected to become increasingly important in the Microsoft certification program. For example, studies have shown that there is a very high correlation between the ability to perform simulated tasks on a computer-based test and the ability to perform the actual job tasks. Thus, simulations enhance the validity of the certification process.

Another truly wonderful benefit of simulations is in the area of test security. It is just not possible to cheat on a simulation question. In fact, you will be told exactly what tasks you are expected to perform on the test. How can a certification candidate cheat? By learning to perform the tasks? What a concept!

# Study Strategies

There are appropriate ways to study for the different types of questions you will see on a Microsoft certification examination.

## Knowledge-Based Questions

Knowledge-based questions require that you memorize facts. There are hundreds of facts inherent in every content area of every Microsoft certification examination. There are several keys to memorizing facts:

- **Repetition** The more times your brain is exposed to a fact, the more likely you are to remember it.

- **Association** Connecting facts within a logical framework makes them easier to remember.

- **Motor Association** It is often easier to remember something if you write it down or perform some other physical act, like clicking on a practice test answer.

We have said that the emphasis of Microsoft certification is job performance, and that there are very few knowledge-based questions on Microsoft certification exams. Why should you waste a lot of time learning file names, IP address formulas, and other minutiae? Read on.

## Performance-Based Questions

Most of the questions you will face on a Microsoft certification exam are performance-based scenario questions. We have discussed the superiority of these questions over simple knowledge-based questions, but you should remember that the job task orientation of Microsoft certification extends the knowledge you need to pass the exams; it does not replace this knowledge. Therefore, the first step in preparing for scenario questions is to absorb as many facts relating to the exam content areas as you can. In other words, go back to the previous section and follow the steps to prepare for an exam composed of knowledge-based questions.

The second step is to familiarize yourself with the format of the questions you are likely to see on the exam. You can do this by answering the questions in this study guide, by using Microsoft assessment tests, or by using practice tests. The day of your test is not the time to be surprised by the convoluted construction of Microsoft exam questions.

For example, one of Microsoft Certification's favorite formats of late takes the following form:

**Scenario:** You have a network with...

**Primary Objective:** You want to...

**Secondary Objective:** You also want to...

**Proposed Solution:** Do this...

What does the proposed solution accomplish?

    A. satisfies the primary and the secondary objective

    B. satisfies the primary but not the secondary objective

    C. satisfies the secondary but not the primary objective

    D. satisfies neither the primary nor the secondary objective

This kind of question, with some variation, is seen on many Microsoft Certification examinations.

At best, these performance-based scenario questions really do test certification candidates at a higher cognitive level than knowledge-based questions. At worst, these questions can test your reading comprehension and test-taking ability rather than your ability to use Microsoft products. Be sure to get in the habit of reading the question carefully to determine what is being asked.

The third step in preparing for Microsoft scenario questions is to adopt the following attitude: Multiple-choice questions aren't really performance-based. It is all a cruel lie. These scenario questions are just knowledge-based questions with a little story wrapped around them.

To answer a scenario question, you have to sift through the story to the underlying facts of the situation, and apply your knowledge to determine the correct answer. This may sound silly at first, but the process we go through in solving real-life problems is quite similar. The key concept is that every scenario question (and every real-life problem) has a fact at its center, and if we can identify that fact, we can answer the question.

### Simulations

Simulation questions really do measure your ability to perform job tasks. You must be able to perform the specified tasks. There are two ways to prepare for simulation questions:

1. Get experience with the actual software. If you have the resources, this is a great way to prepare for simulation questions.

2. Use official Microsoft practice tests. Practice tests are available that provide practice with the same simulation engine used on Microsoft certification exams. This approach has the added advantage of grading your efforts.

# Signing Up

Signing up to take a Microsoft certification examination is easy. Sylvan operators in each country can schedule tests at any testing center. There are, however, a few things you should know:

1. If you call Sylvan during a busy time period, get a cup of coffee first, because you may be in for a long wait. Sylvan does an excellent job, but everyone in the world seems to want to sign up for a test on Monday morning.

2. You will need your social security number or some other unique identifier to sign up for a Sylvan test, so have it at hand.

3. Pay for your test by credit card if at all possible. This makes things easier, and you can even schedule tests for the same day you call, if space is available at your local testing center.

4. Know the number and title of the test you want to take before you call. This is not essential, and the Sylvan operators will help you if they can. Having this information in advance, however, speeds up the registration process.

# Taking the Test

Teachers have always told you not to try to cram for examinations, because it does no good. Sometimes they lied. If you are faced with a knowledge-based test requiring only that you regurgitate facts, cramming can mean the difference between passing and failing. This is not the case, however, with Microsoft certification exams. If you don't know it the night before, don't bother to stay up and cram.

Instead, create a schedule and stick to it. Plan your study time carefully, and do not schedule your test until you think you are ready to succeed. Follow these guidelines on the day of your exam:

1. Get a good night's sleep. The scenario questions you will face on a Microsoft certification examination require a clear head.

2. Remember to take two forms of identification—at least one with a picture. A driver's license with your picture, and social security or credit cards are acceptable.

3. Leave home in time to arrive at your testing center a few minutes early. It is not a good idea to feel rushed as you begin your exam.

4. Do not spend too much time on any one question. If you are taking a form test, take your best guess and mark the question so you can come back to it if you have time. You cannot mark and revisit questions on an adaptive test, so you must do your best on each question as you go.

5. If you do not know the answer to a question, try to eliminate the obviously wrong answers and guess from the rest. If you can eliminate two out of four options, you have a 50 percent chance of guessing the correct answer.

6. For scenario questions, follow the steps we outlined earlier. Read the question carefully and try to identify the facts at the center of the story.

Finally, I would advise anyone attempting to earn Microsoft MCSE certification to adopt a philosophical attitude. Even if you are the kind of person who never fails a test, you are likely to fail at least one Microsoft certification test somewhere along the way. Do not get discouraged. If Microsoft certification were easy to obtain, more people would have it, and it would not be so respected and so valuable to your future in the IT industry.

# MCSE
## MICROSOFT CERTIFIED SYSTEMS ENGINEER

# Part 1

## Windows NT Workstation 4.0

## EXAM TOPICS

Overview of Windows NT Workstation 4.0

Installing Windows NT Workstation 4.0

Configuring Windows NT Workstation 4.0

Managing Users and Groups

Windows NT File System Support

Understanding Windows NT 4.0 Security

Understanding Windows NT Networking

Installing and Configuring TCP/IP

Connecting to NetWare Servers

Remote Access Service and Dial-Up Networking

Workgroups and Domains

Printing

Configuring Applications

Performance Tuning

Booting, Troubleshooting, and Service Packs

# Workstation
# Practice
# Questions

$Q$

$\&$

$A$

Part of being successful on a Microsoft exam is understanding what is actually being asked. Read all questions and choices carefully. Also, realize that some questions will require selecting more than one answer. In these cases, choose all correct answers for the question.

The following questions are structured in a format similar to what you'll find on the Windows NT Workstation 4.0 exam. Knowledge-testing questions are mixed with situational style questions in random order, as you would find on the exam. However, for your convenience, the questions presented here are ordered by chapter. This will not be the case in the Workstation 4.0 exam. It is provided here so that you can easily reference additional information.

# Overview of Windows NT Workstation 4.0

1. Which file system is not supported by Windows NT Workstation 4.0? (Choose all that apply.)

   A. FAT

   B. VFAT

   C. HPFS

   D. NTFS

2. You are running three 16-bit applications designed for Windows 3.1, a DOS application, and a 32-bit Windows NT application on your Windows NT Workstation. The DOS application locks up. What will happen to the remaining applications running on your computer?

   A. All applictions will lock up on the workstation.

   B. All 16-bit applications will lock up.

   C. Only the DOS application will lock up.

   D. The entire workstation will lock up.

**3.** In Windows NT's architecture, where do the environmental subsystems reside?

   A.  User mode

   B.  Kernel mode

   C.  HAL

   D.  Environmental mode

**4.** You have a Pentium computer with 32MB of RAM, four processors, and three 2GB hard disks. You need to install an operating system that will take advantage of this computer's hardware. What operating system will you choose?

   A.  Windows NT Server 4.0

   B.  Windows NT Workstation 4.0

   C.  Windows 95

   D.  DOS 7

**5.** Julie has installed RAS on her Windows NT workstation. She is getting complaints that some users can't connect to her computer through RAS. What is the most likely reason?

   A.  There can be only one connection at a time.

   B.  There can be only 10 client sessions at a time.

   C.  The maximum concurrent connections is set too low.

   D.  The maximum client sessions is set too low.

exam
ⓦatch

*The exam will present a scenario with a mix of applications, such as DOS and Windows applications, and ask you what would be the result if application x were to crash. How would the other applications currently running be affected? Study how the subsystems react to each other, and how the applications run within the subsystem.*

**6.** By default, MS-DOS and Windows 3.*x* programs execute differently on a Windows NT workstation. Which of the following best describes the difference between how DOS applications execute, and how 16-bit Windows applications execute?

A. 16-bit programs do not share memory with one another and are preemptively multitasked, while DOS programs share memory and are cooperatively multitasked.

B. 16-bit programs share memory with one another and are preemptively multitasked, while DOS programs do not share memory and are cooperatively multitasked.

C. 16-bit programs do not share memory with one another and are cooperatively multitasked, while DOS programs share memory and are preemptively multitasked.

D. 16-bit programs share memory with one another and are cooperatively multitasked, while DOS programs do not share memory and are preemptively multitasked.

**7.** There are 15 workstations on your network. Everyone on the network needs to access files on Julie's Windows NT workstation. She is getting complaints that some users can't connect to her computer. What is the most likely reason?

A. There can be only one inbound client session at a time.

B. There can be only 10 inbound client sessions at a time.

C. The number of inbound client sessions is set too low.

D. None of the above. Windows NT Workstation can handle unlimited inbound client sessions.

**8.** You are planning to set up a network consisting of nine Windows NT workstations. You do not want to risk the network having a central point of failure, and want it to be easy to install. In addition, each user on the network is to control the resources on his or her workstation. Centralized control of user accounts is not important. Which network model will you choose?

A. Workgroup model

B. Workstation model

C. Domain model

D. Primary Domain model

**9.** Which of the following is responsible for creating, managing, and scheduling threads?

A. Kernel

B. NT Executive

C. HAL

D. Environment Subsystem

**10.** You are planning to set up a network consisting of nine Windows NT workstations for a group of inexperienced users. Which network model will you choose?

A. Workgroup model

B. Workstation model

C. Domain model

D. Primary Domain model

**11.** Jennifer's computer dual boots between Windows NT Workstation 4.0 and Windows 95. Jennifer complains that while using Windows 95, she can't use one of her hard disks. What is most likely the reason?

A. Windows 95 isn't compatible with Windows NT Workstation's Master Boot Record.

B. Windows 95 is using DriveSpace 3.0.

C. The partition is NTFS, which is not visible to Windows 95.

D. The partition is VFAT, which is not visible to Windows 95.

exam
ⓦatch    *Novell integration is heavily tested on almost every MCSE exam.*

## QUESTIONS AND ANSWERS

| | |
|---|---|
| I want central control... | Use the domain model. It gives you central control over user accounts. |
| I have a large number of users... | Use the domain model. The workgroup model is unwieldy for more than ten users. |
| We have inexperienced users... | Use the domain model. The workgroup model requires that users know how to share and manage accounts for other users on their own systems. |
| We do not have a server... | Use the workgroup model. This is one advantage of the workgroup. You do not need to dedicate a machine to authenticating user accounts. |

**12.** You have just upgraded Alicia's computer to Windows NT Workstation 4.0. She now complains that a DOS-based finance program, which directly accesses the printer on her computer to print checks, will not run. What is most likely the problem?

A. The printer driver wasn't upgraded during installation of Windows NT Workstation.

B. The printer wasn't installed during installation of Windows NT Workstation.

C. Windows NT does not support DOS-based programs.

D. Windows NT does not allow hardware access, which is why the DOS program will not run.

**13.** You are planning to install an operating system on a computer that uses a RISC CPU. On such a system, what operating systems can you use? (Choose all that apply.)

A. OS/2 Warp

B. Windows 95

C. Windows NT Server 4.0

D. Windows NT Workstation 4.0

*The test will have you choose an appropriate protocol for use in a given situation. Nothing tricky here, just make sure you know what each protocol is used for.*

# Installing Windows NT Workstation 4.0

**1.** You are preparing to install Windows NT Workstation 4.0 on a computer that contains some older hardware. Before installing, what will you consult to make certain that the legacy hardware has been tested by Microsoft to be compatible with Windows NT Workstation?

A. HCL

B. Windows NTHQ

C. HAL

D. HQTOOL

**2.** During an upgrade of Windows 95 to Windows NT Workstation 4.0, all of the installed programs and Registry settings are replaced. What caused this?

A. Windows NT was not installed in the same directory as Windows 95.

B. Windows NT was installed in the same directory as Windows 95.

C. Windows 95 cannot be upgraded to Windows NT, and so defaulted to a full install instead.

D. Windows 95 upgrade to Windows NT is like a full installation. This is normal.

**3.** The active partition is also known as which of the following?

A. Boot partition

B. System partition

C. Primary partition

D. Secondary partition

**4.** You have installed Windows NT Workstation 4.0 on a computer, and find you are unable to specify access at the directory and file level. In addition, other operating systems are able to access your hard disk. What is the problem, and how can you remedy it?

A. The partition is formatted in FAT, and should be converted to NTFS.

B. The partition is formatted in NTFS, and should be converted to FAT.

C. Windows NT Workstation doesn't support this kind of security at the directory and file level. Upgrade the workstation to Windows NT Server.

D. Windows NT Workstation needs to be configured to support directory and file level security, and also to hide partitions from other operating systems. Use Disk Administrator to configure these settings.

**5.** You have decided to delete a partition on your Windows NT computer. What tools can you use to perform this task? (Choose all that apply.)

A. FDISK

B. Disk Administrator

C. DELTREE

D. FREEDISK

**6.** Darren has misplaced the three setup floppies that came with Windows NT Workstation 4.0. Unfortunately, a new computer needs Workstation installed immediately. What can he do to quickly and easily replace these setup disks?

A. Contact Microsoft and have them mail three new setup disks to him.

B. Use the WINNT.EXE /OX command to make a new set of floppies.

C. Use the WINNT.EXE /S command to make a new set of floppies.

D. Use the WINNT.EXE command and select the "Create New Setup Disks" option.

exam
Ⓦatch

*The protocol required to connect to a Hewlett-Packard printer is often a test question.*

**7.** You are passing by Julie's workstation. Her screen looks like the one shown in the next illustration. What kind of installation is she performing?

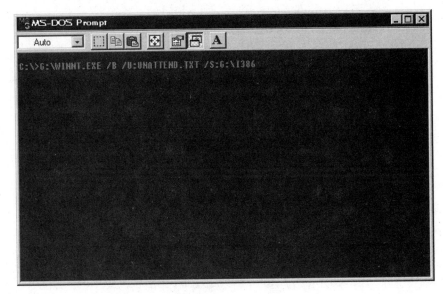

A. Unattended upgrade

B. Unattended full installation

C. Floppyless, unattended upgrade

D. Floppyless, unattended full installation

**8.** You are installing Windows NT Workstation 4.0, and reach the part of installation where you are offered a choice of protocols to install. There are several protocols that Windows NT offers during this phase. If you don't add or remove any protocols offered here, which of the following will Windows NT Workstation install?

A. TCP/IP, NWLink, AppleTalk

B. TCP/IP, NWLink, IPX/SPX

C. TCP/IP, NetBEUI, DLC

D. TCP/IP, NWLink, NetBEUI

**9.** You are installing Windows NT Workstation 4.0 on a computer that doesn't yet have a network adapter card installed. Even though the card isn't on the computer, what can you do to install your protocols?

A. Choose TCP/IP as your protocol and use the IP address of 127.0.0.1.

B. Use the MS Loopback adapter.

C. Choose an 803.2 network adapter card.

D. Skip installation of the adapter, and just bind the protocols as normal.

10. You have just added a new Hewlett Packard laser printer to the network. The HP printer appears to be functioning, and is attached correctly to the network. Despite this, no one can print to the printer. What is most likely the reason for this?

A. TCP/IP is not installed on the network workstations.

B. FTP is not installed on the network workstations.

C. DLC is not installed on the network workstations.

D. NWLink is not installed on the network workstations.

11. You are implementing a network of 100 desktop computers and 25 laptop computers. All of the desktop computers are identical to each other, as are all of the laptop computers. What is the minimum number of answer files and UDF files required to perform unattended installations?

A. 125 answer files and one UDF file

B. One answer file and 125 UDF files

C. Two answer files and one UDF file

D. One answer file and two UDF files

12. Pat's computer currently runs Windows NT Workstation 3.5 on a single HPFS partition. She wants the operating system upgraded to version 4.0, and doesn't want to lose the existing access settings for file and directory security. How can you install Windows NT Workstation 4.0, yet still preserve the existing security settings?

A. Upgrade Workstation on the existing partition.

B. Convert the partition to NTFS, then upgrade Workstation.

C. Convert the partition to FAT, then upgrade Workstation.

D. Upgrade Workstation, then convert the partition to NTFS.

exam
ⓦatch   *You need to know the hardware requirements for Windows NT 4.0
Workstation: 12MB RAM for an Intel processor or 16MB RAM for a
RISC processor, a 120MB hard disk, and a 486/33Mhz processor. Also
remember that you cannot upgrade or install Windows NT 4.0 on a
386 no matter how much memory the computer has.*

**13.** You are using Setup Manager, shown in the next illustration, to create
unattended answer files, so that you can specify answers to questions that
would otherwise have to be entered during installation. Having started the
program, where would you go to specify adapter cards and their
communication parameters?

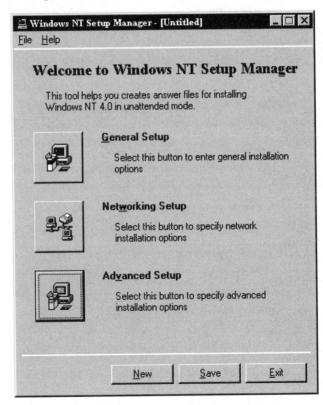

A. File Menu

B. General Setup

C. Networking Setup

D. Advanced Setup

---

**exam ⓌatchⒽ**

*If you ever misplace or lose the three setup floppies included with Windows NT 4.0, you can make a new set using the NT setup utilities WINNT.EXE or WINNT32.EXE. If you are running Windows NT, you can use WINNT32.EXE with the /OX switch. If you are running any other version of Windows, use WINNT.EXE with the /OX switch. This question often appears on the NT 4.0 Workstation exam, so be prepared.*

---

# Configuring Windows NT Workstation 4.0

**1.** Which subtrees of the Registry contain information on object linking and embedding (OLE)?

A. HKEY_LOCAL_MACHINE

B. HKEY_CURRENT_CONFIG

C. HKEY_CLASSES_ROOT

D. HKEY_CURRENT_USER

**2.** The following operating systems were installed on a computer in the order given: DOS 6.22, Windows 95, Windows NT Workstation, Windows NT Server. You go into System Properties, and click the Startup/Shutdown tab. Which operating system is configured to start as the default operating system on this computer?

A. DOS 6.22

B. Windows 95

C. Windows NT Workstation

D. Windows NT Server

**3.** While working in Microsoft Word, you notice the virus scanner that is also running appears sluggish. What can you do to boost the virus scanner's performance from the tab shown in the next illustration in System Properties?

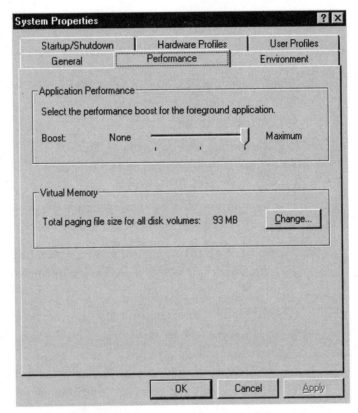

A. Decrease the Boost to None.

B. Leave the Boost level where it is.

C. Increase the Boost level to Maximum.

D. Change the virtual memory to 26MB.1

**4.** Visiting the Microsoft web site, you see that there is a service pack that will update your Windows NT Workstation to a certain version number. How can you tell whether your workstation is already at that version or in need of the service pack update?

A. In Internet Explorer, click About on the Help menu. This will show the version.

B. In System Properties, click the General tab. This will show the version.

C. In System Properties, click the Environment tab. This will show the version.

D. In Control Panel, click About on the Help menu. This will show the version.

5. In the case of a system crash, you want your Windows NT workstation to send an administrative alert. Where can you go to configure your workstation to do this?

A. User Profiles tab of System Properties

B. Hardware Profiles tab of System Properties

C. Startup/Shutdown tab of System Properties

D. Environment tab of System Properties

6. An application is having trouble finding certain files it commonly uses to run. You decide to modify the PATH statement. What will you modify so that it will look for files in the directories you specify?

A. Modify the path statement in the Services applet in Control Panel.

B. Associate the path to the software with the Add New Programs applet in Control Panel.

C. Modify the path statement in the Performance tab of System Properties.

D. Modify the path statement in the Environment tab of System Properties.

7. You want to change certain configuration information about your hardware profile through the Registry. Which of the following keys will you use to change this information?

A. HKEY_USERS

B. HKEY_CURRENT_USER

C. HKEY_CURRENT_CONFIG

D. HKEY_CLASSES_ROOT

**8.** In which subtree of the Registry does the Security Accounts Manager (SAM) reside?

A. HKEY_USERS

B. HKEY_CURREWindows NT_USER

C. HKEY_LOCAL_MACHINE

D. HKEY_CLASSES_ROOT

**9.** You have just purchased a new laptop to use at work and home. At work, you connect the laptop to a docking station, allowing you to be part of the network. However, while at home, you don't want any of the network services to start when you use the laptop. What can you do to configure the laptop to run differently, depending on which environment it's in?

A. Change settings in the Environment tab in System Properties.

B. Create two different user profiles.

C. Create two different hardware profiles.

D. Modify the BOOT.INI file.

**10.** Darren wants to install a MIDI device to his Windows NT workstation. What would you use in Control Panel to install this device's drivers?

A. Sounds

B. Devices

C. Multimedia

D. System

exam
ⓦatch

*The exam doesn't ask complex Registry questions. Prepare for a question or two on what type of information is stored under a major Registry key.*

**exam**
**ⓦatch**

*The exam will ask you which Control Panel icon you would select to configure a certain device. They can be tricky!*

**11.** Julie is having problems with her computer, and thinks the Registry has been corrupted in some way. Marni is also using Windows NT Workstation, and helps out by installing a copy of her computer's Registry on Julie's computer. Now Julie complains that she can't get into Workstation at all. What is the problem?

    A. Marni is using a different version of Windows NT than Julie is.

    B. Julie needs to reboot her computer before the new Registry takes effect.

    C. The Registry is unique to each computer.

    D. The system files also need to be copied over for the Registry to work.

**12.** Pat is frustrated with herself. Every time she leaves her computer for lunch, she forgets to log off. As a result, security problems have arisen from people accessing the network under her account. What can you configure on her Windows NT workstation to restrict access after it hasn't been used for more than 10 minutes?

    A. Enable Password Protection in the Network applet.

    B. Set the HKEY_LOCAL_MACHINE\PASSWORD key value to 10.

    C. Set the Password Protect on the Screensaver tab of the Display applet.

    D. Set the Password Protect on the Environment tab of the System applet.

**13.** Your workstation needs to connect with the Internet. All installations and configurations necessary to do this have been made, except for installing TCP/IP. Which applet in the Control Panel would you use to install TCP/IP so that you can connect to your Internet Service Provider?

    A. Devices

    B. Services

    C. Network

    D. Modems

exam
ⓦatch    *You may get a question on the exam concerning the correct paging file size for a given situation. Remember the recommendations.*

# Managing Users and Groups

**1.** You are told by your supervisor to implement account policies for your network. Which of the following does an account policy apply to? (Choose all that apply.)

   A. Passwords

   B. SIDs

   C. Security Account Manager (SAM)

   D. Account permissions

**2.** The Administrator account is a "known" account, which is automatically created when Windows NT is installed. Since everyone familiar with Windows NT knows this account exists (and knows it is the only account that won't lock you out from an incorrect password), it is a potential security risk from would-be hackers who try to guess the password. To protect your system, you decide to set up a new account with administrator privileges and delete the existing account. When you attempt to delete the Administrator account, you find you cannot. Why?

   A. You are logged on as Administrator, and cannot delete the account while you're using it.

   B. You cannot delete the Administrator account, only rename it.

   C. The Administrator account is automatically deleted when a new account with administrator privileges is created.

   D. You can only delete the Administrator account by modifying the SAM.

**3.** You attempt to create a global group on your Windows NT Workstation for members of Sales. Unfortunately, Windows NT Workstation will not allow you to create this group. Why?

A. Global groups can only be created on a Windows NT server functioning as a domain controller.

B. You must create the global group from within a local group.

C. You do not have the necessary permissions to create a local group.

D. You must be a member of a global group to be able to create global groups.

4. You attempt to place a local group inside of a global group, but Windows NT won't allow you. What is the most likely reason for this?

A. You do not have the proper permissions.

B. Global groups can only contain other global groups.

C. Only local groups exist on Windows NT.

D. Global groups cannot contain local groups.

5. You want to set up account policies on your network, but only want the policies to affect the local computer. Which program will you use?

A. User Manager's Account menu

B. User Manager's Policy menu

C. User Manager for Domains

D. Account Policy applet in Control Panel

6. You are concerned that one user may be causing problems on the network. You want events resulting from his actions to be logged, so that you can view them later in the Event Viewer. How can you do this?

A. Enable auditing through User Manager.

B. Enable security through User Manager.

C. Enable auditing through Event Viewer.

D. Enable security through Server Manager.

7. What identifies a user to a Windows NT workstation or server?

A. The password

B. The account name

C. The SID

D. The user

**8.** You have just made changes to Howard's account from the PDC. When you check at his workstation, the changes haven't taken effect. What must you do to his Windows NT workstation for the changes to take effect?

A. Have Howard reboot his computer.

B. Have Howard log off the network, then log back on.

C. Remove Howard from the Everyone group.

D. Nothing. You must reboot the server.

**9.** You have accidentally deleted an account. To remedy the situation, you create a new account with the same name, but find that it does not have the same permissions as the original. Why?

A. The SID is different.

B. The SAM is different.

C. The Access Token is different.

D. You do not have the proper permissions to create a duplicate account.

**10.** You are regularly using different Windows NT workstations, located within the same domain. You have decided to set up a roaming profile for yourself. Where is the profile information stored?

A. In a file called DEFAULT in the WINNT/SYSTEM32/CONFIG directory.

B. In a file called USERDEF in the WINNT/SYSTEM32/CONFIG directory.

C. It is replicated to all computers in the domain.

D. It is located on the domain controllers.

**11.** You want to audit whether a particular user makes any changes to user rights. Which activity will you audit?

A. Use of User Rights

B. User and Group Management

C. Security Policy Changes

D. File and Object Access

**12.** You want to add Jennifer to a default group that will give her the right to load and unload device drivers. What group must you add her to if she is to perform this action?

A. Power Users

B. Server Operators

C. Backup Operators

D. Administrator

**13.** You are setting up a small network for training seminars that last seven days. You want to use standard accounts that rotate from class to class, for which you set the passwords. You set passwords to expire every seven days, but are worried that some students from previous classes may change their expired password to continue their access. How can you prevent this?

A. Disable the User Must Logon to Change Password check box in Account Policy.

B. Enable the User Must Logon to Change Password check box in Account Policy.

C. Enable the User Account Disabled check box in Account Policy.

D. Nothing. Once the password has expired, their access is denied.

---

exam
ⓦatch

*Nearly every student who has taken the Windows NT Workstation test has reported that they were given a question about the renaming of an account. You will receive at least two questions concerning when it's appropriate to copy, delete, disable, or rename an account.*

# Windows NT File System Support

**1.** Julie's computer has Windows 95, and she has just installed Windows NT Workstation 4.0. The computer dual boots between the two of them. She uses CONVERT.EXE on her single hard disk. Now she complains that one of her operating systems won't boot. What has happened?

A. She has converted her FAT partition to FAT32, so Windows NT can't boot.

B. She has converted her FAT partition to NTFS, so now Win 95 can't boot.

C. She has converted the FAT32 partition to NTFS, so now Win 95 can't boot.

D. She has converted the FAT partition to VFAT, so now Windows NT can't boot.

**2.** You have decided to create a volume set on your Windows NT computers. Which of the following cannot be part of a volume set? (Choose all that apply.)

A. Boot Partition

B. System Partition

C. Primary Partition

D. Secondary Partition

**3.** You want to implement fault tolerance on your system. The level of RAID you choose should enable you to simply remove a failed drive and replace it with a new one, to restore the data. In addition, you don't want to waste vast amounts of space for redundancy. Which method of fault tolerance should you choose?

A. Disk striping

B. Disk striping with parity

C. Volume set

D. Disk duplexing

**4.** The file system you are using is NTFS. You bring up the file property sheet shown in the next illustration and click the Compressed check box. What will happen? (Choose all that apply.)

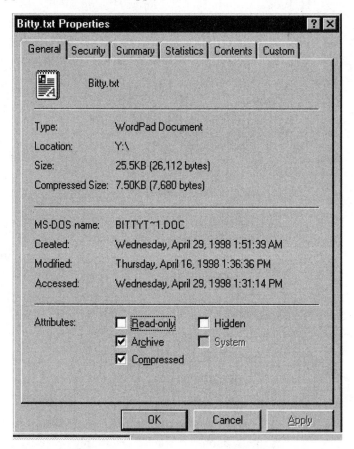

A. Only the file will be compressed.

B. DRVSPACE.BIN will be loaded the next time you start Windows NT.

C. DBLSPACE.BIN will be loaded the next time you start Windows NT.

D. The file will be added to a zip file.

**5.** You want to name a file to be saved on a VFAT drive. Which of the following would be a valid filename? (Choose all that apply.)

A. This is a FileName.TxT
B. ThisFile.TXT
C. THISFILE.TEXT
D. THIS:TXT.TXT

**6.** Jennifer has just realized that she deleted an important file yesterday. Since then, she has emptied her Recycle Bin in Windows NT Workstation. She is desperate to have the file recovered. What options does she have? (Choose all that apply.)

A. Restore the file from an existing backup.
B. Using MSDOS Prompt, use the UNDELETE command to recover the file.
C. Use Norton Disk Utilities to salvage the file.
D. Use the SALVAGE command to recover the file.

## QUESTIONS AND ANSWERS

| | |
|---|---|
| I want greater disk performance... | Do not use a volume set. Use a stripe set. |
| I want to increase my capacity later... | Do not use a stripe set. Use a volume set. It can be extended, whereas a stripe set cannot. |
| I want to use free space from several areas... | Do not use a stripe set. Use a volume set. It can combine multiple areas of free space, including space within partitions on the same drives. |
| I have the same amount of space on two separate disks... | Use a stripe set. |
| I want to include the system and boot partitions... | You cannot include the system or boot partitions in stripe or volume sets. |

**7.** You want your computer to dual boot between Windows NT Workstation 4.0 and Windows 95. Which file system will allow you to use both operating systems?

A. FAT32

B. NTFS

C. FAT

D. HPFS

**8.** You create a new partition on a computer that has three existing partitions named C:, D:, and E:. Two network drives are also mapped. When you go to name the drive, what will happen?

A. The next available drive letter will be F:.

B. The next available drive letter will be H:.

C. The drive cannot be named, because there are mapped network drives on the computer. You must remove the mappings from your computer before you can give the partition a drive letter.

D. The next available drive letter will be the first letter assigned to a mapped drive, because this drive does not actually exist on the computer. All new mappings automatically will be incremented one drive letter.

**9.** You want to use RAID to increase performance on your system. What will you use to allow the best possible reads and rights? Fault tolerance is not an issue.

A. Stripe set without parity

B. Stripe set with parity

C. Disk mirroring

D. Disk duplexing

exam
ⓦatch  *Very likely, you will be asked to choose the 8.3 version of a given long filename.*

## QUESTIONS AND ANSWERS

| | |
|---|---|
| I am installing NT and I have HPFS... | Convert it before you upgrade. NT 4 does not like HPFS. |
| I do not require the capability to assign permissions or use compression... | Use FAT. Dead giveaway. |
| My hard disk is 120MB... | Use FAT. NTFS is not as efficient for a drive that size. |
| My hard disk is 1.2GB... | Use NTFS. FAT is not very effective on a large drive. |
| I have a RISC processor... | Then use FAT on your system partition. The remainder can be NTFS. FAT is required for the bootup files on the system partition. |

10. You have decided to implement disk striping with parity on a Windows NT workstation with two hard disks and three partitions. You attempt this, but find you cannot. Why?

    A. Stripe set with parity requires three partitions on the same physical disk.
    B. Stripe set with parity requires two physical hard disks, with one partition on each.
    C. Stripe set with parity requires three physical disks.
    D. Windows NT Workstation doesn't have RAID level 5.

11. Jennifer moves a file to a folder on the same NTFS partition. The file was compressed before she moved it. What will happen to the file once it is moved?

    A. The file will retain its attributes and remain compressed.
    B. The file will adopt the attributes of the new folder, and become uncompressed.
    C. The file will not be copied, but just become a pointer to the original file.
    D. An error message will occur saying that the file cannot be copied.

**12.** You have just created a new partition on your Windows NT Workstation. You now want to format it as NTFS. What must you do?

   A. Run FORMAT from a command line, and specify NTFS as the format type.
   B. Run CONVERT from a command line, and format the partition to NTFS.
   C. Use Disk Administrator to format the partition, then run CONVERT to change the files to NTFS.
   D. Use Disk Administrator to format the partition as NTFS.

**13.** What feature of NTFS keeps track of whether disk writes have been completed or not?

   A. Hot Fix
   B. WriteGuard
   C. Lazy Write
   D. Compression

**14.** During installation, you did not have any floppy disks handy to create an emergency repair disk. Now, you are concerned that this might be a serious matter, should you ever require this disk. What can you do to create the disk, now that installation of Windows NT Workstation is completed?

   A. Nothing. Only Windows NT Server requires an emergency repair disk.
   B. Use ERD to create the emergency repair disk.
   C. Use RDISK to create the emergency repair disk.
   D. Use Disk Administrator to create the emergency repair disk.

exam
Ⓦatch

*Don't be surprised to see a question concerning which file system to use: FAT or NTFS. You should know the differences between the two, and when it is appropriate to choose one over the other.*

# Understanding Windows NT 4.0 Security

**1.** Howard is a member of the Graphic Design, SQL User, and Marketing groups. He requires access to a shared folder. The folder's ACL allows Full Control to the SQL User group. Howard's user account allows Read. Graphic Design allows Read and Write. The Marketing group has No Access permissions. Based on these permissions, what access does Howard have?

A. Full Control

B. Read and Write

C. No Access

D. Read

**2.** Julie has Full Control on an NTFS directory. She needs to use a file in a subdirectory. She's been granted Read and Write permissions on the subdirectory, and Read permissions on the file. What are her permissions for the file?

A. Full Control

B. Read

C. Write

D. Read and Write

**3.** Your account has Read permissions. You are also a member of the Sales and Marketing groups. Sales has Write permissions, while Marketing has Read and Delete. What permissions do you have?

A. Read

B. Read and Write

C. Read and Delete

D. Read, Write, and Delete

**4.** What uniquely identifies a user or group on a Windows NT network?

A. SID

B. Name

C. Password

D. ACL

**5.** Jeannette has accidentally deleted Jennifer's account. To restore the account, she creates a new account and gives it the same name. Will this work?

A. No, all permissions will be lost.

B. Yes, the new account now has the same permissions as the old one.

C. No, because Jeannette doesn't know the password, Jennifer won't be able to access the system.

D. Yes. Because the name of the account is the same, Windows NT can now restore the old account's values.

**6.** Which of the following is only used by the POSIX subsystem?

A. Owner Security ID

B. Group Security ID

C. Discretionary Access Control List

D. System Access Control List

**7.** You want to take ownership of a file. What file-level permission will you need to accomplish this task?

A. File Ownership

B. Create

C. Full Control

D. Change

exam
Watch

*Permissions are cumulative, except for No Access. You don't have to belong to a group that has all the proper permissions. If your account has Read access and you belong to a group with Write access, you will be granted Read and Write access.*

**8.** You are worried about hackers breaking into your system by guessing passwords. You decide to set Windows NT to lock out an account after a certain number of attempts. Which accounts will not be affected by implementing this Account Policy?

A. Power Users

B. Members of the Administrator group

C. The Administrator account

D. The Guest account

**9.** You want to automate the logon process, so that you don't have to input a username and password during logon. You do this by supplying the Windows NT Workstation with a default name and password. Where must you supply the default username and password?

A. The Registry

B. User Manager

C. Account Policy

D. Boot Manager

**10.** Windows NT Workstation supports four types of logons. What are they?

A. Domain, Workgroup, Remote, and Passthrough

B. Local, Domain, Workgroup, and Passthrough

C. Local, Remote, Domain, and Passthrough

D. Local, Remote, Domain, and Workgroup

exam
ⓦatch   *Many people think an administrator can do anything. That isn't true, especially when it comes to resource ownership. Remember that once you take ownership, you can't give it back to the previous owner. For the previous owner to become the owner, he must have permissions to take ownership.*

**11.** A user executes a program. What permissions will the program have?

A. Whatever the user who has taken ownership of the executable has given.

B. Whatever Windows NT Workstation allows it.

C. The same rights and permissions as the user who is running it.

D. The rights and permissions designated in the Registry.

**12.** You are reading the newspaper, and come across an article about how the government once lost a case against a computer hacker because—as silly as the legal system is—the logon screen said "Welcome". You don't want this ever happening to your company. How can you add a legal notice to your logon screen?

A. Change the LegalNoticeCaption string value of Winlogon.

B. Enter a string in System Properties.

C. You can't change the screen. Your only option is to create a VB program that issues a warning, and will run before the logon screen appears.

D. You can't. This is why the government lost the case.

**13.** Which of the following file systems support user-level security on Windows NT Workstation? (Choose all that apply.)

A. FAT

B. NTFS

C. VFAT

D. FAT32

exam
ⓦatch

*There is another permission type called File Delete Child. File Delete Child is a POSIX function that allows a user with full control of a folder to delete a top-level file within that folder, even though the user doesn't have permissions to delete that file. Let's say you have full control of a folder called Sales Reports. Within that folder there is a file called MARY.XLS in which you have No Access permissions assigned. Since you have full control of the Sales Reports folder, you can delete the file MARY.XLS, even though you don't have access to that file.*

# Understanding Windows NT Networking

**1.** In the Windows NT networking model, what allows redirectors to be written without regard to the protocol being used?

A. OSI

B. NDIS

C. TDI

D. NIC

**2.** Which of the following allows multiple protocols to bind to a single network adapter card?

A. ISO

B. NDIS

C. TDI

D. NIC

**3.** You are connecting your Windows NT workstation to the Internet. The workstation will be connecting directly, and not going through Proxy Server. Which protocol must you install?

A. NetBEUI

B. NWLink

C. AFP

D. TCP/IP

**4.** You are setting up a small bus network consisting of Windows NT workstations for training purposes. The network will not grow, and will actually be torn down in two weeks time. What is the best protocol to use for this type of network?

A. NetBEUI

B. NWLink

C. TCP/IP

D. AFP

**5.** You want to increase the access time for a protocol, on a computer where multiple protocols are bound to multiple adapter cards. How would you change the binding order, so that the object is accessed faster?

    A. Lower the protocol in the binding order.

    B. Raise the protocol in the binding order.

    C. Lower the adapter card in the binding order.

    D. Raise the adapter card in the binding order.

**6.** Your network is spread over several floors of the same building. Routers are used to connect the different subnets. You have one HP laser printer that people need to use. How can you enable users on the different subnets to communicate with this printer?

    A. Enable DLC routing on the router.

    B. Set up a gateway server using NWLink or TCP/IP that will then use DLC to communicate with the printer.

    C. Set up a gateway using DLC that will then use NWLink or TCP/IP to communicate with the printer.

    D. Configure the subnet mask in DLC, so that all subnets can communicate with the printer.

**7.** You have just created a share on your Windows NT Workstation. Which application is best suited for managing this shared resource?

    A. Network applet in Control Panel

    B. Server applet in Control Panel

    C. Resource applet in Control Panel

    D. User Manager

exam
ⓦatch

*Know which protocols are routable (NWLink and TCP/IP) and which ones aren't (NetBEUI and DLC). Also know when you should use each protocol in a given situation. For example, you need to communicate with the Internet. Which protocol should you use?*

**8.** What hidden shares are created on your Windows NT workstation during installation? (Choose all that apply.)

    A. Admin$

    B. C$

    C. A$

    D. User$

**9.** What service allows your computer to be seen on the network?

    A. Server service

    B. Services for Microsoft Clients

    C. Computer Browser

    D. The protocol being used to access the network

**10.** Two new users to your Windows NT network are exploring the fun side of networking by using the Chat program and playing MS Hearts. Which type of interprocess communication are they using?

    A. Named Pipes

    B. Mailslots

    C. Telephony

    D. NetDDE

**11.** When your computer starts, it announces its presence to the network through a broadcasted message. Which type of interprocess communication is being used?

    A. Mailslots

    B. Named Pipes

    C. NetBIOS

    D. NetDDE

exam
Ⓦatch

*Be sure to understand that the TDI layer and the NDIS layer allow transport protocols to communicate with applications and networks seamlessly.*

**12.** Which layer of the OSI model corresponds to the NDIS Interface?

    A. Session

    B. Data Link

    C. Physical

    D. Network

**13.** You are having a problem with your network. After some investigation, you find that there is a break in the coaxial cable. You get new cable and fix the problem. At which level of the OSI model are you working?

    A. Session

    B. Data Link

    C. Physical

    D. Network

# Installing and Configuring TCP/IP

**1.** The World Wide Web is based on which protocol?

    A. FTP

    B. HTTP

    C. TCP

    D. DHCP

**2.** You have just installed TCP/IP on a Windows NT workstation, on a network that is a single subnet of 10 computers. What is the default subnet mask you will use?

    A. 255.255.255.255

    B. 255.0.0.0

    C. 255.255.255.0

    D. 255.255.0.0

**3.** You want host names to be resolved to IP addresses. Which of the following will you implement?

A. WINS

B. DNS

C. DHCP

D. DLC

**4.** Your workstation is connected to the Internet. You try to connect to www.odyssey.on.ca/~mcross. After a wait, you get a message saying that the web site cannot be found. You try again with www.microsoft.com, and the same thing happens. Each address you type in this manner has the same results. When you type in IP addresses, however, you connect. What is missing from your configuration?

A. Address of Primary and Secondary WINS Server

B. Address of Primary and Secondary DNS Server

C. Subnet Mask

D. IP Address

## QUESTIONS AND ANSWERS

| | |
|---|---|
| You need to configure TCP/IP in a routed environment... | You will need to configure the default gateway. |
| You need to configure TCP/IP in a non-routed environment... | You do not need the default gateway. The default gateway is for sending information that is not on your network. |
| You would like to automatically configure... | Use Dynamic Host Configuration Protocol (DHCP). |
| You require dynamic resolution... | Use either WINS or DNS depending on the scenario. These are dynamic alternatives to static files like HOSTS and LMHOSTS. DNS is to HOSTS as WINS is to LMHOSTS. |

**5.** You are installing TCP/IP on your Windows NT workstation, and have decided to manually enter the IP address. The network you are connecting to is a single subnet in a meeting room. What other information is required to complete installing TCP/IP?

A. Subnet mask

B. Default Gateway

C. DNS Server

D. WINS Server

**6.** What are the layers of the TCP/IP protocol suite?

A. Application, Transport, Network, Network Interface

B. Application, Presentation, Session, Transport, Network, Data Link, Physical

C. Application, Presentation, Internet, Network Interface

D. Application, Transport, Internet, Network Interface

---

exam
ⓦatch     *You may be asked what is required to automatically configure client workstations.*

---

**7.** You are installing TCP/IP on your Windows NT Workstation 4.0. The network you are connected to is spread across a large campus through several routers. You manually assign an IP address to this machine. What other information must you supply to install TCP/IP?

A. WINS Server

B. Subnet Mask

C. Default Gateway

D. DHCP Server

**8.** Howard has called you in as a consultant for his TCP/IP network. He wants to implement a server that will resolve IP addresses to Fully Qualified Domain Names, but isn't sure what to use. Which of the following will you suggest?

A. WINS

B. DNS

C. DHCP

D. Default Gateway

**9.** You have just installed TCP/IP on your Windows NT Workstation, and now you want to verify that your computer can connect with the Default Gateway. What utility will you use?

A. Telnet

B. ICMP

C. Pong

D. Ping

**10.** Jennifer has just sent you e-mail over the Internet. You decide to reply to the message. Your Windows NT workstation is on a network that uses NetBEUI. Mail is actually sent to a mail server on your network, which then sends it onto the Internet on your behalf. Which protocol is used to send this message to Jennifer?

A. SMTP

B. ICMP

C. FTP

D. NetBEUI

**11.** You want to separate a group of computers in a training room from the network, but don't want to create a new subnet. How can you keep this group from communicating with the network, and keep the network from interacting with this group of workstations?

A. Give the group of computers in the training room the same NetBIOS scope ID.

B. Give the group of computers in the training room the same NetBIOS name.

C. Give the each computer in the training room a different NetBIOS scope ID and name.

D. Give all of the computers on the network the same NetBIOS scope ID.

12. You cannot afford an expensive router, so you decide to use a Windows NT computer to forward packets between two subnets. The computer you are using is multihomed, and TCP/IP has been configured correctly. Despite this, the Windows NT computer still isn't routing packets. How do you fix this?

A. You need to configure TCP/IP.

B. You need to activate the "Enable IP Routing" from the checkbox of the Forwarding tab in TCP/IP properties.

C. You need to activate the "Enable IP Forwarding" checkbox from the Routing tab of TCP/IP properties.

D. You need to purchase a router, and use it to route packets.

13. You cannot afford an expensive router, and have decided to use a Windows NT computer to forward packets between two subnets. Everything is configured correctly, and two NICs have been installed in the computer. What must you do to each NIC before you can use it as a router?

A. Enable multihoming from TCP/IP properties.

B. Assign different IP addresses to each NIC.

C. Enable active routing in the NIC's setup program.

D. Enable active routing in the TCP/IP properties.

# Connecting to NetWare Servers

1. Your company has gone through a merger with a company that uses NetWare for their network. Your network uses Windows NT. You want to connect for the first time to a NetWare 3.12 server with your Windows NT workstation. What information must you provide?

   A. Default Tree
   B. Context
   C. Preferred Server
   D. NetWare ID

2. After a company merger, your company uses a mixed network of Windows NT and NetWare. You want to connect for the first time to a NetWare 4.0 server with your Windows NT workstation. What information must you provide?

   A. Default Tree
   B. NetWare ID
   C. Preferred Server
   D. Context

3. What protocol is used by default on NetWare servers?

   A. NWLink
   B. IPX
   C. TCP/IP
   D. NetBIOS

## QUESTIONS AND ANSWERS

| | |
|---|---|
| I only want to use one frame type although several are in use on the network... | Select the frame type you wish to use in the NWLink IPX/SPX Properties dialog box. |
| I need to use multiple frame types... | Use a registry editing tool to add the frame types you need. |
| There is only one frame type in use on my network... | Select Auto Detect in the NWLink IPX/SPX Properties dialog box. |
| I used Auto Detect and I need to know which frame type it detected... | Use IPXROUTE CONFIG from the Windows NT command line. |

4. You want to install a new protocol so that your Windows NT workstation can communicate with a NetWare server. Which transport protocol is based on the protocol used by default on NetWare servers?

   A. IPX
   B. SPX
   C. NWLink
   D. NetBIOS

5. You have installed CSNW on a Windows NT workstation. You realize that you forgot to install the default protocol used by the NetWare server you want to connect to. What must you do?

   A. Install IPX/SPX on your Windows NT workstation.
   B. Install NWLink on your Windows NT workstation.
   C. Install NWLink on the NetWare server.
   D. Nothing.

6. Darren is having trouble interacting with other computers on a NetWare network. He is using Windows NT Workstation 4.0. You check the other workstations using this network, and they appear to have no problem. What is the most likely cause for Darren's problems?

    A.  A possible computer virus

    B.  IPX/SPX is not installed

    C.  Incorrect frame type

    D.  Incorrect version of NetWare

**7.** Jennifer is unable to connect to a NetWare network from her Windows NT workstation. You check her configurations, and find that everything is as it should be. Checking the server, you find that two things are mismatched between Windows NT and NetWare. What two things must match for Jennifer to connect to NetWare?

    A.  Password

    B.  Logon script

    C.  Account name

    D.  DNS Server address

**8.** You have installed CSNW on your Windows NT workstation, and noticed that the throughput to the NetWare network is quite slow. You check both the frame type on your workstation and the one used by the network, and notice they're different. Why is this slowing the throughput?

    A.  All network traffic is being forced to go through a Windows NT Server, which is translating the frame type.

    B.  All network traffic is being forced to go through a NetWare server, which is translating the frame type.

    C.  Your Windows NT Workstation is being forced to translate the frame type.

    D.  The frame types are causing your computer to be isolated from the network, so you can't communicate at all.

---

exam
**Ⓦatch**

*The Windows NT Help file for CSNW and NWLink, NWDOC.HLP, contains an abundance of valuable information. Click on the Overview button in the Client Service for NetWare dialog box to bring up this help file. Taking the time to read through its contents before taking the Windows NT Workstation exam will be an excellent review of the material for connecting to NetWare services.*

---

9. You attempt saving a file with a long filename to a NetWare server. The server has not loaded any special NLMs. What will happen?

   A. The file will be saved with the long filename.
   B. You will be forced to save the file using the 8.3 naming convention.
   C. An OS/2 name space NLM will be loaded.
   D. A DOS name space NLM will be loaded.

10. You notice that the full name of GSNW is Gateway (and Client) Services for NetWare. You want to install this on your Windows NT workstation. Which of the following is true?

    A. To install GSNW on a workstation, you must also be running NWLink.
    B. To install GSNW on a workstation, you must also be running IPX/SPX.
    C. To install GSNW on a workstation, the Server service must be running.
    D. You can't install GSNW on a workstation.

11. Your company has just merged with a company whose network uses NetWare 4.*x* servers. You decide to switch the frame type on your Windows NT workstations to the default frame type used by these servers. You switch the frame type to 802.3, but notice degraded performance. Why?

    A. The default frame type of NetWare 4.*x* is 802.2.
    B. The default frame type of NetWare 4.*x* is 802.5.
    C. The default frame type of NetWare 4.*x* is Ethernet II.
    D. The default frame type of NetWare 4.*x* is Ethernet SNAP.

12. You want to have a single authentication on your mixed Windows NT and NetWare network. You plan to merge accounts from multiple NetWare servers into one account database. Which will you need to install to enable this?

    A. GSNW
    B. FPNW
    C. CSNW
    D. DSMN

## QUESTIONS AND ANSWERS

| | |
|---|---|
| We are migrating from a NetWare server to a Windows NT server... | Since your Windows NT Workstations already have CSNW installed, all you need to do is uninstall CSNW on the workstations when the server migration is complete. |
| We need permanent access to a NetWare server, but we need it NOW! | Install GSNW on a Windows NT Server. As time permits, install CSNW on each Windows NT Workstation. |
| We need temporary access to a NetWare server for a large number of users... | Install GSNW on a Windows NT Server for the short time needed. |
| We need temporary access to a NetWare server for a few users... | Install CSNW on each Windows NT Workstation that needs to access the NetWare server. |
| We need to copy files from a NetWare server to a Windows NT server... | Install CSNW on a Windows NT Workstation to connect to both servers. |

**13.** Where would you change the frame type used by Windows NT Workstation?

    A. NWLink IPX/SPX Properties

    B. Modems

    C. Services

    D. The NetWare server

exam
ⓦatch

*Although GSNW is not a part of Windows NT Workstation, the certification exam for NT Workstation can contain general questions regarding how GSNW works and how NT Workstation users can benefit from it. It is not necessary to have in-depth knowledge about GSNW.*

# Remote Access Service and Dial-Up Networking

**1.** A user complains that he can't connect to your RAS server. He is using TCP/IP with SLIP on a Windows NT workstation. Why can't he connect?

A. You can't run SLIP from a Windows NT workstation.

B. RAS can only answer using PPP.

C. RAS cannot dial out using SLIP.

D. The TCP/IP settings are incompatible between your RAS server and the workstation.

**2.** How many simultaneous inbound sessions is Windows NT Workstation 4.0 limited to?

A. 1

B. 10

C. 256

D. Unlimited

**3.** What utility can you use to test a RAS connection?

A. SLIP

B. TAPI

C. NETTEST

D. Ping

exam
ⓦatch

*The exam draws heavily upon the DUN configuration parameters, so spend some time dissecting the installation. Work forwards from the RAS port installation to the phonebook entry configuration, paying strict attention to how the different settings interact with each other. If you have any questions about an option, select it and press the F1 key to receive some context sensitive help.*

## QUESTIONS AND ANSWERS

| | |
|---|---|
| I'm working from home and the office is a long-distance call for me... | Use PPTP for connectivity. By utilizing the Internet as your WAN backbone, you can avoid long distance charges. |
| I work off of a legacy UNIX server which doesn't support PPP... | SLIP is the right one for you. SLIP predates PPP and has a lot of support in UNIX environments. |
| I work from home but I need more bandwidth... | Use PPP-MP. Creating a logical pipe with multiple RAS ports increases your speed. |
| I use NetBIOS applications that access non-NetBIOS hosts... | Use the NetBIOS gateway. Clients can access TCP/IP or IPX hosts through the RAS server, which does a protocol conversion to allow access to NetBIOS clients. |
| I'm a traveling user and I need access back to the office... | Use PPP because it's simple. PPP does all the necessary negotiation and allows multiple protocols. |

**4.** You have RAS configured to receive calls on your Windows NT workstation. You notice that no sessions are in progress, and attempt to send a fax through the same port. An error occurs. Why?

A. The fax machine has locked the port because it is incompatible with RAS

B. RAS has locked the port because it's still waiting for a call

C. RAS will not allow any other communication software to run on Windows NT Workstation while it's in use

D. The fax you're sending is over 64KB in size. It's too large, and RAS refuses to give up the port.

**5.** Alicia has two 14.4 Kbps modems attached to her Windows NT workstation. The two modems are connected to two separate phone lines. She enables Multilink, and is now curious as to what bandwidth she has. What would you tell her?

A. 14.4 Kbps

B. 28.8 Kbps

C. 56 Kbps

D. ISDN comparable

**6.** On your Windows NT workstation, you are running a program that uses the telephone to call a person when you click that person's name. What kind of application is this?

A. TAPI

B. PPP

C. SLIP

D. CRAPI

**7.** Which of the following are serial protocols? (Choose all that apply.)

A. PPP

B. IPX

C. SLIP

D. TCP/IP

**8.** Julie is using Windows NT Workstation to dial in to a Windows NT host. When RAS authenticates her, what authentication protocol will be used?

A. MS-CHAP

B. DES

C. SPAP

D. SPAM

**9.** You want to ensure that events are logged, in order to be sure that nothing unusual is happening with RAS. That way, you can view this logged information with Event Viewer. What can you check to make certain that RAS events are being logged?

A. Check that the HKEY_LOCAL_MACHINE\SYSTEM\ ControlSet001\Services\RemoteAccess\Parameters\EnableAudit key is set to 1 in the Registry.

B. Ensure that Enable RAS Event Logging is checked in the Network Configuration dialog box.

C. Ensure that Enable RAS Event Logging is checked in RAS Monitor.

D. Nothing. RAS automatically logs events.

10. Your Internet Service Provider uses SLIP. Where will your IP address come from?

A. It will be automatically assigned by the ISP's DHCP server.

B. It must be manually entered by you into your computer.

C. It will be automatically supplied by InterNIC.

D. None of the above.

11. You want to connect with RAS to an older UNIX server. You are using Windows NT Workstation. Which serial protocol is your best choice for connection?

A. TCP/IP

B. PPP

C. SLIP

D. PPTP

---

exam
ⓦatch

*TAPI is the groundwork for Microsoft's development of computer telephony integration (CTI). Much of this information may seem to relate more to programmers, but Microsoft wants to get the word out, so look carefully at this information. The best way to understand the API is to spend some time browsing the settings in Control Panel under Telephony and Modems. The settings here relate directly back to the RAS and DUN parameters. Again, the key is to focus on what you know Microsoft cares about, because it will be on the exam.*

**12.** Darren uses a Windows NT computer at home, and uses RAS to connect with his head office. He has a 28.8 Kbps modem in his computer, and an older 14.4 on the bookshelf. He wants to increase his bandwidth, but doesn't want to buy yet another modem. What would you suggest?

A. Use PPP-MP with a NetBIOS gateway.

B. Use PPP-MP with the 28.8 modem that's in the computer.

C. Leave the 28.8 modem in the computer, install the 14.4 modem as well, get two phone lines, and use PPP-MP.

D. Buy another modem, and quit being so cheap.

**13.** You are deciding which transport protocols will be supported by your RAS server. Which of the following are your choices? (Choose all that apply.)

A. TCP/IP

B. IPX

C. NWLink

D. NetBEUI

**14.** You want to add a server, and modify the protocols used to connect with Dial-Up Networking. What would you use to make these changes?

A. Dial-Up Networking Monitor

B. RAS Monitor

C. RAS Phonebook

D. Dial-Up Networking Phonebook

---

---

# Workgroups and Domains

**1.** Of the following choices, which contains a list of all resources in a domain and can be accessed by other computers?

A. PDC

B. BDC

C. Browser

D. Master Browser

**2.** Jennifer must use two Windows NT workstations on a TCP/IP network. Each Windows NT workstation is located in a different part of the building. Both computers have identical software setups. What can you do so that, no matter which workstation Jennifer is using, she will have the same desktop settings?

A. Set up a user profile for Jennifer.

B. Set up a roaming profile for Jennifer.

C. Rename both workstations so they each have the same NetBIOS name, making the network think it's the same computer with the same settings.

D. Give each workstation the same IP address, making the network think it's the same computer with the same settings.

**3.** You are setting up a network consisting of 10 Windows NT workstations and no server. What model will you use?

A. Single Domain

B. Workgroup

C. Master Domain

D. Complete Trust Domain

exam
**watch**     *While the Workstation exam doesn't emphasize domain models, a basic understanding of them adds to your understanding of domains.*

**4.** Where is account information kept in a domain? (Choose all that apply.)

A. PDC

B. BDC

C. Member Server

D. Master Browser

**5.** Your network consists of 29 computers. How many Master Browsers and Backup Browsers are there on a network this size?

A. One Master Browser and one Backup Browser

B. One Master Browser and two Backup Browsers

C. Two Master Browsers and one Backup Browser

D. One Master Browser and 29 Backup Browsers

**6.** Julie is a new network administrator. She is somewhat confused about when to promote a BDC to a PDC. When should she do so?

A. If an election is held

B. If the Master Browser becomes unstable

C. If the BDC is expected to be shut down or offline for awhile

D. If the PDC is expected to be shut down or offline for awhile

**7.** The Master Browser's browse list is limited to what size?

A. 16KB

B. 32KB

C. 64KB

D. 128KB

# QUESTIONS AND ANSWERS

| | |
|---|---|
| My home office business uses three Windows NT Workstation computers... | Use a common workgroup. |
| I'm setting up a SQL Server on a new Windows NT Server in an existing domain... | Install the Windows NT Server as a member server, then install SQL Server on it. |
| I commonly work on two different domains. How do I set up my Windows NT Workstation for both? | If at all possible, a trust relationship should be set up. If one domain trusts another, set up your workstation in the trusted domain. If you have two-way trust, add it to the domain you use most. A computer can't be a member of multiple domains. |
| I'm in a domain, but would like to share the printer attached to my workstation with others... | Set up a share with permissions for a local group, to which you've added the domain users or global groups you want to allow to print there. |
| I want to log on to the domain but still have administrative access to my Windows NT Workstation... | Log onto your workstation as an administrator, and add your domain account to the local Administrators group. |
| I don't want my Windows NT Workstation to be in a workgroup or domain... | You have to be in one or the other. You may choose a workgroup not in use. |
| I have trouble with users keeping their Windows 95 and domain passwords synchronized... | If feasible, migrate to Windows NT Workstation. Then you'll only need one password. |

8. You have joined your Windows NT workstation to a domain. When you try to manage domain user and administrator accounts, you find you cannot. Why?

   A. You must use the User Manager for Domains program that comes with Windows NT Workstation.
   B. You must use the Domain Administrator program that comes with Windows NT Workstation.
   C. User Manager, which comes with Windows NT Workstation, can't administer such accounts.
   D. You do not have the proper permissions.

**9.** You have a domain of 200 computers. How many Primary Domain
Controllers will you have?

A. 20

B. 16

C. 50

D. 1

**10.** What does the next illustration show about the Windows NT workstation it
was taken from?

A. The workstation is a preferred Master Browser.

B. The workstation is not a preferred Master Browser.

C. The workstation is a PDC.

D. The workstation is a BDC.

**11.** How often does a Backup Browser receive an updated copy of the
browse list?

A. Every 5 minutes

B. Every 10 minutes

C. Every 15 minutes

D. Every 20 minutes

**12.** Darren is working on a Windows NT workstation that is part of a domain called STKITTS. A one-way trust has been set up with STKITTS as a trusting domain and LONDON as the trusted domain. Darren tries to access resources on LONDON, but finds he can't access anything. Why?

    A. Darren doesn't have an account on LONDON.

    B. Darren isn't part of the Complete Trust Model.

    C. STKITTS isn't trusted.

    D. LONDON isn't trusted.

**13.** All of the domain controllers are down. When you try to log onto your Windows NT workstation, what will happen?

    A. You won't be able to log on, because authentication can't take place.

    B. You won't be able to log on, because the workstation won't be able to interact with the network.

    C. Cached information from your last successful logon will be used to authenticate you.

    D. Your LastKnownGood option will be evoked from the BOOT.INI.

exam
Ⓦatch

*Now that the Internet is so popular, you may be familiar with another usage of the word domain. An Internet domain like "microsoft.com" is in the Internet domain namespace, and lets you know that systems within it, like "www.microsoft.com" are within that domain. The Internet meaning and the Windows NT meaning are entirely different. For Windows NT 4.0 usage, you can ignore the Internet meaning. The usage will blur once Windows NT 5.0 is released with its DNS-based active directory, but we'll have a new book for that.*

# Printing

**1.** You have just downloaded a new printer driver off of the Internet. After installing the driver, users start to complain that the printouts are illegible. What is most likely the problem?

A. You downloaded a virus from the Internet.
B. You have installed the wrong print driver.
C. The print spooler is corrupt.
D. The print spooler has stalled.

**2.** Your network consists of 10 Windows NT workstations. There is one printer attached to a single workstation, and it is shared by the network. You have just acquired a new printer driver off of the Internet. What is the easiest way to get everyone to use the updated driver?

A. Install the print driver on each workstation.
B. Create a new printer that uses the new driver, and instruct everyone to use this new printer.
C. Create a shared directory, then send e-mail to everyone on the network instructing them to download the driver and install it on their computer.
D. Install the print driver only on the computer acting as a print server.

**3.** You have just added a new Windows NT workstation to the network. The workstation is able to interact with the network, but cannot connect to a Hewlett Packard printer that is directly attached to the network. You check the user's permissions, and everything seems fine. What is most likely the problem?

A. DLC is not installed on the new workstation.
B. TCP/IP is not installed on the new workstation.
C. The user doesn't have the proper permissions to access the printer.
D. You forgot to enter a subnet mask for the workstation, keeping it from connecting to the printer.

**4.** What is responsible for routing print jobs to the appropriate port?

A. Print router

B. Print spooler

C. Print drivers

D. Print Prioritizing Service

**5.** A user has just begun printing the wrong document. Being new to the network, he is unsure as to who can manage and stop this print job. Since default settings exist, what can you tell him?

A. Only the print queue can stop the print job.

B. Only a member of the administrator group can stop the print job.

C. The creator owner of the print job can manage and stop the job.

D. The print job cannot be stopped.

**6.** You have taken ownership of a printer by mistake, and now want to give back the ownership. What must you do?

A. Select Return Ownership from the Printer Properties.

B. Return the ownership from the Printers applet in Control Panel.

C. Return the ownership from Windows NT Explorer.

D. You can't return ownership.

**7.** The Engineering department is always printing huge documents to a printer located in the meeting room. The printer is particularly noisy, and always disturbs the meeting. What can you do to remedy this?

A. Change the setting of the Availability check box in Print Router.

B. Change the setting of the Availability check box in Print Spooler.

C. Change the Availability settings from Date/Time Properties.

D. Change the Availability settings of the printer from the Scheduling tab of the Printer Properties.

*Be sure to understand that Hewlett-Packard JetDirect cards require the DLC protocol to be loaded on your system. DLC is not a routable protocol, so the print server and the printing device must be on the same side of a router.*

8. What controls the display of graphics on your monitor and printer?

    A. Graphic Device Monitor

    B. Graphic Device Adapter

    C. Graphic Device Interface

    D. Graphic Display Interface

9. What provides a user interface for configuration management of the print driver?

    A. Printer Interface Driver

    B. Printer Device Driver

    C. Printer Graphic Interface

    D. Printer Display Interface

10. A printer with a high priority needs to use a print device currently used by a printer with a low priority. What will happen?

    A. The printer with low priority will stop printing.

    B. The printer with the higher priority will have to wait for the low-priority printer to finish printing.

    C. The printer with the high priority will wait until the current page of the low-priority printer finishes printing, then it will start printing.

    D. The printer with low priority will attempt printing faster, so the higher-priority printer can print its job.

**11.** You decide to take ownership of a printer. Where will you go to do this?

A. Ask the network administrator nicely

B. Share tab of the Printer Properties

C. Security tab of the Printer Properties

D. Network applet in Control Panel

**12.** You decide to audit print events. Before you can audit these events, what must you do?

A. Turn auditing on in User Manager.

B. Turn auditing on in Print Manager.

C. Turn auditing on in Services.

D. Turn auditing on in Printer Properties.

**13.** You have implemented a print audit on a printer, and now want to see the results. What will you use for this?

A. Printer Manager

B. Printer applet in Control Panel

C. Event Viewer

D. The Print Audit screen in Printer Properties

---

exam

ⓦatch

*Be sure to understand that changing the priority of a printer doesn't affect the priority of the print queue. When you use two printers, printing to the same printer device, a printer with a higher priority will print to the device, when it's available, before a printer with a lower priority. If the lower-priority printer is busy printing a document, it finishes printing the job before releasing control to a higher-priority printer.*

---

# Configuring Applications

1. Which has the capability to access hardware directly in Windows NT?

   A. User mode
   B. Kernel mode
   C. Process
   D. Thread

2. You want to run a 16-bit Windows 3.x program in its own address space. What actions must you perform to do this?

   A. From the Start menu, choose Run, and select the Run in Separate Memory Space check box.
   B. From Object Manager, select the program, and select the Run in Separate Memory Space check box.
   C. Do nothing. 16-bit programs already run in a separate memory space.
   D. Do nothing. This objective can't be accomplished.

3. You are running several 16-bit Windows 3.x programs in Windows NT. One of these 16-bit programs crashes. What will happen to the other 16-bit programs and Windows NT itself?

   A. Only the program that crashed will be affected.
   B. Windows NT will freeze up.
   C. All of the 16-bit programs will crash, and Windows NT will freeze up.
   D. All of the 16-bit programs will crash, but Windows NT will be unaffected.

4. How are 32-bit and 16-bit programs multitasked?

   A. 32-bit and 16-bit programs are cooperatively multitasked.
   B. 32-bit and 16-bit programs are preemptively multitasked.
   C. 16-bit programs are cooperatively multitasked with each other, and 32-bit programs are preemptively multitasked.
   D. 16-bit programs are preemptively multitasked with each other, and 32-bit programs are cooperatively multitasked.

# QUESTIONS AND ANSWERS

| | |
|---|---|
| You have a 16-bit application suite and one application is faulty... | Run the faulty application in a separate memory space so it cannot affect the other applications running. Be aware that running every 16-bit application in a separate memory space is an option, too. |
| One 32-bit application crashes... | Don't worry. It will not affect the other applications running on the system. |
| Three 16-bit applications are running in the default space, and one crashes... | Once the faulty application that has frozen the message queue has been terminated, the other applications should be able to continue processing. You must know the defaults that these applications are run in. All three shouldn't crash, just the faulty application. Once the faulty application that has frozen the queue is terminated, the other two applications should be able to continue processing. |
| You want to start a program minimized and in a separate memory space... | Remember the syntax for starting applications from the command prompt. You know the command is START, and you know the switch for separate is /SEPARATE, and you know the switch for minimized is /MIN. Look for the answer with these choices, and of course, in the correct order. Here is the proper syntax for the command: START /MIN /MAX /SEPARATE application_name. |
| You would like to start a program with a higher priority level... | Start the application using the HIGH priority class. This too is done from the command prompt. Know the syntax and the correct order. Once again, here is the proper syntax for the command with priority levels: START /LOW /NORMAL /REALTIME /HIGH application_name. |
| How are 32-bit applications run in relation to... | They are preemptively multitasked with other applications in the system. |
| How are DOS applications run in relation to... | They also are preemptively multitasked with other applications in the system, including other DOS applications. |
| How are 16-bit applications run in relation to... | They are cooperatively multitasked within their own VDM and preemptively multitasked with other applications in the system. |

**5.** Windows NT won't allow a program to directly access hardware, yet many programs must print, save to a hard disk, and access other hardware devices. What allows Windows NT to control the hardware, yet make the application think it is accessing hardware devices?

A. Virtual Device Drivers

B. Virtual Access Drivers

C. Virtual Control Devices

D. Virtual Subsystem

**6.** How are POSIX and OS/2 programs multitasked in Windows NT Workstation?

A. POSIX applications are preemptively multitasked, while OS/2 applications are cooperatively multitasked.

B. POSIX applications are cooperatively multitasked, while OS/2 applications are preemptively multitasked.

C. POSIX and OS/2 applications are both cooperatively multitasked.

D. POSIX and OS/2 applications are both preemptively multitasked.

**7.** On Windows NT Workstation, what provides Windows 3.*x* emulation?

A. KRNL386.EXE

B. USER.EXE

C. GDI.EXE

D. WOWEXEC.EXE

**8.** You want to start a program from the command line with a priority of 13. What command will you type if the program is called MICHAEL.EXE?

A. START MICHAEL /LOW

B. START MICHAEL

C. START MICHAEL /REALTIME

D. START MICHAEL /HIGH

e x a m
ⓦa t c h

*You probably will be asked on the test to choose the correct command line for starting an application, based on the situation. This will include the priority levels, separate memory space, and whether it will be minimized or maximized. Know your syntax! You can type START /? |MORE at the command prompt for an overview.*

**9.** What purpose does the Hardware Abstraction Layer serve in Windows NT Workstation?

    A. It contains the device drivers for hardware on your system.

    B. It allows Windows NT to be portable to other architectures.

    C. It shadows your BIOS to its memory space.

    D. It is used by Networks only.

**10.** You want to start a 16-bit program from the command line in a separate memory space. What must you type?

    A. START *<program name>* /MEM

    B. START *<program name>* /SEPARATE

    C. START *<program name>* /HIGH

    D. START *<program name>* /UMB

**11.** Part of the microkernel's function is scheduling. What is the smallest unit it can schedule?

    A. Thread

    B. Executable

    C. Process

    D. Thunk

e x a m
ⓦa t c h

*The exam may ask what types of applications are supported in Windows NT.*

**12.** You want to run an OS/2 application in a VDM, rather than have it use the OS/2 subsystem. What must you type?

A. START *<program name>* /VDM

B. START *<program name>* /FORCEDOS

C. FORCEDOS, then wait for the dialog box to appear

D. FORCEDOS *<program name>*

**13.** Rosa is using the START command to start a program. What is the highest priority level she can set from the command line?

A. Default

B. Low

C. High

D. Realtime

# Performance Tuning

**1.** Jennifer's Windows NT workstation has several hard disks that are single partitioned. Her system and boot drives are the first hard disk. Her computer uses more resources than memory, and she is experiencing sluggishness on her computer from things being swapped out of memory to the page file. How can you optimize this workstation?

A. Create multiple page files, with one on each hard disk.

B. Create multiple page files, with one on every hard disk except the system/boot drive.

C. Implement a stripe set across all disks.

D. Implement a stripe set with parity across all disks.

**2.** You want to view the performance of a single physical disk in a stripe set. You start performance monitor, but none of the counters appear. What is the problem?

A. You need to run DISKPERF for the counters to appear.

B. You need to run DISKPERF –YE for the counters to appear.

C. You need to run DISKPERF –Y for the counters to appear.

D. Since it's a stripe set, you can't view the counters of just one disk, only the set.

**3.** Which of the following is the single biggest bottleneck on most computers?

A. Hard disks

B. RAM

C. Processor

D. NIC

**4.** Windows NT implements numerous methods of performance optimization. Which of the following isn't supported?

A. Swap files across multiple disks

B. Thread and process prioritizing

C. Symmetric multiprocessing

D. Caching API requests

**5.** You are using Performance Monitor and want to monitor the % Network Utilization counter. When you check Performance Monitor, you find these counters are missing. What can you do to fix this problem?

A. Run DISKPERF

B. Install Network Monitor Agent

C. Install SMS

D. Install SMTP

exam
ⓦatch

*You must use DISKPERF –YE if you want to monitor a physical drive in a stripe disk set. Using DISKPERF –YE installs the Disk Drive Performance Statistics Driver low in the disk driver stack, so that it can see individual physical disks before they are logically combined.*

**6.** Windows NT can automatically adjust an application's priority by which value?

   A. 2

   B. 3

   C. 7

   D. 24

**7.** You have just installed a new Windows NT Workstation. You plan to use Performance Monitor for optimization. What is the first thing you should do to start an optimization plan with Performance Monitor?

   A. Check the counters in Chart View.

   B. Create a baseline.

   C. Create a Crashdump file.

   D. Optimize Performance Monitor.

**8.** You go into System Properties, and click the Performance tab. There you move the Application Performance Boost slider bar to Maximum. What is the value of the application's priority level now?

   A. The foreground application has a priority of three.

   B. The foreground application has a priority of seven.

   C. The foreground application has a priority of ten.

   D. The foreground application is unchanged. The background application has a value of three.

**9.** How many processors will Windows NT Workstation 4.0 support out of the box?

   A. 1

   B. 2

   C. 16

   D. 32

**exam**
**Watch**

*Many people taking the exam get confused by the number of processors that are supported by Windows NT Workstation and Windows NT Server. Be sure to recognize the differences in supported quantities of processors between the two different operating systems as they are shipped.*

**10.** You are preparing to create a baseline with Performance Monitor. Which view mode should you be in to do this?

A. Chart

B. Report

C. Log

D. Standard

**11.** Which is the form of processing that is best for system performance?

A. Symmetric

B. Asymmetric

C. Both symmetric and asymmetric

D. Neither

**12.** You are certain that an application or Windows NT service has become a CPU or memory bottleneck. What tool is best suited to determine this quickly?

A. Task Manager

B. Dr. Watson

C. Performance Monitor

D. MSD

**13.** You turn on the disk counters, and check disk activity in Performance Monitor. You find there is a sustained disk activity rate of 85 percent. You check the counters for the number of Page Fault/sec and find they are low. What is causing the bottleneck?

A. Network
B. Memory
C. Hard disk
D. CPU

---

exam
**Ⓦatch**

*Windows NT Workstation can create Volume and Stripe sets with the Disk Administrator. Windows NT Server is also capable of creating certain levels of RAID from the Disk Administrator. Some people taking the exam get confused on the differences in Disk Administrator between the two operating systems.*

---

# Booting, Troubleshooting, and Service Packs

**1.** You boot your Windows NT Workstation, and the following message appears: "Windows NT could not start because the following file is missing or corrupt: WINNT\SYSTEM32\NTOSKRNL.EXE." Why is this message probably appearing?

A. IO.SYS is missing.
B. NTLDR is missing.
C. BOOT.INI file is missing or contains wrong information.
D. NTDETECT.COM is missing.

**2.** Which of the following activities can be performed by an Emergency Boot Disk? (Choose all that apply.)

A. Inspect the boot sector.
B. Inspect the Registry.
C. Inspect the startup environment.
D. Verify system files.

**3.** You have installed a UPS on your computer for protection from power outages. Every time your computer starts, the UPS shuts off. How can you fix the problem?

    A. Add the /NODEBUG switch to your BOOT.INI.

    B. Add the /BASEVIDEO switch to your BOOT.INI.

    C. Add the /CRASHDEBUG switch to your BOOT.INI.

    D. Add the /NOSERIALMICE=COMX switch to your BOOT.INI.

**4.** Julie's computer dual boots between Windows NT Workstation and Windows 95. She has changed the display driver on her Windows NT Workstation. Now, when she boots into Windows NT, all she sees is a blank screen. She can't even see the display sheet to change her settings back! How can she get into Windows NT and change the display driver to something else?

    A. From the Dual Boot menu, choose Windows 95 and change the display driver from there.

    B. From the Dual Boot menu, choose Windows NT Workstation VGA mode. Change the display.

    C. Boot into DOS, then change the display settings from there.

    D. She can't. She must reinstall Windows NT.

**5.** Some files have been corrupted on Darren's computer, and Julie has helped him out by providing him with a backup of her computer's files. You get a frantic call saying that the situation is worse. You try booting Windows NT Workstation, but fail. You then boot your computer from a floppy created for Darren's original system, and receive the following message: "Windows could not boot because the following file was missing or corrupt: WINNT\SYSTEM32\NOSKRNL.EXE. Please Reinstall a copy of the above file". What can you do to fix the problem?

    A. Install the Service Pack for Windows NT.

    B. Specify the correct ARC path in the BOOT.INI file.

    C. Specify the correct ARC name in the BOOT.INI file.

    D. Replace the BOOT.INI file with an LMHOSTS file.

**e x a m**
**ⓦa t c h** *The importance of the BOOT.INI cannot be stressed enough. Know what will happen if the BOOT.INI file is damaged, missing or otherwise errant. You must also know how to edit it, and be very familiar with reading it.*

6. Which boot file will examine the hardware on an Intel machine, and build a list of components that is passed on to the NTLDR?

   A. NTDETECT

   B. BOOT.INI

   C. NTOSKRNL

   D. BOOTSECT.DOS

7. You are informed that a computer in your company is having a problem with a SCSI drive. New SCSI drivers have been installed to optimize the system, but now it won't work. The BIOS on the SCSI controller is enabled. You check the BOOT.INI file and see the following: "[boot loader] timeout=30 default=SCSI(0)DISK(0)RDISK(0)PARTITION(1)\WINNT". What does this tell you about the problem?

   A. The SCSI drivers don't work.

   B. The disk information is in the wrong section.

   C. Since the BIOS is enabled, the ARC path should read MULTI(0)DISK(0)RDISK(0)PARTITION(1)\WINNT.

   D. The wrong partition is set in the ARC path.

8. What switch, when used in BOOT.INI, will cause the names of device drivers to be displayed as they are loaded?

   A. /BASEVIDEO

   B. /IMG

   C. /SOS

   D. /DEVICE

**9.** You can share files with other Windows NT workstations through peer services, but no one can access the server. What is the most likely problem?

    A. Network

    B. Workstation configurations

    C. The server

    D. None of the above

**10.** Jennifer takes BOOTSECT.DOS and places it on another workstation. Now, when she selects Windows 95 from the Dual Boot menu, the operating system won't load on that workstation. Why?

    A. The problem isn't with BOOTSECT.DOS, but with the hard disk itself.

    B. It calls NTDETECT.

    C. It loads the NTLDR.

    D. It stores partition information specific to the computer it was originally installed on.

**11.** Which file loads the Windows NT operating system on a computer with a RISC processor?

    A. BOOTSECT.DOS

    B. NTOSKRNL

    C. OSLOADER

    D. NTDETECT

**12.** Your computer has been producing STOP errors. You know that these are logged to the SYSTEM.LOG file. What would you use to view these logged errors?

    A. Event Viewer

    B. System Editor

    C. Registry Editor

    D. Performance Monitor

*If your BOOT.INI does not list the SCSI ARC name, then NTBOOTDD.SYS will not be used.*

13. You are having difficulties with Windows NT Workstation. Unfortunately, your modem isn't working. Which of the following resources are available to you under these circumstances? (Choose all that apply.)

   A. TechNet
   B. MSDL
   C. Microsoft Knowledge Base
   D. Windows NT Help files

14. You want to view information regarding interrupt requests (IRQ), I/O ports, direct memory access (DMA), memory and device drivers. What tool comes with Windows NT, and can be used to investigate such information from one screen?

   A. Windows NT Diagnostics
   B. Disk Administrator
   C. Server Manager
   D. Performance Monitor

*The Security Accounts Manager (SAM) and security files are not automatically updated by RDISK. To update those files, you need to use the /S switch in conjunction with RDISK.*

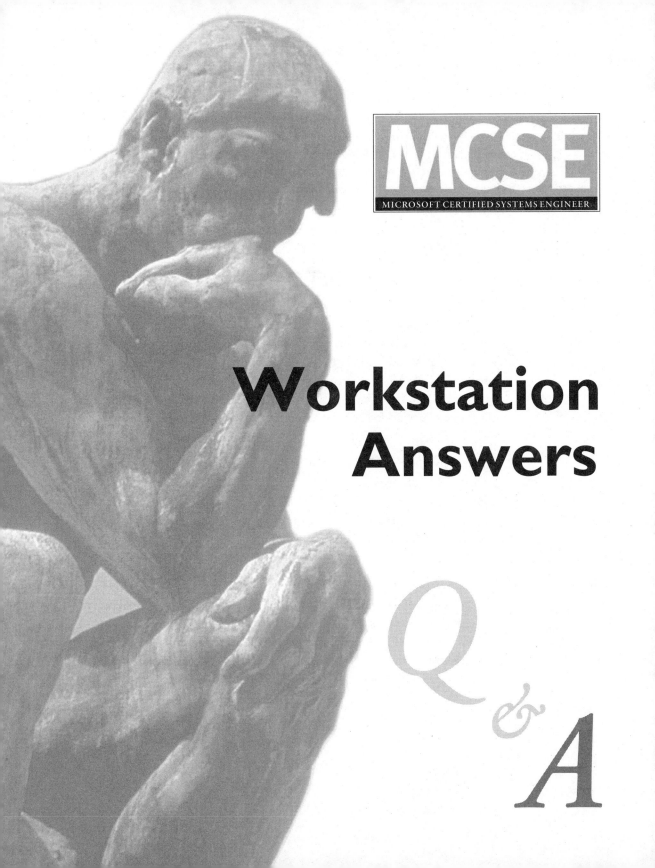

The answers to the questions are in boldface, followed by a brief explanation. Some of the explanations detail the logic you should use to choose the correct answer, while others give factual reasons why the answer is correct. If you miss several questions on a similar topic, you should review the corresponding section in the Study Guide before taking the MCSE test.

# Answers:
# Overview of Windows NT Workstation 4.0

1. **C.** High Performance File System (HPFS) was supported by previous versions of Windows NT, but is no longer. FAT, NTFS, and VFAT are all supported by Windows NT. FAT (File Allocation Table) is the file system used with DOS, VFAT (Virtual File Allocation Table) is a file system introduced in Windows 95, and NTFS (New Technology File System) is the file system available only on Windows NT.

2. **C.** Only the DOS application will lock up, because it is running in its own virtual MS-DOS machine (VDM). Because it's running in its own memory space, only the DOS application will be affected. This is different from 16-bit Windows programs that share common space, where one application can crash all other 16-bit Windows programs.

3. **A.** The environmental subsystems reside in the User mode of Windows NT Workstation's architecture. The environmental subsystems contain Application Programming Interfaces (APIs) that emulate an application's native operating system. In short, a POSIX application thinks it's actually running on a UNIX machine rather than on a Windows NT workstation. See the next illustration for additional information on Windows NT's architecture.

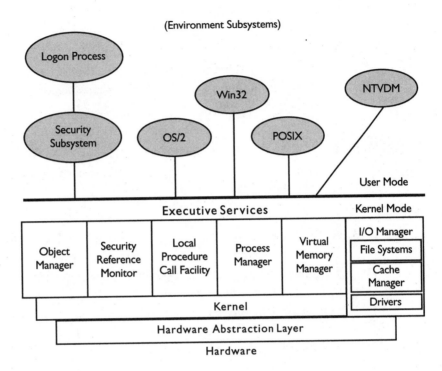

4. **A.** Windows NT Workstation can only handle two processors. The other OSs can only handle one. Windows NT Server supports four processors out of the box, but can use up to 32 processors.

5. **A.** Windows NT Workstation can only have one RAS connection at any one time. This is unlike Windows NT Server, which can handle 256 connections.

6. **D.** Windows NT Workstation handles 16-bit Windows applications and DOS applications differently. DOS applications run in their own virtual DOS machine (VDM). To the application, this makes it seem that it is the only program running on the computer, and so has no need of sharing

memory with other applications. Also, since each DOS program is running in its own VDM, they can be preemptively multitasked and given different priorities. 16-bit Windows applications run together in a single VDM (just as if they were running in Windows 3.x), share memory, and use cooperative multitasking.

7. **B.** There can be only 10 inbound client sessions at one time on a Windows NT workstation. Windows NT Server, however, can handle an unlimited number of client sessions.

8. **A.** The Workgroup model is ideal for networks with 10 or fewer computers, and is easy to set up. There is no centralized control of user accounts and resources. Users of this model should be somewhat adept with computers, as they control their own resources and access to their workstations. A positive point to this type of model is that one does not have to use Windows NT Server (which is more expensive than Workstation) for authenticating users, and there is no central point of failure for the network.

9. **A.** The Kernel is responsible for creating, managing and scheduling threads. In User mode, applications make requests to the Kernel. The Kernel then executes the request and returns the data that results from the execution. There are 32 thread priority levels in Windows NT, and the Kernel schedules based on a priority level.

10. **C.** The Domain model is the best choice for networks consisting of inexperienced users. This is because the Workgroup model requires users to have the ability to set up shared resources and manage accounts. With the Domain model, accounts and resources can be centrally controlled from a PDC.

11. **C.** NTFS partitions are not visible to operating systems that aren't Windows NT (Windows NT Server or Workstation). Though a file on a NTFS partition would be visible to non-Windows NT systems on a network, it would not be seen by a non-Windows NT operating system that was dual booted on the computer that contains the NTFS partition. This is because the computer viewing the file off the network is viewing the file through Windows NT. In other words, the computer on the network "sees" the file through the "eyes" of the Windows NT Server or Workstation that is allowing access to the file.

12. **D.** Windows NT doesn't allow direct access to hardware, which is why DOS-based programs that require such access will not run. In these cases, it is important to plan whether the program can be upgraded or is even necessary, before installing Windows NT.

13. **C, D.** Both Windows NT Server 4.0 and Windows NT Workstation 4.0 are portable to Reduced Instruction Set Computing (RISC) processors. Examples of processors that are based on the RISC design include MIPS, DEC Alpha, and PowerPC. RISC allows for fast and efficient processing of smaller numbers of instructions. Windows NT also supports x86 processors, such as Intel, which are based on the Complex Instruction Set Computing (CISC) design.

# Answers:
# Installing Windows NT Workstation 4.0

1. **A.** The Hardware Compatibility List (HCL) is an inventory of all hardware that Microsoft has tested to be compatible with Windows NT. This list includes much of the hardware on the market today, and even hardware that hasn't been manufactured for years. By consulting this list, you can avoid hardware conflicts that will result immediately during installation or over time after installation is completed.

2. **C.** When Windows 95 is upgraded to Windows NT, it is like a full installation. Registry settings are replaced and installed programs need to be reinstalled. This is because the Registries of the two operating systems are different. Future releases of the two products will not have this problem according to Microsoft.

3. **B.** The active partition is the partition on the hard disk that Windows NT will boot from. It is also known as the system partition.

4. **A.** File Allocation Table (FAT) partitions are unable to take advantage of the file and directory security offered by NTFS. With NTFS you can specify directory and file access levels, and even specify who will get what kind of access to these objects. In addition, computers that dual boot to operating systems other than Windows NT, will not be able to view or access files or directories on the NTFS partition.

5. **A, B.** Fixed Disk setup program (FDISK) and Disk Administrator can both remove partitions. FDISK is a DOS utility, while Disk Administrator comes with Windows NT Workstation and Server. While FDISK can create and delete FAT partitions, Disk Administrator can create and remove both FAT and NTFS partitions. No matter what you use to remove a disk, be careful that you really want to remove the partition, and that you choose the correct partition. There is no way to "unremove" a partition!

6. **B.** Using the WINNT.EXE /OX or WINNT32.EXE /OX commands creates new setup floppies. This is convenient should you ever lose, misplace or damage the floppies that come with Windows NT Workstation. It is important to remember this, not just in case you lose your floppies, but because this question tends to pop up on Windows NT Workstation exams!

7. **D.** The command used in this question uses several switches. The WINNT.EXE starts a full installation of Windows NT, while the /B switch makes it floppyless. The /U:UNATTEND.TXT signifies an unattended installation, and uses a text file named UNATTEND.TXT to take installation information from. This text file could have any name, but the name you specify must match the text file's name. Usually on Microsoft exams, the file's name is what we used here. The /S switch specifies the source location of UNATTEND.TXT. In this case, it resides in the D:\I386 directory. It is important that you familiarize yourself with these switches, as any combination of them may appear on your exam.

8. **D.** TCP/IP, NetBEUI, and NWLink are the protocols you get to choose from when installing Windows NT Workstation. More protocols can be added to the list (such as AppleTalk or DLC), and installed at this time. Protocols also can be added after installation is completed.

9. **B.** The MS Loopback adapter allows you to install protocols, even if there isn't a network adapter card on your computer. Also, it is particularly useful for diagnosing problems that might occur as a result of incorrect configurations. In installing the MS Loopback adapter, the only configuration information you have to supply is the frame type (802.3 or Ethernet, 802.5 or Token Ring, or FDDI).

10. **C.** DLC is a protocol used to allow computers to interact with mainframes and Hewlett Packard printers. It can be installed either on individual workstations, or on a gateway used to communicate with the printer. If there is a problem communicating with a HP printer, always consider DLC as a reason.

11. **C.** Since all of the desktop computers and all of the laptop computers are identical, one answer file would be required for each type. One would be needed for the hardware configuration of the desktop computers, and another would be needed for the laptops. A single UDF would be needed, with a separate section for each computer and user. This would allow users who are installing Windows NT to specify just the answer file, and allow UDF to automate installation.

12. **B.** Unlike previous versions, Windows NT Workstation 4.0 doesn't support HPFS. The HPFS partition must first be converted to NTFS first. NTFS will preserve the existing file and directory security settings. Once this is done, you will then be able to perform the upgrade.

13. **C.** Once presented with the initial startup screen of Setup Manager, the options are fairly straightforward. General Setup controls user information, hardware settings, the computer's role on the network, installation directory, display settings, time zone, and license mode. Networking Setup controls adapters, protocols, services, Internet services, and modem information. The Advanced Setup controls advanced settings, such as converting FAT partitions to NTFS, that should only be used by experienced users.

# Answers:
# Configuring Windows NT Workstation 4.0

1. **C.** The HKEY_CLASSES_ROOT contains information used for object linking and embedding. Applications register this information when they are installed.

2. **D.** The last operating system installed will be the default operating system listed in the Startup/Shutdown tab of System Properties. In this case, the default would be Windows NT Server. To change the default operating system, simply choose another OS from the drop-down list. The next time

you reboot, the OS you choose will appear as the default operating system. This information appears in the BOOT.INI file, and can also be changed by editing this file.

3. **A.** Since the virus scanner is working in the background, you would want to decrease the foreground application's priority. Therefore, you would lower the boost to None. The Performance Boost applies to the foreground application, which is the application you are working in at the time. Raising the boost increases its priority. Lowering it lowers its priority, and thereby raises the performance of applications running in the background.

4. **B.** On the General tab of System Properties, you can find user information, version number, and product ID. This information about Windows NT Workstation is not found in any of the other sources. Such information is particularly useful when obtaining updates and service packs from Microsoft.

5. **C.** The Startup/Shutdown tab of System Properties allows you to set how Windows NT Workstation will behave during a Stop error (system crash). You have the choice of writing the event to the system log, sending an administrative alert, or writing debugging information to a file of your choosing.

6. **D.** The Environment tab of System Properties allows you to modify a number of things about your system. Admittedly, it would be pointless to change many of the items here, but the path statement is useful. If the system cannot find a file in the current directory, it will search through each of the directory paths that you specify in this field. It is the same as changing the path statement found in the AUTOEXEC.BAT.

7. **C.** The HKEY_CURRENT_CONFIG contains the configuration information for the current hardware profile. While most changes to the hardware are usually made through the HKEY_LOCAL_MACHINE, this key can also be used for making changes to hardware.

8. C. The Security Accounts Manager resides in the HKEY_LOCAL_ MACHINE key of the Registry. This subtree is in binary format as a safety feature to keep curious or malicious users from altering security information.

9. C. By creating different hardware profiles, you can specify which services you want to start according to your needs. In this case, one hardware profile would start network services, while another hardware profile would run the computer off the wire. All you need to do is specify which hardware profile you wish to use, depending on your needs, when you start the computer.

10. C. The Multimedia applet in Control Panel is used to install MIDI devices and their drivers. The MIDI tab has features that will run a wizard to help you install and configure such a device.

11. C. The Registry is unique to each computer. It contains information about all devices and software on the computer. If it is copied over to another computer, the Windows NT workstation receiving the Registry will not work.

12. C. By setting Password Protect on the Screensaver tab of the Display applet, anyone who attempts to use the computer once the screensaver has started will be greeted with a password dialog box. If that person doesn't know the correct password, he won't be able to use the workstation.

13. C. You install protocols such as TCP/IP through the Network applet. Although the Internet uses TCP/IP, the Internet applet configures settings for using the Internet. The Network applet installs, binds and configures the protocols themselves.

# Answers: Managing Users and Groups

**1. A.** Account policy deals with the items in the Account Policy Box, shown in in the next illustration. Changes here affect every user logging onto the computer. User Manager's Policy menu is used to change account policies on just that computer, while changes to account policies in User Manager for Domains affects every user in that domain.

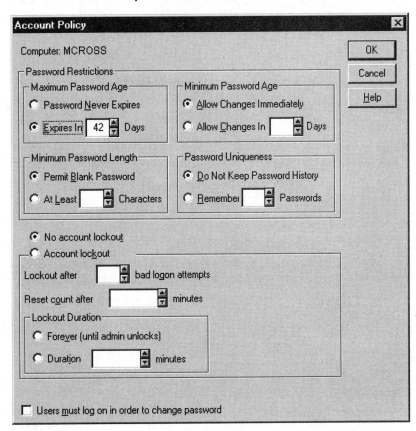

**2. B.** You cannot delete the Administrator account. Since it is created by Windows NT upon installation, it does pose a potential security risk. Because of this, many people rename the account. The other way to secure your system from this avenue of entry is more difficult. Choose an impossible-to-guess password, made up of both numbers and letters, write down the password, and lock it away somewhere safe (such as in a safe). Then create an account under a different name that you will use for administration. The original Administrator account still exists, and acts as a failsafe should anything go wrong with the account you regularly use for admin purposes.

**3. A.** Global groups can only be created on a Windows NT server functioning as a domain controller. They are used to ease the administration burden of individually assigning rights to domain users. Local permissions are assigned through global groups to the domain users, who need access or permissions to certain resources. Windows NT workstations aren't capable of creating global groups, only local groups. Workstation is capable of adding existing global groups to local groups.

**4. D.** Global groups cannot contain local groups. You can place a global group into a local group, but not the other way around. Global groups affect the entire domain, and are stored in the directory service database.

**5. B.** The Policy menu in User Manager allows you to set account policy on the local computer. The policies set here will not affect the entire domain, only that computer.

**6. A.** You enable auditing of a user through User Manager. Auditing allows you to track system events that result from an audited user's actions. It can record invalid logon attempts, attempts to access resources that a user hasn't permission to use, and much more. It is useful for determining whether a user, or a user's account, is being used improperly.

7. **C.** The Security Identifier (SID) identifies an account to a Windows NT computer. It is neither the account's name nor password that identifies an account to a Windows NT computer, but the SID. The SID is created when the account is created. It is unique and cannot be modified. To discover first hand that the SID is used to identify an account, you only have to delete an account, then recreate it with the same name. The access the new account enjoys will be different from the original account, because the new account's SID is different than the first one.

8. **B.** The user must log off, and then log back onto the network before the changes take effect. Many of the changes to a user's account will not take place immediately. In many cases, a user remains unaffected by the changes while logged on. The changes will appear when the user logs back onto the network, and a new access token is created containing these changes.

9. **A.** The Security Identifier is unique. It is created when an account or group is created, and cannot be changed or modified. This means that if you delete an account or group, and then create another by the same name, the new one will have a new SID generated for it. Since the SID identifies the account to a Windows NT server or workstation, the new account is viewed as different from the original.

10. **D.** Roaming user profiles are kept on the domain controllers (generally, replicated between the PDC and BDCs). When a user logs onto the domain, his or her profile is copied onto the computer he is using. This is what allows the profile to be "roaming".

11. **C.** Security Policy Changes audits changes to user rights or audit policies. Use of User Rights audits whether a user succeeded or failed in the use of any right other than logon or logoff. User and Group Management audits whether a user created, modified, or deleted a user or group account. File and Object Access audits whether a user accessed an object (such as a directory or printer) or file that was set to be audited.

12. **D.** Members of the Administrator group are the only default group with the right to load and unload device drivers. No other group membership allows the right to perform this action.

13. **B.** Users Must Logon To Change Password is the setting you must change to prevent users with expired passwords from changing their password. Since they cannot log on to change the expired password, users must go to an administrator to change it.

# Answers: Windows NT File System Support

1. **B.** CONVERT.EXE will convert a FAT partition to NTFS, without deleting any of the existing files. NTFS is a file system only supported by Windows NT systems, while FAT32 is an enhanced version of FAT that only Windows 95 supports. Since the single disk drive has been changed to NTFS, Windows 95 is unable to boot.

2. **A, B.** The system and boot partitions cannot be part of a volume set. This is because the volume set is viewed through Windows NT. Since it hasn't loaded yet, it can't be viewed. As such, if the system and boot partitions were on the set, it couldn't be seen, and thus couldn't be loaded.

3. **B.** Disk striping with parity offers fault tolerance. Volume sets and disk striping without parity do not. With disk striping with parity, if one disk fails, one need only replace the failed hard disk and regenerate its data. Since parity information spreads the mixing data over the other disks, very little storage space is used (in comparison to disk mirroring or disk duplexing).

4. **A.** NTFS uses file compression that is different from systems that use disk compression, such as DoubleSpace, DriveSpace, and Stacker. Rather than compressing the entire partition, and then loading drivers to use the drive, NTFS can compress each file individually.

**5. A, B, C.** VFAT is an enhanced version of FAT supported by Windows NT. It allows 255 character names, preserves case, and allows spaces between characters. It breaks from the standard 8.3 DOS naming convention, though you can still use that convention. It is important to remember that VFAT is not the same as FAT32, which is only supported by Windows 95.

**6. A.** Once the Recycle Bin has been emptied, files deleted in Windows NT are gone for good. Your only option is to restore the file from an existing backup. When files are deleted in Windows NT, they are sent to the Recycle Bin. If you decide not to resurrect the files, they are completely lost to you when the Recycle Bin is emptied. Even if you drop to DOS, and try using UNDELETE, you won't be able to recover them.

**7. C.** FAT is an old file system that is widely supported, and widely in use. Both Windows 95 and Windows NT can read from a FAT file system, and it is the only real option for a computer that dual boots between the two.

**8. B.** The next available drive letter will be the one that isn't currently used. This includes all mapped network drives. If C, D, and E are drives on the computer, and F and G are mapped drives used on the computer, then the next available drive letter would be H. If this isn't satisfactory, you can always choose the option of not designating a drive letter at this time (see the next illustration). Remove the mapped drives, then assign the next available drive letter, which now would be F.

**9. A.** Disk striping without parity is RAID level 0. It is excellent for increasing read/write performance, but offers no fault tolerance. If one disk fails in a stripe set, the data on every hard disk is lost! It should only be used for performance issues, but never as an option for disaster recovery.

**10. D.** This one was a bit of a trick question, as Windows NT Workstation doesn't support RAID level 5 (disk striping with parity). Windows NT Server does support disk striping with parity, which requires three physical hard disks to implement. This is because the parity information is spread out across the physical disks, so that if one fails, the other two (or more) can regenerate the missing data.

**11. A.** If a compressed file is moved to a folder on the same partition, the file will retain its attributes and remain compressed. However, if this same file were moved to a different partition, it would adopt the attributes of the target folder, and could become uncompressed.

**12. A, D.** Since this is a new partition, there are no existing files to worry about. Because CONVERT changes the file system over to NTFS, without deleting any files, it isn't needed here. CONVERT also can not be used, because no file system exists yet. It's a new partition, remember? FORMAT can be used to format a partition to NTFS, while Disk Administrator is the other valid way to format the partition as NTFS. With Disk Administrator, you just need to remember to choose Commit To Changes, otherwise the disk won't be formatted.

**13. C.** The Lazy Write feature of NTFS is a transaction log that tracks whether writes have been made properly to a disk.

**14. C.** An emergency repair disk (ERD) can be made during installation, or with RDISK. RDISK is a utility that allows you to recover information that deals with disk configuration, and to create and update ERDs. The emergency repair disk is used to restore missing or corrupt system files.

# Answers:
# Understanding Windows NT 4.0 Security

1. **C.** The No Access setting overrides any permissions that might have been set. It does not matter what other permissions you might have; this setting overrides everything else.

2. **B.** File permissions override directory permissions. If a user has Full Control on a directory, Read and Write permissions on a subdirectory, and Read permissions on a file, that user will only have Read permissions to that file.

3. **D.** Permissions are cumulative. The various permissions assigned to your user account are combined with the permissions set for any groups that you belong to.

4. **A.** The Security Identifier (SID) is what identifies users and groups on the network. When an account is created, a unique SID is also created that identifies the user or group. This is similar to a Social Security or Social Insurance number. While the person does in fact have a name, the system doesn't use it to recognize you. It uses the number associated with you instead.

5. **A.** Creating a new account with the same name as a deleted one will not create the same account. Because the SID is created as a unique number when an account is created, deleting an account and creating a new one by the same name won't result in the original account being re-created. This is because a new SID has been created. When the user logs on, the SID will be looked at, seen as different from the original, and the original permissions won't be allowed.

6. **B.** The Group Security ID is only used by the POSIX subsystem. It is part of the Security Descriptor, which describes the security attributes of an object. The Security Descriptor contains the ACL.

7. **C.** Full Control is needed to take access of a file. The following table explains each of the file-level permissions available in NTFS.

| Access Level | Permissions | Description |
|---|---|---|
| No Access | None | This level overrides all others. |
| Read | RX | Can read or execute a file. |
| Change | RXWD | Can read, execute, write, Delete a file. |
| Full Control | RWXDPO | Can read, execute, write, change permissions, and take ownership of a file. |

**8. C.** The Administrator account is unaffected by account lockout settings (shown in the next illustration) in Account Policy. After a number of invalid logon attempts, the Administrator account will experience a short delay before further attempts can be made. However, this is not a result of any Account Policy settings.

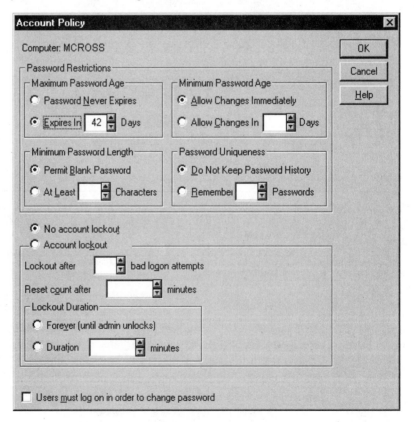

**9.** **A.** By editing the Registry, you can supply the system with a name and password, which will automate the logon process. The account you specify here should never be the Administrator account. Though this is used in low-security settings, the Administrator account falling into inexperienced hands can still result in considerable damage to a system.

**10.** **C.** Windows NT Workstation supports Local, Remote, Domain, and Passthrough logon types

**11.** **C.** A program will have the same rights and permissions as the user who is running it. If Microsoft Word attempts to open a file, Windows NT Workstation determines what rights and permissions the program has, which will be the same as the user running that program. If the program is allowed access to the file, the operating system will then open it.

**12.** **A.** By changing the value of the LegalNoticeCaption in WinLogon to a warning message, you can have a legal notice appear on the logon screen.

**13.** **A, B, C.** All file systems supported by Windows NT can use user-level security. This is because such security is implemented through the operating system, not the file system. In this question, FAT32 isn't correct, because Windows NT doesn't support that particular file system.

# Answers:
# Understanding Windows NT Networking

**1.** **C.** The Transport Driver Interface (TDI) is what allows redirectors to be written without regard for the protocol on your system. Rather than having to write one redirector for each protocol, or one redirector that works with several protocols, only one redirector has to be written to work with the TDI. Information is passed from the redirector down to the TDI, which then passes it on to the Transport protocol. The process is similar to that used for the NDIS Interface.

2. **B.** NDIS allows multiple protocols to bind to a single network adapter card (or NIC), or a single protocol to bind to multiple network adapter cards. Because of this, separate protocol stacks aren't required for each NIC.

3. **D.** TCP/IP is the protocol of the Internet. Since the Internet is a giant router, it requires a protocol that efficiently routes packets. TCP/IP does just that.

4. **A.** NetBEUI is a small, fast, and non-routable protocol. Because this network is small and will never grow, a protocol with larger overhead (TCP/IP and NWLink) is overkill. These larger protocols would slow down your network. AFP is the AppleTalk Filing Protocol. It is used by Windows NT to communication with Macintosh computers, but all the computers in this example are PCs.

5. **B.** To increase access to a protocol, you raise it in the binding order. This means moving the protocol higher up the list in the binding order. The higher a protocol is on the binding list, the faster the computer can access it.

6. **B.** By using a gateway with a routable protocol on the computer side, and DLC on the printer side, computers throughout the network will then be able to use the printer.
(I'll expand on this a-bit, so it becomes clearer. Since DLC isn't routable, you need to implement a gateway. You set up one computer with two network adapter cards in it. You bind DLC to the NIC connected to the segment that has the HP printer to which you want network-wide access. On the other NIC, you bind a routable protocol that the network uses, such as TCP/IP. Now, when users send a print job to the HP printer, it goes through the gateway. The gateway takes the data sent with TCP/IP off the wire, repackages it with DLC as the protocol, and sends it out the NIC connected to the section that has the printer. Fortunately, this all takes less time to occur than it does to explain!)

**7. B.** The Server applet in Control Panel is best suited for managing shares. With this applet, you can monitor the total number of active sessions, the number of open files currently accessed from the network, the number of file locks place by remote users, and the number of open pipes between your computer and the remote clients who are accessing the share. In addition, you can use it to disconnect users, and to close resources.

**8. A, B.** Windows NT creates two hidden shares during installation for administration purposes. Admin$ shares the root system directory, while C$ allows administrators to drive C's root directory. A similar share is created for each additional partition. However, floppy drives and CD-ROMs do not have such directories created for them.

**9. C.** A network wouldn't be a network if you couldn't see the other computers. The Computer Browser service allows your computer to be seen on the network, and maintains a list of available servers. Without it, Windows NT Workstation would be blind on the wire!

**10. D.** Network Dynamic Data Exchange (NetDDE) is a type of interprocess communication that creates a constant link between two applications, so that they can communicate. NetDDE provides these capabilities by keeping open two one-way pipes.

**11. A.** Mailslots is a type of interprocess communication (IPC) that provides connectionless communication between two computers. Because it is connectionless, delivery of messages sent by this method is not guaranteed. Mailslots is generally used for broadcasts.

**12. B.** The NDIS Interface corresponds to the Data Link layer of the OSI model.

13. **C.** The network cable corresponds to the Physical layer of the OSI model. It is important to remember what each layer of the OSI model does. Questions relating to OSI do tend to pop up on the Microsoft exams for Windows NT.

# Answers: Installing and Configuring TCP/IP

1. **B.** The World Wide Web is based on the Hypertext Transfer Protocol (HTTP). This is what enables the web to transfer web pages written in Hypertext Markup Language (HTML) from a web server to your Internet browser.

2. **C.** The default subnet mask for a single subnet is 255.255.255.0. This allows for 254 unique hosts to be part of the subnet. The subnet mask is used to distinguish the network from the host in an IP address. It masks part of the IP address so that this distinction can be made.

3. **B.** Domain Name Service (DNS) resolves DNS host names to IP addresses.

4. **B.** DNS servers resolve host names to IP addresses. Because you can connect with the IP address, but not the host name, the error in configuration of TCP/IP on your system is the absence of addresses of Primary and Secondary DNS Server. This is common in new installations of TCP/IP.

5. **A.** Because this is a non-routed network, you don't need to provide a default gateway, just the IP address and subnet mask. This is because there is only a single subnet, so the workstation won't need to go through a default gateway to connect with other subnets.

6. **D.** The layers of TCP/IP don't map exactly to the OSI layers, because the OSI model came out almost a decade after TCP/IP was introduced. This illustrates how far ahead of its time the TCP/IP suite was. The layers are

Application, Transport, Internet, and Network Interface. The next table shows how they map to the OSI model.

| OSI | TCP/IP |
| --- | --- |
| Application | Application |
| Presentation | |
| Session | |
| Transport | Transport |
| Network | Internet |
| Data Link | Network Interface |
| Physical | |

**7. B, C.** Because this is a routed network, both the subnet mask and default gateway must be specified during the installation. The subnet mask allows the computer to establish whether a message is for the segment this computer is on, or for another segment of the network. If it's for a different segment, it sends the packets to the default gateway. The default gateway then begins the process of sending it to the destination computer.

**8. B.** Domain Name System (DNS) servers resolve IP addresses to Fully Qualified Domain Names. DHCP assigns IP addresses to host computers, while WINS is used to resolve NetBIOS names to IP addresses.

**9. D.** Ping uses Internet Control Message Protocol (ICMP) to send an echo request to a destination computer. The destination computer responds, thereby proving that a connection exists. PING is a tool that comes with Windows NT Workstation.

**10. A.** Simple Mail Transfer Protocol (SMTP) is the protocol used to send and receive messages over the Internet. Since your message is going through the Internet, the mail server on your network—not your computer—is the actual computer sending this message. The server uses SMTP, not NetBEUI, to send the message.

11. **A.** By giving a group of computers the same NetBIOS scope ID, you can isolate them from the rest of the network. This group of computers will be able to communicate with each other, but they won't be able to interact with the rest of the network, and the network won't be able to interact with them.

By doing this, you can also set up different computers on the network with the same name (so long as they have different scope IDs). This means that SERVER.MRK, SERVER.SAL, and SERVER.STF can all exist on the same network, although they wouldn't be able to communicate with each other.

12. **C.** If everything is configured correctly and the multihomed computer isn't routing packets, the problem is often that the "Enable IP Forwarding" check box isn't enabled. Until this is box is checked, Windows NT won't route the packets.

13. **B.** For a multihomed Windows NT computer to act as a router, a different IP address must be assigned to each NIC. This is because one NIC will be part of one subnet, and the other will be part of another subnet. When one NIC on the multihomed computer receives a packet for the other subnet, it will send the packet onto the wire through its other NIC. This is what allows packets to be passed from one subnet to another.

# Answers: Connecting to NetWare Servers

1. **C.** When connecting to a NetWare 3.12 server for the first time, you must provide the preferred server you want to attach to. This is done through the Select NetWare Logon dialog box shown in the next illustration. If this information isn't provided, you won't be able to connect.

**Select NetWare Logon** ✕

Username:     twhinkle

◉ Preferred Server

Preferred Server:     `<None>` ▼

○ Default Tree and Context

Tree:     [                    ]

Context:     [                    ]

☐ Run Login Script

[ OK ]     [ Cancel ]     [ Help ]

2. **A, D.** When connecting to a NetWare 4.*x* server for the first time, you must provide the Default Tree and Context. This is because NetWare Directory Services, used in NetWare 4.*x*, is structured differently than 3.*x* was. In 3.*x*, information was stored in the bindery, while newer 4.*x* uses NDS. NDS allows resources and account databases to be shared between servers from a central location. It is only available on NetWare 4.*x*.

3. **B.** IPX is the default protocol used by NetWare servers. NWLink is Microsoft's implementation of the IPX/SPX protocol, and used by Windows NT machines to communicate with NetWare servers.

4. **C.** NWLink is an IPX/SPX-compatible transport protocol used by Windows NT Workstation to communicate with NetWare servers. IPX/SPX is the standard protocol of NetWare. While NetWare is fully capable of using other protocols, IPX/SPX is often used. This is because IPX/SPX is a reliable, routable protocol with less overhead than TCP/IP. It is ideal for use in medium-sized networks that require routing.

**5.** **D.** If you forgot to install NWLink before installing Client Services for NetWare, don't worry about it. NWLink will automatically be installed if its not already present during the installation of CSNW. This is because CSNW cannot function if NWLink isn't running.

**6.** **C.** The key point in this question is that only the user is having a problem. When one computer can't interact with a NetWare network from a Windows NT machine, while other users of the network aren't having a problem, always consider incorrect frame type. If the frame types used by two computers are different, then communication problems result.

**7.** **A, C.** The account name and password used on the Windows NT machine must match the one on the NetWare server. If a user has mismatched user account name and/or password, he or she will not be able to connect.

**8.** **B.** NetWare servers can translate different frame types on a network. Since the frame type on your computer is different from the rest of the network, all traffic between your computer and the network is being passed through the NetWare server so that the frame type can be translated.

**9.** **B.** If a NetWare server doesn't have the OS/2 name space NLM enabled, then Windows NT users will be forced to use the 8.3 naming convention for filenames saved to the NetWare server. If the NetWare server has this NLM loaded, they can use long filenames.

**10.** **D.** You can't install GSNW on a workstation. GSNW is used on Windows NT Server to provide connectivity with NetWare servers. Client Services are also installed with GSNW on the server. However, it can only be installed on a Windows NT server, not a workstation.

**11. A.** The default frame type of NetWare 4.*x* operating systems is 802.2, also known as Source Routing. It is the IEEE standard known as Logical Link Control. NetWare 3.*x* uses the 802.3 frame type.

**12. D.** Directory Service Manager for NetWare (DSMN) enables a single authentication for NetWare and Windows NT networks. It merges user accounts from multiple servers into a single database that is then distributed to the various NetWare servers. It is sold as part of the Services for NetWare package.

**13. A.** NWLink IPX/SPX Properties (shown in the next illustration) is where you would change the frame type used by Windows NT Workstation. Generally, you would leave the frame type set to auto, unless your workstation was having trouble interacting with a NetWare network.

# Answers:
# Remote Access Service and Dial-Up Networking

**1.** **B.** When a Windows NT machine is acting as a RAS server, it can only answer incoming calls with Point to Point Protocol (PPP). While it can dial out using either PPP or Serial Line Internet Protocol (SLIP), inbound sessions are limited to using PPP. This is because PPP is the newer, and better of the two protocols. SLIP is supported for calling out, so that it can still connect to older systems.

**2.** **A.** Windows NT Workstation is limited to one incoming session at a time. Windows NT Server, however, can handle up to 256 simultaneous inbound sessions.

**3.** **D.** Ping can be used to test a RAS connection. It is easy to use, and can check whether a connection has actually been established. As shown in the next illustration, by PINGing a server, you can see whether you're actually connected to it.

```
C:\WINNT40\System32\cmd.exe                              _ □ ×

C:\>ping dialupserver

Pinging dialupserver [207.158.5.104] with 32 bytes of data:

Reply from 207.158.5.104: bytes=32 time<10ms TTL=128
Reply from 207.158.5.104: bytes=32 time<10ms TTL=128
Reply from 207.158.5.104: bytes=32 time<10ms TTL=128
Reply from 207.158.5.104: bytes=32 time=10ms TTL=128

C:\>
```

**4.** **B.** When RAS is set to receive calls, it locks the COM port and modem. This port then becomes unavailable for other communication software, such as fax machines.

**5. B.** Multilink combines multiple serial data streams into a single bundle. While generally used with two ISDN channels, it can also be used with modems and standard phone lines. Therefore, if you have two 14.4 modems connected to two phone lines, and Multilink is enabled, your bandwidth is 28.8 Kbps. To enable Multilink, simply check the Enable Multilink check box found in the Network Configuration dialog box shown in the next illustration.

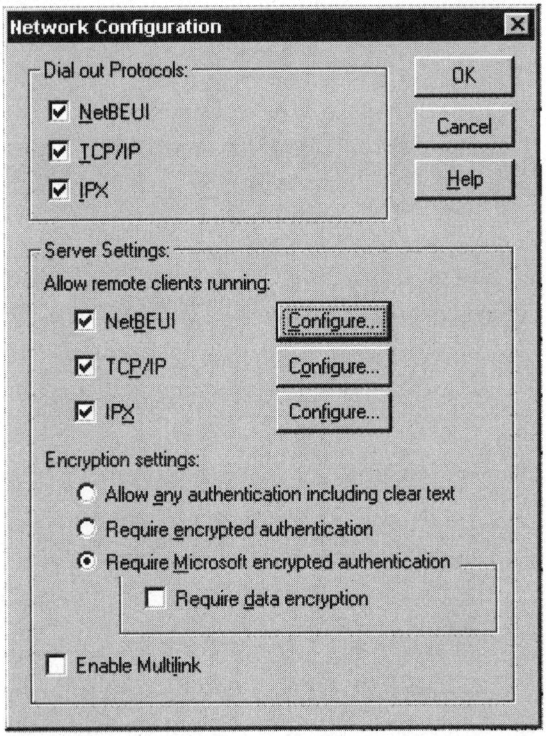

**6. A.** Telephony Application Programming Interface (TAPI) works between applications and hardware. It provides an abstraction between the two, so that programmers write programs to the API, rather than for specific communication hardware. An example of how TAPI is used is a Personal Information Manager (PIM) program. A user clicks a person's name, and the computer accesses the Public Switched Telephone Network (a fancy word for the phone company's telephone lines), and calls the person.

**7. A, C.** The two serial protocols that RAS supports are Point to Point Protocol (PPP) and Serial Line Internet Protocol (SLIP). The others listed in this question are not serial protocols.

**8. A.** When one client using Windows NT dials in to another Windows NT computer with RAS, MS-CHAP authentication protocol is used. This is because MS-CHAP is the safest encrypted authentication protocol offered by Windows NT.

**9. A.** By setting the HKEY_LOCAL_MACHINE\SYSTEM\ControlSet001\ Services\RemoteAccess\Parameters\EnableAudit key to 1, RAS can log detailed information that can later be viewed by Event Viewer.

**10. B.** If an Internet Service Provider uses PPP, then IP addresses can be assigned to your computer. If the ISP is using SLIP, it cannot automatically assign you an IP address. In such a case, you must manually enter it. This is because the DHCP servers require PPP to assign the address.

**11. C.** SLIP is an older serial protocol that is ideal for use when connecting to older computers. PPP is newer, and many older systems don't support it. This is not uncommon when dealing with Internet Service Providers who still require scripts to log into their system.

**12. C.** PPP-MP is a multilink protocol. It allows multiple serial data streams to be aggregated into a single bundle. This means that the bandwidth of both modems will be combined, thereby increasing the overall bandwidth. It is mainly used for combining channels on ISDN lines, but can be used to increase the bandwidth of modems by using multiple modems with multiple phone lines.

**13.** **A, B, D.** RAS supports TCP/IP, IPX, and NetBEUI as dial-in and dial-out transport protocols. Don't get SLIP and PPP confused with these. While you can dial out with PPP and SLIP, and dial in with PPP, neither is a transport protocol; they are serial protocols.

**14.** **D.** The Dial-Up Networking Phonebook contains settings to handle multiple connection protocols, logon validation protocols, and scripted connections. In addition, configurations can be made for handling multiple servers, locations and network protocols.

# Answers: Workgroups and Domains

**1.** **A.** The Domain Master Browser contains a list of all resources in a domain. The information is obtained from master browsers in the network, which share their information with the domain master browser. The PDC is always the Domain Master Browser.

**2.** **B.** With a roaming profile, the user's desktop environment will be preserved. This means that no matter which Windows NT workstation this user logs onto, the desktop settings will be identical.

**3.** **B.** A Workgroup model is used when centralized control of accounts and security isn't an issue. With this type of model, you can have a mixture of workstations and servers. However, as is the case with this question, the Workgroup model is also used when there is no server. Why? Because with no server, there can be no Primary Domain Controller and therefore no domain. In this situation, a network consisting of 10 workstations and no server, the Workgroup model is ideal.

4. **A, B.** All account information in a domain is kept on the domain controllers: the Primary Domain Controller and Backup Domain Controller. It is replicated between them, so that the information on both remains up to date. The main database is kept on the PDC, where changes to accounts are made. Updated information is then replicated to BDCs on the network.

5. **A.** In a network of 2 – 31 computers, there is one Master Browser and one Backup Browser. For every 32 computers added to the network after this, one additional Backup Browser is added. These figures are constant, and aren't affected by any other conditions.

6. **D.** If you're expecting to shut down the PDC, or it is offline for awhile, you should promote the BDC to a PDC. This way, authentication and account administration will be unaffected by the PDC not being online.

7. **C.** The Master Browser's browse list is limited to 64KB in size.

8. **C.** Windows NT Workstation's User Manager cannot administer domain user and administrator accounts. The program doesn't have this capability. However, User Manager for Domains, in Windows NT Server, can administer these accounts.

9. **D.** There is only one Primary Domain Controller per domain. There can, however, be multiple Backup Domain Controllers per domain. The PDC and BDCs work together. The BDC can authenticate logons, and receive replicated information from the PDC so that they are always in synch.

10. **B.** Two of the choices in this question can be eliminated immediately. Remember, a Windows NT workstation cannot be either a PDC or a BDC; only a computer running Windows NT Server can. What the screen capture for this question shows it that the computer isn't a preferred Master Browser, because the Registry entry has the IsDomainMaster set to FALSE. To make it a preferred Master Browser, change the value to TRUE.

**11.** C. The Backup Browser receives an updated copy of the browse list from the Master Browser every 15 minutes. This is the default time limit.

**12.** C. STKITTS isn't trusted by LONDON. Since this is a one-way trust, LONDON is the only domain trusted to access resources from the other domain. (Here's a way to remember how trusts work: Ed is a user on the network who wants to use a thing on another network. TrustEd can use the resource. TrustThing has the resource.)

**13.** C. When users log on at their usual Windows NT workstations, and all of the domain controllers are down, cached information will be used to authenticate them. This information comes from their last successful logon. This does not mean they will have the same access to the network, however. File shares, printer shares, logon scripts, roaming profiles, and other services on the domain controllers will be unavailable to the user.

# Answers: Printing

**1.** B. When you install a new print driver, and printouts are illegible garbage, it is an indication that an incorrect print driver has been installed. To correct such a problem, try changing the driver to a previous version that worked, or try a different driver.

**2.** D. You only need to install an updated printer driver on the print server. When the Windows NT workstations use the shared printer, the new driver will be automatically sent over the wire to the workstations and used by them as well. This is because Windows NT Workstation automatically checks to see if there is a newer printer driver available when it connects with the server. If there is, it uses the new one.

**3.** A. When a workstation is unable to connect to a Hewlett Packard printer, always consider that the DLC protocol hasn't been installed on the workstation. DLC is a protocol that enables computers to connect not only with mainframes, but also with HP printers that are network attached.

**4. B.** The print spooler routes print jobs to the proper port. The print router routes print jobs from the spooler to the appropriate print processor.

**5. C.** By default, the person who creates and owns the print job can manage his or her own print jobs. The user can start, stop, pause, or delete the job. This is done through the Print Manager window that appears when you double-click the printer icon. From Printers in Settings on the Start menu, select the printer you sent the job to. Double-click it, and the screen shown in the next illustration appears. From here you can manage any print job you've started.

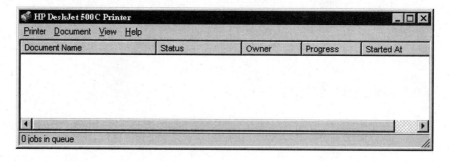

**6. D.** Once you take ownership of a printer, you can't give it back. It doesn't matter whether you're a plain old user or a member of the Administrators group.

**7. D.** You can establish the times that a printer is available to process print jobs by changing the Availability settings of the Scheduling tab of the Printer Properties. With this, you can control when the printer will print. Simply specify in the Availability section on the Scheduling tab (see the next illustration) what times you want this printer to be available. If you want the printer always available to accept print jobs, simply check Always.

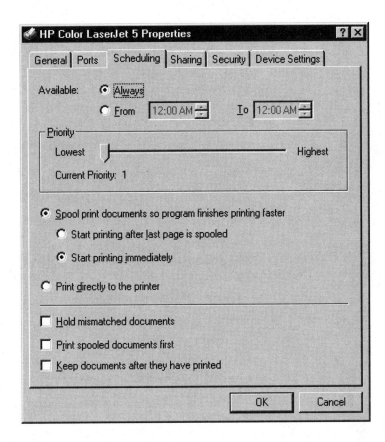

**8. C.** The Graphic Device Interface controls the display of graphics on both your monitor and printer. It allows applications to communicate with these different devices, and controls the display so that the application doesn't have to be involved.

**9. A.** The Printer Interface Driver provides a user interface for configuration management of the print driver. It allows users to easily change the configuration of a print driver, without the need of additional programs.

**10. B.** When a printer with a high priority attempts printing to a print device being used by a low-priority printer, it will wait for the current job of the low-priority printer to finish. The reason for this is that if a low-priority printer were interrupted by a high-priority one, and the high-priority was allowed to print, the resulting printouts would be all mixed up. An example will make this clearer. I have a printer that's low priority, and it's printing my document. Half-way through, your high-priority printer sends a job to the print device. If your printer is allowed to interrupt, your job would print out in the middle of mine, then be covered up by the rest of my job.

11. **C.** The Security tab of Printer Properties is used to take ownership of a printer. If you have the proper permissions to do so, you can take ownership from here.

12. **A.** Before you can audit print events, you must enable auditing through User Manager. Attempting to set up a print audit does not automatically enable auditing. It must be done separately.

13. **C.** To view the results of a print audit, use Event Viewer. Event Viewer is used to read events (problems and important occurrences) which are logged to a file on the hard disk. Rather than putting cryptic messages on a screen, print audits are recorded to a log file. This allows you to review the information as often as you need.

# Answers: Configuring Applications

1. **B.** Kernel mode has the capability to access hardware directly. Applications must go through the operating system to access hardware in Windows NT. They cannot access the hardware directly, because applications run in User mode.

**2.** **A.** You can run a 16-bit program in its own memory area by using Run. From the Start menu, choose Run. There is a check box under the field where you type the program you wish to run. By checking the check box, the 16-bit program will run in a separate address space, in its own Virtual DOS Machine (VDM). See the next illustration.

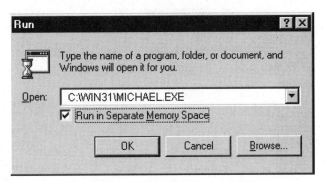

**3.** **D.** By default, a 16-bit Windows 3.*x* program runs in a shared memory space with other 16-bit programs. If one crashes, all of the 16-bit programs also running will crash. Though all these 16-bit programs will now not run, it won't affect Windows NT itself. This is because all of the 16-bit programs are running in a single VDM. The VDM encases the 16-bit programs, so that they only interact and affect each other in memory.

**4.** **C.** 16-bit programs are run within their own VDM, and are cooperatively multitasked. This gives them the natural environment they expect. Windows 3.*x* didn't run programs in separate VDMs, but allowed applications to interact in memory. In other words, they could stomp all over each other. In Windows 3.*x*, the applications were cooperatively multitasked, allowing one program to keep control of the processor until it was ready to relinquish it. This allowed a single program to bring down the system.

Windows NT needed to provide these programs with an environment they expected, but also keep one program from crashing the system. Windows NT uses 32-bit programs, which are preemptively multitasked. Since the VDM itself is 32-bit, it is preemptively multitasked with other programs running on the system. By placing 16-bit programs in a single VDM, the applications get the environment they expect, while Windows NT is protected. The VDM acts like a protective shell, so that while one 16-bit program may crash, the other 16-bit programs, Windows NT and other 32-bit programs remain unaffected.

5. **A.** Windows NT does not allow programs to access hardware. Any access a program has to hardware goes directly through Windows NT. Virtual Device Drivers trick an application into thinking that it is actually accessing a hardware device in Windows NT, when actually, it is the operating system that retains control over the devices.

6. **D.** OS/2 and POSIX applications are both preemptively multitasked. This is because both are 32-bit. Because of this, even though both use their own separate subsystems, each passes messages through the Win32 subsystem.

7. **D.** WOWEXEC.EXE is used on Windows NT Workstation to provide Windows 3.x emulation for 16-bit Windows 3.x programs.

8. **D.** The command would be START *<program name>* /HIGH to start a program with a priority of 13. It is difficult to remember the priorities, but here's a suggestion for the exam: If you remember the default priority level of a program is 8, then Low would be lower, and High would be higher. After that, just remember that REALTIME is superhigh; it has a priority of 24!

**9. B.** The Hardware Abstraction Layer (HAL) allows Windows NT to be portable to other architectures. Rather than needing to write a new operating system for a computer with multiple processors, or a different architecture, you only need to write a new HAL.

**10. B.** By typing START *<program name>* /SEPARATE from the command line, you can start a 16-bit program in its own separate memory area. The 16-bit program will then run in its own VDM, separate from other 16-bit Windows applications that are running.

**11. A.** A thread is the smallest unit that can be scheduled by the microkernel. A process is a running program, while a thread is a task that the program needs to have processed. The full name of a thread is "thread of execution".

**12. D.** FORCEDOS *<program name>* will force an OS/2 application to use a VDM rather than the OS/2 subsystem.

**13. D.** Realtime has the highest priority level you can set with the START command. It has a priority of 24. However, it is not the only priority you can set with this command. The default priority is 8, while Low is 4 and High is 13.

# Answers: Performance Tuning

**1. B.** Since you are optimizing the paging files, you want to create a page file on every disk except the system\boot disk. This will enable the operating system to write and read from the drive with the system on it, and enable reads and writes to swap files to be spread across the other hard disks.

**2. B.** You must run DISKPERF –YE to enable the counters on a single physical disk in a stripe set. Without running this, you will not be able to view any counters with Performance Monitor. This is the same as what happens with regular disks when counters aren't initialized. It will appear, as is shown in the next illustration, that no disk activity is occurring.

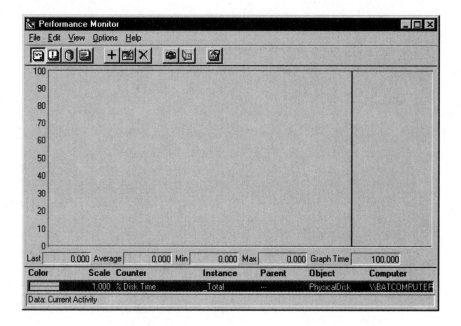

**3. A.** On a majority of computers, the biggest bottleneck encountered is hard disks. This is not difficult to understand, when you consider that so much is written to it, and so little is removed. The hard disk isn't just used for files, but also for virtual memory, file caching, and much more.

**4. D.** Windows NT provides symmetric multiprocessing, swapping across multiple disks (such as stripe sets), and thread and process prioritizing. Each of these is a method of improving performance, and makes Windows NT such a robust operating system.

**5. B.** Network Monitor must be installed to use the % Network Utilization counters in Performance Monitor. Without it, the counters won't appear. This is similar to what happens with disk counters when they aren't initialized. Network Monitor loads the network counters, which can then be used by Performance Monitor.

**6. A.** Windows NT Workstation can automatically adjust an application's priority by a value of two.

**7. B.** By creating a baseline, you are recording how the system functions normally. Without one, you can only guess as to what a problem might be. This is because, when you suspect a problem, you won't know whether it is normal for that particular system to be doing what it's doing. With a baseline, you can analyze current findings by comparing them to the baseline. This will make it easier to establish what the real problem with the system is.

**8. C.** The Priority Boost slider bar changes the responsiveness of programs running in the foreground. By moving the slider bar to Maximum, the priority is increased by two, and the priority level becomes ten.

**9. B.** Windows NT Workstation will support two processors. This should not be confused with Windows NT Server, which supports four processors out of the box, and up to 32 processors in total. Windows NT Workstation can only handle two out of the box, although it can be modified by OEMs to support up to 32 processors.

**10. C.** When creating a baseline with Performance Monitor, you should be in Log view. This is the only view mode in which you can record counters, so that they can be referenced later. The other view modes can only display the data, but cannot record them to a log.

11. **A.** In asymmetric multiprocessing, computer time is wasted as the operating system is monopolizing one of the processors. Everything the operating system does runs off one processor, and everything else must run on the others. This wastes the power of a processor at times, as the operating system could benefit from the processor during times when it is available. In symmetric multiprocessing, all threads of execution are spread evenly across all processors, and there is no waste of processor time and power.

12. **A.** Task Manager is useful for short-term monitoring of the system. It is useful for detecting CPU or memory bottlenecks caused by applications or Windows NT services. In Task Manager, you can view both the number of applications and the number of processes running. In addition, from the Performance tab, you can also view the number of threads these processes are running. The real clue to this question is the word applications, which is the heart of what Task Manager monitors.

13. **C.** Sustained rates of 85 percent or higher in disk activity means that the hard disk has become a bottleneck in the system. While occasional high rates aren't enough to worry about, sustained rates are a problem.
It is also important to realize that when this happens, you should also check the number of page faults that are occurring. If information in memory constantly is being swapped to disk, it would mean that disk thrashing is occurring. Under these conditions, memory would then be the bottleneck.

# Answers: Booting, Troubleshooting, and Service Packs

1. **C.** The message from this question usually appears when the BOOT.INI file is missing or damaged. It could be that the file is completely gone, or the ARC pathname is wrong. In either case, the operating system can't be found, causing Windows NT not to load.

**2. A, B, C, D.** The Emergency Repair Disk (ERD) can be used to verify system files, inspect the Registry, inspect the startup environment, and inspect the boot sector.

**3. D.** If a UPS suddenly switches off when your Windows NT workstation boots, it is usually because the system is checking the com port that the UPS is attached to for a mouse. This can cause the UPS to switch off. Adding the /NOSERIALMICE switch will cause the system not to check the com port that you specify for a mouse.

**4. B.** The VGA mode that appears on the boot menu will load Windows NT with a generic VGA driver that works for all display devices. This is mainly of use when display drivers are changed. If the improper one is chosen, you won't be able to see anything when you reboot. Because VGA mode loads a generic driver that works with any display device, you are able to change your settings to either a new driver or the original one that worked. After this, it's just a matter of rebooting, and entering Windows NT as normal.

**5. B.** Since the BOOT.INI file specifies the location of the operating system, different computers will have different paths. In this case, BOOT.INI is from another computer, so that was the source of the wrong ARC path in the BOOT.INI. To make a long story short, BOOT.INI is causing the system to look for the operating system on another partition, controller, disk, or even on a disk that may not exist!

**6. A.** NTDETECT examines hardware and passes a list to the NTLDR. After finding the current hardware configuration of your workstation, it passes the information to NTLDR, which then passes it on to the Registry.

**7. C.** ARC has SCSI as the first section of its naming convention. This entry should read MULTI, since the BIOS is enabled on the SCSI controller. If BIOS is disabled, the ARC path reads SCSI, but if it's enabled, it reads MULTI.

**8.** **C.** The /SOS switch in BOOT.INI will cause the names of device drivers to be displayed as they are loaded. It is generally used to visually detect if a particular device driver isn't loading, or if one is loading that isn't supposed to be.

**9.** **C.** If the workstations can communicate with each other but not the server, the problem is most likely the server. Because communications exist between the workstations, there isn't a problem with the cable, or your network operating system. I've seen people scrambling around an office, fiddling with cables or even reinstalling Windows NT Workstation, when the real problem is that someone shut off the server. This is really a logical troubleshooting question, but don't be surprised if it comes up on your Windows NT exam.

**10.** **D.** BOOTSECT.DOS stores information specific to the computer it is on. It is an MS-DOS boot sector, and is used when another operating system (DOS or Windows 95) is selected from the Boot menu. It cannot be borrowed and placed on another computer.

**11.** **C.** On RISC machines, the OSLOADER.EXE is the operating system loader. It is the equivalent of the NTLDR on *x*86-based computers, and is loaded by the boot sector routine. It finds and loads the Windows NT operating system. Like NTLDR, it is a hidden, read-only file.

**12.** **A.** Event Viewer can be used to view errors that have been logged to the SYSTEM.LOG. It can also view events to security and application logs. As is shown in the next illustration, events recorded to the log are displayed with icons designating why the event was recorded. For logs that are of considerable size, Event Viewer can also filter what it displays, so that only certain events or those within a specified time period appear.

| Date | Time | Source | Category | Event |
|------|------|--------|----------|-------|
| i 5/12/98 | 5:31:32 AM | BROWSER | None | 8015 |
| 5/12/98 | 5:31:27 AM | BROWSER | None | 8015 |
| 5/12/98 | 5:29:02 AM | EventLog | None | 6005 |
| 5/12/98 | 5:30:13 AM | Dhcp | None | 1003 |
| 5/10/98 | 8:20:47 PM | BROWSER | None | 8033 |
| 5/10/98 | 8:20:47 PM | BROWSER | None | 8033 |
| 5/10/98 | 8:20:20 PM | Srv | None | 2013 |
| 5/10/98 | 8:20:20 PM | Srv | None | 2013 |
| 5/10/98 | 8:16:29 PM | BROWSER | None | 8015 |
| 5/10/98 | 8:16:24 PM | BROWSER | None | 8015 |
| 5/10/98 | 8:14:00 PM | EventLog | None | 6005 |
| 5/10/98 | 8:15:11 PM | Dhcp | None | 1003 |
| 5/9/98 | 4:43:43 PM | BROWSER | None | 8033 |
| 5/9/98 | 4:43:43 PM | BROWSER | None | 8033 |
| 5/9/98 | 4:42:42 PM | Dhcp | None | 1003 |
| 5/9/98 | 4:41:48 PM | Srv | None | 2013 |

Event Viewer - System Log on \\BATCOMPUTER
Log   View   Options   Help

**13.** **A, D.** Because your modem is down, you only have two of the four options available to you. The obvious answer is Windows NT's Help files, which are on your workstation. While TechNet sounds like an Internet service, it is actually a CD-ROM. You are given one when you become Microsoft Certified, and can get more by subscription after that. It contains the complete MS Download Library (MSDL). MSDL is an electronic bulletin board (BBS) that can be connected to, via modem, at (206) 936-6735. Through it, you can download service packs, articles, handy text and program files, upgrades, and more. The Knowledge Base is Microsoft's official repository of support information. It contains answers to technical questions, and is available at the URL http://www.microsoft.com/search/default.asp.

**14.** **A.** The Resources tab of Windows NT Diagnostics will display details on hardware resources. By simply clicking one of five buttons, you can view IRQs, I/O ports, DMA, physical memory, and device drivers.

# MCSE

MICROSOFT CERTIFIED SYSTEMS ENGINEER

# Part 2

## Windows NT Server 4.0

## EXAM TOPICS

Introduction to Windows NT Server 4.0

Planning Windows NT 4.0 Installation

Installing Windows NT Server 4.0

Configuring Windows NT Server 4.0

Managing Resources

Windows NT 4.0 Security

Windows NT 4.0 Domains

Replication and Data Synchronization

Printing

NetWare Integration

Remote Connectivity

Backup

Windows NT 4.0 Monitoring and Performance Tuning

Troubleshooting

# Server
# Practice
# Questions

$Q_{\&}A$

J ust as we have made every effort to supply questions similar to those you will see on the MCSE Server exam, you should make an effort to take this practice test in an environment similar to exam conditions. Go straight through the test once, before looking at the answers. Remember that you are looking for the *best* answer, not just an acceptable one. In some cases you will need to choose all correct answers.

The purpose of taking a practice test isn't simply to go over the material once again. It is a tool to help you gauge your readiness to take the actual exam. In other words, you should not only know the correct answers; you should understand why each answer is correct.

# Introduction to Windows NT Server 4.0

1. A program running on NT Server spawns a thread with an initial priority level of 30. What's the highest level that the thread can be executed?

   A. 30
   B. 31
   C. 32
   D. 33

2. Windows NT can use more than one processor to execute more than one thread at a time. When executing more than one thread across multiple processors, NT automatically assigns threads to idle processors, including the OS threads. This is known as _____ multiprocessing.

   A. asymmetric
   B. symmetric
   C. cooperative
   D. preemptive

3. You're setting up a server and want to use Windows NT's built-in RAID capabilities. Your requirements are to ensure that all data is maintained on at least two hard disks, so that if a hard disk fails the other drive will be able

to take its place. You also want to have redundancy on the disk controllers, so that you'll run each hard disk on it's own controller. What type of redundancy is this?

A. Striping with Parity (RAID 5)

B. Disk mirroring (RAID 1)

C. Striping without Parity (RAID 0)

D. Disk duplexing

**4.** Your network has three Windows NT servers, one is a PDC and the other two are member servers. Your PDC's hard disk has failed beyond repair. What should you do to recover the PDC as soon as possible?

A. Promote one of the other servers to the PDC.

B. Build a new PDC with the same computer name and domain name.

C. Build a new PDC with the same domain name and a different computer name.

D. Build a new PDC and restore from backup tape.

**5.** You have two network subnets, Subnet A and Subnet B. Subnet A has 55 Windows 95 clients running TCP/IP. Subnet B has 30 Windows 95 clients running NetBEUI. There is an NT server on both subnets. Your company doesn't have a lot of money to spend on network equipment. In fact it only has about $300. What should you do to connect the two subnets, without increasing the amount of broadcasts on each subnet? (Choose all that apply.)

A. Remove NetBEUI and install TCP/IP on Subnet B clients.

B. Buy a second Network card and install it on one of the servers, and connect the other subnet to it.

C. Set NT to serve as a gateway to translate NetBEUI to TCP/IP.

D. Buy a second Network card and install it on both of the servers, and connect the other subnet to it.

**6.** You want to set an NT server to replicate three files to another NT server. Where should you place the files?

A. Place the files in the C:\SYSTEMROOT\SYSTEM32\REPL\EXPORT directory.
B. Place the files in the C:\SYSTEMROOT\SYSTEM32\REPL\IMPORT directory.
C. Place the files in any directory under the C:\SYSTEMROOT\SYSTEM32\REPL\EXPORT DIRECTORY.
D. Place the files in any directory under the C:\SYSTEMROOT\SYSTEM32\REPL\IMPORT DIRECTORY.

7. You're a very proficient administrator. In fact, many consider you the best in your field. You've heard that Windows NT has an administrative wizard. Should you use it? Why or why not?

A. Yes, the administrative wizards allow you to perform more admin functions than the standard tools.
B. Yes, the administrative wizards allow you to perform basic functions at a quicker pace.
C. No, The administrative wizards don't add any functionality to the admin tools, and they require more time to use.
D. No, wizards are only for lamers.

8. Why is Windows NT so stable?

A. Because of its architecture. It has two modes: User and Kernel. User mode is not allowed to directly access the hardware, whereas Kernel mode is. Applications run in the User mode. If it misbehaves, it won't bring down the entire operating system.
B. Because it is a 32-bit operating system. 16-bit operating systems were unstable because they couldn't use multiple threads. Now that the OS supports multiple threads, programs can manage themselves.
C. Because the Kernel mode allows drivers to access the hardware directly. This ensures that all drivers can manipulate the hardware no matter what type it is. A programmer can write a driver for a video card, which can dynamically allocate memory from the network adapter if it isn't being used.
D. Because the HAL can be replaced on different platforms of Windows NT. If the HAL couldn't be replaced we wouldn't be able to run NT on various hardware platforms.

9. Your NT Server appears to be running very slowly. It only has 16MB RAM and 150MB available disk space. You notice that the hard disk is continually running, even when no one is accessing it. What should you do to increase its performance?

   A. Add another hard disk.
   B. Buy a faster processor.
   C. Disconnect users that aren't needed.
   D. Add more RAM.

10. When Windows NT swaps RAM to virtual memory, what size is the page?

    A. 1KB
    B. 2KB
    C. 4KB
    D. 8KB
    E. 16KB
    F. 32KB

11. How much address space is available for applications?

    A. 1GB
    B. 2GB
    C. 4GB
    D. 8GB
    E. 16GB
    F. 32GB

exam
Ⓦatch

*During the exam you will be asked to choose the correct fault-tolerant strategy for a situation. You must understand the features of each method, and know when it is appropriate to use each.*

**12.** The OS/2 and Win32 subsystems operate in the _____
_____. Use the illustration to help answer the question.

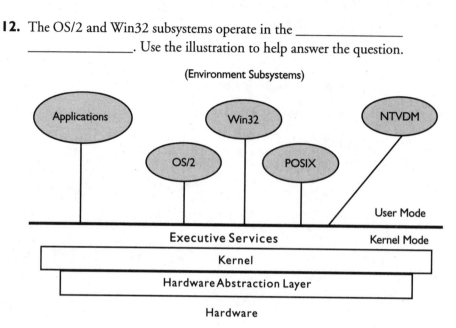

(Environment Subsystems)

A. User mode
B. Kernel mode
C. Executive services
D. Environment subsystems

exam
ⓦatch *When you take the Networking Essentials exam for your MCSE, you will see scenario questions regarding fault tolerance for networks. For example, if one network connection were to go down in one city, how could you ensure that all cities could remain communicating while the direct connection is restored? This would involve multiple routes between cities. On a smaller scale, you can have multiple routes between segments of the network in your organization to ensure fault tolerance. This could be accomplished by using the NT Server with multiple network controllers.*

# Planning Windows NT 4.0 Installation

**1.** How can you install Windows NT? (Choose all that apply.)

A. RIPL from an NT server

B. Over the network

C. CD-ROM

D. Floppy disk

**2.** You have a laptop with NT Server installed on it. When it's at your office it is docked in a docking unit. The docking unit adds hardware to the laptop, such as a 17-inch monitor, sound card, and 100MB Ethernet card. You configured NT while it wasn't docked. What should you do to get the docked hardware detected and used by NT?

A. NT has a plug and play service that will auto detect the changes, so you don't have to do anything. If it needs drivers it will prompt you for the device drivers.

B. Reinstall NT in a different directory and dual-boot between docked and undocked modes.

C. Simply add the new device drivers while the laptop is docked.

D. Create two hardware profiles, one docked and the other undocked. In each profile configure the proper hardware devices. Then when you boot the system choose which hardware profile you want to use.

**3.** You're upgrading your NT Server from a 10MB Ethernet card to a 100MB Ethernet card. After attempting to install the device driver from the NT CD-ROM, you notice that there isn't a driver for your new Ethernet card. You check the hardware compatibility list (HCL) and your card is not listed. What should you do? (Choose the best answer.)

A. Contact Microsoft and request a new driver.

B. You'll need to get a different Ethernet card since it's not listed in the HCL.

C. Contact the vendor of the Ethernet card for a compatible driver.

D. Try using different drivers until you find one that works.

**4.** You want to install NT Server on your 486/33 computer. You have 16MB RAM and 120MB of available disk space. Will you be able to install NT Server on this computer? Why or why not?

    A. Yes, this system meets the minimum requirements.

    B. No, you need to have at least a 486/66Mhz processor.

    C. No, the minimum amount of RAM required is 24MB.

    D. No, you need to have at least 125MB of available disk space.

**5.** You want to dual-boot between Windows NT and Windows 95. Your computer currently has NT Server installed and the entire hard disk (1GB) is formatted as an NTFS partition. What should you do first to ensure you can dual-boot between both operating systems?

    A. Install Windows 95 and edit the BOOT.INI file.

    B. Reformat the drive for a FAT partition.

    C. Convert the NTFS partition to a FAT partition.

    D. Use Disk Administrator to enable the NTFS partition to emulate a FAT partition while being accessed by Windows 95.

**6.** You're installing a new 9GB hard disk. You want to format it using one partition. Which type of file system should you use?

    A. NTFS.

    B. FAT.

    C. CDFS.

    D. NT can't recognize volumes over 8GB; therefore, you'll need at least two partitions.

exam
ⓦatch

*A common problem with using NWLink (IPX/SPX) is that it will default to auto-detect the frame type. Make sure that you choose the correct frame type when you are configuring the protocol.*

**7.** The next illustration shows the screen you'll see when you run the
following command:

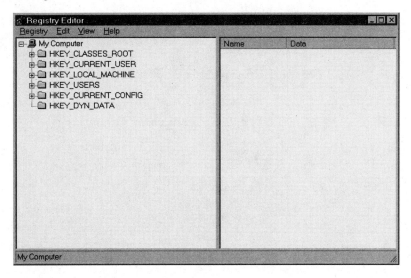

A. REGEDIT32.EXE
B. REGEDT32.EXE
C. REGEDIT.EXE
D. Registry Editor

**8.** You move a file named MIKE'S SALES REPORT.XLS from your C: drive
to your D: drive. The file is compressed on the C: drive. The D: drive has
no compressed files or directories. After the file is moved will it be
compressed? Why?

A. Yes, the original compression attributes are maintained when copying
and moving files.
B. Yes, the original compression attributes are maintained only when
moving files between partitions.
C. No, when you move a file between partitions the compressions attribute
is inherited from the parent directory.
D. No, when you move a file it always inherits the compression attribute
from its parent directory.

**9.** Which of the options shown in the next illustration would you check to assign special permissions to allow users to execute and delete files? (Choose all that apply.)

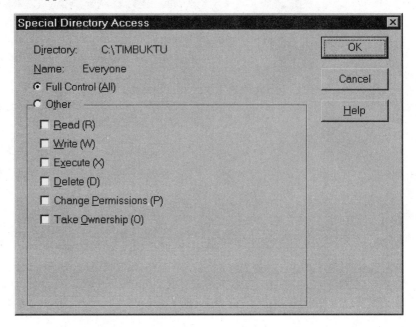

A. Read

B. Write

C. Execute

D. Delete

E. Change Permissions

F. Take Ownership

G. Other

**10.** Your network has five subnets. Each subnet has at least one NT server physically attached to the subnet. You want to use DHCP, but you don't want to manage five separate DHCP servers. Without configuring the routers can you do this? How?

A. No, this can't be done. You must configure the routers.

B. Yes, purchase a UNIX DHCP server, which is capable of supporting multiple subnets.

C. Yes, enable the NT servers to forward DHCP requests to a central DHCP server.

D. Yes, enable IP routing on all the NT servers.

**11.** You're the best Windows NT administrator in the world. You know so much about NT you don't even need to use the Control Panel applets to make changes to your system. Instead you edit the Registry to make changes. Everyone is always impressed that you manage your servers using only REGEDT32.EXE. Is this a good idea? Why?

A. No, editing the Registry is always a bad idea and should never be done, no matter what!

B. No, although you can edit the Registry without breaking your system, it is always best to use the proper Control Panel tools to modify the Registry. You may make a mistake while editing the Registry, making your entire server unstable.

C. Yes, computers are known to make errors. If you can eliminate an additional step in managing your server, like using the Control Panel applets, you should do it.

D. Yes, it's always better to be impressive than safe. If you can wow people with your abilities, you might get a promotion or a raise.

**12.** Your computer is setup to dual boot between NT Server and OS/2. Which type of file system should you use?

A. FAT

B. NTFS

C. HPFS

D. CDFS

**13.** You have 20 computers on a subnet. All 20 computers only need to communicate with the NT server on the same subnet. The server provides simple file and print capabilities. Which protocol should you use?

A. NetBEUI

B. TCP/IP

C. NWLink

D. AppleTalk

**14.** Your network consists of UNIX servers running TCP/IP, Macintosh servers running AppleTalk, and Novell servers running IPX/SPX. You're installing your first NT server. You want it to communicate with all other servers on your network. Which protocol(s) should you install? (Choose all that apply.)

A. NetBEUI

B. TCP/IP

C. NWLink

D. AppleTalk

**15.** Your computer has one hard disk and one partition. You created an uncompressed file called JESSE'S HOMEWORK.DOC on an NTFS partition. You later move this file to the Homework directory, which is compressed. What will occur?

A. The file will be compressed.

B. The file will be uncompressed.

C. You'll be prompted if you want to compress the file.

D. It depends on how you've configured compression.

exam
Ⓦatch
*A frequent test questions asks you to identify the principal function of the DLC protocol. DLC is used primarily to connect to a Hewlett-Packard printer.*

## QUESTIONS AND ANSWERS

| | |
|---|---|
| Your server will be configured to run SQL and SMS at the same time, being a domain controller. Do you want to use the minimum requirements? | No way. If you are going to be running complex server applications on your NT server, you will need to configure a quick processor to run SQL and will need a lot of memory to deliver packages with SMS. |
| You have a 1000 node network that requires your server to handle file and print services. What kind of hardware requirements should you use? | Since your computer will not be doing too much work, a dual or quad processor is not required. You might want to use at least 128MB of RAM to process the handling of files on your network. |
| You just got in a new computer from your buddy who makes them using extra parts from old computers. It is configured with 64MB of RAM, Pentium 133, and a 2GB hard disk. You try installing Windows NT 4.0 Server on the computer, but it will not load. What is the problem? | Even though you have the right "hardware requirements," you have to make sure that each hardware device is on the HCL. This is what is prohibiting the computer from correctly installing. |

## QUESTIONS AND ANSWERS

| | |
|---|---|
| You are connecting to a Novell NetWare server and have Gateway Services for NetWare installed. What protocol do you want? | NWLink. If you are connecting to a NetWare Server, NWLink is required. |
| You have a small LAN of about 15 workstations in a workgroup environment. You want a quick protocol compatible with Windows computers. What protocol do you want? | NetBEUI. It is a quick, non-routable protocol that is predominantly used for small networks. |
| You will be connecting to the Internet to allow people to come to your Web site and buy from your online store. What protocol do you want? | TCP/IP. It is the standard protocol of the Internet. |
| You have a few Hewlett-Packard printers that are using HP Jet-Direct cards installed on your network. What protocol should you install to allow your clients to connect to the printers? | DLC, which enables computers to connect to HP printers and also enables workstations to connect to mainframe computers. |

# Installing Windows NT Server 4.0

1. You have one Windows NT server and 100 workstations. There will never be more than 50 users connected to the server at a time, since 50 workers work the morning shift and 50 workers work the evening shift. What type of licensing should you use and how many licenses should you buy? (Choose the best answer.)

   A. 100 licenses and configure as per seat. This allows the 100 computers to connect to the NT server and any other NT server you deploy in the future.

   B. 100 licenses and configure as per server. This allows 100 connections to the server. Since 100 total users will be accessing the server, you must buy 100 licenses.

   C. 50 licenses and configure as per seat. This will allow the 50 computers to connect in the morning and 50 to connect in the evening.

   D. 50 licenses and configure as per server. This allows 50 simultaneous server connections. When the 51$^{st}$ connection is attempted it won't be permitted until another user logs off.

2. How would you create the three NT setup boot disks after installing Windows NT?

   A. Run the program WINNT.EXE /B.

   B. Run the program WINNT32.EXE /B.

   C. Run the program WINNT.EXE /OX.

   D. Run the program WINNT32.EXE /OX.

3. You want to install a BDC at your New York office. You currently have a dial-up connection between your New York office and your headquarters in Charlotte. Currently your RAS server in the Charlotte office is offline and won't be running for five days. You have people onsite at both locations ready to assist in installing the BDC. This BDC must be up in two days. How should you install the BDC in New York?

A. Install the BDC in the New York office as a BDC and wait until the RAS server is running to fully synchronize with the PDC.

B. Install the BDC in the Charlotte office and ship the server to the New York office overnight.

C. Install the BDC in the New York office as a PDC. When the RAS server is running, connect the two PDCs and demote the PDC in the New York office to a BDC.

D. Ship the PDC to the New York office, then install the BDC and ship the PDC back to the Charlotte office.

4. You've recently installed a new BDC. The new hardware on the BDC makes it a better server than the PDC, so you want to switch their roles. How can this be done?

A. In Server Manager, demote the current PDC, then promote the new BDC.

B. In Server Manager, demote the current PDC. While the current PDC is being demoted you'll be prompted for a new PDC.

C. In Server Manager, promote the new BDC, then demote the old PDC.

D. In Server Manager, promote the new BDC.

5. Your network currently has one server running as a PDC. You've recently purchased a new server to run SQL 6.5. How should this new server be configured?

A. Member server and SQL 6.5.

B. BDC and SQL 6.5.

C. PDC and SQL 6.5, then demote the old server to a BDC.

D. BDC, member server, and SQL 6.5.

**6.** Your Windows NT 3.51 server has the shell preview and some various third-party utilities that aren't compatible with Windows NT 4.0. What should you do before upgrading to NT 4.0?

   A. NT 4.0 will automatically upgrade the components or disable them if it can't upgrade them.

   B. Remove the shell preview and other utilities that are incompatible.

   C. You can't upgrade until you completely reinstall NT 3.51.

   D. Run the program NTHQ.EXE to determine if they are compatible. Remove them if they aren't.

**7.** You are ready to upgrade from Windows NT 3.51 to Windows NT 4.0. What command do you enter at the command shell?

   A. WINNT.EXE.

   B. WINNT32.EXE.

   C. WINNT.EXE /U.

   D. You can't upgrade to NT 4.0 from previous versions of NT.

**8.** You are ready to upgrade from Windows 95 to NT 4.0. What command do you enter at the command shell?

   A. WINNT.EXE.

   B. WINNT32.EXE.

   C. WINNT.EXE /U.

   D. You can't upgrade to NT 4.0 from Windows 95.

---

exam
Ⓦatch

*You may see one or two questions about Per Seat and Per Server licensing. Be sure to keep in mind that you can make that one-time switch only from Per Server to Per Seat. You cannot switch in the other direction.*

---

**9.** You want to install Windows NT 4.0 on 100 machines. You don't want to sit at each computer and answer each question that SETUP asks. How should you install? (Choose all that apply.)

A. Create an UNATTEND.TXT file for each computer.

B. Use the /UDF switch to replace computer-specific sections in the UDF file.

C. Start SETUP at each computer and run around to each one in round-robin fashion, answering the questions.

D. As with NT 3.51, you must answer the questions sitting at the console.

**10.** You are about to install Windows NT 4.0 on a computer running Windows 95. Before you do so, you wish to obtain some information about the hardware. You run the program NTHQ.EXE, which is shipped on the NT 4.0 CD. What does this utility tell you? (Choose all that apply.)

A. Determines whether the hardware on the machine is on the HCL.

B. Determines whether the machine has PCI devices installed.

C. Determines whether the machine has ISA devices installed.

D. This is a trick question as NTHQ.EXE only runs on NT.

**11.** As you installed Windows NT 4.0, you chose not to create an emergency repair disk (ERD), knowing that you would need to update it after you installed other programs. You have now configured everything the way you like and installed all your programs. How do you create an ERD?

A. You can't, because you chose not to create one during install. You can only update an existing ERD.

B. Run the ERD.EXE program.

C. Run the RDISK.EXE program.

D. Run SETUP.EXE again, and choose the option create ERD.

# QUESTIONS AND ANSWERS

| | |
|---|---|
| I want to install Windows NT Server. I do not have a bootable CD-ROM drive, and one of my boot disks is giving me a read error consistently. | On a working computer with a CD-ROM drive, use the WINNT.EXE setup utility to recreate the floppy disks by using the /OX switch. |
| I am getting ready to install Windows NT Server 4.0 on a computer with Windows 95 already on it. I want to keep Windows 95 available as a boot option and allow the Windows 95 operating system to view the contents on my NT 4.0 Server drives created with Disk Administrator. What do I have to do? | In this scenario you need to use FAT for two reasons. The first reason is to enable Windows 95 to boot. If you install NT into an existing FAT partition, you want to retain the FAT partition so the original OS can still boot. Windows 95 can only read FAT partitions. If you were to create a new drive letter from within Windows NT Disk Administrator using NTFS, Windows 95 would not be able to read the contents of that drive. |
| I am installing across the network and do not want the setup program to even mention using the boot floppy disks. What command or switch do I need to use in this instance? | In this instance you would use the /b switch. |
| I want to create a network boot disk with Network Client Administrator (NCA). I've never run NCA before. In which subdirectory of the Windows NT Server 4.0 CD are the files kept? What is the default share name specified upon first-time setup? | \Clients and Clients |
| I am setting up a new computer and I want to name it NEWSALESCOMPUTER12A. I consistently get errors when I try to name the computer. Why? | NetBIOS names are limited to 15 characters. |
| I have only 80MB of free space left on my main hard disk in my Intel computer, and I want to install Windows NT Server 4.0. Can I install it? | You need at least 124MB of free space to install Windows NT Server 4.0. It is recommended that you have more, but 124MB is the bare minimum. |

# QUESTIONS AND ANSWERS

SERVER QUESTIONS

| | |
|---|---|
| I want to set up a server that will not be bothered with maintaining account information. What do I want to install? | You should set up a member server, which has no responsibility with the user account database. |
| My PDC just crashed and I need to keep the domain running. What do I do? | Use Server Manager to promote a BDC to PDC. |
| As a new member of Technical Support, I got a call from an Administrator who said that she was having a problem setting up a second PDC in her Domain Ajax. What should I tell her? | Only one PDC is allowed per domain. |
| I am the administrator of a domain that has one PDC and one BDC designated for each satellite office, but they are located in our local office. 15,000 client workstations are spread across the country in various satellite offices. (On the exam you will see questions that have network scenarios as big or bigger than this). Users complain that it takes a very long time to log on. The satellite offices are connected via T1 connections. What can I do to remedy this situation? | This question leans toward the Windows NT Server in the Enterprise exam, but it is still relevant here. An efficient way to speed logons in a WAN environment is to locate a BDC in the remote office. Logging on across the WAN link can slow the process considerably. |
| I am the administrator of a Windows NT network that has one PDC and no BDCs. The PDC has crashed and will not boot. The last known good backup is from yesterday. What can I do to bring the server back online? | Without a BDC to promote to PDC, your only choice is to reinstall Windows NT Server 4.0, and then restore from backup. Any changes between the backup and the server crash will be lost. |
| I am about to start the installation process with the boot disks. As I boot the machine, what do I have to type to get the installation process started? | Nothing. When you use the boot disks or CD-ROM drive for installations, the setup process starts automatically as the machine boots. |
| I have a machine whose CD-ROM drive is not compatible with Windows NT. What can I do to install Windows NT Server? | Copy the installation file to your hard disk and run the installation from there. Until you obtain an NT-compatible CD-ROM drive, you cannot install Windows NT Server from a CD-ROM. |
| I want to create an answer file for unattended installation. What utility is available to help me do this? | SETUPMGR on the Windows NT Server CD-ROM. You'll find it in the Support/Deptools/i386 subdirectory. |

**12.** You're attempting to install Windows NT 4.0 on a computer with an IDE CD-ROM. When SETUP attempts to detect your CD-ROM, it fails. What should you do?

A. Nothing, since NT is already accessing your IDE CD-ROM to install from, it's just a minor bug that is fixed in SP2.

B. Select S from the mass storage screen and select Other, then use your vendor OEM driver disk to install the driver.

C. Edit the CDROM.INF file to include the type of CD-ROM.

D. Rerun SETUP using the /CDROM option.

**13.** When would you use NTFS instead of CDFS on your CD-ROM drive? (Choose all that apply.)

A. When security is the primary concern.

B. When you have a read/write CD-ROM.

C. When you are not concerned about the speed of the CD-ROM.

D. You can't use NTFS on a CD-ROM drive.

**14.** Security, security, security! Security is your number one concern. How should you configure your hard disks? (Choose all that apply.)

A. Use a FAT partition and use physical security to protect it.

B. Use an NTFS partition and use physical security to protect it.

C. Use a FAT partition and use file-based security to protect it.

D. Use an NTFS partition and use file-based security to protect it.

**15.** Your CD-ROM drive isn't supported by NT, but it is supported by Windows 95. When you try to install NT, it fails when detecting where the source files are located. You don't have a driver for your CD-ROM drive. Your hard disk has over 3GB of free space. Your computer currently has Windows 95 installed. What should you do to get NT installed on your computer?

A.  Buy a compatible CD-ROM drive.

B.  Upgrade to a compatible driver.

C.  Contact the vendor.

D.  Copy the source files to the local hard disk while in Windows 95. Then run the install from the local hard disk.

16.  You're planning to roll out an entire Windows NT domain over the weekend. You've done much planning and preparation for this project. You're going to use an unattended installation to install over 20 servers. Your domain will cross two separate geographic areas. One is in Atlanta, the other is in Orlando. The Orlando site is your Headquarters and will house the PDC. You figure that since the remote site only has two servers (one member server and one BDC), you should go ahead and fly out to Atlanta on Friday and return later that night. This way, if anything goes wrong in Orlando, you won't have a scheduled trip hanging over your head. When you try to install the BDC you get an error. Why are you getting this error?

A.  The Atlanta site isn't communicating with the Orlando site.

B.  You need to install WINS before you can bring up a remote server.

C.  You haven't installed the PDC.

D.  First, you need to install all member servers.

17.  You are planning to install Windows NT on Windows For Workgroups 3.11 clients and Windows 95 clients. You want to be able to dual boot the systems.  What directory should you install it in?

A.  WFW clients install in the same directory and Windows 95 clients install in a separate directory.

B.  WFW clients install in a separate directory and Windows 95 clients install in the same directory.

C.  Install on both clients in a different directory.

D.  Install on both clients in the same directory.

18. When creating a Network Installation Startup Disk, which of the following steps must be accomplished?

   A. You need to specify a shared directory where the installation files will be copied.
   B. You need to create the disk using Disk Administrator.
   C. You need to select Make Network Installation Startup Disk from the Network Client Based Administrator dialog box.
   D. You need to run the program from a DOS client.

exam
ⓦatch

*Be sure to understand the difference between the /U and /UDF switches and their respective purposes.*

# Configuring Windows NT Server 4.0

1. Which of the following are valid IPX frame types? (Choose all that apply.)

   A. 802.2
   B. 802.3
   C. SNAP
   D. II

2. You are configuring your server's TCP/IP properties so that it can communicate with all computers in your intranet. Your network consists of three subnets. Each subnet has an NT server. You assign the computer an IP address of 172.117.25.5 and a subnet mask of 255.255.255.0. The other two subnet addresses are 172.117.26.0 and 172.117.27.0. You attempt to connect to the other servers, but your connection times out. Only computers on your local subnet appear while browsing the network. What should you do to fix the problem?

   A. Register the server in a DNS server.

    B. Make sure WINS is operating properly and that the server is registered in the WINS database.

    C. Configure the default gateway.

    D. 172 is reserved for special purposes. It won't work properly as an address.

**3.** Your network is currently configured as two separate subnets. Your main objective is to enable communication between the two subnets. As a side objective, you want to minimize broadcast traffic between the two subnets. Your solution: You attach both segments together with a hub and configure all machines to use NetBEUI .
What is the result?

    A. You meet both your main objective and your side objective.

    B. You only meet your main objective.

    C. You don't accomplish either objective.

**4.** You are setting up a scope for a DHCP server. You have created a pool of addresses, entered a valid subnet mask for that pool, and excluded all the addresses you wanted to leave out. What else must you do to set up the scope?

    A. Activate the scope.

    B. Establish the broadcast type.

    C. Enter the WINS addresses.

    D. Configure the duration of the lease.

**5.** You have two disk drives. The first drive is formatted with two NTFS partitions (C: and D:). The second drive is formatted as one NTFS partition (E:). Drive C: and E: have no data on them and each has 1GB of available disk space. Drive D: only has 200MB of available disk space. You want to optimize the performance of your paging file. How should it be configured?

    A. Put the entire paging file on C:.

B. Split the paging file across the C:, D:, and E: drives.

C. Split the paging file across the C: and D: drives.

D. Split the paging file across the C: and E: drives.

6. You have three 1GB drives. Your main objective is to provide a fault-tolerant disk set. One side objective is to allow for the most available disk space. A second side objective is to have at least three logical drives. Your solution: Create a volume set across the three disks.
What is the result?

A. Meets your main objective and both side objectives

B. Meets your main objective and one side objective

C. Meets only your main objective

D. Doesn't meet your main objective

7. You have three 1GB drives. Your main objective is to provide a fault-tolerant disk set using all the available disks. One side objective is to allow for the most available disk space. A second side objective is to have at least three logical drives.
Your solution: Create a stripe set with parity across all three drives. Then create an extended partition and create three logical drives.
What is the result?

A. Meets your main objective and both side objectives

B. Meets your main objective and one side objective

C. Meets only your main objective

D. Doesn't meet your main objective

8. You have four disk drives with the following free space available: 100MB, 200MB, 400MB, 600MB. What is the largest stripe set you can create?

A. 400MB

B. 600MB

C. 800MB

D. 1300MB

9. Two drives in your stripe set with parity have failed. The stripe set with parity consists of eight disks. What must you do to recover the data on the failed drives?

    A. In Disk Administrator, click Fault Tolerance | Regenerate.

    B. Recover from backup tape.

    C. Replace the failed drives. Then, in Disk Administrator, click Fault Tolerance | Regenerate.

    D. Nothing. A stripe set with parity automatically recovers with the available disks.

10. You are installing Windows NT on a computer and wish to use software RAID to provide redundancy on the operating system files. Which type of RAID should you use to provide the best fault tolerance?

    A. Mirror

    B. Volume set

    C. Stripe set

    D. Stripe set with parity

11. You've enabled auditing on your Windows NT server as follows:
    WRITE: Success
    WRITE: Failed
    Change Permissions: Success
    The permissions only apply to files in the root folder. What action will cause an entry in your audit log? (Choose all that apply.)

    A. A user makes a change to a file in a sub folder.

    B. A user unsuccessfully tries to delete a file.

    C. A user unsuccessfully tries to modify an existing file.

    D. A user successfully modifies an existing file.

12. You want to install Windows 95 on 100 computers. In order to install Windows 95 on all machines as fast as possible you want to install it via the network. How should you do this? (Choose all that apply.)

A. Share Win95 Installation files.

B. Make installation startup disk with Network Client Administrator.

C. Make Installation disk set with Network Client Administrator.

D. Install from disk.

E. Install from disk set.

13. The power supply your server is plugged into is very unreliable. At least once per week the power goes out, causing the server to turn off and lose data. After three weeks, you wake up and realize you need a UPS. After buying the UPS, you need to connect it to your server. Which port do you use?

A. Port 110

B. UPS Port

C. COM Port

D. Parallel Port

14. You are installing an external tape on your Windows NT Server. The external tape drive requires a SCSI controller, so you install a compatible SCSI controller. What must you do to use the new tape drive with NT? (Choose all that apply.)

A. Install the NTBACKUP software.

B. Restart the NTBACKUP service.

C. Install the SCSI device driver.

D. Install the tape drive device driver.

15. You want to use disk duplexing for fault tolerance and performance gains. What hardware do you need to use disk duplexing?

A. Two hard disks and two controllers

B. Two hard disks and one controller

C. Three hard disks and one controller

D. Three hard disks and two controllers

**16.** You have four disks, each 300MB. What is the most useable disk space available if you create a stripe set with parity?

    A. 300

    B. 600

    C. 900

    D. 1200

**17.** Your network is growing by leaps and bounds. To help performance, you've standardized on TCP/IP as the only protocol on the servers and workstations. Even after changing all computers to TCP/IP you still have too many broadcasts on your network. What should you do?

    A. Install a DHCP server.

    B. Install a WINS server.

    C. Install more bridges.

    D. Replace hubs with switches.

**18.** You're creating a new partition on the free space on one of your hard disks. You've already entered the size of the partition you want to create and the new drive appears in Disk Administrator. What should you do next?

    A. Mark the partition active.

    B. Assign a volume label.

    C. Format the partition.

    D. Commit the changes.

e x a m
ⓦa t c h    *When using DHCP and WINS, your WINS renewal interval must be at least one-half the time of the DHCP lease. This ensures that the registered computer names have the proper IP addresses assigned to them.*

**19.** When the power fails to a server using the UPS configuration shown in the next illustration, what does the file POWEROUT.BAT do?

SERVER
QUESTIONS

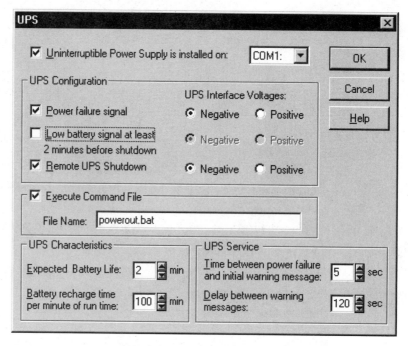

A. It automatically shuts down the computer.

B. It warns users that the power is out.

C. It starts the UPS battery.

D. It executes whenever the power fails.

*Be careful when setting the lease duration. You should set a lease duration that best meets your needs. If you have a lot of IP addresses but relatively few computers, you can set a long lease duration. Conversely, if you have only a few IP addresses and many computers you should set a short lease. If you have many IP addresses you may be tempted to choose Unlimited, that isn't recommended because DHCP not only assigns IP addresses, but also client configuration information. If you set the lease duration to Unlimited, your clients won't ever update their configuration information if it changes, unless you manually update DHCP at each client.*

# Managing Resources

1. You need to create 10 user accounts that have the same Description, Groups, Profile, and Dial-in permissions. What's the best way to add all 10 users via the User Manager program?

   A. Create each account individually.
   B. Create the first account, then use the copy user account option to create new users.
   C. Import a .CSV file with all the users names.
   D. Create the first account, then use the clone user account from the command shell.

2. Sally recently quit the company under not so good terms (she was fired). Her boss comes to you and asks you to delete her account because he was concerned she may delete or copy sensitive files on the server. Sally has extensive user rights and groups assigned to her account, which will take quite some time to recreate when her replacement is hired. What should you do?

   A. Immediately delete the account—security is the number one concern.
   B. Rename the account to a name Sally will never guess.
   C. Disable the account, then when her replacement comes in you can rename it and enable the account.
   D. Copy the account, then delete the account.

3. You want to give three users access to a shared folder on your NT server, which is running as a member server. How should you do this?

   A. Create a global group on your server, put the users in the global group, and give the global group permissions to the shared folder.
   B. Create a global group on the domain controller, add the users to the global group, and give the global group permissions to the shared folder.
   C. Create a local group on your server, add the users to the local group, and give the local group permissions to the shared folder.
   D. Give the users permissions to the shared folder.

**4.** There are 50 people in the sales department and 30 people in the marketing department who need access to a printer located in the front office. What is the best way to grant access to these two departments?

A. Create two global groups called SALES and MARKETING. Place all the sales department people in the global group named SALES and the marketing department users in the MARKETING global group. Create a local group called FRNT-OFC-PRT and place the SALES and MARKETING groups in the local group. Finally, grant the local group FRNT-OFC-PRT permissions to the printer.

B. Create two global groups called SALES and MARKETING. Place all the sales department people in the global group named SALES and the marketing department users in the MARKETING global group. Finally, grant each group permissions to print to the printer.

C. Create two local groups called SALES and MARKETING. Place all the sales department people in the local group named SALES and the marketing department users in the MARKETING local group. Create a global group called FRNT-OFC-PRT and place the SALES and MARKETING group in the global group. Finally, grant the global group FRNT-OFC-PRT permissions to the printer.

D. Create two local groups called SALES and MARKETING. Place all the sales department people in the local group named SALES and the marketing department users in the MARKETING local group. Finally, grant each group permissions to print to the printer.

exam
ⓌatchⒽ  *A number of people who have taken the NT Server exam reported being asked how to change file permissions on a Windows NT Server from a Windows 95 machine. One of the answers provided is Server Manager, which is part of the client administration tools, but this is not the correct answer. It seems tricky, but you use Windows Explorer to assign file permissions.*

**5.** A user in the domain you manage complains that every time he logs on he gets a different desktop. The user typically logs onto six different NT workstations per day. How can you help the user?

   A. Create a policy file on each of the workstations.

   B. Synchronize each desktop on the workstations he uses using the directory replicator service.

   C. Ensure the directory replication service is working properly.

   D. Create a roaming profile for the user.

**6.** You created two home directories for two users on your Windows NT server. One user logs onto an NT workstation and the other user logs onto WFW 3.11. Only the user who logs onto NT Workstation can access his home directory. How can you fix this problem?

   A. You can't give home directories to WFW 3.11 clients.

   B. Relocate the WFW 3.11 user's home directory on his local machine.

   C. Map a drive to the home directory for the user on WFW 3.11.

   D. Enter the entire UNC path in the Home Directory dialog box.

**7.** A user connects to a share on your NT server. What special group is he a member of?

   A. Creator Owner

   B. Interactive

   C. System

   D. Network

**8.** You are going to shut down your Windows NT server to add new hardware. You want to see how many users are currently connected to it before you shut it down. Which tool should you use?

A. Server Manager

B. User Manager

C. Explorer

D. Network Neighborhood

9. After you installed client-based administrative tools on your Windows 95 computer, which tool would you use to manage a printer on an NT server?

A. Server Manager

B. Explorer

C. User Manager for Domains

D. File Manager

10. You want to allow an administrator in DOMAIN X to administer DOMAIN Z as well. What is the best way to allow this?

A. Create a local group in DOMAIN X.

B. Create a global group in DOMAIN Z.

C. Create an identical account in the other domain and place it in the local administrator group.

D. Add the user account in DOMAIN X to the local administrator group in DOMAIN Z.

---

exam
ⓌatchⒽ

*You may be asked how the mandatory profile reacts in the event of a server crash. If for some reason the server that contains your mandatory profile is not on the network, one of two things will happen: If you have never logged onto the domain before, the default user profile is used. If you have successfully logged onto the domain before, the local cache profile on your computer is used.*

---

11. Your network is configured as a single domain that has two domain controllers, three member servers, and 34 NT workstations. For security you assign mandatory profiles for all user accounts using the .MAN

extension to make the profile mandatory. The server that has the profiles fails. What will happen when users attempt to log onto the domain while the server is down?

A. Users will log on successfully and receive the default user profile.

B. Users won't be allowed to log on until they can access the mandatory profile.

C. If the user has logged on before, he'll use the default profile for his account; otherwise, he won't be able to log on.

D. The user will automatically be redirected to a different domain controller.

12. After you installed client-based administrative tools on your Windows 95 computer, which tool would you use to create a network shared folder on an NT workstation?

A. Server Manager

B. Explorer

C. User Manager for Domains

D. File Manager

13. You just deleted a user account by accident. How should you recover the user account and its permissions?

A. You must recreate the user account with the same name and assign it the same permissions and groups.

B. If the PDC hasn't synchronized the domain yet, log onto a BDC and copy the account to a new account with a different name.

C. Use the resource kit utility GETSID.

D. Use CACLS to retrieve the account and its permissions.

*For the exam, make sure you know how and why to configure a roaming profile.*

**14.** Your network has six BDCs running on it. You've upgraded the hardware in all six computers, so now you only need three BDCs. How should you demote the BDC to a member server?

A. Use Server Manager and choose Demote from the Computer menu.

B. Take the server offline, then use Server Manager and choose Demote from the Computer menu.

C. Run the command NET START /MEMBER.

D. Reinstall Windows NT.

**15.** You ask Lori to help you add users to the network. You don't want her to have full administrative rights on the domain. How should you set Lori's account up so that it can add users, but doesn't have full administrative rights?

A. Add her account to the Account operators group.

B. Add her account to the Server Operators group.

C. Add her account to the Power Users group.

D. Create a separate domain for Lori to add the users in.

exam
ⓦatch

*Local and global groups (as well as trust relationships) are not covered in much depth during the Windows NT Server 4.0 exam. They are covered in great depth in the Windows NT 4.0 Server in the Enterprise exam. However, it is very important to understand the differences between the two. It will also make studying easier for the next exam, when you will need this background. Local and group administration can be a very complex issue, especially when Microsoft gets their hands on it for the exam.*

**16.** You want to assign a logon script to the new user account you're creating in the next illustration. Which button should you click to enter a logon script name?

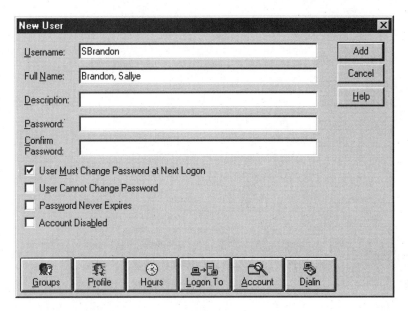

A. Groups

B. Profile

C. Hours

D. Logon To

E. Account

F. Dialin

**17.** You copy a file from an NTFS partition to a FAT partition. The file name is NT DOMAIN SECURITY PLAN. Administrators have Full Control and all other groups have No Access. What will happen to the file name and permissions when it is copied to the FAT partition?

A. Both permissions and long file name will be discarded.

B. The permissions will be retained, but the long file name will be discarded.

C. The permissions will be discarded and the long file name will be retained.

D. Both permissions and long file name will be retained.

**18.** What type of group does the next illustration represent?

   A. Local group

   B. Global group

   C. Domain group

   D. Computer group

## QUESTIONS AND ANSWERS

| | |
|---|---|
| I only have one domain and I need to assign permissions or rights… | Use a local group. This is the correct group if you only have one domain. You can add users, and also other global groups if you need to give permissions to members of another domain later. |
| I need to place a group within… | Use local. Only local groups can contain a global group. In fact, that is the only way one group can be placed in another group. |
| I need to give users permissions on workstations or member servers… | Use a global group. You cannot create a global group on a member server or workstation, but you can add this global group to the member server or workstations local group. You can then grant permissions to the local group. |
| I need to group users so they can access resources from another domain… | Use a global group. Global groups can be placed in the other domain's local groups. The other domain can then grant permissions to the local group. |
| I need a group to include users from other domains… | Use a local group. Although the group cannot be used outside the local domain, it can be used to hold global groups that contain users from other domains. |

# Windows NT 4.0 Security

**1.** You are copying a file from an NTFS partition to a FAT Partition. The original file's permissions allow administrators Full Control and Everyone Read Access. What are the permissions of the copied file?

A. Administrators Full Control and Everyone Read Access.

B. Everyone Full Control.

C. Everyone Read Access.

D. FAT doesn't support file-level permissions.

**2.** You were auditing users logging onto your server and you noticed the administrator account was logged on. You're the only one with the password, and you haven't logged on using the administrator account for three months. What should you do? (Choose all that apply.)

A. Rename the administrator account.

B. Change the administrator's password.

C. Disable the administrator account.

D. Delete the administrator account.

**3.** The folder MANAGEMENT has the following NTFS permissions:

■ RESEARCH group: List

■ SALES group: Read

■ MARKETING group: No Access

■ MANAGERS group: Add

User LoriL belongs to the RESEARCH group, SALES group, and MANAGERS group. What permissions will she have to the folder?

A. Full Control

B. Read

C. Add

D. Read and Add

**4.** You have a shared folder on your server named PUBLIC. All users have Change permissions to the folder. Everyday files are being deleted that shouldn't be. No one is confessing to deleting the files. What should you do?

A. Only allow users to have Read permissions to the folder.

B. Audit for Delete on the folder and files within the folder.

C. Use a network sniffer to identify who is deleting the files.

D. You can't do anything as long as all users can delete the files.

**5.** You want to change the permissions on many files and directories on an NTFS partition. Many of the permissions will vary from file to file within a directory. What is the fastest way to do this?

A. Use File Manager and set it on each directory and file.

B. Use Explorer and change permissions on each folder, and choose to update all files and folders in its directory.

C. Use the CACLS program from the command shell.

D. Edit the Registry and update all the ACEs.

**6.** You've enabled auditing to detect whenever a file is deleted. You notice that user LoriL is deleting files she should not be deleting. You confront her and ask her why she is doing this. She promises you it wasn't her, someone else must be doing it and the audit is wrong. What should you do?

A. Tell her boss so she'll get fired. She's obviously lying.

B. Tell her she is wrong and she is lying. If she admits to deleting the files, you won't tell on her.

C. Audit for logons. The next time she logs on, run a network sniffer to capture everything she does. This way you'll have proof that she did it.

D. Tell her to change her password and not to share it with anyone.

exam
**ⓦatch**

*Permissions are cumulative, except for No Access. This may confuse people because you don't have to belong to a group that has all the proper permissions. If your account has read access and you belong to a group with write access you will be granted read and write access.*

**7.** You've upgraded all your Windows 95 machines to Windows NT. All your hard disks are formatted with NTFS. Whenever a user creates a local file, who is the default owner of that file?

A. The administrator

B. The user who created the file

C. Everyone

D. All users in the creator's groups

**8.** Your users don't like to be responsible for managing their own security. It's just too much pressure on them. Besides, that's why they hired you. They want you to be the owner of all files created on their workstations. How can you do this?

A. Edit the Registry key HKEY_LOCAL_MACHINE\CurrentConfig\ System\Security\defaultowner on the domain controller.

B. Edit the Registry key HKEY_LOCAL_MACHINE\CurrentConfig\ System\Security\defaultowner on each workstation.

C. Manually take ownership of the root directory, then all files created in that directory will set you as the owner.

D. You can't have the owner of new files be set to anyone other than the creator.

**9.** Your system has recently been hacked. In order to help prevent further hacking incidents in the future you've enabled auditing and taken some other security measures. You set auditing up on all files and folders for every type of access. After you do this, your servers have slowed down to a crawl. Why?

A. Your security log needs to be set to a larger size to handle the increased auditing.

B. You haven't run DISKPERF –Y to enable the hard disk performance counters.

C. The increased logging writes to the disk drive. The increased logging impacts the overall performance of the server. You should reduce auditing or install more servers to handle the load.

D. It's just an anomaly. Auditing requires very little overhead.

**10.** You have a file named RYAN'S MARKETING REPORT.DOC. The file permissions are set to Everyone Full Control. The file is moved to a folder named REPORTS on a different partition. The folder REPORTS has Everyone with Change permissions. What will the permissions be on the file after it is moved?

A. Everyone Full Control

B. No Access

C. Everyone Change

D. Everyone Change, Ryan Full Control

**11.** Your server has a FAT partition with a folder called PUBLIC. You want to make this folder available to everyone on the network so they can read, write, and execute files within the directory. You don't want anyone to be able to delete files. How should you set the permissions? (Choose all that apply.)

A. Give everyone Read share permissions.

B. Give everyone Change share permissions.

C. Give everyone Add share permissions.

D. Give everyone Change NTFS file/folder permissions.

E. Give everyone Read, Write, and Execute Special File/folder permissions.

F. Convert the drive to NTFS.

---

exam
Ⓦatch

*The key to assigning and removing a user to a group is that the user must be logged off before the change can take effect. If the user isn't logged on when the change is made, the change will reflect the next time the user logs on. If the user is logged on when the change is made, he must first log off, then log back on to apply the changes. This can be tricky if you see it on the test.*

---

**12.** How many users will be allowed to connect to the share JESSE if you change the User Limit from 1 to Maximum Allowed in the next illustration?

A. 1

B. 10

C. 225

D. unlimited

exam
Watch

*There is one more permission type called File Delete Child. File Delete Child is a POSIX function that allows a user who has Full Control of a folder to delete a top-level file within that folder, even though the user doesn't have permissions to delete that file. Let's say you have full control of a folder called "Sales Reports". Within that folder there is a file called "Mary's Sales.xls" in which you have No Access permissions assigned. Since you have full control of the "Sales Reports" folder you can delete the file "Mary's Sales.xls" even though you don't have access to that file.*

# Windows NT 4.0 Domains

**1.** Your network has 2,000 users, and over the next year you plan to increase to about 2,500 users. How many BDCs should your network have?

A. One

B. Two

C. Three

D. Four

**2.** You have five research scientists running Windows NT. They need to ensure that only they have access to their own research. When they want to share information on the network, each scientist needs to control access to his own computer. Which model should you use?

A. Workgroup

B. Single Domain

C. Master Domain

D. Complete Trust

**3.** You currently have 250 trusts in your domain model. How many more trusts can you create?

A. Four

B. Five

C. Six

D. About 250, but it depends on the hardware

E. There is no limit to the number of trusts you can create with Windows NT 4.0.

**4.** You manage two domains, HQ and SALES. SALES trusts HQ. You want a user in HQ to access a resource in SALES. How can you do this while creating only one group?

A. Create a local group on the server in the SALES domain and add the user to it.

B. Create a global group on the server in the SALES domain and add the user to it.

C. Create a local group on the server in the HQ domain and add the user to it.

D. Create a global group on the server in the HQ domain and add the user to it.

**5.** You have two domains, DOMAIN A and DOMAIN B. The guest account is disabled in both. You want all users in both domains to have access to a folder in DOMAIN A. You want to manage only one group. What three steps must you perform?

A. Create a local group on DOMAIN A.

B. Create a local group on DOMAIN B.

C. Add all users to the local group in DOMAIN A.

D. Add all users to the local group in DOMAIN B.

E. Create one-way trust in which DOMAIN A trusts DOMAIN B.

F. Create one-way trust in which DOMAIN B trusts DOMAIN A.

**6.** You have 150 users and six servers in a central office. The MIS department wants to keep complete control over user accounts and resources. Which domain model should you use?

A. Single Domain

B. Master Domain

C. Multiple Master Domain

D. Complete Trust Domain

**7.** You have 132,000 users. The MIS department wants to control user accounts and account security. Local department managers need to manage local resources. Which domain model should you use?

A. Single Domain

B. Master Domain

C. Multiple Master Domain

D. Complete Trust Domain

**8.** You have 10,000 users. Each department wants to control its own user accounts and resources. Which domain model should you use?

A. Single Domain

B. Master Domain

C. Multiple Master Domain

D. Complete Trust Domain

**9.** A_____ is a link that combines two separate domains into one administrative unit that can authorize access to resources on both domains.

**10.** You're the lead network project manager who needs to merge 20 separate Windows NT domains. The first phase of the project is going to interconnect all the domains using the complete trust model. How many trusts must you create to have each domain trust every other domain?

A. 20

B. 370

C. 380

D. 390

E. 400

---

e x a m

ⓦat c h

*Be sure to understand local and global groups. When you create a local group on a domain controller, it can only be used on other domain controllers within the same domain. The local group created on a domain controller can't be used on member servers and workstations. A global group created on a domain controller can be used on member servers, workstations, and in other domains.*

---

**11.** Your server needs to be rebooted for a new device driver to take effect. You don't want to do this while users are logged on. What should you do to see who is currently logged onto the server?

    A. Run Server Manager and double-click the computer you need to reboot. Then click the Users button.

    B. Run Server Manager and double-click the computer you need to reboot. Then click the Shares button.

    C. Use User Manager for Domains and select the Current Users Logged On.

    D. Use the NET USE command at the command shell.

**12.** You're a server operator on a domain. You need to install two NT workstations on the domain. How do you do this?

    A. On the workstation joining the domain, provide your username and password in the proper dialog box.

    B. Use Server Manager and add the computer to the domain. Then, on the workstation joining the domain, do not provide your username and password in the dialog box.

    C. Anyone can join the domain. You don't need to be the server operator. Just have the user join the domain.

    D. You can't. Only administrators can add computers to the domain.

**13.** Since your domain is a single domain and there aren't any trusts, you don't have to use global groups. Instead, you decide to use local groups only. Is this a good idea?

    A. Yes, it helps ease the management of groups by requiring only one type—local.

    B. No, it doesn't follow the domain model and it won't work.

    C. No, it doesn't follow the domain model, even though it will work. If you need to add trusts in the future you'll need to create global groups.

    D. Yes, it doesn't follow the domain model, but the domain model is flexible to allow customization.

**14.** If you create a local group on the PDC, what other computers can use this local group?

    A. Member servers

    B. NT workstations

    C. BDCs

    D. Only the PDC

**15.** What type of domain model does the next illustration represent?

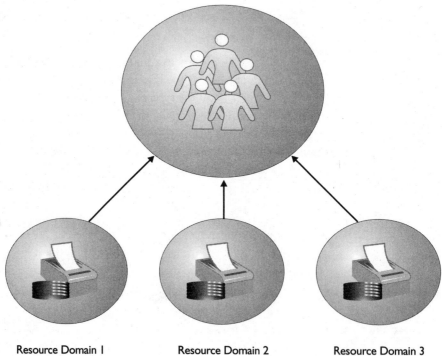

Resource Domain 1       Resource Domain 2       Resource Domain 3

    A. Single Domain

    B. Master Domain

    C. Multiple Master Domain

    D. Complete Trust Domain

**16.** What type of domain model does the next illustration represent?

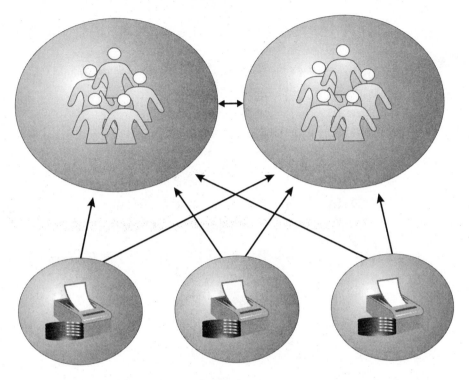

Resource Domain 1            Resource Domain 2            Resource Domain 3

A. Single Domain
B. Master Domain
C. Multiple Master Domain
D. Complete Trust Domain

exam
ⓦatch

*Be sure to know which way the arrows point for trusts. You may see several diagrams with arrows representing trusts on your test. If you forget that the arrows point from the trusting domain to the trusted domain, you'll probably miss the question.*

# Replication and Data Synchronization

1. You have five files that are commonly read throughout the day by all users in your organization. Many users are connecting over slow links, which causes unacceptable delays. What should you do to help reduce the slow file access? (Choose the best answer.)

   A. Increase the link speed to at least a T1.
   B. Replicate the data to each remote site by exporting the data to servers and/or workstations on the remote segment.
   C. Manually copy the files to each remote site whenever they are changed or updated.
   D. Use file compressions to speed up transmissions.

2. You want to set up directory replication. Which of the following can be an export server? (Choose all that apply.)

   A. NT Workstation
   B. PDC
   C. BDC
   D. Member Server

3. You need to establish logon scripts for about 30 percent of your users. You expect to update the logon script at least once per month. You have one PDC and three BDCs. How can you configure the logon scripts so that they are available to the users every time they log on?

   A. Place the logon script on the PDC. For redundancy, export the file to all import servers.
   B. Place the logon script on the PDC. Set up the PDC as the export server and all the BDCs as an import server.
   C. Place the logon script on the PDC and all BDCs.
   D. Place the logon script on the BDCs and configure them as an export server. Configure the PDC as an import server.

4. You're trying to install directory replication. You've created an account called SYNCH to serve as the service account. It belongs to the following groups: Domain User, Backup Operators, and Server Operator. You've tried everything you can think of to get the files to replicate, but it just doesn't happen. What's wrong?

    A. You need to reboot the server to have the changes take place.

    B. You need to add the SYNCH account to the Replicator group.

    C. You need to verify that the password used for the service account is correct.

    D. You need to add the SYNCH account to the Administrators group.

5. You are trying to create the service account that the directory replication service will use. You use User Manager for Domains to create the account named Replicator, but you can't create the account. Why?

    A. You need to use User Manager, not User Manager for Domains.

    B. You need to give it the right to log on as a service.

    C. You can't use the name Replicator, because there is a group already named Replicator.

    D. You need to add it to the Replicator group.

6. Why must the Directory Replication Service account be added to the Replicator group?

    A. So NT can track its usage.

    B. It is allowed access to the REPL$ share on the export server.

    C. It is allowed access to the REPL$ share on the import server.

    D. Because this group is only allowed one account assigned to it, so that no user can hack the Replicator group.

exam
ⓦatch    *Only computers that are running Windows NT Server can be configured as export servers. The Windows NT Server does not have to be a domain controller to be used in this configuration.*

**7.** What is the REPL$ share?

    A. It's the share on the export directory that allows the import servers access to the files and folders that need to be replicated.

    B. It's the share on the import directory that allows the export server to write the replication files to their import directory.

    C. It's an admin share that gives the administrator group access to the logon directory.

    D. It's the directory users access to execute logon scripts.

**8.** You need to set up an import directory on a remote Windows NT workstation. What tool should you use?

    A. You can't do it remotely. You'll need to access the workstation locally.

    B. Server Manager.

    C. The Server applet in Control Panel.

    D. Replication Manager in the NT Resource Kit.

**9.** You are replicating many directories that have subdirectories. You notice that the import servers only have the root directory data. They don't have the subdirectories of the exported directory. What should you do?

    A. Resynchronize all the directories.

    B. Select the Entire Subtree check box.

    C. Select the Wait Until Stabilized check box.

    D. Change the password of the service account.

**10.** When looking at the Manage Imported Directories dialog box, you see the message No Master. What does this mean?

    A. This server isn't set up to replicate data.

    B. You need to redefine the export server.

    C. You need to define a service account.

    D. The server is not receiving updates from the export server.

11. You have a BDC connected to the PDC via a slow WAN link. What should you do to help improve the performance of the SAM replication, so that it doesn't use up the available bandwidth? (Choose all that apply.)

    A. Reduce the value of the ReplicationGovernor.

    B. Reduce the value of the change log.

    C. Increase the value of the ReplicationGovernor.

    D. Increase the value of the change log.

    E. Stop and restart the Netlogon service.

12. You changed the default import directory on all your import servers (three BDCs) about two months ago. Your PDC is the export server. Now you need to use logon scripts to map drives for all your users. You place the logon scripts in %SYSTEMROOT%SYSTEM32\REPL\EXPORT\ SCRIPTS directory to replicate them to all your import servers. All the scripts are replicated properly, but they aren't executed when users log on. Why?

    A. You need to change the import directory path to %SYSTEMROOT%SYSTEM32\REPL\IMPORT\SCRIPTS.

    B. You need to specify the logon script path on all the domain controllers.

    C. You need to set the PDC up as both an import and export server.

    D. You need to specify the logon script in the users profile.

exam
ⓦatch
*You can name the replicator service account by any name that you want, with the exception that it cannot have the same name as a group. That is the reason it is named dReplicator— not just Replicator—because a group by that name already exists.*

13. In the next illustration, what is the directory replication service on the server CONAN set up to do?

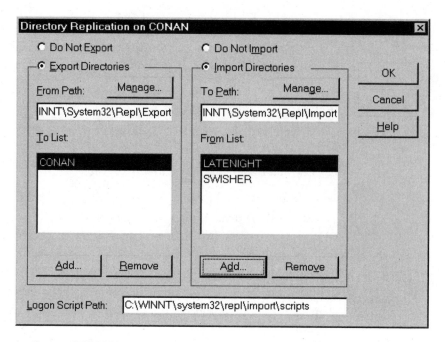

A. Server CONAN is set up to import data from the servers LATENIGHT and SWISHER.

B. Server CONAN is set up to export data to the servers LATENIGHT and SWISHER.

C. Servers LATENIGHT and SWISHER are set up to import data from CONAN.

D. Servers LATENIGHT and SWISHER are set up to export data to CONAN.

exam
ⓦatch   *The logon script path cannot be changed for member servers. You need to store logon scripts in %SYSTEMROOT%SYSTEM32\ REPL\IMPORT\SCRIPTS or in subdirectories of that path.*

# Printing

1. A network printer has catastrophically failed. The paper is jammed, the toner cartridge has exploded leaving toner all over the office, and the power supply is on fire. Needless to say, that printer won't be up anytime soon. In fact, your boss has declared the office where the printer is located a disaster area and no one is allowed in unless they have a bio suit. How can you redirect jobs from that printer to another printer in a different office?

   A. Drag all of the print jobs from the printer and drop them onto another printer.
   B. Purge all the print jobs and tell users to re-send their print jobs to a different printer.
   C. On the Ports tab in Printer Properties on the print server, create a new port with the UNC name of another shared printer that uses the same driver.
   D. Violate your boss's order and install another printer with the same model number next to the failed printer.

2. Sally calls you, complaining that a she can't print to a shared printer. She's using Windows 95 and all other users are using Windows NT. You check her permissions and notice she has No Access assigned to that printer. You change her permissions to give her full control of the printer. She tries again, but she still can't print. What is the problem?

   A. She used the wrong password.
   B. She changed her password after logging on, causing a password caching problem.
   C. The group change won't take place until she logs off and back on.
   D. The printer uses a trusted connection, and Windows 95 can't connect with a trusted connection.

**3.** You are setting up a member server to maintain about 20 printers. The clients connecting to the printer include NT 4.0, NT 3.51, Windows 95, and Windows 3.11. How many different drivers should you install?

A. One

B. Two

C. Three

D. Four

**4.** Al currently uses Windows NT 3.51 and does a large number of time-consuming, graphically intense print jobs. Which of the following NT 4.0 improvements in printers will help Al the most?

A. EMF file spooling

B. Point and print

C. Ability to establish a printer pool

D. Postscript capabilities

**5.** You've installed an HP LaserJet on a UNIX server. You're trying to print to it via your NT server. What protocol must be installed on NT Server?

A. DLC

B. IPX/SPX

C. DEC

D. TCP/IP

**6.** You're setting up a printer using LPD. What information do you need about the printing device?

A. IP Address

B. Subnet mask

C. The paper size

D. Default gateway

7. Your server's spooler stopped running. You restart the service, but it fails. You think there is a corrupt file in your print spooler. What should you do?

   A. Check for a corrupt file in C:\WINNT_ROOT\SYSTEM32\ SPOOL\*printername* and delete it.

   B. Check for a corrupt file in C:\WINNT_ROOT\SYSTEM32\ SPOOLER\*printername* and delete it.

   C. Check for a corrupt file in HKEY_LOCAL_MACHINE Registry and delete it.

   D. Check for a corrupt file in the Printers applet and delete it.

8. Your HP printer came with an HP JetDirect card. It's the latest model JetDirect card, so it supports DLC, IPX, TCP/IP, and AppleTalk. You want to use the HP network port print monitor that comes with NT. You are trying to set up the printer, but you don't have the option to use the HP Network Print Monitor. What should you do?

   A. Use TCP/IP instead.

   B. Use IPX.

   C. Contact HP for updated firmware.

   D. Install DLC.

9. You have a dual-homed Windows NT server. The first adapter card has three HP printers attached to it. It uses the HP network port print monitor that comes with NT. You are trying to install a fourth HP printer using the same print monitor. Instead of attaching it to the first adapter card subnet you attach it to the second adapter card subnet. While setting up the fourth printer, NT fails to detect the JetDirect Card. What should you do? (Choose all that apply.)

   A. Attach the printer to the first subnet.

   B. Use a different print monitor (like LPD).

   C. Update the firmware.

   D. Install DLC.

**10.** Your network has three subnets and one Windows NT server. You have an HP JetDirect-enabled printer on Subnet A. The JetDirect card supports several protocols including DLC, TCP/IP, and IPX. The NT server is located on Subnet C. How should you configure the printer so that it uses the HP JetDirect card?

A. Use the HP print port monitor that comes with NT.

B. Use the DLC protocol to print to the printing device.

C. Use the LPD service to print to the printing device.

D. You can't print to it, since DLC isn't routable.

**11.** You have a shared printer that everyone is allowed to print to. Your manager says he hates printing because he has to wait behind at least five other people to receive his print job. How should you configure the printer, so he doesn't have to wait as long?

A. Buy your boss a new printing device and attach it to his computer.

B. Schedule the printer to print his print jobs before everyone else's.

C. Create two printers printing to the same printing device. Give him permissions to print to one of the printers and everyone else can print to the other printer. Assign his printer a priority of 50 and assign the other printer a priority of 5.

D. Select to print documents after the last page is spooled.

**12.** You're having a problem printing to one of your printing devices. You attempt to troubleshoot it. One of the steps you take is to print directly to the printer. After making this change, you can print. Where is the problem?

A. In the cable connection to the shared printer.

B. In the cable connection to the local printer.

C. In the spooler.

D. You don't have enough information to answer.

**13.** You have a user on the network who often sends a job to be printed, then realizes the job isn't ready to print. She doesn't want to waste company resources by printing unnecessary documents, so she calls you and asks you to delete her print job. After she did this eight times in one week, you think it's time to allow her to delete her own print jobs. What should you do? (Choose all that apply.)

A. Give her Full Control of the printer.

B. Give her Manage Documents permissions on the printer.

C. Make her a member of the Power Users group.

D. Teach her how to delete print jobs.

14. Several users on your network select the incorrect print driver when printing to your HP 5 printer. Every time this happens it causes the printer to hang. What should you do?

A. Stop sharing the printer.

B. Don't allow those users to print to your shared printer.

C. Select Hold Mismatched Documents check box.

D. Select to print spooled pages first.

15. Where does the server spooler pass its data?

A. To the local print provider

B. To the printing device

C. To the down level client

D. To the print monitor

16. You are creating a printer pool with six printing devices. Which of the following conditions must be true to create a printer pool? (Choose all that apply.)

A. All printing devices must be defined to the same printer.

B. All printing devices must use the same driver.

C. All printing devices must be located in the same room.

D. All printing devices have to be connected to the same printer port.

**17.** After creating the Windows NT gateway to a NetWare resource, what must you do to activate the gateway?

   A. Create the NTGATEWAY group on the NetWare server.

   B. Add user accounts to the NTGATEWAY group.

   C. Move NWLINK to the top of the binding order.

   D. Map a drive to the NetWare shared resource or add a printer.

**18.** In the next illustration, which printer tab would you select to configure the print processor?

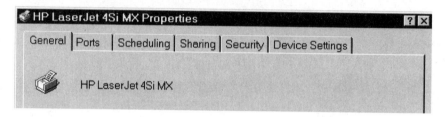

   A. General

   B. Ports

   C. Scheduling

   D. Sharing

   E. Security

   F. Device Settings

e x a m
ⓦatch

*Be sure to understand that Hewlett-Packard JetDirect cards require the DLC protocol to be loaded on your system. Because DLC is not a routable protocol, the print server and the printing device must be on the same side of a router.*

**19.** What events will get recorded in your security log in Event Viewer if you have auditing enabled as shown in the next illustration? (Choose all that apply.)

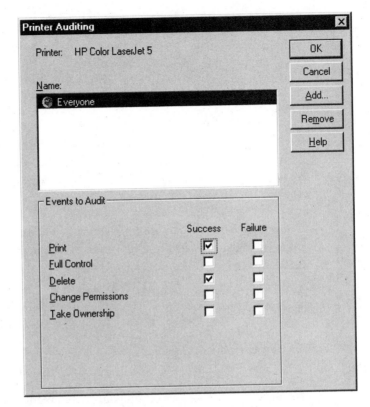

A. A user prints a document on the printer.

B. A user tries to print a document but his permissions are insufficient.

C. A user tries to print a document, but the spooler hangs. The administrator stops and restarts the spooler to start the printer.

D. A user tries to delete another user's print job, but fails because his permissions are insufficient.

exam
ⓦatch

*Be sure to understand that changing the priority of a printer doesn't affect the priority of the print queue. When you have two printers printing to the same printer device, a printer with a higher priority will print to the device, when it's available, before a printer with a lower priority. If the lower priority printer is busy printing a document, it will finish printing the job before releasing control to a higher priority printer.*

# NetWare Integration

1. You are setting up a gateway from an NT server to a Novell 3.12 server. What account and/or group must you install?

   A. An account on the Novell server named NTGATEWAY

   B. A global group on the NT server named NTGATEWAY

   C. A group on the Novell server named NTGATEWAY

   D. An account on the NT server named NTGATEWAY

2. You have a Windows 95 computer with client administration for NT installed, and an NT server. You want the computer to connect to a Novell 3.12 server. How should you connect to the Novell server?

   A. Map the drive on the Netware server

   B. GSNW

   C. Server Manager

   D. User Manager for Domains

3. You've installed an NT server on your Novell Network. What will the Novell clients be able to access on the NT server?

   A. Shared directories

   B. Shared printers

   C. NetBIOS client/server applications

   D. Nothing

4. Your network uses IPX/SPX with 30 clients using 802.3 frame type and 20 clients using 802.2 frame type. You need all clients to access NT. How should you do this?

   A. Install NetBEUI on all the clients.

   B. Use Manual Frame.

   C. Use Auto Frame detection.

   D. Install two drivers: one for the 802.3 frame type, and one for the 802.2 frame type.

**5.** You are planning on using the NetWare Migration utility. What must you first install on the server?

A. GSNW

B. IPX/SPX

C. Novell's NetWare redirector

D. NCP filter

**6.** What happens to NetWare file attributes that aren't recognized by Windows NT when you migrate files from NetWare to NT?

A. They are ignored.

B. They are translated to a similar attribute.

C. The files aren't transferred until the problem is corrected.

D. All file attributes are recognized by NT.

**7.** You have 200 NetWare 3.12 clients on your network that need to access files on your Windows NT server. What should you do? (Choose all that apply.)

A. Install GSNW.

B. Install CSNW.

C. Install FPNW.

D. Install NWLink.

exam
ⓦatch

*Be sure to install GSNW and take a look at the interface. Even if you don't have a NetWare server, you can still get a feel for the GSNW interface. Installing it and checking out the different options will help you to remember them. Running the Migration Tool is helpful as well, but you need a NetWare server to explore all its capabilities.*

**8.** In the next illustration, how many frame types are assigned to Adapter (0)?

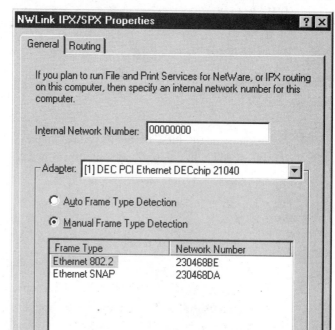

A. One

B. Two

C. Three

D. Don't know

*Knowing the exam material isn't the only thing necessary to pass certification exams. Being relaxed and focused during the exam enables you to apply your knowledge to the exam questions. Learn some relaxation and focusing exercises, and use them before and during the exam.*

## QUESTIONS AND ANSWERS

| | |
|---|---|
| I want to use the command line to map a drive to a NetWare server using bindery services... | NET USE G: \\SERVER\VOLUME\DIRECTORY |
| I want to use the command line to map a drive to a NetWare server using NDS... | NET USE G: \\TREE\VOLUME.ORGUNIT.ORGUNIT |
| I want to use the command line to connect to NetWare print queue using bindery services... | NET USE LPT1 \\SERVER\PRINTQUEUE |
| I want to use the command line to connect to a NetWare print queue using NDS... | NET USE LPT1 \\TREE\PRINTQUEUE.ORGUNIT.ORGUNIT |

# Remote Connectivity

**1.** Your network has three NT servers. One server is a file and print server, a second server is a RAS server, and the third server is a SQL server. When clients dial in to the RAS server and try to connect to the other servers, it takes about 30 seconds to make the initial connection to the servers. What should you do to help reduce the connection time?

A. Install a HOSTS file on the RAS server.

B. Install a LMHOSTS file on the RAS server.

C. Install a HOSTS file on the clients.

D. Install a LMHOSTS file on the clients.

E. Install WINS on the clients.

F. You can't do anything unless you upgrade the connection speed.

**2.** Your Windows NT workstation is set up to dial into a RAS server. It's set up to dial out using PPP with TCP/IP and NetBEUI protocols. The selected encryption type is Clear Text. The server is set up to allow TCP/IP, IPX/SPX, and NetBEUI protocols. The server is also running Gateway Services for Novell. When the NT workstation connects to the RAS server, what is it allowed to do on the network? (Choose all that apply.)

A. Access resources on the RAS server

B. Use applications that require WINSOCKS

C. Use applications using NetBEUI

D. Access a Novell server via the Gateway

**3.** You have various types of dial-up clients that use different types of security. How should you configure your RAS server to allow the users to decide which type of authentication they want to use?

A. Require Microsoft encryption.

B. Require any encryption.

C. Allow anything including plain text.

D. Text only.

**4.** Your users are dialing into your RAS server and are getting disconnected intermittently. What should you do to investigate the problem?

A. Check the system log in Event Viewer and find the error code associated with the problem.

B. Enable the modem log and check the MODEM.LOG file the next time a user is disconnected.

C. Enable the device log and check the DEVICE.LOG file the next time a user is disconnected.

D. Use a network sniffer to see if another administrator is manually disconnecting the user.

**5.** How do you grant permissions to a user to connect to a RAS server? (Choose all that apply.)

A. User Manager

B. Remote Access Admin

C. Server Manager

D. Explorer

exam
ⓦatch

*Although Windows NT Workstation and Server have identical implementations of the RAS, Windows NT Server allows a whopping 256 simultaneous inbound connections while Windows NT Workstation allows only one.*

6. What is the highest level of authentication you can use that ships with Windows NT RAS?

   A. PAP
   B. CHAP
   C. MS-CHAP
   D. Clear text

## QUESTIONS AND ANSWERS

| | |
|---|---|
| I have clients currently using third-party SLIP client software to connect to an existing UNIX server at my site. I want to replace the UNIX dial-up server with a Windows NT RAS server. Are there any additional considerations I should make? | If you implement a Windows NT Server as your dial-up server, you will need to install PPP client software on your users' workstations. RAS does not provide a SLIP server component. If your users are using Windows 95 or Windows NT Workstation, consider installing DUN on those machines. |
| Users on my network currently connect to my RAS server using the NetBEUI protocol. I want these users to be able to browse Internet web sites through my network's current Internet gateway. | Install TCP/IP on the users' workstations. TCP/IP is the language we speak on the Internet and users will need it if they want to browse Internet resources. |

**7.** PPTP can reduce the costs associated with remote clients by doing which of the following? (Choose all that apply.)

   A. By providing faster remote connections over direct dial-up lines

   B. By protecting your intranet from authorized users

   C. By allowing remote network users to use their local ISPs to access the main network

   D. By allowing RAS connections over ISDN

**8.** Users in your company are allowed to log onto the RAS server from home using their personal computers. Users have various different types of clients. Your main objective is to provide them the ability to log onto the corporate network. What's the highest level of authentication security you should use?

   A. Require Microsoft Encryption

   B. Require any encryption

   C. Allow anything including plain text

   D. Text only

## QUESTIONS AND ANSWERS

| | |
|---|---|
| Is there a way to start or stop RAS from a command prompt? | Yes. RAS is a service and can be started with the NET START function. To start the Remote Access Service, type:<br>**NET START "REMOTE ACCESS SERVER"**<br>To stop the RAS service, type:<br>**NET STOP "REMOTE ACCESS SERVER".** |
| What other methods can I use to start and stop the RAS service? | The RAS service can be started and stopped with the Services icon within Control Panel or with the Remote Access Admin program. |

**9.** Your RAS server supports PPP clients. Which types of communications are allowed by your clients?

A. WINSOCK applications using TCP/IP and IPX

B. RPC

C. Named Pipes

D. NETBIOS

**10.** Which of the following statements are not accurate about RAS autodial? (Choose all that apply.)

A. It's automatically enabled.

B. It needs at least one TAPI dial location.

C. It works with IPX.

D. It works with TCP/IP.

**11.** How many users can dial in using TCP/IP with your RAS server configured as shown in the next illustration?

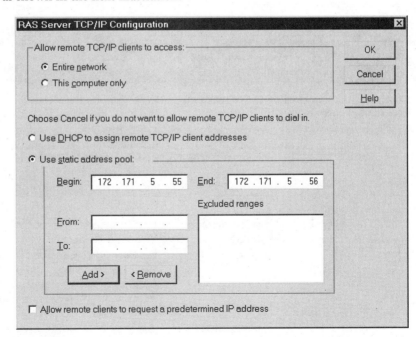

A. One

B. Two

C. Three

D. Four

E. unlimited

---

exam
**W**atch

*Gateway Services For NetWare (GSNW) is a Windows NT Server network service that changes SMB packets to NCP packets so NetWare computers can receive them. Files, print queues, and some NetWare utilities on NetWare servers are then available to all clients, even though they may not be running a NetWare-compatible protocol or client. This applies as well to DUN clients dialing in to a RAS server.*

---

## QUESTIONS AND ANSWERS

| | |
|---|---|
| What methods can I implement to make my RAS server more secure? | A secure physical facility with a locked door is a basic necessity. You can also implement callback so you can confirm where calls are being made from, monitor Windows NT auditing, apply PPTP filtering if required and implement a third-party intermediary device if you want more security than RAS itself provides. |
| If MS-CHAP is the best encryption method available to me in RAS, why wouldn't I always use it? | MS-CHAP is supported by Microsoft Windows clients but is not widely adopted by many other types of clients. Therefore, if you have UNIX hosts on your network or third-party dial-up clients, you will need to select another encryption method for those clients. |

# Backup

1. You have two servers on a switched Ethernet network: server X and server Y. Server X has a DAT backup unit installed and backs up both server X and server Y every night with no problem. Server Y has no backup device attached to it. A workstation recently had a hard disk fail and lost all its data, so now you back up all workstations via the network using server X as the backup unit. The first night you back up the servers and workstation, the backup doesn't finish until 8:30 A.M. This is unacceptable. All backups must be completed by 6:30 A.M. What should you do?

   A. Install a second tape backup device on server X. Configure the first tape backup device to back up the servers, and the second tape backup device to back up the workstations.

   B. Install a tape backup device on server Y. Configure the first tape backup device to back up both servers, and have the second tape backup device on server Y back up all the workstations.

   C. Remove the backup device from server X and install it on the faster server Y.

   D. Install a backup device on each workstation and back up the workstations on the local machine. Appoint one workstation as the master backup to back up both servers.

2. Your network consists of the following: one Windows NT server, ten Windows 95 clients, and six Windows NT Workstation clients. You need to back up the server everyday, and back up the clients once per week. Where should you place your tape backup device(s)?

   A. Put a tape device on the workstations.

   B. Put a tape device on the server.

   C. Put a tape device on the server and a tape device on one client.

   D. Put a tape device on all the workstations and the server.

exam
ⓦatch

*It is important to know when you need to add another tape drive to your network and where it should be located.*

**3.** How do you back up the Registry using the NTBACKUP program?

   A. Perform a differential backup.

   B. Stop the Server Service, then back up the Registry.

   C. Use RDISK.

   D. Specify a folder that contains at least one file that is associated with the Registry and choose to back up the Registry.

**4.** You need to add a tape backup device to your system. Currently you're using only IDE drives. The tape backup device is a SCSI device. You don't have a SCSI controller. How should you configure the tape backup device? (Choose all that apply.)

   A. Buy a SCSI controller.

   B. Add the tape device using the Tape Devices applet in Control Panel.

   C. Add the SCSI controller using the SCSI Adapters applet in Control Panel.

   D. Reboot the server.

**5.** You need to maintain a backup copy of your server in case the hard disk fails. You have three 4GB tapes. The server has 3.8GB of data that need backing up. You don't ever want to use more than two tapes to restore the data. How should you schedule your backup?

   A. Perform a normal backup on Sunday, overwriting the existing data. Then every night do a differential on a second tape, overwriting the existing data.

   B. Perform a normal backup on Sunday overwriting the existing data. Then every night do an incremental on a second tape, overwriting the existing data.

   C. Perform a normal backup on Sunday overwriting the existing data. Then every night do a daily backup on the same tape, overwriting the existing data.

   D. Perform a normal backup every other day without overwriting the existing data.

**6.** What's a differential backup?

A. It copies files that have been created or changed since the last normal or incremental backup, but it doesn't mark the files as having been backed up.

B. It copies files that have been created or changed since the last normal or differential backup, and it marks the files as having been backed up.

C. It copies files that have been created or changed since the last normal or daily backup, but it doesn't mark the files as having been backed up.

D. It compares two drives and only backs up those files that are different.

**7.** Which of the following is not a good idea for a backup strategy?

A. Do a normal backup every night onto a different tape. After three months, rotate through the tapes again.

B. Storing the backup tapes in a lock box in a secured room down the hall from the server.

C. Using a rotational backup system where you perform incremental backups during the week.

D. Using verification when doing a large backup.

E. Using verification when doing a small backup.

**8.** You started your server without the tape drive powered on. Your server is a mission-critical server and can't be rebooted without at least one week's notice. How should you backup the data?

A. Turn the tape drive on and back up as usual.

B. Turn the tape drive on and run a SCSI bus identifier utility.

C. Turn the tape drive on and run NTBACKUP in verbose mode.

D. You need to reboot the server.

---

exam
ⓦatch    *Windows NT Backup can be used to backup the Registry, which includes security settings and user account information, while the system is running.*

---

9. What's wrong with the following tape name: NT Backup of Our PDC and All the BDCs Within the Master Domain?

   A. The tape name can't contain spaces.

   B. The tape name can't be over 32 characters.

   C. The tape name must be all upper case.

   D. You can't name a tape with NTBACKUP.

# Windows NT 4.0 Monitoring and Performance Tuning

1. Your server has six disks, and each disk has two partitions. The boot and system partitions are located on the first partition of the first disk. How should you optimize the page file?

   A. Place the page file on the second partition of the first disk.

   B. Place the page file on any disk other than the fist disk.

   C. Split the page file across all partitions on all disks, except the first disk.

   D. Split the page file across all disks, placing it on only one partition per disk.

2. You want to monitor the available disk space on your Windows NT server and be notified when there is only 15 percent available disk space left. How can you do this? (Choose all that apply.)

   A. Server Manager. Use the Alert option.

   B. Performance Monitor set to Alert on 15% Free Space counter.

   C. Start DISKPERF with the AT command and schedule it to run every hour.

   D. Run DISKPERF –Y.

3. You have a network with three Windows NT servers and 75 Windows NT workstations. All computers are using TCP/IP as their only protocol. Once in a while a select group of users needs to copy a 125MB data file to one of

the servers. Copying this file over the network causes a noticeable slowdown of the entire network. How can you prevent the network from slowing down when users copy a 100MB file to the server?

A. Install a new network adapter card on a different subnet and enable IP routing.

B. Install NetBEUI on all the clients that need to copy large files to the server.

C. Give the same network adapter card two IP addresses.

D. Use fewer hubs on your network.

**4.** One of the servers you're responsible for never has more than 10 users connected at a time. What should you do to minimize the memory used?

A. Change the Server Service to maximize throughput.

B. Change the Server Service to balance memory.

C. Change the Server Service to minimize memory used.

D. Change to Windows NT Workstation, since it can support 10 concurrent connections.

**5.** Your server's performance the past two weeks has been quite poor. You've added 50 more users to the network recently, but really don't think that could have caused a problem. You run Performance Monitor and determine the page file is paging excessively. What should you do?

A. Buy a faster hard disk.

B. Increase the page file size.

C. Optimize the page file by spreading it across many disks.

D. Add RAM.

E. Remove the 50 users you recently created to determine if they are causing the problem.

exam
ⓦatch *Many people taking the exam get confused by the number of processors that are supported by Windows NT Server and Windows NT Workstation. Be sure to recognize that NT Workstation, as shipped, supports only two processors, while NT Server supports four.*

**6.** You suspect your server is paging excessively, but you're not certain. Before your boss will allow you to purchase more RAM to alleviate what you believe to be excessive paging, he needs proof. What should you do?

A. Create a Performance Monitor log and log the following counters: Memory: Pages/Sec and Physical disk: % Disk Time.

B. Create a Performance Monitor alert to notify your boss when the following counters exceed a given threshold: Memory: Pages/Sec, Page Faults/Sec, and Processor: % Processor Time.

C. Limit your boss's capabilities on the network until he allows you to buy more RAM.

D. Quit your job, because any boss that won't accept what you say at face value isn't worth working for.

**7.** You installed a new application on your Windows NT server, but it fails when it starts. What should you do first?

A. Reinstall the application.

B. Remove the application and contact the vendor.

C. Check the System Log.

D. Check the Application Log.

**8.** When viewing the Security Log what does the key graphic represent?

A. Audit Success

B. Audit Failed

C. Security violation

D. Security is enforced

**9.** You are trying to identify a faulty NIC on a remote subnet. You plan to use network monitor to identify the traffic on the remote subnet. Why won't this work?

A. You need to run Windows NT on the remote subnet.

B. You need to install a network monitor agent on the remote segment.

C. The Network Monitor that ships with NT only monitors traffic to and from the server running Network Monitor.

D. There are too many variables between the subnets that may cause problems.

**10.** You want to monitor disk performance of your stripe set with parity. What do you need to do?

    A. Run Performance Monitor from the command shell.

    B. Run the command DISKPERF –Y.

    C. Run the command DISKPERF –YE.

    D. Run the command DISKPERF –N.

**11.** You are finished monitoring your hard disks and want to regain optimal performance. What should you do?

    A. Delete all log files.

    B. Stop performance monitor.

    C. Run the command DISKPERF –Y.

    D. Run the command DISKPERF –N.

**12.** You've installed a Windows NT server to serve as a common directory for users to share Word and Excel files. What should you do to optimize the server?

    A. Configure the Server Service to Minimize Memory Used.

    B. Configure the Server Service to Balance.

    C. Configure the Server Service to Maximize Throughput for File Sharing.

    D. Configure the Server Service to Maximize Throughput for Applications.

**13.** While using the Processor: %Processor Time counter in Performance Monitor, you see it spike to 100 percent when starting an application, but then it drops to 85 percent. What do you need to do?

    A. Upgrade to a faster processor.

    B. Increase the size of your page file.

    C. Add more physical memory to your system.

    D. Nothing, the system is performing within acceptable parameters.

**14.** You want to increase the priority of a thread. Which of the following tools should you use? (Choose all that apply.)

    A. Performance Monitor

    B. Thread Analyzer

    C. Task Manager

    D. None of the above

**15.** Your network has a PDC, two BDCs, two member servers, and 75 Windows NT workstations. Your workstation has a high-speed connection to all servers. You want to be alerted if the available disk space is less than 10 percent on any drive. How should you do this? (Choose all that apply.)

    A. Enable disk drive performance counters.

    B. Create five performance monitor alerts on your workstations so that there is one for each server. Set the alert so that it sends a network message to your user name.

    C. Monitor Logical Disk: % Free Space.

    D. Create five administrative alerts on your workstation so that there is one for each server. Set the alert to send a network message to both your username and computer name.

---

exam
ⓌＷatch

*A program might not work correctly when you use Run Program on Alert because Performance Monitor passes the Alert condition as a parameter to the program. If it does not work correctly, you should create a batch file to run the program and call the batch file from Performance Monitor.*

---

**16.** You have 300 workstations and three servers. The following protocols are loaded on all workstations and servers: TCP/IP, NetBEUI, and NWLink. The binding order is as follows: NetBEUI, TCP/IP, and NWLink. Your clients mostly use NWLink. You want to improve the performance of your network. What should you do?

    A. Move NWLink to the top of the binding order on the workstations.

    B. Move NWLink to the top of the binding order on the severs.

    C. Move NWLink to the top of the binding order on the workstations and servers.

    D. None of the above.

**17.** What steps can you take to help alleviate the problems associated with excessive paging? (Choose all that apply.)

A. Reduce the paging file size.

B. Increase the paging file size.

C. Add more RAM.

D. Distribute the paging file across multiple disks.

E. Move the paging file off the boot partition.

**18.** Use the next illustration to answer the following question. How many hard disks is the paging file on?

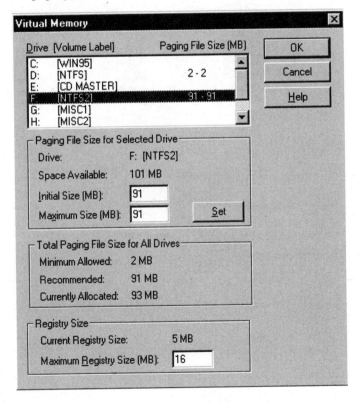

A. One

B. Two

C. Three

D. Don't know

**19.** The following two illustrations are examples of what? (Choose two.)

A. The first is asymmetric processing.

B. The second is asymmetric processing.

C. The first is symmetric processing.

D. The second is symmetric processing.

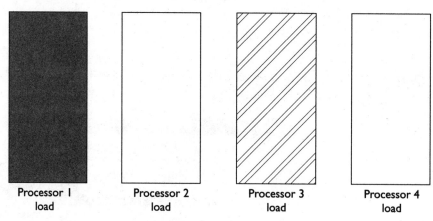

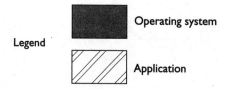

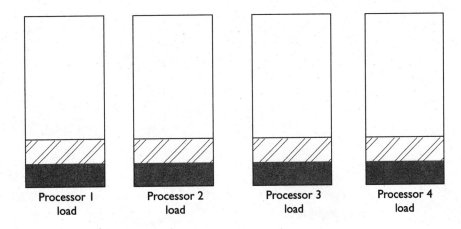

Processor 1 load     Processor 2 load     Processor 3 load     Processor 4 load

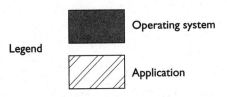

Legend

Operating system

Application

# Troubleshooting

1. You're trying to install Windows NT on your computer, but NT doesn't detect any hard disks on your computer. You have a SCSI hard disk and you've verified that it doesn't contain any viruses. What should you do? (Choose all that apply.)

   A. Use a different virus checker, because it must have a virus.

   B. Use the SCSITOOL program to obtain the SCSI information of your drive.

   C. Ensure the SCSI Bus is properly terminated.

   D. Use an IDE drive.

**2.** While you're installing Windows NT, Setup hangs while copying files to your hard disk. What should you do? (Choose all that apply.)

A. Replace the HAL.

B. Use a different installation media.

C. Make sure Setup isn't using reserved memory.

D. Edit the BOOT.INI file and change the partition number.

**3.** Your computer failed to boot after you installed an incorrect SCSI device driver. What should you do to recover from this mistake as quickly as possible?

A. Restore the server from the ERD.

B. Restore the server from tape backup.

C. Boot with an MS-DOS disk and delete the driver.

D. When you boot, choose the LastKnownGood Configuration.

**4.** You have a mirror set with SCSI disks and BIOS enabled and one disk fails. How do you set up the ARC path on your boot disk? The disks are partitioned as follows:

- Disk 0: System | Data | Data

- Disk 1: Data | Mirror set | Data

A. MULTI(0)DISK(0)RDISK(0)PARTITION(1)

B. MULTI(0)DISK(0)RDISK(0)PARTITION(2)

C. MULTI(0)DISK(0)RDISK(1)PARTITION(1)

D. MULTI(0)DISK(0)RDISK(1)PARTITION(2)

E. SCSI(0)DISK(0)RDISK(1)PARTITION(2)

F. SCSI(1)DISK(0)RDISK(1)PARTITION(2)

5. Your print server appears to have stopped running. There are several print jobs waiting to be printed, but they aren't going anywhere. You try to delete the print jobs, but this fails. What should you do next?

   A. Copy the print jobs to a different printer.

   B. Reboot the server.

   C. Recreate the printer on a different server.

   D. Stop and restart the spooler service.

6. During installation, SETUP fails to detect your third SCSI hard disk. How should you resolve this problem? (Choose all that apply.)

   A. Press S to specify additional mass storage devices during installation.

   B. Press C to cancel and rerun Setup.

   C. After Setup finishes, specify the third SCSI drive using SCSI adapters in Control Panel.

   D. Edit the DEVICE.LOG file and the Setup.INF file.

7. Your server only has one drive, and its paging file size has increased beyond its initial size. What are the results?

   A. The disk will become more fragmented.

   B. The number of disk I/Os will increase.

   C. Applications will take longer to start.

   D. Your hard disk will eventually fail.

8. Which of the following is the proper ARC path name for a SCSI drive, without BIOS enabled, whose Target ID is 0 on the first disk controller, and the boot partition is the second partition?

   A. MULTI(0)DISK(0)RDISK(0)PARTITION(1)

   B. MULTI(0)DISK(0)RDISK(0)PARTITION(2)

   C. MULTI(0)DISK(0)RDISK(1)PARTITION(3)

   D. SCSI(0)DISK(1)RDISK(1)PARTITION(3)

   E. SCSI(0)DISK(0)RDISK(1)PARTITION(2)

   F. SCSI(1)DISK(0)RDISK(1)PARTITION(2)

   G. SCSI(0)DISK(0)RDISK(0)PARTITION(2)

**9.** What happens when you click the Update Repair info in the next illustration?

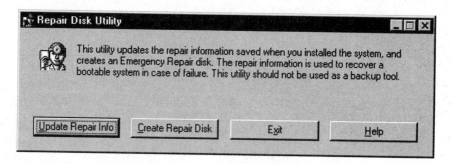

A. Updates the %SYSTEMROOT%\REPAIR directory only

B. Updates the %SYSTEMROOT%\REPAIR directory and the ERD disk

C. Updates the %SYSTEMROOT%\REPAIR directory, and prompts you to update the ERD disk

D. Backs up your Registry to tape backup

**e x a m**
**Ⓦ a t c h**    *If you encounter a permission problem with a network share, be sure to verify the effective permissions for the user.*

**10.** Which of the tabs in the next illustration would you select to see if your UPS is running?

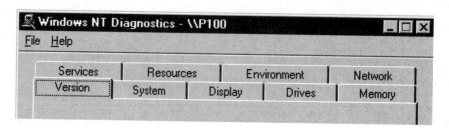

A. Version

B. System

C. Display

D. Drives

E. Memory

F. Services

G. Resources

H. Environment

I. Network

11. When you encounter a STOP error (Blue Screen of Death) data is displayed on the screen. What is this information used for?

A. Nothing. It is garbage outputted to the screen.

B. To help engineers troubleshoot the problem.

C. To dump the contents of RAM to the paging file.

D. To confirm the state of the video driver at the time the computer received the error.

---

exam
ⓦatch    *The Security Accounts Manager (SAM) and Security files are not automatically updated by RDISK. To update those files you need to use the /S switch in conjunction with RDISK.*

---

# MCSE
## MICROSOFT CERTIFIED SYSTEMS ENGINEER

# Server
# Answers

# Q & A

Threadhe answers to the questions are in boldface, followed by a brief explanation. Some of the explanations detail the logic you should use to choose the correct answer, while others give factual reasons why the answer is correct. If you miss several questions on a similar topic, you should review the corresponding section in the *MCSE Windows NT Server 4.0 Study Guide* (Osborne/McGraw-Hill) before taking the MCSE test.

# Answers:
# Introduction to Windows NT Server 4.0

1. **B.** Normally a thread can be increased two priority levels, but the initial priority level was already at 30 and 31 is the highest priority level, so the highest level this thread can execute at is 31. There are 32 priority levels numbered 0-31.

2. **B.** Windows NT uses symmetric multiprocessing (SMP) to execute threads across multiple processors. Asymmetric multiprocessing (ASMP) keeps the operating system on one processor and allows non-operating system threads to execute on the remaining processors.

3. **D.** Disk duplexing is just like disk mirroring except that it uses multiple disk controllers for added redundancy. Disk mirroring uses two disk drives, each maintaining the exact same data. If one drive fails the other drive has a mirror image of the other drive.

4. **D.** The only option is to restore from tape. This network should have used a BDC for redundancy. Then, if the PDC failed, you could simply promote the BDC to a PDC.

5. **A, B.** You must set up Windows NT as a router in order to route IP traffic between the two subnets. None of the answers mentioned turning on IP routing, but you need to pick the best answers available. If one part of the process isn't mentioned, assume you need to do that step.

6. C. Be sure to understand that files located in the root of the export directory will NOT get exported. Only files in subdirectories of the export directory get exported.

7. C. The administrative wizards are typically used to assist people who are unfamiliar with Windows NT to do administrative functions. If you're proficient in using NT you'll find the wizards slow and boring.

8. A. NT only allows applications to run in User mode, thereby keeping applications away from the hardware. Device drivers run in the Kernel mode. If you have a buggy device driver your system can become unstable.

9. D. This is important to know and understand for the test. Just because your hard disk is getting used a lot doesn't mean you need more hard disk space or a faster hard disk. Typically, your hard disk will get used a lot because your paging file is swapping memory in and out of the hard disk and RAM. To alleviate this problem you need to add more RAM.

10. C. This is one you'll need to have memorized. NT swaps virtual memory in 4KB sizes.

11. B. Windows NT has 4GB of address space, but 2GB are dedicated to the operating system. This means that applications have the remaining 2GB of address space.

12. A. User mode houses the following subsystems: OS/2, Win32, POSIX, and NTVDM. This mode doesn't allow the components to directly access the hardware. Hardware requests are done in Kernel mode at the hardware abstraction layer.

# Answers:
# Planning Windows NT 4.0 Installation

1. **B, C.** Windows NT 4.0 doesn't support a floppy installation like NT 3.51. You can install NT from a network share point or from the CD-ROM.

2. **D.** Windows NT 4.0 supports hardware profiles similar to Windows 95. However, it doesn't auto detect the hardware configuration at startup. You must tell the operating system which hardware profile you wish to use.

3. **C.** The best answer is to contact the vendor. NT 4.0 is a widely supported operating system, so there is a good chance the vendor will have a driver that will work. If not they should be able to tell you whether or not any other drivers are compatible with the hardware. Choice B is a viable option, but it isn't the best answer. First, contact the vendor. If they can't supply a driver, you should try to get a different Ethernet card.

4. **D.** The minimum requirements for NT are as follows: 486/33, 16MB RAM, 125MB available disk space, VGA card, CD-ROM, or access to a network NT installation share point, compatible pointing device.

5. **B.** You'll need to reformat the drive for a FAT partition. Windows 95 doesn't recognize NTFS partitions. You can use more than one partition on your hard disk and format other partitions with NTFS, but Windows 95 won't be able to read these volumes.

6. **A.** NTFS allows for partition up to 16 exabytes, whereas FAT only allows up to 4GB. CDFS isn't an option, as it is only used for CD-ROMs.

7. **C.** This is the Registry editor that ships with Windows 95. A lot of people find it easier to work with this than REGEDT32.EXE. However, REGEDIT doesn't allow you to set security permissions on the keys.

**8.** **C.** When you move a compressed file between partitions it's like making a copy. The compression attribute is inherited from its parent directory. If the file was moved on the same partition the file would remain compressed even if the parent directory wasn't compressed.

**9.** **C, D, G.** To assign execute and delete permissions, simply check the Delete and Execute check boxes. Once you select one of the check boxes the Other radio button will automatically be selected.

**10.** **C.** You need to enable DHCP forwarding in the TCP/IP properties. This will capture the DHCP request from local computers and forward them to the DHCP server.

**11.** **B.** No matter how good an administrator you are, you shouldn't edit the Registry directly unless it is the only way to accomplish a task. The Control Panel applets can usually provide the customization you need on your system.

**12.** **A.** Windows NT no longer supports HPFS. Therefore, FAT is the only file system that both NT and OS/2 recognize. You may have heard that you can edit the Registry to get NT to recognize HPFS, but if you're asked on the test you'd better say NT doesn't support HPFS.

**13.** **A.** NetBEUI is the best choice here. Since all computers are on the same subnet you don't need a routable protocol. NetBEUI has the least amount of overhead and configuration of the available protocols, and it is very efficient in small LANs.

**14.** **B, C, D.** You need to install all three protocols that are in use on your network. This is one thing that NT is really known for: the capability to communicate with heterogeneous networks.

**15.** **B.** This is a case where you move a file within the same partition. When this occurs the file attributes are unchanged. The pointer to the file is changed, showing it under a new directory, but the attributes remain the same.

# Answers: Installing Windows NT Server 4.0

1. **D.** This is the preferred licensing because it saves you money. Per server licensing is controlled by the server. The server monitors the number of connections and when the total licensed connections are reached it doesn't allow any new connections until current users log off. Option A may sound like a good idea if you are planning to buy more NT servers in the future; however, you are allowed a one-time switch from per server to per seat. So you should still use Option D and then, when you buy a new server, you can buy an additional 50 licenses and change to per seat licensing.

2. **D.** You must run the program WINNT32.EXE instead of WINNT.EXE, since you've already got NT installed. WINNT32.EXE is for use on NT and WINNT.EXE is used in Windows 95 and DOS. The /OX switch creates the boot disks without installing NT. The /B switch installs NT without using the boot disks. These are two common questions on the exam. Know the difference between these switches and when to use WINNT32.EXE and WINNT.EXE. Also know that some of the switches between the two programs are different. To see the available switches, run the program with the /? switch.

3. **B.** The best way to get a BDC up and running in your New York office would be to create the server in the Charlotte office where it can connect to the PDC. You can never install a BDC without being able to communicate with the PDC. Therefore, the installations at the New York office would fail. Many organizations create their BDCs on the same subnet as the PDC so the directory can be quickly replicated. Then they send the BDC to its destination.

4. **D.** Since both servers are functioning when you promote the new server to become the PDC, the current PDC automatically demotes itself to the BDC role. If the PDC was offline when you promote a BDC, it must be demoted when it comes back online.

5. **B.** Although a SQL server should be configured as a member server, having only one domain controller allows for a single point of failure for your network. With 100 users or fewer, the BDC role won't take much away from the SQL server. If this network had a PDC *and* a BDC, this server should be configured as a member server.

6. **B.** You must remove the incompatible programs to upgrade from NT 3.51 to NT 4.0. If you don't, setup will fail.

7. **B.** Since NT is a 32-bit operating system, you need to run WINNT32.EXE.

8. **D.** You would run the WINNT.EXE command, but it isn't an upgrade. NT 4.0 can only upgrade from NT 3.51. You need to run WINNT.EXE, even though Windows 95 is a 32-bit operating system. Windows 95 has some legacy code and 16-bit code, which makes it backwards-compatible with previous versions of DOS. Therefore, it can't use the WINNT32.EXE command.

9. **A, B.** If you create an UNATTEND.TXT file for each computer you can use the /UDF switch when you run WINNT.EXE to install in unattended mode. This is the fastest way to install 100 computers. When you view the other answers it is pretty simple to guess the correct answer, but you'd need to know that both A and B are correct.

10. **A, B, C.** NTHQ.EXE is shipped on the media disk to allow users to examine their hardware before installing NT 4.0. NTHQ.EXE only runs on DOS and Windows 95, because they allow direct access to the hardware. NT won't run this utility.

11. **C.** In order to update or create the ERD you should use the RDISK.EXE program. If you wish to back up the SAM database you need to use the /S switch. The ERD should be protected as a secure item, since it has the entire SAM database on it.

**12. B.** You'll need to install a driver for the CD-ROM. If your mass storage device (which is reading the NT install files or storing the OS) isn't detected, you can't install NT. You must have an updated driver that NT 4.0 can use in order to complete the install.

**13. D.** CDFS is the file system on your CD-ROM drive. You can't use NTFS, FAT, or any other file system to read standard CD-ROM drives.

**14. B, D.** You need to choose NTFS as your file system to ensure file- and folder-level security is available, but you'll also need to protect it with physical security. If you don't have physical security, a person can steal your hard disks, install them in a different NT system, take ownership of the files, and view all the files on your hard disk.

**15. D.** The quickest way to get NT installed on this computer is to copy the source files to the local hard disk and run WINNT.EXE. You'll probably want to buy a compatible CD-ROM drive later, but it isn't necessary to install NT on the computer.

**16. C.** You can never add a BDC or member server without communicating with the PDC. If you can't connect to the PDC, you can't add a server to the domain.

**17. B.** You could argue that you want to install them all in separate directories; however, you have to understand what Microsoft is testing. Installing Windows NT in the same Windows directory as WFW doesn't hurt anything. In fact it allows you to use the same program groups. If you install Windows NT in the Windows directory of a Windows 95 machine, Windows 95 will no longer work.

**18. A, C.** You need to know how to create a Network Installation Startup Disk. If you've missed this question you should actually create a Network Installation Startup Disk. Some information just needs to be reinforced by hands-on application. This is one of them.

# Answers: Configuring Windows NT Server 4.0

1. **A, B, C, D.** Novell uses all four frame types. If your network has more than one frame type you'll need to configure NT to use the appropriate frame type. Older versions of NetWare use 802.3, but the newer versions of NetWare, 4.*x*, use 802.2.

2. **C.** The default gateway is required to communicate outside of the server's local subnet. The default gateway is typically the IP address of the router port that connects to your local subnet. This question can be misleading. A likely troubleshooting effort would have you check the WINS database to ensure it was registering properly, but the best answer is that it needs a default gateway. Without a default gateway it doesn't matter if it is registered in WINS or not. After configuring the default gateway, if the problem still occurs, you should check the WINS database.

3. **B.** This meets only your main objective. By connecting both subnets with a hub, you enable both of them to communicate with each other. However, the broadcast traffic is passed through the hub to both subnets.

4. **D.** The best answer is to configure the duration of the lease. This is the last required step to set up the scope. To set up a scope, it doesn't need to be active, nor does it need the WINS addresses or broadcast type. The only available answer is to configure the duration of the lease, even though it defaults to three days if you don't change it.

5. **D.** It doesn't increase performance to place the paging file on partitions that are on the same drive (unless space is an issue). Therefore, answers B and C aren't the best answer. Placing the paging file on more than one physical drive provides better throughput to the disks.

6. **D.** A volume set is used to combine 2 – 32 areas of free space on the same or multiple drives. A volume set doesn't provide any fault tolerance. It simply allows you to group areas of free space as one drive letter.

7. **A.** This solution meets all your objectives. A stripe set with parity gives you the fault tolerance that is required. This is the only solution available. It maximizes the available disk space. A stripe set with parity (RAID 5) uses 3 – 32 drives with the same size partition. It manages the data just like a stripe set, except it writes a parity bit across all the disks. The parity bit is used to recreate the data in case one of the drives fails.

8. **C.** Remember a stripe set combines two or more equal areas of free space. You don't need to use all four hard disks to create a stripe set. The largest stripe set can be achieved by combining 600MB drive and the 400MB drive. Combining these two drives will give you an 800MB stripe set.

9. **B.** Since two drives have failed, you don't have enough parity bits to recreate the lost data. You must recover from tape backup. If only one drive had failed, then option C would be the correct answer.

10. **A.** There are only two types of RAID in NT that provide fault tolerance (mirror and stripe set with parity). The key to this question is that the RAID set is going to be used on the system and boot partitions. The only type of software RAID that NT supports that can be used on the system and boot partitions is mirroring (RAID 1).

11. **C, D.** The only log events from the given answers occur when a user attempts or succeeds to write to an existing file. When a user modifies a file he is actually writing to the file; therefore, the WRITE: Success and Failed are recorded. The auditing wasn't applied to the subfolders, so no audit was created when a user changed a file in a subfolder. Attempting to delete a file isn't writing to the file. If you wish to audit this function, you need to turn auditing on for DELETE.

12. **A, B.** You need to do two things. You need to share the installation files for Windows 95, so the clients can run the setup program via the network. You'll also want to create an installation startup disk using the Network Client Administrator so you can simply put the disk in a computer and boot the PC. Then the computer will automatically access the network share to start the setup process.

13. **C.** You need to plug the UPS into the COM port (also known as a serial port). After plugging in the UPS you'll need to configure NT to communicate with the UPS. When configuring the UPS values, refer to the UPS owner's manual to obtain the correct values.

14. **C, D.** First, you need to install the SCSI device driver. After installing the SCSI device driver, you'll need to restart the computer so that the tape drive will be detected. Next install the tape drive device driver. (You'll also need to restart the server to get each new driver to take effect, but that wasn't among the listed options.)

15. **A.** Disk duplexing is like disk mirroring, except it uses redundant disk controllers. Each hard disk is connected to it's own disk controllers. If either a hard disk or controller fails, the data is still accessible.

16. **C.** The largest stripe set with parity is only 900MB because 300MB is used for parity. You need to be careful with the way the question is worded.

17. **B.** You need to install a WINS server to cut down on broadcasts. Of course you'll need to ensure the clients are configured for H-node type broadcast, but that is an assumption you have to make to answer this question correctly. WINS is the best answer available. Using a WINS server to locate computers on the network will minimize broadcasts. Instead of sending out a broadcast first, clients will query the WINS server.

18. **D.** You need to commit the changes you made before you can format a partition. Windows NT provides this functionality to protect users from their own mistakes. Assigning partitions and formatting drives can have a disastrous effect on your computer if not done properly.

19. **D.** Just by looking at the file name you don't know exactly what this file does. However, you do know it is triggered when the power fails. You may want to put a batch file in here that copies an import file to a different server. This option allows you to trigger a batch file when the power fails. You shouldn't use a batch file that requires user intervention because it will fail to run, since a user would need to be logged on and waiting to answer the questions when the power fails.

# Answers: Managing Resources

1. **B.** Copying a user account doesn't copy the Username, Full Name, or Password, since this is different for each user. Copying a user account speeds things up by copying the Description, Groups, Profile, and Dial-in permissions. If your users belong to several groups, copying the account can really save you time.

2. **C.** Although all these options will work, disabling the account is the best answer. That's why the function exists and Microsoft expects you to know this.

3. **C.** This is the proper way to assign permissions in this scenario. You only have three user accounts, so it is unlikely that these users will be grouped together in a global group on the domain controller. It is best to create the local group on the server that has the shared folder, and to add the users directly to the local group. Then give the local group permissions to access the folder.

4. **A.** Remember AGLP. Accounts get added to global groups, global groups get added to local groups, and local groups get assigned permissions.

**5. D.** A roaming profile allows a user to log onto any NT workstation or server within the domain and receive the same desktop. The user must log onto a domain in order for the roaming profile to work. Also know that Windows 95 and Windows NT profiles are NOT compatible. You can setup profiles for both operating systems on your network, but a user that logs onto NT and 95 will receive different desktops.

**6. C.** In order for WFW to access a home directory you must map a drive to that directory. The User Environment Profile dialog box is for managing profiles, as well as a user's home directory. It is accessed by clicking the Profile button on a user's account in User Manager for Domains.

**7. D.** In addition to the built-in groups mentioned, there are groups are created by the system and used for special purposes. Because the memberships of these groups cannot be altered, the groups are not listed in User Manager for Domains. The network group is assigned to everyone connecting to your computer over the network. Users working locally on a computer are added to the Interactive group.

**8. A.** Server Manager lets you view the properties of remote computers by letting you view open files and resources, create alerts, and remotely disconnect users. Server Manager also lets you create, modify, and delete shares, as well as adjust the number of users allowed, and the permissions associated with the shares. You can stop and start services as if you were directly in front of the machine. The remote computer's Services dialog box appears exactly as your local services utility, with no features disabled.

**9. B.** In addition to the things mentioned in the preceding question, you can also manage printers with Explorer. Using Explorer, you can add printers to your computer by double-clicking them.

**10. C.** This question may have tricked you, because D seems like a viable option if a trust exists between DOMAIN X and DOMAIN Z. The question doesn't mention that a trust exists, so choice C is the best answer.

If you set the same password and username, NT will allow the user to go seamlessly between domains.

11. **B.** This question has caused many heated discussions among administrators, because it depends on what type of mandatory profile you're referring to. If it is a normal roaming profile that has Read permissions only, the user will receive the cached profile (or the default profile if the user has never logged on). If the mandatory profile is specified with a .MAN extension, the user must be able to access the profile when logging onto the domain.

12. **A.** Server Manager allows you to manage shared directories on remote NT computers. If you select a computer, then click Computer | Shared Directories, you can view all the shares on the selected computer. From here you can stop or start sharing a directory (including shared directories) and you can assign or change share permissions.

13. **A.** You can't recover a deleted user account, unless you restore the PDC from tape backup. That would be a lot of work to recover one user account, and it could cause more problems, because any changes applied to the SAM after the last backup would be lost.

14. **D.** You can't change the role of an NT server (except from BDC to PDC and vice versa). In order to change a domain controller to a member server, you must reinstall the operating system.

15. **A.** The key to this question is that you need help adding a user to a domain. If the object were to add users to a workstation, you should add Lori to the Power Users group. Since you are adding users to a domain and you don't want to give her full administrator rights, you should use the Account Operators group.

**16. B.** To add a logon script, choose the Profile option. In the next dialog box, fill in the Logon Script Name field with the name of the script file the user needs to execute when he logs on.

**17. C.** When moving a file from an NTFS partition to a FAT partition all long file names will be preserved, because FAT does support long file names in NT. FAT doesn't support permissions, though. They are discarded.

**18. A.** The icon with the computer in the background represents a local group. If it had a globe in the background it would be a global group.

# Answers: Windows NT 4.0 Security

**1. D.** Once again, FAT partitions do NOT allow file permissions. The only permissions you can use are when you share a folder on the network, you can apply share level permissions.

**2. A, B.** You need to change the password, so the hacker can't log on using the administrator account. Next you'll want to rename the account, so the hacker can't break into the account again using the same username.

**3. D.** User LoriL has Read and Add permissions, because the permissions are cumulative. Each ACE is processed sequentially comparing the access mask with the user's access token once all requested permissions are allowed access is granted.

**4. B.** You need to audit the folder and files for Delete. The next time the file is deleted you should check the security log in Event Viewer.

**5.** **C.** You could use Explorer to assign the permissions, but this will take quit a bit of time. It will be quicker to use the CACLS program located in the %SYSTEMROOT%\SYSTEM32 folder.

**6.** **D.** It sounds like MaryS has given her password to someone, or someone has broken into her account. You should have her change her password ASAP, so the problem can be resolved.

**7.** **B.** This is a key to managing security on an NTFS system. Users must understand that they control the permissions to their files and folders. If security is a concern, you'll need to educate your users on managing their file permissions.

**8.** **D.** Once again, this is a key aspect of NTFS. If you don't need file-level permissions you could use FAT instead of NTFS. You can't turn off the creator/owner aspects of NTFS.

**9.** **C.** Understand that auditing does have a price—it impacts your system performance. You need to balance auditing requirements and performance needs. The function of your servers and the type of business you're in should be considerations when deciding how much to audit.

**10.** **C.** When you move a file to a different partition, it inherits the permissions of the parent folder. When you move a file on the same partition, only the pointer to the file is changed, so the original permissions remain.

**11.** **B, E, F.** You must convert the FAT drive to NTFS first. FAT partitions don't support file/folder-level permissions, so the required security scheme can't be achieved using FAT.

**12.** **D.** With Windows NT, the maximum number of connections is unlimited when you use per seat licensing. If you use per server licensing, the server

will stop users from accessing the share when the maximum number of
licensees is exceeded. This question doesn't mention anything about the
type of licensing; you must assume it is per seat, since unlimited is the only
answer that makes sense.

# Answers: Windows NT 4.0 Domains

1. **A.** If you have fewer than 5,000 users, one BDC should be sufficient. It
   helps with user logon and provides redundancy in case the PDC fails. Make
   sure to read the question carefully. If it asked how many domain controllers
   you need for 2,500 users, the answer would be 2. The key is domain
   controllers versus backup domain controllers. Domain controllers include
   both the PDC and the BDC.

2. **A.** Since the scientists need to ensure that their computer can only be
   accessed by them, and only grant access to those they choose, a workgroup
   model is the proper selection. Any domain model would grant an
   administrator access to the workstation, so the security the scientists require
   wouldn't be enforced. Also, since there are only five scientists, managing the
   user accounts shouldn't be very difficult.

3. **E.** LSA secrets is unlimited, so the number of trusts you can create is
   unlimited. You may need to add more memory if you have hundreds of
   trusts, but NT doesn't limit the number of trusts you can create. You are
   only limited by hardware.

4. **A.** By creating a local group in the SALES group you can add users from the
   trusted domain to it. Assign the local group permissions to the resource in
   SALES. This doesn't follow the Microsoft model of Users in Global groups,
   Global groups in Local groups, and Local groups getting assigned
   permissions, but expect to see similar questions on the test.

5. **A, C, E.** You must create a one-way trust in which Domain A trusts Domain B. This allows you to add the users in domain B to the local group you created in Domain A. After adding all the users to the local group you need to assign the local group permissions.

6. **A.** The Single Domain model is excellent for very small organizations that want to manage resources from a central office.

7. **C.** The same reasons for choosing a Master Domain stated in the preceding answer would apply to this domain, except it has 132,000 users. The Master Domain model can't scale that high, so you need to use a Multiple Master Domain.

8. **D.** The Complete Trust Domain is the domain model of choice when you don't want any central administration. It allows all departments to manage their own users and resources.

9. **TRUST.** You may think this is a tough question because you aren't given any options to choose from, but questions in this format might be on the test, so be prepared.

10. **C.** The formula to determine the number of trusts is $n(n-1)$. $20(20-1)=380$.

11. **A.** Using Server Manager, you can view the users that are currently connected and the resources they are using. Users may be connected and not using any resources, so it's probably a good idea to see if they are using any resources.

12. **B.** You can't add a computer to the domain as a server operator using the Join The Domain function within network Control Panel, or using the SETUP program. Instead, you must add the computer to the domain using Server Manager before installing the computer or joining the domain.

**13. C.** This isn't a good idea. Not only does it cause problems if you create a trust later on, but if you need to add groups of users to workstations and member servers, you'll need to create local groups on each and add all the users to those groups. If you used global groups on the domain controllers you could simply add the global group to the local group on the member servers.

**14. C.** One thing that may have confused you is that the PDC isn't part of the answer. The question asked what OTHER computers can use this group. Local groups are only accessible on the computer they are created on, unless it is a domain controller. Domain controllers share their SAM database, therefore, local groups created on a domain controller can be used by other domain controllers within the same domain.

**15. B.** The Master Domain model has a one-way trust between the master domain and the resource domains. The master domain is the trusted domain, and the resource domains are the trusting domains.

**16. C.** The Multiple Master Domain model is like the Master Domain model, except it has more than one master domain joined by a two-way trust. This allows the domain to scale past 40,000 users.

# Answers:
# Replication and Data Synchronization

**1. B.** Using the directory replicator service is the best way to improve file access. The users are just reading the file, so they don't all have to work from a single file. By replicating the files to the remote sites, the clients can access the files by higher network speeds.

**2. B, C, D.** Any NT server can be an export server. NT Workstation can only be an import server.

**3. B.** This is the most common way to replicate logon scripts. You could set one any server to be an export server and export the logon script to all the BDCs and PDCs; however, this isn't the typical way to do this.

**4. B.** The SYNCH account needs to be part of the Replicator group so it can connect to the Export servers REPL$ share.

**5. C.** Windows NT will not allow you to name a group and user account to the same name. The name Replicator is already used by the group, so you have to choose a different name.

**6. B.** The import computers need access to the REPL$ on the export computer. This is where the export directories are shared out.

**7. A.** The REPL$ is the share point that the import servers access on the export server to copy the replicated data. When they copy this data they do a complete image copy, replacing anything that is different in it's import directory.

**8. B.** Server Manager allows you to manage the replication process across your network. Just double-click the computer you want to manage and click the Replication button to access the computer's replicator service properties.

**9. B.** If you don't select the Entire Subtree option, only the root directory will be exported. You'll usually want to have this option checked.

**10. D.** No Master means that the import server isn't receiving update notifications from the export server. Check to make sure the service is running on the export server and that both computers can communicate with each other.

**11. A, D.** You need to reduce the value of the Replication Governor to reduce the amount of bandwidth used from updates by the PDC. In order to ensure that you don't miss updates, increase the change log to accommodate the longer delays in receiving updates.

**12. B.** You need to edit the logon script path on all the domain controllers to point to the new import directory.

**13. B.** This screen is used to manage which computers export and import directories. CONAN is the export server and LATENIGHT and SWISHER are the import computers. Notice the Logon Script Path in the bottom of the Illustration. This is where you tell NT where your logon scripts are located on the local machine. This path only affects the server CONAN. To edit the path on the other service you need to open their properties in Server Manager.

# Answers: Windows Printing

**1. C.** You simply need to change the port that the printer currently uses. You don't have to point it to another shared printer. You can point it to any local port. By changing the port you will automatically reroute the print jobs to a different printer.

**2. C.** She is still using the same access token that she originally logged on with. In order for the new permissions to take place she needs to log off and back on.

**3. C.** You should only add three drivers. Since Windows 3.11 doesn't use point-and-print functions, it can't automatically download the drivers. You may be wondering why you don't need more drivers, because Alpha and Intel versions of Windows NT use different drivers. If the question states you have NT 4.0 running, it assumes that one version is running. If you were running two different builds of NT the question would state that. The MCSE tests are the same way.

**4. A.** Although choices C and D are beneficial, they aren't new to NT 4.0. Point and print capabilities are a great improvement to NT, but they won't help Al print faster. The last choice is EMF file spooling. The EMF has two advantages: it returns control of the application to the user immediately, without waiting for printer calls to be interpreted by the print driver; and EMF files can be printed on any printing device.

**5. D.** Since this is a UNIX server and TCP/IP is the standard protocol for UNIX servers, you must assume that you need to use TCP/IP. The UNIX server could be running the IPX/SPX protocol, but the best answer is TCP/IP.

**6. A.** Actually you need to know the server name (or IP address) and the printer name. However, the options listed only allow you to choose IP address. This is the only correct answer listed.

**7. A.** Check the path where the file would be stuck. If you get a question like this on the exam, you may not know the path name, but you can eliminate answer choices such as C and D, because you know the answer should include a path.

**8. D.** Once again, you must have DLC loaded to use the HP network port print monitor. You can't even choose this port unless you have DLC loaded. Be sure to know this for the test.

**9. A, B.** The HP network port print monitor only supports one Ethernet card on your server. If you have a dual-homed computer, all your HP printers that use the HP network port print monitor must be on the same subnet. You can either move the printer to the first subnet or you can use a different port monitor that will work with the JetDirect card.

10. **C.** DLC isn't routable so you can't use it or the HP network print port monitor that ships with NT. Your only alternative is to use TCP/IP, which uses the LPD service to print to the printer.

11. **C.** You need to create two printers printing to the same printing device. By giving your boss's printer a higher priority his jobs will be sent to the printer before the other printers jobs will be sent. If a job is already sent from the other printer, it will finish printing, then your boss's job will be sent next.

12. **C.** If you can print directly to the printer, bypassing the spooler, but you can't print using the spooler, the problem is usually found in the spooler.

13. **D.** The only thing you need to do is teach her how to delete her own print jobs. The creator of a print job can manage their own print jobs, so she doesn't need any extra rights and permissions. A little education is all she needs.

14. **C.** Although you may like to keep those users from printing to your shared printers, as an administrator we usually aren't afforded that luxury. The only real option is to Hold Mismatched Documents. This option checks the driver before printing the document. If it is the incorrect driver the print job won't get sent to the print device.

15. **A.** The local print provider polls the print processors. Once the print processor recognizes the job's data type, it receives the print job and modifies it, if necessary, according to its data type.

16. **A, B.** When creating a printer pool you must use the same driver for all the printing devices. Also, the entire printing pool must be managed by the same NT printer object. You can't have half the printers managed by one NT server and the other half by another NT server. They all must reside on the same server and the same printer on that server.

17. **D.** The gateway will not be active until you map a drive or add a printer from the NetWare server. If you haven't played with the GNSW, you really should experiment with it before taking the test. A basic familiarity with the interface can go a long way toward helping you understand and answer the questions.

18. **A.** The General tab has a button located near the bottom of the screen that allows you to edit the print processor. Adjusting the print processor allows you to specify the data type: RAW, EMF, TEXT, and so on.

19. **A, C.** The audit is only set up to record successful prints and deletes on the printer. Therefore, it won't detect when a user attempts to delete or send a print job in which he doesn't have the proper permissions.

# Answers: NetWare Integration

1. **C.** You need to install a group called NTGATEWAY on the NetWare server. It is NOT an NT group. You have a very good chance of seeing a question like this on the test. It's easy to get confused when taking the test. Remember the NTGATEWAY group is created on the NetWare server.

2. **B.** Although Windows 95 comes with its own NetWare redirector, you need to choose GSNW. It's the only choice among the given options. Using a redirector on Windows 95 would also be possible, but that wasn't an option here.

3. **D.** You may have been able to choose A and B, but you were only allowed to choose one, so it couldn't be A or B. If A is correct, so is B. Your only choice was D—nothing. This is a dead giveaway that FPNW isn't installed on the NT server.

4. **B.** In order for NT to detect both frame types you'll need to set the frame type manually. If you use autodetect it will default to the first frame type it detects on the network.

5. **A.** After you install GSNW you'll be able to use the NetWare Migration utility.

6. **A.** NetWare has many more file attributes than NT does. When a file attribute is encountered that NT doesn't recognize or support, it is just ignored.

7. **C, D.** You'll need to install File and Print Service for NetWare along with the NWLink protocol. Installing FPNW on NT allows NetWare clients to see NT as a NetWare server.

8. **D.** This is a trick question. Notice you were asked about Adapter(0); the adapter on this screen is Adapter(1). Since you don't know the parameters of Adapter(0) you can't know how many frame types are assigned to it. If you had been asked about Adapter(1), the correct answer would be two.

# Answers: Remote Connectivity

1. **D.** Installing an LMHOSTS file will allow the clients to resolve the names of the logon servers without going through WINS. When the clients use WINS to resolve the server names, it takes time to communicate the request and answer over a modem. Using WINS allows the client to find the servers without using the slow connection to resolve the computer name.

2. **A, B, C, D.** A RAS client using PPP is just like any other client on your network once it is validated. The only difference is that it is a much slower client. Although you can do anything on the network, some operations may be unacceptably slow.

**3. C.** Since you don't know what type of clients will be getting authenticated, you need to allow any type of authentication, even clear text.

**4. C.** Enabling the DEVICE.LOG file will record the transaction that occured while users were connected. You should use this file to help determine the cause of the failure.

**5. A, B.** You can use User Manager and click the dial-in button, or you can use the Remote Access Admin utility to give people permissions to dial-in. The dial-in button is new to Windows NT 4.0.

**6. C.** MS-CHAP is the Microsoft implementation of the Challenge Handshake Authentication Protocol (CHAP), which provides encrypted authentication and can also be configured to provide data encryption. MS-CHAP is used by Microsoft RAS servers and clients to provide the most secure form of encrypted authentication.

**7. C.** Once PPTP is installed on the server, you will be able to establish a connection to it over the Internet with a PPTP-enabled client, such as Windows NT Workstation. To initiate a Virtual Private Network (VPN), a user will first need to use DUN to dial an ISP and establish an Internet connection. The user would then use DUN again to "dial" the RAS server, using the IP address of your RAS server as the phone number and the VPN number as the port.

**8. A.** By requiring Microsoft Encryption you are requiring MS-CHAP, which is the highest level of authentication security on RAS.

**9. A, B, C, D.** Once again, RAS with a PPP connection is just like another node on your network. It supports various protocols, although some connections may be unbearably slow.

**10.** C. RAS autodial works with NetBEUI and TCP/IP, but it doesn't work with IPX.

**11.** B. There can only be two users dialed in at one time on this RAS server, because you only have two IP addresses to give out. A computer can never share an IP address, not even a RAS client. Once the client logs off, the IP address can be given back out to the next RAS client.

# Answers: Backup

**1.** B. The backups need to occur on two different servers since one server can't do it quickly enough. By adding a tape drive to the second server, you should be able to back up all the clients and the server in time.

**2.** B. Although option D is a valid choice, B is the best answer for this question. Since you could only choose one you should choose the answer that does the same job, with less money.

**3.** D. If you are backing up from a local drive that contains the Registry, you can include a copy of it in the backup set. Keep in mind that this option is only available if the drive containing the Registry is selected for backup. Windows NT Backup will not back up the Registry or event logs located on remote systems. If it is possible for you to back up the Registry, Backup Local Registry on the Backup Information window will not be ghosted.

**4.** A, B, C, D. The steps to add the backup devices are as follows: first, buy the SCSI controller; second, install the SCSI controller using the SCSI Adapters applet; next, reboot the server; finally, install the Tape Drive driver using the Tape Devices applet and reboot the server.

**5. A.** A differential backup will back up the data since the last normal backup on Sunday, but it won't mark the data as being backed up. Then every night of the week you can do a differential swapping between the two tapes you have left. On Sunday you can start all over again.

**6. A.** A differential backup copies files that have been created or changed since the last normal or incremental backup. The differential backup does not mark files as having been backed up. If you are doing normal and differential backups, restoring requires only the last normal and last differential backup tape. If you perform two differential backups in a row, the files backed up during the first backup will be backed up again, even if they have not changed. This is because files are not marked as having been backed up.

**7. B.** You must find an off-site location for storage of backup tapes. This way, if your building catches fire or otherwise becomes inaccessible, you can at least be sure that your data can be recovered. The location can be a vault, a safe deposit box at a bank, or a fireproof safe at home. If you decide to use a fireproof safe, make sure it is specifically designed to protect magnetic media.

**8. D.** You need to reboot the server in order for the tape drive to be detected. The SCSI bus needs to assign it an ID, then Windows NT needs to initialize it. This can only be done by booting the system.

**9. B.** If the tape was previously used for a backup, the existing name will be in the Tape Name section. If it is a new tape, it will be blank. You can use up to 32 characters to name the tape.

# Answers: Windows NT 4.0 Monitoring and Performance Tuning

**1. D.** You should split the paging file across all disks (not all partitions). Placing the paging file on multiple partitions doesn't increase its performance, since all the data is still on the same disk. You may be concerned that it is still on the boot and system partition, but this was the best answer available.

2. **B, D.** First, turn on disk counters by running DISKPERF –Y. Next, set an alert on Performance Monitor to alert you when there is 15 percent space or less available on the %Free Space counter.

3. **A.** You may look at this question and say option A only applies if you put the computers on the same subnet as the new adapter card on the server. This is true, but it is the only answer that makes sense. You have to assume you'll do the other correct steps to make the solution in option A work. Many of the test questions on the exam will be like this. The key to answering these questions is to eliminate all the wrong answers first, then choose the best answer from the remaining questions.

4. **C.** Options for NT Server Service optimization areas follows:

   ■ Minimize Memory Used, which can handle up to 10 users simultaneously using Windows NT Server. You should not use this option on a file server unless the network is very small.

   ■ Balance, which serves up to 64 users and is useful for departmental servers.

   ■ Maximize Throughput for File Sharing, which is for 64 or more users. When you choose this option, access to the file cache has priority over user application access to memory. It also allocates as much memory as is required for file sharing. This option is the default setting.

   ■ Maximize Throughput for Network Applications, which is for 64 or more users. This option allows users' application access to have priority over file cache access to memory. This setting is a good choice for servers that run primarily network applications.

5. **D.** Whenever you have excessive paging you should add more RAM. By adding more RAM you'll reduce the need for NT to swap memory from RAM to the hard disk. By having as much physical memory as possible, you increase the amount of disk caching and reduce the amount of paging to the hard disk. This will increase the performance of your system immensely. Normally when you increase physical memory you also increase the size of the page file, especially if you write a dump file when the system crashes.

6. **A.** This counter watches pages that are swapped and written to your disk drive. Remember that the virtual memory of your system is kept in a file named PAGEFILE.SYS that is located on your disk drive. If you monitor this counter and the %Disk Time counter ,you will see how much the PAGEFILE.SYS affects the overall performance of your system. The Memory:Pages/Sec value should be <5.

7. **D.** The event viewer can display three separate logs. The log you open depends on the type of items you need to view:

   ■ The System Log contains events that are provided by the Windows NT internal services and drivers.

   ■ The Security Log contains all security-related events when auditing has been enabled.

   ■ The Application Log contains events that have been generated by applications.

     By default, each log file is a maximum of 512KB in size and overwrites events older than seven days. However, these parameters can be reset by changing the Maximum Log Size and Event Log Wrapping options in each of the three individual log files. The maximum size of the log can be changed in 64 KB increments. The three event log wrapping options are: Overwrite Events as Needed; Overwrite Events Older Than *x* Days; and Do Not Overwrite Events (clear log manually).

8. **A.** An audited security access attempt was successful. For example, access to an audited directory was granted.

**9.** C. The Network Monitor is an outstanding tool for monitoring the network performance of your system. The Network Monitor that comes with Windows NT Server will only display the frames that are sent to or from your system. It will not monitor your entire network segment. A *frame* is an amount of information that has been divided into smaller pieces by the network software to be sent out across the wire.

**10.** C. You must use DISKPERF –YE to monitor a physical drive in a RAID set. Using DISKPERF –YE installs the Disk Drive Performance Statistics Driver low in the disk driver stack, so that it can see individual physical disks before they are logically combined.

**11.** D. Remember that the disk performance counters are disabled by default, and you want them that way for normal operation. Enable them at the command line by running DISKPERF –Y and rebooting. Don't forget to disable them when you are done. The command is DISKPERF –N.

**12.** C. The key to this question is that the server is performing the role of a file server. Although they are Word and Excel files, the users will be running Word and Excel either locally or from a different server, so it isn't an application server.

**13.** A. This counter indicates how busy the processor in your system is. There is no need to be alarmed if your processor has spikes of 100 percent; this is expected in some situations, such as when starting up an application. However, a bottleneck can occur if your processor is so busy that it does not respond to service requests for time. If you are experiencing a consistent processor load of 80% or more, you have a processor bottleneck.

**14.** D. You can't manually change the priority of a thread. However, you can use Task Manager to change the priority of a process.

**15.** A, B, C. First, turn on disk drive performance counters. Next, create a performance monitor alert for each server that monitors the Disk: % Free Space to alert you at less than 10 percent space available.

**16.** A. Changing the binding order on the servers won't improve the overall network performance, because the clients mostly use NWLink to communicate. The server will respond with the same protocol it was addressed with. So if a client initiates a communication with NWLink, a server will respond with NWLink.

**17.** C, D, E. You should add more RAM to alleviate the paging problem. By distributing the paging file across multiple disks you increase the performance of the paging file, but you don't reduce the amount of paging. Finally, you should move the paging file off the boot partition, because the OS needs to access the paging file and the boot partition the most.

**18.** D. You can't tell how many hard disks (physical drives) the swap file is on. All you can tell is that the swap file is on two logical drives. A drive letter represents a logical drive, not a physical drive, unless you have the entire drive partitioned as one logical drive.

**19.** A, D. Notice in the first illustration that the OS is on one processor and an application is running on a different processor. This is ASMP, whereas the second illustration is SMP. The OS and applications are spread across multiple processors.

# Answers: Troubleshooting

**1.** B, C. When hard disk detection fails with a SCSI bus, you should do the following:

Scan the drive for viruses. If the Master Boot Record is infected, Windows NT Server may not see the hard disk drive. If the hard disk is SCSI, use SCSITOOL to obtain SCSI information. Check to see if there is a valid boot sector on the drive. Check that all SCSI devices are properly terminated.

**2.** A, C. The Hardware Abstraction Layer (HAL) is a likely problem source when accessing hardware and your system fails, because HAL controls User mode access to the hardware. Also, if NT is using reserved memory, it could fail while copying data to the hard disk.

**3. D.** LastKnownGood is the configuration that was saved to a special control set in the Registry after the last successful logon to Windows NT. Instead of reloading the entire operating system you can restart the computer without logging on, then select LastKnownGood during the boot sequence. This will load the previously known good control set, and bypass the bad device driver. LastKnownGood can also be initiated if Windows NT has a fatal error at boot time.

**4. D.** A SCSI controller that has its resident BIOS disabled uses the SCSI ARC name. All other controllers (both IDE and SCSI controllers with their BIOS enabled) are listed as *multi*. The numbers that follow SCSI or multi start counting with 0. This number indicates which controller the disk is attached to. Disk is always part of the ARC name, but it is only actively used if SCSI is listed as the first word of the ARC path. If Disk is actively used, then the SCSI bus number is used here. It starts counting with 0. If you have multi in the first space, then Disk will always be 0. Rdisk indicates either the SCSI Logical Unit Number (LUN) when SCSI is the first word in the ARC path, or the ordinal number of the disk, if it is multi. Remember the counting here also starts with 0. This is simply the partition number on the disk. The important thing here is that the counting starts with one!

**5. D.** Typically this is a condition that occurs when the print spooler has stalled. To restart the spooler, stop and restart the spooler service using the Services applet in Control Panel.

**6. A, C.** You can either try to fix the problem while loading Windows NT by pressing S and specifying the SCSI drive, or you can wait to add it after SETUP has finished. I would wait until SETUP had finished, if I didn't need the hard disk to finish SETUP.

**7. A, C.** If your paging file has increased in size, that means Windows NT is swapping more memory to the hard disk. Using more memory, and writing a lot of it to the hard disk can only slow down application start times. Before your application can start, NT must make room for it in RAM by swapping current RAM to the paging file. Also, since the disk is fuller, the files will become more fragmented.

8. **G.** Be sure to know the ARC path naming conventions. See Question 4 for details of ARC path naming.

9. **C.** If you choose the Update Repair Info button, the Repair Disk Utility will overwrite some of the files located in the %SYSTEMROOT%\ REPAIR directory. After the %SYSTEMROOT%\REPAIR directory has been updated, the program prompts you to create an Emergency Repair Disk. The disk it creates is the same as if you had chosen the Create Repair Disk option.

10. **F.** The Services tab reports the current status of services—whether they are running, stopped, starting, or stopping. This is a good place to check to see if a service is stopping and starting. If you use the Services applet in Control Panel, it will only report if the service is running or stopped. If the service is stopping, it will still report it as running until it completely stops. Use NT Diagnostics to see the current state of the service.

11. **B.** The words "blue screen of death" are about the worst thing you can tell someone about their Windows NT server. The blue screens are actually text mode STOP messages that identify hardware and software problems that have occurred while running Windows NT Server. The reason for producing the blue screen is to visibly alert users to the fact that an error message has been generated. The blue screen is intended to provide information to help in troubleshooting the problem, rather than allowing the system to fail in an "invisible" manner.

# MCSE
## MICROSOFT CERTIFIED SYSTEMS ENGINEER

# Part 3

## Networking Essentials

## EXAM TOPICS

Networking Basics

Network Models

Protocols and Packets

Data Link Protocols

Network Operating Systems

Network Applications

Multi-Vendor Environments

Transmission Media

Network Interface Cards

Network Connectivity Devices

Wide Area Networks (WANs)

Network Security and Reliability

Network Monitoring and Management

Network Troubleshooting

Internet Technologies

# Networking
# Essentials
# Practice
# Questions

## Q & A

Τ he following questions will help you measure your understanding of the material presented on the Networking Essentials exam. There are 300 questions divided up by the applicable chapter. Read all the choices carefully, as there may be more than one correct answer. Choose all correct answers for each question.

# Networking Basics

1. Your company has temporarily rented office space on the 5th floor, and it needs to network the four computers in that office so that the employees can share a printer. What topology is best suited for this situation?

   A. The star topology
   B. The ring topology
   C. The bus topology
   D. The star ring topology

2. Which of the following statements best describe a star topology?

   A. It uses more cable than the bus topology.
   B. It is more difficult to troubleshoot than the ring topology.
   C. It is less reliable than the ring topology because a single computer can bring down the entire network.
   D. It is less reliable than the bus topology because a single break in the cable can bring down the entire network.

3. Which of the following occurs if the number of broadcast messages on the network exceeds the capacity of the network bandwidth?

   A. Beaconing
   B. A broadcast tornado
   C. Crosstalk
   D. A broadcast storm

4. Which of the following is an example of a LAN?

   A. Two computers in Biloxi connected by leased line to computers in Rapid City.
   B. A computer in San Antonio connects via modem to a computer network in Charlotte.
   C. 1,700 computers are connected to a network located in a 17-story office building.
   D. The office in Louisville is connected to the office in Naples by a Public Data Network.

5. What is the difference between a file server and an application server?

   A. Data stays on the file server, whereas data transfers to the client from the application server.
   B. Data stays on the application server, whereas data transfers to the client from the file server.
   C. Data cannot be written to on a file server.
   D. Data cannot be written to on an application server.

## QUESTIONS AND ANSWERS

| | |
|---|---|
| The computers on your office floor are connected and hooked up to the printer. | This is a LAN since the computers are all close to each other. |
| A freelance computer book writer in New York uses his modem to send his document to a colleague in L.A. for cross-referencing. | There are only two computers connected but since they are far apart, this is a WAN. |
| The 5000 computers at an Air Force base are all hooked up to a high-speed network. | Even though the number of computers is high, and an Air Force base can be quite large, it's still the same geographical location; therefore this network is also a LAN. |
| The university campus has a network that connects all workstations and offers students who are away from campus the possibility to use a dial-in-modem. | The fact that people in remote locations can connect to the network makes this a WAN. |

**6.** Which of the following statements best describe client/server networks?

A. Tasks are divided between the front end and the back end.

B. All processing occurs at the front end.

C. The back end answers requests from the front end.

D. All processing occurs at the back end.

**7.** You have been hired to be the network administrator for a small insurance company. Currently there are 12 employees and all of them have computers on their desks. The company plans to expand within the next nine months by hiring an additional eight people. The majority of the computers contain confidential customer information. Your boss asks you to design and install a network for the company. What type of network would you design and install?

A. A server-based network

B. A peer-to-peer network

C. A client-based network

D. A workgroup network

**8.** Which of the following statements best describe a peer-to-peer network?

A. It requires a dedicated administrator.

B. It provides broad resource protection.

C. It requires a centralized server for logon validation.

D. It provides each user the ability to administer his or her own resources.

**9.** Which of the following is an example of client/server networking?

A. A workstation application accessing data from a remote database.

B. A workstation application accessing data from the local hard disk.

C. A workstation application accessing data from a local database.

D. A workstation application accessing data from a floppy diskette.

**10.** What type of topology is shown in the next illustration?

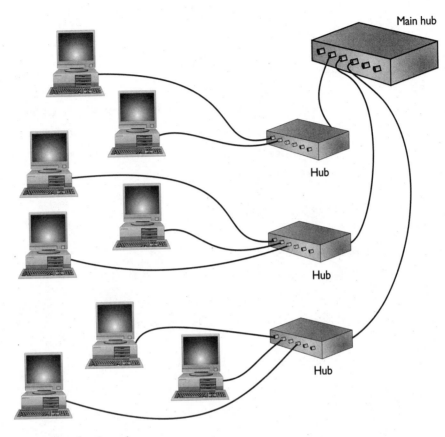

A. Star-bus topology
B. Bus topology
C. Star ring topology
D. Ring topology

**11.** What is another name for a peer-to-peer network?

A. Client/server
B. Workgroup
C. Transitional
D. Server-based

**12.** You are called out to troubleshoot a network outage in one of the remote buildings of the company that you work for. The person that called in the outage said that the network for the entire building is down. Looking over your wiring diagrams, you see that the network uses a star ring topology. As you are driving out to the location, you ponder what could cause the entire network to go down. What possibility comes to your mind?

A. A cable came loose from one of the computers.

B. A cable is no longer terminated.

C. One of the office hubs has failed.

D. The main hub has failed.

**13.** Your star topology network is starting to see a lot of network traffic. What can you do to alleviate the traffic load?

A. Replace the star topology network with a bus topology network.

B. Replace the hubs with powered hubs.

C. Replace the wiring with all new wiring.

D. Replace the hubs with switched hubs.

**14.** You work at the main company headquarters located in Boston. A new regional office is being set up in Ocean Springs. You have decided that it is more economical for you to buy capacity on the Public Data Network (PDN) of a third-party provider. What types of PDNs are available for consideration?

A. X.24

B. Frame Relay

C. X.25

D. Front Relay

# Network Models

1. Current Situation: You have been hired to develop the network architecture for a local law firm. All of the computers are less than 80 meters from the wiring closet.
   Required Result: Select the correct cable type to use.
   Optional Desired Results: Minimize the cost of maintenance; minimize the cost of the installation.
   Proposed Solution: Use 10Base2 cable.
   Which results does the proposed solution produce?

   A. The proposed solution produces the required result and produces both of the optional desired results.
   B. The proposed solution produces the required result and produces only one of the optional desired results.
   C. The proposed solution produces the required result but does not produce any of the optional desired results.
   D. The proposed solution does not produce the required result.

2. Current Situation: You have a computer located 210 meters away from the 10Base2 network.
   Required Result: Allow the computer access to the network.
   Optional Desired Results: Act as a print server; minimize broadcasts.
   Proposed Solution: Use 10BaseT cable.
   Which results does the proposed solution produce?

   A. The proposed solution produces the required result and produces both of the optional desired results.
   B. The proposed solution produces the required result and produces only one of the optional desired results.
   C. The proposed solution produces the required result but does not produce any of the optional desired results.
   D. The proposed solution does not produce the required result.

**3.** The _____ is a network layer device.

**4.** Current Situation: You are responsible for two separate networks. One is based on 802.3 and the other one is based upon 802.5.
Required Result: Allow data to pass between the two networks.
Optional Desired Results: Minimize installation; minimize maintenance.
Proposed Solution: Use a repeater.
Which results does the proposed solution produce?

A. The proposed solution produces the required result and produces both of the optional desired results.

B. The proposed solution produces the required result and produces only one of the optional desired results.

C. The proposed solution produces the required result but does not produce any of the optional desired results.

D. The proposed solution does not produce the required result.

**5.** Current Situation: Your network is becoming very congested with traffic.
Required Result: Open up multiple paths so that the data can flow more quickly.
Optional Desired Results: Allow for future growth; monitor the Data Link layer.
Proposed Solution: Add routers to your network.
Which results does the proposed solution produce?

A. The proposed solution produces the required result and produces both of the optional desired results.

B. The proposed solution produces the required result and produces only one of the optional desired results.

C. The proposed solution produces the required result but does not produce any of the optional desired results.

D. The proposed solution does not produce the required result.

**exam**
**Watch** *Microsoft will expect you to know the characteristics and purpose of the media used in the 802.3 and 802.5 standards! Be sure to study for 802.3 media types and the IBM Cabling System for 802.5 media.*

6. _____ communication ensures reliable delivery of data from the sender to the receiver.

7. Current Situation: The office has four computers networked using the bus topology. Five additional computers are not networked.
Required Result: Add the five computers to the existing network with minimal effort.
Optional Desired Results: Monitor the network for broadcast storms; monitor the network's bandwidth usage.
Proposed Solution: Use 10BaseT cable to add the five computers to the network.
Which results does the proposed solution produce?

A. The proposed solution produces the required result and produces both of the optional desired results.

B. The proposed solution produces the required result and produces only one of the optional desired results.

C. The proposed solution produces the required result but does not produce any of the optional desired results.

D. The proposed solution does not produce the required result.

8. You are designing a network with a coworker who suggests that you use the 802.4 standard. The network you are designing will have seven users, who need to share a laser jet printer and share document files with each other.

A. You should adopt the usage of 802.4 because it was designed for networks of fewer than ten users.

B. You should not adopt the usage of 802.4 because it was designed for automating machinery.

C. You should adopt the usage of 802.4 because it was designed for optimizing laser jet printing on networks.

D. You should not adopt the usage of 802.4 because it was designed for operating at 100 Mbps, which exceeds the requirements for the network.

9. You have been monitoring your network and have noticed an increase in broadcast storms. Your boss has told you to solve the problem immediately, no matter how much it costs. What do you do?

A. Replace the routers with repeaters.

B. Replace the bridges with repeaters.

C. Replace the repeaters with routers.

D. Replace the routers with gateways.

## QUESTIONS AND ANSWERS

| Question | Answer |
| --- | --- |
| I have two 10BaseT networks that I need to connect together. What is the cheapest way to do this? | Use a repeater. It will pass *all* traffic from one network to the other and vice versa. |
| I have a 10BaseT network and a 10Base2 network, both of which use the 802.3 frame type. How can I connect them together? | Since they are using the same frame type, either a repeater or a bridge will work. The deciding factors would be cost and network usage. |
| My company has many departments wanting to be networked together, but there are many different networks being used. How can I possibly interconnect them all? | Larger, more complicated networks need routers. A router can join together many complex networks, even those using different types of networks. |
| I want to connect three high-volume Ethernet networks together, but I have a limited budget. | Use a bridge. It will segment the traffic, only allowing traffic to pass that is destined for another network. |

*The Networking Essentials test will always test your understanding of different network devices and which layer they function on in the OSI model. You must also know which device is most appropriate in a given situation.*

10. What establishes formal communication between two computers on an internetwork using a well-defined path?

A. A virtual circuit

B. A handshake

C. A mailslot

D. A session

11. The Data Link layer of the OSI model is broken down into two sublayers. What are they?

A. Medium Access Control sublayer

B. Logical Link Central sublayer

C. Media Access Control sublayer

D. Logical Link Control sublayer

12. What layer of the OSI model uses logical network addresses to route packets?

A. Session

B. Transport

C. Physical

D. Network

*It is important for the Networking Essentials test that you understand the difference between connection-oriented and connectionless communication, and in what situations each one is appropriate.*

# Protocols and Packets

**1.** Current Situation: You manage a network of 180 computers in a single building.

Required Result: Allow the 180 computers to communicate with the corporate network located 200 miles away using routers.

Optional Desired Results: You need to monitor network traffic; you want to gather software inventory statistics.

Proposed Solution: Install the NetBEUI protocol on the 180 computers. Which result does the proposed solution produce?

A. The proposed solution produces the required result and produces both of the optional desired results.

B. The proposed solution produces the required result and produces only one of the optional desired results.

C. The proposed solution produces the required result but does not produce any of the optional desired results.

D. The proposed solution does not produce the required result.

**2.** You have recently been hired to support a network that consists of seven Windows NT servers and 246 Windows 95 client computers. All computers are using IPX/SPX to communicate. The management of your company has decided that they want all employees to have direct Internet access to allow for instantaneous research capability. They have tasked you to make it happen. What must be done so that each computer will be able to communicate on the Internet?

A. You have to install the Client for Internet service on each Windows NT server.

B. You have to install DLC on each of the client machines.

C. You have to install TCP/IP on each of the client machines.

D. You have to install the Client for Internet service on each Windows 95 client.

exam
ⓦatch  *IPX/SPX is the fastest routable network protocol suite available.*

**3.** You have recently been hired to design a network for a hospital that will consist of ten Windows NT servers, ten UNIX servers and 300 Windows 95 clients. The Windows 95 clients need to have access to the complete network. You are not using routers so you have decided to use the NetBEUI protocol. What is the result of this decision?

A. The client machines will have access to the entire network.

B. The client machines will have access to the Windows NT servers.

C. The client machines will have access to the UNIX servers.

D. The client machines will not be able to access the network.

exam
ⓦatch

*TCP/IP, IPX/SPX NWLink, Appletalk, and DECnet are routable protocols while NetBEUI and DLC are not.*

## QUESTIONS AND ANSWERS

| My network will have . . . | The protocol(s) I should use is . . . |
|---|---|
| Five Windows 95 workstations that will not be connected to the Internet. | NetBEUI because NetBEUI is a fast protocol that works well in small workgroups that do not require Internet connectivity. |
| 20 Windows 95 and NT workstations that will be connected to the Internet. | TCP/IP because TCP/IP is the protocol used on the Internet. |
| 100 Windows NT workstations, five Windows NT servers, and 100 Macintosh workstations. | TCP/IP with AppleTalk installed on the Windows NT servers because TCP/IP can be used with either Windows NT or Macintosh. AppleTalk will be used to connect the Macintoshes to the Windows NT server. |
| 100 Windows 95 workstations, ten preexisting Novell NetWare servers, and ten UNIX servers. | TCP/IP and IPX/SPX because TCP/IP can be used to connect to the UNIX servers, while IPX/SPX can be used to connect to the NetWare servers. |

4. The sales department in Nashville needs a reliable method of transferring files to the accounting department in Austin. It is imperative that the data arrive successfully so that the books are straight. Your network uses TCP/IP, so what do you recommend they use?

   A. You recommend that they use TFTP.
   B. You recommend that they use SNMP.
   C. You recommend that they use FTP.
   D. You recommend that they use DLC.

5. _____ is the fastest routable network protocol suite available.

6. Which of the following protocols are routable?

   A. DLC
   B. NetBEUI
   C. TCP/IP
   D. IPX/SPX

7. You are being interviewed for a network position with a large manufacturer of appliances that has office locations throughout the world. The interviewer says that they have been thinking about converting their entire existing network so that it exclusively uses the DLC protocol. He asks what your opinion is on the matter. What do you tell him?

   A. You tell him that it is a wise move as DLC is a small, fast protocol that would work fine for the entire corporation.
   B. You tell him that it is not a wise move because DLC uses a lot of overhead when it routes packets.
   C. You tell him that it is a wise move because DLC is the protocol used for communication on the Internet.
   D. You tell him that it is not a wise move because DLC is not a routable protocol so it will not work for the entire corporation.

**8.** What type of access method does Asynchronous Transfer Mode use?

    A. CSMA/CD

    B. Token Passing

    C. CSMA/CA

    D. Demand Priority

**9.** At what layer of the OSI model does the NetBEUI protocol operate?

    A. Physical

    B. Network

    C. Transport

    D. Session

**10.** You are setting up a user at a remote location with access to one of the UNIX servers on the company network. The user needs to access the text-based system, just as if he were sitting in front of it. What could you configure for the user to be able to do this?

    A. FTP

    B. TFTP

    C. SMB

    D. Telnet

**11.** What protocol defines the structure of Internet mail messages?

    A. SNMP

    B. TFTP

    C. SMTP

    D. TRAX

exam
ⓦatch

*It is important to remember that NetBEUI is capable of binding with up to eight different drivers. Protocols prior to NetBEUI frequently did not have the capability to bind with more than one driver.*

**12.** Name the IEEE standard that defines the Carrier Sense Multiple Access with Collision Detection access method.

A. 802.2

B. 802.3

C. 802.4

D. 802.5

# Data Link Protocols

**1.** Current Situation: You have 38 standalone computers on the second floor of your headquarters building.

Required Result: Network the computers so that the users can share data.

Optional Desired Results: Minimize the cost of installation; monitor the network for unauthorized access.

Proposed Solution: Use a single segment of thinnet to network the computers on the second floor.

Which results does the proposed solution produce?

A. The proposed solution produces the required result and produces both of the optional desired results.

B. The proposed solution produces the required result and produces only one of the optional desired results.

C. The proposed solution produces the required result but does not produce any of the optional desired results.

D. The proposed solution does not produce the required result.

**2.** You see an advertisement in the paper from a company looking for someone who can help install a network that conforms to IEEE 802.5. When you call the company, they ask you if you have experience with the type of Ethernet network that they need installed. What do you tell them?

A. Yes, you have experience installing 802.5 Ethernet networks.

B. No, you do not have any experience, because it is impossible, since 802.5 is a bus network.

C. Yes, you have experience configuring 802.4 Ethernet networks.

D. No, you do not have any such experience, because it is impossible, since 802.5 is a token ring network.

3. Current Situation: Your college has 14 buildings on its main campus, and each building has its own LAN.
Required Result: Connect all 14 LANs.
Optional Desired Results: High speed access; fault tolerance.
Proposed Solution: Install a Fiber Distributed Data Interface topology.
Which results does the proposed solution produce?

A. The proposed solution produces the required result and produces both of the optional desired results.

B. The proposed solution produces the required result and produces only one of the optional desired results.

C. The proposed solution produces the required result but does not produce any of the optional desired results.

D. The proposed solution does not produce the required result.

4. You are hired by a large law firm to troubleshoot their newly installed thicknet network. As you analyze the drawings of the network they have provided, you see that they have 128 computers spread out over six segments located throughout the firm's 49 offices. Where do you begin your troubleshooting?

A. You need to begin in the office closest to the administration office since it has the majority of computers.

B. You need to tell the law firm officials that the network exceeds the amount of computers that can be on a thicknet network.

C. You need to tell the law firm officials that the network exceeds the 5-4-3 rule.

D. You need to begin in the office of the CEO, as that is where the thicknet terminates.

**5.** Your company expanded its network by running FDDI out to a research and development building that was located 3000 meters away from the administration building. They call you in to troubleshoot because they are receiving errors on the network since the expansion was completed. What do you do?

   A. You replace the fiber optic cable with a better quality fiber optic cable.

   B. You tell them to use the alternate FDDI ring to clear up the errors.

   C. You replace the fiber optic cable with shielded twisted pair cable.

   D. You tell them that the distance exceeds the maximum allowed for FDDI.

**6.** You're troubleshooting a newly installed token ring network that fails to work. The token ring is set up to operate at 16 Mbps. You inspect the MSAU, and it seems to be operating correctly. What else can be causing the problem?

   A. One of the network interface cards is set to operate at 4 Mbps

   B. One of the computers is not turned on.

   C. One of the computers has been removed from the network

   D. One of the network interface cards is set to operate at 100 Mbps.

**7.** You're designing a network and one of the criteria that has been levied on you is that it must perform at 100 Mbps. There will be 28 computers on the network, and the network needs to be fault tolerant. What high-speed network architecture will you use?

   A. FDDI

   B. Fast Ethernet

   C. CDDI

   D. Token ring

exam
ⓦatch

*It is highly likely you will see many questions on the exam relating to maximum cable distance for each of the above data link protocols. This can appear in complex scenario questions where a number of factors are presented. It may not be immediately obvious that the cable length has been exceeded.*

8. Current Situation: 10BaseT network consists of 93 computers using Category 5 cable.
   Required Result: Upgrade it to 100 Mbps.
   Optional Desired Results: Minimize costs; minimize installation time.
   Proposed Solution: Install 100BaseFX.
   Which results does the proposed solution produce?

   A. The proposed solution produces the required result and produces both of the optional desired results.

   B. The proposed solution produces the required result and produces only one of the optional desired results.

   C. The proposed solution produces the required result but does not produce any of the optional desired results.

   D. The proposed solution does not produce the required result.

9. What type of cabling do 10Base2 networks use?

   A. Thin coaxial

   B. Thick coaxial

   C. Shielded twisted pair

   D. Unshielded twisted pair

10. According to studies, what is the most common Ethernet implementation?

   A. 10Base2

   B. 10BaseT

   C. 10Base5

   D. 10BaseFL

**e x a m**
**Ⓦ⓪ a t c h**

*Be prepared to answer questions on the exam where you must choose the correct topology and media for the data link protocol you are using.*

**11.** What is the maximum amount of nodes that can be on a 10Base5 segment?

A. 30

B. 100

C. 1000

D. 1024

**12.** _____ networks use multistation access units.

**exam** *The exam leans quite heavily on Ethernet technology, due to*
**Watch** *Ethernet's dominance in the marketplace. Pay special attention to*
*special characteristics of the various media types of Ethernet.*

# Network Operating Systems

**1.** You have received a new computer that will be configured as a mail server. As you are installing Windows NT Server you find that setup disk 2 has errors. What can you do to get Windows NT Server installed on the computer?

A. Install Windows NT Server using WINNT.EXE /UDF.

B. Install Windows NT Server using WINNT.EXE /Z.

C. Install Windows NT Server using WINNT.EXE /B.

D. Install Windows NT Server using WINNT.EXE /D.

**exam** *It is a good idea to install and reinstall Windows NT Server multiple*
**Watch** *times to become very comfortable with the installation process. This*
*will help on various questions within the MCSE core track of exams.*

**2.** You work for a company that has a network with several LAN Manager 2.2c for MS-DOS clients on the network. Your boss wants those clients to be able to access data on the Novell NetWare network. What do you need to do to enable this functionality?

   A. Install IPX/SPX on the LAN Manager 2.2c for MS-DOS clients.

   B. Install LAN Manager 2.2c support on the Novell NetWare servers.

   C. Nothing, LAN Manager 2.2c for MS-DOS clients automatically configure themselves to see the Novell NetWare network.

   D. Nothing, LAN Manager 2.2c for MS-DOS clients do not support IPX/SPX so they cannot see the Novell NetWare network.

**3.** Martha works in the Sales department but has been assigned to work on a special project with Marissa from Marketing and Justin in R&D. A directory has been set up on a Windows NT server so that they can store the project data they are working on. No one else needs to have access to the data right now, although that may change in the future. What method allows only those people to access the directory?

   A. Add them to a group and give that group access to the directory.

   B. Copy the directory to each of their computers.

   C. Add them to a locale and give the locale access to the directory.

   D. Add them to the list of authorized visitors.

exam
ⓦatch

*On various exam questions there will be possible answers that talk about adding the user to the administrators group to give them the appropriate permissions. The rule of the thumb on these questions is you never want to give an end user administrator permissions. There will usually be a better answer. With exam questions, discard answers you know are not correct, to give yourself better odds at choosing the right answer.*

**4.** Steven calls the help desk and tells you that he cannot reach p333.biloxi.ms.us. You check his HOSTS file as shown in the next illustration. Why can't Steven reach p333.biloxi.ms.us?

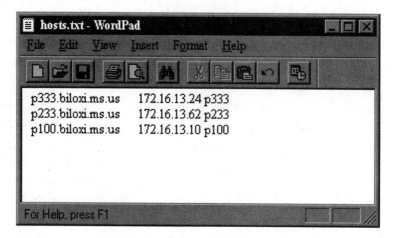

A. There are not enough spaces between the IP addresses and the single names.

B. There are too many spaces between the domain names and the IP addresses.

C. The IP addresses are in the wrong location.

D. The single names are in the wrong location.

**5.** Jim was a member of the Sales group but he recently moved over to the Marketing department. He needs to access the latest marketing data that is located in the \MARKETING directory on the file server. The Marketing group, as well as the Administrators group, has Full Control permission, the Everyone group has Read permission, and the Sales group has No Access permissions to the \MARKETING directory. When Jim logs on as a member of the Marketing group and tries to access the \MARKETING directory, it won't let him in. What do you have to do to fix Jim's problem?

A. Delete Jim's account and recreate it, since it has a problem.

B. Add Jim's account to the Everyone group.

C. Remove Jim's account from the Sales group.

D. Delete the Sales group.

**exam**
**ⓦatch**

*Remember the acronym AGLP (accounts-global-local-permissions) for the exam. This will help you remember that accounts are added to global groups which are added to local groups which are assigned permissions.*

**6.** Your network is expanding into other buildings on the college campus, and you expect to gain several hundred new users in the next week. You are busy with the network expansion, so you need assistance with creating the new user accounts. Raymond has volunteered to help you out, but you don't want to give him Administrator access to the network. Since you don't want to give Raymond Administrator access, how can he create the new user accounts?

A. Add him to the Domain Users group.

B. Add him to the Power Users group.

C. Add him to the Account Operators group.

D. Add him to the Server Operators group.

**7.** Lynn is having a problem printing to a network printer. After troubleshooting, you find that the application she is using is not communicating with the printing device. How do you fix the problem so that Lynn is able to use the printing device?

A. Change the printing device to use Lynn's serial port.

B. Reinstall the correct printer driver to her machine.

C. Add a new toner cartridge to the printing device.

D. Reinstall the correct printer queue to her machine.

**8.** When should you allow someone to use the Guests group?

A. For one-time access to resources

B. For permanent access to resources

C. For temporary access to resources

D. For weekly access to resources

**9.** Edward is configuring a Windows NT computer to be the print server for a Hewlett-Packard JetDirect card. But he is having problems installing the printer. What is causing the problem?

A. The printer queue is full.

B. The NetBEUI protocol is not installed on the print server.

C. The printer is out of paper.

D. The DLC protocol is not installed on the print server.

**10.** While looking over your security logs, you see that someone is attempting to log on as Administrator. What is the best thing you can do to prevent the hacker from being successful?

A. Delete the Administrator account.

B. Change the password for the Administrator account.

C. Rename the Administrator account.

D. Disable the Administrator account.

**11.** Applications controlled internally by Windows NT are called _____.

A. Daemons

B. Services

C. NetWare Loadable Modules

D. Applets

**12.** Which of the following is an example of the Universal Naming Convention?

A. //demo1/*sharename*

B. //demo1\\*sharename*

C. \\demo1/*sharename*

D. \\demo1\\*sharename*

# Network Applications

1. Your network has a variety of different mail servers, and the head of IS has directed that the client systems standardize on Microsoft Outlook. As you migrate the clients to Outlook, you start to notice that some of them cannot reach their mail. What do you do to fix the problem?

   A. Install the Microsoft Exchange client software.

   B. Install a multi-vendor gateway.

   C. Install a new operating system.

   D. Install the latest Service Pack for Windows NT.

2. Your network has 160 clients who need access to an older MS-DOS-based application that has very low overhead. You have a 250-user license for the application. What is the best method of implementing access to the application from the 160 client systems?

   A. Install the application on all 160 client systems.

   B. Install the application on your mail server.

   C. Install the application on 80 client systems, and share it from there to the other 80 clients.

   D. Install the application on your application server.

3. ACME Glue Services has hired you to set up a mail server for them. They tell you that one of the requirements that must be met is that all mail must be left on the mail server. What protocol must the software package that you decide to use support?

   A. Internal Message Access Protocol

   B. Post Office Protocol 3

   C. Internet Message Access Protocol

   D. Post Office Protocol 2

# QUESTIONS AND ANSWERS

| My network has . . . | I should implement . . . |
|---|---|
| Many clients that will be using an older DOS-based application that has low overhead, and we have a site license for. | An installation of the application on the application server. No license restriction is necessary since we have a site license. |
| 100 clients that will be accessing data from a database simultaneously. | A client/server database server such as Microsoft SQL Server. |
| 100 users who wish to use Microsoft Word 97. I would rather not install it on each workstation. | An installation of Microsoft Word 97 on each of the workstations. Even though it would be easier to only install one copy on the server, Microsoft Word 97 is fairly extensive and would not perform very well installed on an applications server. |
| 2000 employees that wish to collaborate on projects together, schedule meetings together, and be able to send electronic mail to each other. | Install some type of GroupWare product, such as Microsoft Exchange Server, to help facilitate these activities. |

4. The network you support has a mixture of UNIX, Novell NetWare, Windows NT, OS/2, and Windows 95 systems on it. Management has decided that there is a need for groupware, and they have tasked you to implement it within the next 90 days. What kind of product would you install for use on the network?

   A. SLIP-based groupware
   B. WEB-based groupware
   C. SNMP- based groupware
   D. PPP-based groupware

5. What type of application is shown in the next illustration?

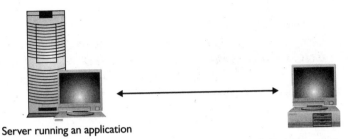

Server running an application

Client displaying output from the server

A. Client/Server

B. Mobilized

C. Centralized

D. Transitional

**6.** Which of the following are common interprocess communications methods?

A. UNIX SPX

B. Remote Procedure Calls (RPC)

C. System Message Blocks (SMB)

D. Windows sockets

**7.** Your network consists of 170 users. 32 of the users are frequently making business trips and need to check their mail while on the road. Your notebook computers use a variety of operating systems, such as MS-DOS, Windows 3.1, and OS/2. You want to make sure that the users can access their mailboxes no matter which notebook they may be assigned for their trip. What mail protocol should you use on you mail server?

A. Post Office Protocol 3

B. Internet Message Access Protocol

C. Point to Point Protocol

D. Serial Line Interface Protocol

*Using a universal naming convention (UNC) is extremely easy. A full UNC consists of the server's name and the name of the share on the server that you wish to use. The names are then put together in the format of \\<Server Name>\<Share Name>\ to form a UNC.*

**8.** What IPC mechanism is exclusive to Microsoft products?

A. Remote Procedure Calls

B. Mailslots

C. Random Procedure Calls

D. NetDDE

**9.** What method of IPC does Windows NT use for connection-oriented communication between processes such as file transfers and authentication?

A. Windows DDE

B. Named pipes

C. NetDDE

D. Windows sockets

**10.** Examining the network trouble tickets for the last week, you notice a trend with users complaining that they can't access the word processing application they always use. You have the word processing application mapped to all the users' S: drive. What can you do to make sure that the users always have access to the word processing application, and eliminate the complaints?

A. Map the word processing application to all the users' T: drives.

B. Move the word processing application to a server closer to the users.

C. Add the word processing application mapping to a logon script for the users.

D. Remove the word processing application mapping from the users' home directory.

**11.** The transfer of e-mail from one location to another is called _____.

**12.** What method of IPC does Windows NT use for connectionless-oriented communication between processes, such as service advertising?

A. Windows sockets

B. NetDDE

C. Windows DDE

D. Mailslots

# Multi-Vendor Environments

**1.** Your network has a mixture of Windows NT servers and Novell NetWare servers. Marissa cannot connect to any of the Novell NetWare servers from her Windows 95 system but she has no problem connecting to the Windows NT servers. You check her system, and see that she has the IPX/SPX-compatible protocol on her system. What can you do so she can connect to the Novell NetWare servers?

A. Add the Microsoft Client for NetWare Networks to her machine.

B. Add the SunSoft PC-NFS network client to her machine.

C. Add the FTP Software NFS Client to her machine.

D. Add the Novell Client32 for Windows 95 to her machine.

**2.** ACME Tunneling Corporation has 2462 clients configured for their Novell NetWare network. ACME management has decided to add a Windows NT server to their network but they are concerned about the need of reconfiguring all the client machines so that they can access it. They ask you how they can solve the dilemma. What do you suggest?

A. Install Gateway Service for NetWare on the Windows NT server.

B. Install File and Print Services for NetWare on the Novell NetWare server.

C. Install Gateway Service for NetWare on the Novell NetWare server.

D. Install File and Print Services for NetWare on the Windows NT server.

## QUESTIONS AND ANSWERS

| | |
|---|---|
| I am installing Windows NT and Novell NetWare servers, but all of my clients are Windows 95. | Use the built-in redirectors for Microsoft Networks and for Novell Networks. They give you full connectivity to both types of servers. |
| I have a Windows NT server and need to allow Macintosh clients on my network. | Install Services for Macintosh on the server, and be certain you have an available volume formatted with NTFS to accept the Macintosh files. |
| My company uses a SQL database to store inventory listings, and we want to make this information available on the Internet. | Install a Web server like Internet Information Server 4.0 and use the database connector to access SQL server for this information. |
| Our company has grown significantly over the last five years, and we now need our LAN users to access our new AS/400 computer. | Install a SNA Gateway like Microsoft's SNA Server that allows LAN protocol access to midrange and mainframe computers. |

3. The network at ACME Clocks consists of 24 Windows NT servers and 1024 Windows 95 clients. The graphics section of the marketing department will be adding 62 new Apple computers to the network, and they will need access to the graphics files stored on one of the Windows NT servers. How can this be accomplished?

   A. Install the IPX/SPX-compatible protocol on the Apple computers.

   B. Install Services for Macintosh on the Windows NT server.

   C. Install the NetBEUI protocol on the Apple computers.

   D. Install Services for Macintosh on the Apple computers.

4. What version of Novell NetWare supports the NetWare Directory Services?

   A. 4.$x$

   B. 3.$x$

   C. 2.$x$

   D. 1.$x$

**5.** The local library wants to make the card catalog database available to its patrons. They have hired you to help them with the project. One of the criteria they have stipulated is that the card catalog database has to be made available to as much of the computer-owning community as possible. What do you recommend to them?

A. Install an NFS server.

B. Install a TFP server.

C. Install a SNA gateway.

D. Install a web server.

**6.** The key to client-based interoperability is the _____.

**7.** What operating systems should Novell's VLM redirectors be used with?

A. Windows 95

B. MS-DOS

C. Windows NT

D. Windows for Workgroups

exam
ⓦatch

*The NetWare NOS is the most common NOS installed in corporate networks today. With the recent explosion of Windows NT, these two products are often found working side by side in the enterprise. Because of this, Microsoft Certification Exams will test your knowledge of Microsoft products and how they interoperate with NetWare and other products. Be aware that these exams are realistic enough to test your ability to function in a real world environment. You should try to develop a sound knowledge and understanding of NetWare whenever possible.*

**8.** What operating system laid the foundation for the Internet?

   A. UNIX

   B. VMS

   C. TCP/IP

   D. LINUX

**9.** Jungle Emporium has Novell NetWare servers, as well as Windows NT servers, on their network. There are 16 MS-DOS clients and 93 Windows 95 clients on the network. The Windows 95 systems access both the Novell NetWare servers and the Windows NT servers. However, the MS-DOS clients currently only have access to the Windows NT servers. How can you give the MS-DOS clients access to the Novell NetWare servers?

   A. Install CSNW on a Novell NetWare server.

   B. Install GSNW on a Windows NT server.

   C. Install CSNW on a Windows NT server.

   D. Install GSNW on a Novell NetWare server.

**10.** What name does Novell give to their redirectors?

   A. Requester software

   B. Demanding software

   C. Relinquishing software

   D. Directive software

**11.** Dan has several files he wants to share with others on the Internet, so he wants to set up an FTP server. He asks for your assistance. He has access to the Windows NT Server system that is in his office. The Windows NT server is used for file sharing in the office, using the NetBEUI protocol. What advice do you give him?

   A. Tell him to install the IPX/SPX protocol on the Windows NT server.

   B. Tell him to install the SNA Server software on the Windows NT server.

   C. Tell him to install the TCP/IP protocol on the Windows NT server.

   D. Tell him to install the VAX OS on the Windows NT server.

**12.** What operating system was the first one written in the C language?

   A. Windows for Workgroups
   B. OS/2
   C. Open VMS
   D. UNIX

# Transmission Media

**1.** You have been contracted to design a network for a company that teaches radar maintenance courses. The building the network will be installed in has a lot of RF (Radio Frequency) noise. Cabling costs need to be kept to a minimum, yet resistant to the interference. What type of cable should your design use for the network?

   A. UTP
   B. Cat 5
   C. Fiber optic
   D. Coaxial

**2.** You have a bus network like the one shown in the next illustration that was working fine for months, but now does not work. What is the problem?

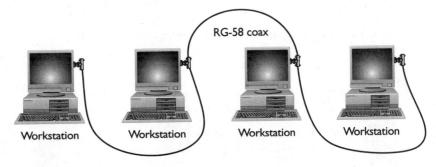

   A. Wrong type of cable being used.
   B. T connector is missing.
   C. Wrong type of NICs in the machines.
   D. Terminator is missing.

3. ACME Barrel Breakers has a 4 Mbps token ring network that they want to upgrade to the 16 Mbps transmission rate. They have installed unshielded twisted pair cable throughout their organization in anticipation of the 16 Mbps upgrade, as well as 16 Mbps NICs in all their computers. ACME has run into problems, so they have hired you to help them out. What advice do you give them?

A. They require the use of IBM Type 1, 2, or 9 cabling.

B. They require the used of IBM Type 4 or 7 cabling.

C. They cannot upgrade a token ring network to 16 Mbps.

D. They need to replace the MSAUs with routers.

4. Jason asks if he can borrow the crimp kit for a few minutes. Curious, you ask him what he needs it for. He says that he needs to put a RJ-45 connector on the end of a 10Base5 cable. What do you tell him?

A. Tell him to use a solder-on RJ-45 connector instead of a crimp-on RJ-45 connector.

B. Tell him to use an RJ-11 connector instead.

C. Tell him that thicknet does not use RJ-45 connectors.

D. Tell him to use an RJ-12 connector instead.

5. Current Situation: There are local area networks in two buildings, side by side.
Required Result: Link the two networks so that data can be shared.
Optional Desired Results: Bypass the use of the telephone company; protect the data from interception by unauthorized parties.
Proposed Solution: Use microwave technology to link the two networks.
Which results does the proposed solution produce?

A. The proposed solution produces the required result and produces both of the optional desired results.

B. The proposed solution produces the required result and produces only one of the optional desired results.

C. The proposed solution produces the required result but does not produce any of the optional desired results.

D. The proposed solution does not produce the required result.

6. Current Situation: Your company has several isolated thinnet LANs located throughout the Research and Development building. Each LAN uses the same operating system. The building is located two miles from the corporate headquarters building.

Required Result: Join the LANs in the Research and Development building together so that data can be shared.

Optional Desired Results: allow data to be sent to the corporate headquarters building; allow network monitoring to be performed from the corporate headquarters building.

Proposed Solution: Use a single 10Base5 cable to connect the thinnet LANs.

Which results does the proposed solution produce?

A. The proposed solution produces the required result and produces both of the optional desired results.

B. The proposed solution produces the required result and produces only one of the optional desired results.

C. The proposed solution produces the required result but does not produce any of the optional desired results.

D. The proposed solution does not produce the required result.

## QUESTIONS AND ANSWERS

| | |
|---|---|
| I want to connect my two computers using twisted-pair wiring. Can this be done? | You have two choices:<br>1. You can buy a small hub and plug each computer to the hub.<br>2. You can connect the two computers together using one wire but it must be wired as a "crossover cable." The transmit and receive pairs are reversed. |
| I've connected my two computers using thinnet, but it doesn't work. What could be the problem? | Even when connecting two computers using thinnet, T-connectors and terminators are required. |

**7.** You're designing a network for a client and trying to decide what type of media you need to use. According to the plans given to you by the client, there will be 28 computers located in two offices situated side by side. The client says that he thinks the company will expand by about seven more computers in those two offices in the next three months. What type of media do you recommend?

   A. 10Base2

   B. 10Base5

   C. 10BaseT

   D. 10BaseFL

**8.** ACME Candle Corporation is worried that their competition may be tapping into their network and stealing trade secrets. The CEO has stated that this situation needs to be resolved immediately and cost is not a problem. What type of media would you recommend they use for their network?

   A. Thinnet

   B. Thicknet

   C. Fiber optic

   D. Unshielded twisted pair

**9.** What type of connector is shown in the next illustration and what type of network is it normally used with?

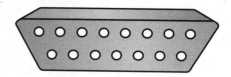

   A. BNC, 10Base2

   B. AUI, 10Base2

   C. BNC, 10Base5

   D. AUI, 10Base5

exam
Ⓦatch

*For each cable medium, the maximum transfer rates, maximum distance, and maximum number of nodes that can be attached are important. Exam questions will include scenarios where an objective is required and other objectives are desired but not required. The question will propose a solution and you are to determine which objectives were met.*

**10.** What is the maximum bandwidth of a Fast Ethernet network?

A. 10 Mbps
B. 16 Mbps
C. 100 Mbps
D. 160 Mbps

**11.** Debra is designing a token ring network using Type 3 cable connected to the MSAU. She asks you to review her design because she feels as though she is missing something. Looking over her design, you see that she forgot to add a vital component. What did she forget?

A. Piercing taps
B. Micro transceiver
C. Plenum connector
D. Media filter

**12.** What type of transmission uses analog signaling?

A. Baseband
B. Narrowband
C. Broadband
D. Wideband

exam
Ⓦatch

*The Networking Essentials exam contains many graphics. Specifically, know how each connector looks, both male and female. Know what each cable type looks like as well.*

# Network Interface Cards

**1.** You are hired by a company to be their network administrator. They have also hired an installation team, who are currently installing the network, but having problems with one of the Windows NT servers. They cannot get the NIC to work in it. They have asked you to look at it for them. What is the first thing you should do?

A. Run MSD.

B. Look in the Device Manager.

C. See if the NIC they are using is on the HCL.

D. Take the NIC out and put it in a different machine.

**2.** William installed a new network interface card in his Windows 95 computer and plugged in the network cable that was next to his desk. He calls you and reports that the network must be down, because he cannot get out to the World Wide Web. What is really wrong with William's system?

A. He forgot to change the jumpers for the parallel port.

B. He forgot to load the NIC software drivers.

C. He forgot to put a terminator on the 10BaseT cable.

D. He forgot to load the USB software drivers.

**3.** Kevin was talking to Amy about her experiences and thought he would have a go at installing the network interface card in his multimedia machine. Since he knew the problems that Amy and William had encountered, he figured that nothing else could happen. He installed the card with an I/O base address of 280h and an IRQ of 5. Upon booting up his system he received the same error message that Amy had received. Something about a device conflict. Kevin leaned around to Amy's cubicle and asked for your phone number. What item could be conflicting with Kevin's network interface card?

A. Keyboard

B. Floppy drive

C. Real-time clock

D. Sound card

**4.** What type of data bus is needed for the network interface card shown in the next illustration?

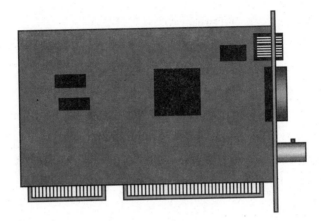

A. ISA

B. MCA

C. EISA

D. PCI

**5.** Jim has installed a new network interface card in his Windows 95 system. He configures the network drive in Windows 95 to operate with an I/O base address of 300h and an IRQ of 7. He receives no conflicts when he boots his system, which makes him very happy. However, when he types in a UNC, nothing happens. Jim calls you up for advice. What do you tell him?

A. Tell him that the network card is bad and he needs to replace it.

B. Tell him to set the configuration parameters on the NIC to the same as those in Windows 95.

C. Tell him to change the I/O base to 280h and the IRQ to 16 from within Windows 95.

D. Tell him that his computer cannot use a network interface card and that he needs a new computer.

## QUESTIONS AND ANSWERS

| | |
|---|---|
| One function of a network interface card is to convert a_____ data stream on the data bus to a _____data stream on the network medium. | parallel, serial |
| Network interface cards communicate with each other using their _____address. | MAC or hardware |
| List four parameters that may have to be configured on the network adapter. | I/O base, IRQ, DMA, transceiver type |
| List three data bus types that use a 32-bit architecture. | MCA, EISA, PCI |
| The network adapter must also have the appropriate _____ to attach to the transmission media. | connector |
| A device responsible for the actual transmission and receipt of electrical signals on the network medium is a _____ , which can be either external or internal to the network adapter. | transceiver |
| An Ethernet NIC card using an external transceiver normally attaches it via the _____ port. | AUI or DIX |

6. You work in the network department of ACME Card Shufflers Inc. They have been experiencing growth over the last several months, and the amount of network clients has almost doubled, while the server farm has stayed the same as when it was installed last year. How can you improve server network performance?

   A. Replace the PCI NICs with ISA NICs.

   B. Replace the EISA NICs with ISA NICs.

   C. Replace the ISA NICs with PCI NICs.

   D. Replace the PCMCIA NICs with PCI NICs.

**e x a m**

**ⓦatch**

*For exam purposes, you should know the functions of a network interface card. You should understand what the hardware or MAC address is used for. You should also know about the data bus types and connector types. Know what a transceiver does. Understand the purpose of DMA, bus mastering, shared memory, and buffering as it relates to NIC performance and choosing the right adapter. You should also know the purpose of the various settings on the card, and there just might be a question on remote boot PROMs.*

**7.** Herb got a good deal on several IBM PS/2 computers, so he decided to set up a network for his office. The computers did not come with network cards, so he asks you if you know where he can get some. What do you tell him?

   A.  Tell him that the EISA network cards he needs are very hard to find.

   B.  Tell him that the MCA network cards he needs are very hard to find.

   C.  Tell him that the IBM PS/2 computers cannot be used on a network.

   D.  Tell him that the IBM PS/2 computers can use any 16-bit network card.

**8.** What type of network driver is needed for Windows NT servers?

   A.  NDIS

   B.  ODI

   C.  NDSI

   D.  OOI

## QUESTIONS AND ANSWERS

| | |
|---|---|
| List all the device settings that might cause a hardware conflict. | I/O base address, IRQ, DMA |
| Once a hardware conflict has been discovered, how can it be resolved? | Change settings on the adapter or on the conflicting device. |
| What can you do if all system IRQs have already been assigned to other devices? | Remove another device, don't install the adapter, and share IRQ. |

## QUESTIONS AND ANSWERS

| | |
|---|---|
| The network adapter must have some software installed that allows the system to communicate with and control the adapter. What is this software called? | Network card driver |
| The network adapter and its software driver exist at what layers of the OSI model? | Physical and Data Link |
| What problem are NDIS and ODI designed to overcome? | Use of more than one protocol at a time |
| The process of connecting the driver to the protocol, and the protocol to high-level network services is called _____ . | binding |
| By default, which network components are bound together under Windows NT? | All of them |

9. Gary put a multi-connector network interface card in his Windows 95 computer. He configured the network driver in Windows 95 for an I/O base address of 280h and an IRQ of 10. He used the software utility supplied with the NIC to configure it for an I/O base address of 280h and an IRQ of 10. Gary boots his system successfully but cannot connect to any network resource. What is causing Gary's problem?

A. He forgot to select the correct NDIS driver.

B. He forgot to select the correct transceiver type.

C. He forgot to select the correct ODI driver.

D. He forgot to select the correct packet type.

exam
ⓦatch

*For installing adapters, Microsoft will stress preparation, particularly checking the HCL. You should know how to install drivers under Windows 95 and NT. You should also know what plug and play does. Nothing can replace the understanding you gain through actually installing an adapter in a system. If possible, do this before taking the exam.*

**exam**

ⓦ**atch**

*Understanding the NDIS architecture, in terms of its purpose and design, will be very valuable for the certification candidate. Microsoft returns to this concept many times during the certification process. NDIS is covered in the NT Server, TCP/IP, and NT Server in the Enterprise exams as well as in the Networking Essentials exam.*

10. What types of network interface cards have on-board transceivers?

A. NICs that have RJ45 receptacles

B. NICs that have AUI connectors

C. NICs that have PCMCIA connectors

D. NICs that have BNC connectors

11. How do network interface cards communicate with each other?

A. IRQ address

B. MAC address

C. PCI address

D. DMA address

12. Thomas's computer uses COM1, COM2, LPT1, and LPT2 with their default I/O base and IRQ settings. His network interface card uses I/O base 280h and IRQ7. What device is conflicting with the network interface card?

A. COM1

B. COM2

C. LPT1

D. LPT2

**exam**

ⓦ**atch**

*The diagnostics part of the exam will focus on defining a hardware conflict and the method for resolving it. It may also ask which diagnostics are available to determine hardware assignments. It may be helpful for you to run the diagnostics on a system and view the information provided.*

**NETWORKING QUESTIONS**

## QUESTIONS AND ANSWERS

| | |
|---|---|
| What are some actions that need to be taken before attempting to install a network adapter? | Check compatibility, check for available system resources and inventory components. |
| In Windows NT, what is the resource provided by Microsoft that lists devices that will work with the operating system? | Hardware compatibility list |
| When configuring DIP switches, how can you determine which way they should be set? | Use the documentation for the adapter and/or check the switch for markings. |
| When configuring settings for a network driver, the I/O port address, IRQ, and DMA settings must match those set on the _____ . | network adapter |

# Network Connectivity Devices

1. ACME Waterworks wants to continue using their mainframe, but they need to replace 47 terminals that no longer work properly. They are concerned about the cost of replacing the terminals. They have contracted with your consulting company to develop a solution for them. How do you propose ACME Waterworks handle the situation?

   A. Recommend that they dispose of the mainframe and replace it with a Windows NT network.
   B. Recommend that they install a router and use their existing desktop computers.
   C. Recommend that they dispose of the mainframe and replace it with a Novell NetWare network.
   D. Recommend that they install a gateway and use their existing desktop computers.

## QUESTIONS AND ANSWERS

| Device | OSI Layer |
|--------|-----------|
| Repeater | Physical |
| Bridge | Data Link |
| Switch | Data Link |
| Router | Network |
| Brouter | Network |
| Gateway | Transport, Session, Presentation, and Application |

2. Current Situation: Token ring network with 218 nodes.
   Required Result: Add an additional 25 users to the network.
   Optional Desired Results: Keep the costs to a minimum; add network monitoring capability.
   Proposed Solution: Add a UTP hub for the additional users.
   Which results does the proposed solution produce?

   A. The proposed solution produces the required result and produces both of the optional desired results.

   B. The proposed solution produces the required result and produces only one of the optional desired results.

   C. The proposed solution produces the required result but does not produce any of the optional desired results.

   D. The proposed solution does not produce the required result.

3. Harmony Musical Notes Publishing has expanded their network to over 200 nodes in the last several months. The network consists of two segments: the Artist Relations department and Sales department on the second floor, and the Administration staff and Printing department on the first floor. The network uses the NetBEUI protocol and the users have recently started to complain that the network is extremely slow. What can you do to alleviate the slow network conditions?

    A. Install a gateway on the network.

    B. Install a bridge on the network.

    C. Install a repeater on the network.

    D. Install a router on the network.

**4.** Turntables R Us has been having a problem with their TCP/IP-based network for the last several weeks. It has slowed to a crawl, and the users are thinking about reverting to sneakernet to get their work done. You have segmented the network with a bridge, but it doesn't seem to be helping. After monitoring the network for several hours, you determine that it is suffering from broadcast storms. What is the best method you can employ to terminate the broadcast storms?

    A. Install a router.

    B. Install another bridge.

    C. Install a repeater.

    D. Install a gateway.

**5.** At what layer of the OSI model does a repeater function?

    A. Physical

    B. Data Link

    C. Network

    D. Transport

---

exam
Ⓦatch

*It is important to know the differences between Category 3 and Category 5 cabling, including the differences in speed capabilities and the number of pairs of wire in each cable.*

---

# QUESTIONS AND ANSWERS

| My network will have . . . | I should use . . . |
|---|---|
| 100 users split into four workgroups each 100 meters from the other. | UTP in a star topology with a thickwire backbone. |
| Five to ten users in one centrally located call center. | UTP in a star topology with a centrally located hub. |
| Five users with all workstations in a row along one wall. | Thinwire coax in a bus topology with the cable terminated with a 50Ω terminator. |
| 50 users in an office with no apparent workgroup configuration. | UTP in a star topology with a hub and patch panel in a wiring closet that is centrally located. |
| 20 graphic artists (who use the network to transfer files between each other intensively) in one workgroup and 20 salespeople in another workgroup 75 meters apart. | UTP in a star topology with a switch centrally located between the graphic artists and a hub centrally located between the salespeople with a UTP or thinwire backbone. |

6. Graphics Express, a small, new advertising company specializing in vivid graphics advertising campaigns, is having a problem with its 10Base2 network. The eight people who design the graphics are having a problem moving the large graphics files amongst themselves. They have hired you to fix the problem. How will you speed up the Graphics Express network?

   A. Add a switch to the existing network and give each person his or her own port from it.
   B. Replace the 10Base2 network with a 10Base5 network and add a switch for the graphics designers.
   C. Add a brouter to the existing network and give each person his or her own port from it.
   D. Replace the 10Base2 network with a 10BaseT network and add a switch for the graphics designers.

7. Margaritaville Mansion Distillers are discussing adding a network to their business. The planned network will connect the administrative offices and

the warehouse located 418 meters apart. They have been told that they should use unshielded twisted pair for the backbone. What do you suggest they use for the backbone?

A. You agree that unshielded twisted pair is the best choice for the backbone.

B. You suggest that they use thinwire for the backbone.

C. You suggest that they use thickwire for the backbone.

D. You suggest that they use fiber optic for the backbone.

8. How do bridges know which side of the bridge to send packets to?

A. From the bridge routing table built by the administrator

B. From the bridge routing chart it builds

C. From the bridge routing chart built by the administrator

D. From the bridge routing table it builds

9. Where does a gateway operate in regards to the OSI model?

A. Presentation

B. Transport

C. Application

D. Session

10. Minor Miracles Corporation has expanded rapidly over the last year. They have quadrupled in size, and it appears that they will double in size during the upcoming fiscal year. Traffic on their Ethernet network is becoming increasingly heavy. What do they need to do in order to have their network be usable and still keep up with the growth?

A. They need to switch to a mainframe network.

B. They need to implement routing on their network.

C. They need to replace the PCs with Amigas.

D. They need to change from 10BaseT to 10Base2.

11. SDC Racing needs to extend their 10Base2 network, as it has already reached 185 meters. What is the easiest way for them to accomplish this?

   A. Add a hub.
   B. Add a switch.
   C. Add a gateway.
   D. Add a repeater.

12. Shoe Town Cobblers want to be able to send data at 100 Mbps on their network. They have hired a contractor to install the Category 3 cable, as well as the 100 Mbps network interface cards and 100 Mbps switches. After the entire network has been installed they are very disappointed, because it does not work like they thought it would. What should they do now?

   A. Replace the switch with a router.
   B. Replace the computers with new computers.
   C. Replace the Category 3 cable with Category 5 cable.
   D. Replace the entire network with a token ring network.

# Wide Area Networks (WANs)

1. Guitar Analyzers Inc. is growing at an amazing rate. The main office is located in Los Angeles and they just opened a store in Seattle. The store in Seattle needs to transfer sales data back to the main office monthly. They have a leased line available for the transfer of the information. Guitar Analyzers have hired you to help them determine if their communications needs are being met in the best manner possible. What do you recommend to Guitar Analyzers?

   A. Yes, their needs are being met perfectly.
   B. No, their needs are not being met, they need to install an OC-12 line.
   C. No, their needs are not being met, they are not using what they are paying for.
   D. No, their needs are not being met, they need to install new XON/XOFF chassis.

---

---

2. String Rollers Inc. has a remote branch office located 30 miles from the main company. They communicate with it daily using an asynchronous modem connection. Recently the data that they have been receiving from the remote office is taking too long to arrive, and sometimes it is corrupt. String Rollers would like to switch to a different method of getting the data, but they would like it to be a one-time cost. How would you recommend String Rollers handle the situation?

   A. Replace the asynchronous modems with a fractional T-1 line.

   B. Replace the asynchronous modems with synchronous modems.

   C. Replace the asynchronous modems with isochronous modems.

   D. Replace the asynchronous modems with a DS-1 line.

3. What is the bandwidth size of an OC-12 circuit?

   A. 51.84 Mbps

   B. 155.52 Mbps

   C. 622.08 Mbps

   D. 1244.16 Mbps

4. You're home relaxing, surfing the web after a long day at work, when all of a sudden you remember that you forgot to bring home an important document to work on. The document is needed for a meeting at 7:00 the next morning. You cannot drive into work, because the building will be locked and you don't have a key. You would access your work machine using RAS since you left it powered on, but the RAS modem is broken. The next illustration shows your current situation. Is there another method you could use to access the document?

Company Network

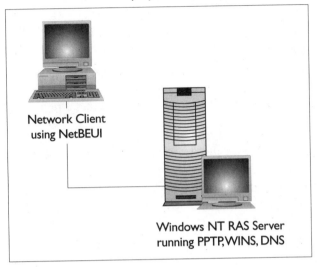

Network Client
using NetBEUI

Windows NT RAS Server
running PPTP, WINS, DNS

Home machine using
NetBEUI and TCP/IP

A. No, since the RAS modem is broken you cannot access your work machine.

B. Yes, you could access your machine using PPTP.

C. Yes, you could access your machine using WINS.

D. Yes, you could access your machine using DNS.

5. Current Situation: The company network has 218 Windows 95 clients, 43 Windows NT workstations, and six Windows NT servers.
Required Result: Set up RAS so the network can be accessed remotely.
Optional Desired Results: Provide support for ISDN communication; provide support for synchronous communication.
Proposed Solution: Configure Windows NT RAS as a SLIP server.
Which results does the proposed solution produce?

A. The proposed solution produces the required result and produces both of the optional desired results.

B. The proposed solution produces the required result and produces only one of the optional desired results.

C. The proposed solution produces the required result but does not produce any of the optional desired results.

D. The proposed solution does not produce the required result.

6. Cones Unlimited are having problems with their RAS. The RAS server is a 386 with 24MB of RAM using an external 28,800 modem. All the users say that they are consistently having problems transferring information, and they might as well not even use the RAS. The management of Cones Unlimited has asked you to help determine what is causing the problem. What do you suspect is the culprit?

A. The serial port in the RAS server uses an INS-8150 UART.

B. The serial port in the RAS server uses a 16450 UART.

C. The serial port in the RAS server uses an INS-8350 UART.

D. The serial port in the RAS server uses a 16550A UART.

7. Jangle Coins Limited has been using X.25 for the last several years but they have become frustrated with the slowness brought on by all of the error checking. They want to switch to another packet-switched protocol that does not conduct so much error checking. They ask you for a recommendation. What protocol do you recommend?

A. ATM

B. SMDS

C. SONET

D. Frame relay

**exam**
**Ⓦatch** *Be sure to know that Microsoft Windows NT Server installs RAS through the Network Icon in Control Panel for the exam.*

exam
ⓦatch   *For the exam, know that ATM uses cell switching which is marked by its small, fixed length cells.*

**8.** What type of modem flow control is faster and more reliable?

A. Software-based flow control

B. RTS/CTS flow control

C. XON/XOFF flow control

D. Hardware-based flow control

**9.** Hijinks Emporium needs a full-time 256 Kbps digital link to one of their suppliers. Hijinks Emporium has hired you to accomplish this for them. How can you establish the link?

A. Set them up with two channels of a T1 line.

B. Set them up with four channels of a T1 line.

C. Set them up with six channels of a T1 line.

D. Set them up with eight channels of a T1 line.

**10.** What layers of the OSI model does the Point to Point Protocol encompass?

A. Physical and Network layers

B. Physical and Data Link layers

C. Network and Transport layers

D. Data Link and Network layers

**11.** _____does not use circuits. Instead it uses connectionless datagram services.

**12.** Thrashing Drives Inc. has been using a dialup connection to transfer data to its three branches located throughout the city. As business has picked up, so has the amount of data that needs to be transferred. They would like to have an increase in speed but do not want to run any additional lines in any location. They have hired your firm to develop a solution for them. What solution do you provide?

A. They need to use ISDN.

B. They need to use ATM.

C. They need to use SONET.

D. They need to use RIP.

# Network Security and Reliability

1. Current Situation: The network consists of eight Windows 95 computers.
   Required Result: Provide protection for resources on the network.
   Optional Desired Results: Audit access to resources; provide multiple permissions to a resource based upon the user.
   Proposed Solution: Implement share-level security.
   Which results does the proposed solution produce?

   A. The proposed solution produces the required result and produces both of the optional desired results.

   B. The proposed solution produces the required result and produces only one of the optional desired results.

   C. The proposed solution produces the required result but does not produce any of the optional desired results.

   D. The proposed solution does not produce the required result.

2. Current Situation: The network in a telemarketing company contains the database that is the core of the business. The company conducts business 24 hours a day, seven days a week.
   Required Result: Provide the capability to swap a failed disk drive while the system is still running (downtime is not an option!).
   Optional Desired Results: Improve I/O performance; provide for future disk drive expansion.
   Proposed Solution: Implement RAID offered by Windows NT.
   Which results does the proposed solution produce?

A. The proposed solution produces the required result and produces both of the optional desired results.

B. The proposed solution produces the required result and produces only one of the optional desired results.

C. The proposed solution produces the required result but does not produce any of the optional desired results.

D. The proposed solution does not produce the required result.

3. Marissa calls the help desk and says that when she turns on her computer it comes up with a screen that has something about missing CMOS settings on it. You go to her cubicle and replace the CMOS battery. No sooner are you back in your office than she is calling you again saying that her screen has the same message on it. What else could cause this problem?

A. Her system has a virus.

B. Her system needs an updated BIOS.

C. Her system needs a new central processing unit.

D. Her system needs an UPS to maintain the settings.

4. Which of the following is a good example of a password?

A. charlie

B. Iltgb0f

C. meerschaum

D. L8SeR=$h0W

5. Bear Surprises Unlimited has been having problems with their Windows NT-based network. The network goes down a lot, especially when reports are due from the Finances department. BSU have hired you to evaluate the situation. You notice that the network server is located next to the water cooler in the reception area. Upon touring the facilities, you see that all the client computers have password-protected screen savers that prohibit you from randomly accessing the network. Running a series of diagnostics on the server proved inconclusive. What do you tell the management of BSU?

A. It must be an intermittent bug, so you need to monitor the server with special diagnostics.

B. The cable to the server does not use the correct connector.

C. The server is not in a secure location.

D. There is no problem with the network.

6. Gold Bullion Exporters are setting up a network that they will use to conduct all of their transactions. Several servers will house the databases of all the sales conducted around the world. They have UPSs on the systems, as well as several hardware RAID 5 subsystems. They think that they have taken care of all the reliability issues, but decide to consult with you just to make sure. What is your evaluation of the situation?

A. GBE has all the reliability issues taken care of.

B. GBE needs to add tape backups as a part of their reliability program.

C. GBE needs to use disk striping with parity as part of their reliability program.

D. GBE needs to use sector sparing as part of their reliability program.

## QUESTIONS AND ANSWERS

| | |
|---|---|
| My virus protection software detected a virus but cannot remove the virus. Is there anything I can do? | Once a virus is in memory, it is often difficult to remove. You need to boot to a "clean" floppy, emergency repair disk, or startup disk. Now there should be no virus in memory, although it still exists on your hard disk. Now launch your virus program to clean it. |
| If I don't have virus detection software, what can users notice that point to an existence of a virus? | Some symptoms that users may notice are:<br><br>My program suddenly takes longer to load.<br>The program size keeps changing.<br>My disk keeps running out of free space.<br>I keep getting 32-bit errors in Windows.<br>The drive light keeps flashing when I'm not doing anything.<br>I can't access the hard disk when booting from the A: drive.<br>I don't know where these files came from.<br>My files have strange names I don't recognize.<br>My computer doesn't remember CMOS settings and the battery is new. |

7. What is the purpose of the parity stripe block on a RAID 5 set?

   A. It is used to notify the operating system that RAID 5 is active.

   B. It is used to modify the File Allocation Table.

   C. It is used to reconstruct data for a failed physical disk.

   D. It is used to separate the boot and system partitions.

8. Silver Bullion Importers has hired contractors to do work in their building. The contractors will be issued accounts on the Windows NT network for the period of the contract. Some of the management are concerned that the contractors may copy confidential data and pass it to their competitors. They have asked you take steps to ensure that the contractors cannot do that. Besides using the Windows NT Server Remoteboot service, what else will you do?

   A. Remove the floppy drive from the systems the contractors are allowed to log on to.

   B. Remove the hard disk from the systems the contractors are allowed to log on to.

   C. Remove the L2 cache from the systems the contractors are allowed to log on to.

   D. Remove the floating point unit from the systems the contractors are allowed to log onto.

9. You are on weekend standby for Paper Pushers, Inc., and your beeper goes off. You call the office, and Greg states that he rebooted one of the Windows NT servers because it was acting "flaky". After you arrive at work you determine that the RAID 5 set cannot be accessed. Where do you begin troubleshooting the problem?

   A. Check to see if NTLDR is corrupt.

   B. Check to see if BOOT.INI is present.

   C. Check to see if FTDISK.SYS is corrupt.

   D. Check to see if WINNT.EXE is present.

10. What type of RAID is in use in the next illustration?

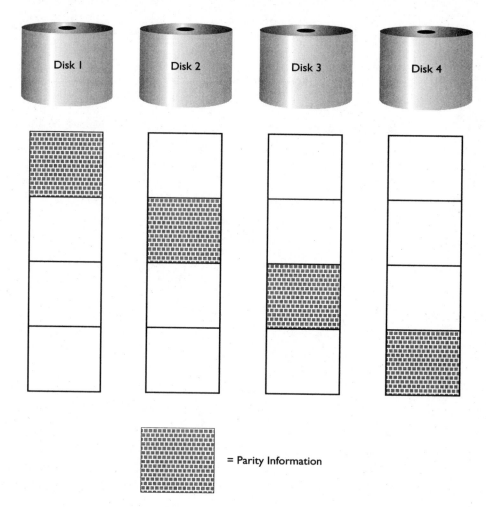

= Parity Information

A. RAID 5
B. RAID 3
C. RAID 1
D. RAID 0

*Access permissions are stressed in the Windows 95 and Windows NT exams. Know which rights are required to do certain tasks.*

## QUESTIONS AND ANSWERS

| | |
|---|---|
| What is the difference between a volume set and a mirror set or stripe set with parity? | A volume set is simply a collection of free space from one or many physical disks, combined in a single logical disk with no fault tolerance. Stripe set with parity or a mirror set provides the ability to recover and restore lost data in case of system or hardware failure. Most fault-tolerant strategies are classified using the RAID system, including disk striping with parity (RAID Level 5) and disk mirroring (RAID Level 1). |
| What is the best way to implement fault tolerance on your computer to allow the maximum amount of storage space using three physical disks? | Disk striping with parity protects the system against data loss in the event that a single disk fails. It can support more than three hard disks. Disk mirroring can only support two hard disks. RAID Level 0 (disk striping without parity) does not provide any fault tolerance because there is no data redundancy. |
| You have four physical disks, each with 200MB free space. You want to create a stripe set with parity. What is the maximum amount of data that can be stored on the stripe set with parity? | 600MB. For striping with parity, there is a parity block for each stripe of data, and parity stripes are distributed across all disks. Therefore, for a stripe set with parity consisting of three disks, one-third of total disk capacity is used for storing parity information. Similarly, for a stripe set with parity consisting of four disks, one-fourth of total disk capacity is used for storing parity information. |

**NETWORKING QUESTIONS**

11. The new database server just arrived for you to configure before placing it into a production environment. You want to configure it for better I/O performance, so you decide to create a stripe set with parity on it. The server has five disk drives and each drive has 4GB of free space. What is the maximum amount of data that can be stored on the stripe set with parity?

    A. 4GB

    B. 12GB

    C. 16GB

    D. 20GB

e x a m
ⓦ a t c h *Know the advantages and disadvantages (including cost feasibility) of using a stripe set, mirror set, and stripe set with parity. There are specific reasons why you would pick one RAID level over another.*

**12.** What elements should be a part of the network security plan for Gophers Delivery Service?

A. C2 security

B. Physical security

C. Verbal security policy

D. User training

# Network Monitoring and Management

**1.** Cup O' Tea Corporation has offices located in 17 metropolitan cities. Each office is connected to the company network. You are the head of the MIS department, and you have stated that passwords must be changed every 60 days. What part of proactive planning are you fulfilling?

A. Monitoring policies

B. Backup strategy

C. User account policies

D. Systems analysis policies

**2.** You have recently been hired by the Day Late Bakeries to work in the network department. You work with one other individual who was hired one day prior to you. Things go smoothly for the first three days, and then the network goes down. The boss is screaming at you to "fix the thing NOW!" It takes you several hours to track down the problem, because you had to trace cables from the first floor up to the third floor. What could have helped you in this situation?

A. Detailed maps of the bakery

B. Event Viewer logfiles

C. Detailed network maps

D. Performance Monitor

3. You just installed a brand-new network server at your company, and you would like to establish a baseline for it. What tool can you use to establish the baseline?

A. Server Manager

B. Network Monitor

C. Disk Administrator

D. Performance Monitor

4. Management of Fake Wood Manufacturing has determined that all the client computers on the network need to have the latest version of an application. The application has changed significantly with the latest release, but you go ahead and roll it out to all of the client computers in the entire organization, using an automated installation procedure. The next day, all of the BrandX computers on the network will not boot properly. How should you have handled this situation?

A. You should have told the users about the server modification first.

B. You should have performed the upgrade on a test group of clients first.

C. You should have refused to install the upgrade on the servers.

D. You should have modified the code with a hex editor.

5. Your server has been acting very sluggish today. You decide to run the Performance Monitor to see if it can help you to isolate the sluggishness. What can be determined from the chart in the next illustration?

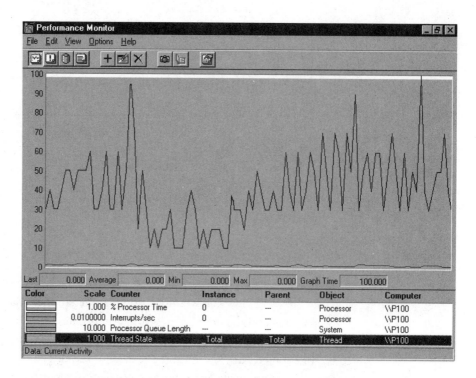

A.  The server is working fine, maybe the network hub has a problem.

B.  An application is using all of the physical memory in the server.

C.  The server needs faster hard disk drives.

D.  An application is using all of the CPU.

**6.** How are Performance Monitor log files saved to disk?

A.  As ASCII files

B.  As comma delimited text

C.  As binary files

D.  As octal text

exam
ⓦatch    *Remember that to audit a file you need to have auditing enabled in the User Manager and also on the file itself.*

7. Jimmy was prompted to change his password when he logged onto the network. He tried to change it, but the system would not let him. He contacts you and tells you that the network is broken. You look at the Account Policies as shown in the next illustration. What do you think is stopping him from changing his password?

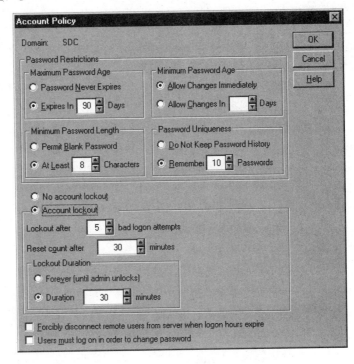

A. The new password is longer than eight characters.
B. The new password is one that Jimmy has used before.
C. The new password is shorter than 14 characters.
D. The new password is not alphanumeric.

**e x a m**
**ⓌⒶⓣⒸⒽ**

*Remember the difference between the version of Network Monitor that comes with Windows NT 4.0 and the version that comes with SMS.*

## QUESTIONS AND ANSWERS

| | |
|---|---|
| The minimum password length will be eight characters. | User account policies |
| All network servers will be locked in a room with limited access. | Security strategy |
| All weekly and monthly media will be stored off site. | Backup strategy |
| Network users will be admonished if they are caught running a sniffer program from their workstation. | Monitoring and systems analysis policies |

8. Management wants to place several of your corporate databases on the Internet to allow customers to search through them. What part of your administrative plan must address this issue?

   A. User Account Policies
   B. Security strategies
   C. Backup strategies
   D. Systems analysis policies

9. What tool would you use to help resolve a bottleneck on your system?

   A. Network Monitor
   B. Performance Monitor
   C. Server Manager
   D. Disk Administrator

10. What is the default size of the three logs that are displayed by the Windows NT Event Viewer?

   A. 512KB
   B. 1024KB
   C. 512MB
   D. 1024MB

**11.** Martha was under pressure to get a graphics presentation to her boss. She completed it and sent it to him via e-mail, as requested. Unfortunately, as the boss was trying to show the presentation to a highly valued client, he could not get the file to open. How could this incident have been avoided?

A. If the software was standardized throughout the company.

B. If Martha had not sent the file through e-mail.

C. If the boss had printed out the presentation for the client.

D. If the PC hardware was standardized throughout the company.

**12.** What is the first action to perform when monitoring your network?

A. Resolve bottlenecks.

B. Identify communities.

C. Determine the source address.

D. Establish a baseline.

exam
ⓦatch

*A program might not work correctly when you use Run Program on Alert because Performance Monitor passes the Alert condition as a parameter to the program. If it does not work correctly, create a batch file to run the program and call the batch file from Performance Monitor.*

# Network Troubleshooting

**1.** You have been hired to design and install a network for ACME Tree Farmers. After doing a site survey you have determined their needs and ordered all the equipment necessary for the completion of the job. To complete the job you will need to run over 12,000 feet of Category 5 cable. What tool should you use to verify the integrity of the cables prior to installation?

A. Digital volt meter

B. Time domain reflectometer

C. Cable tester

D. Oscilloscope

2. You are the network administrator for ACME Building Block Renovators. Your network consists of 28 Windows 95 computers and one Windows NT server using 10Base2. 14 client computers are on the first floor and 14 client computers are on the second floor. The server is located on the first floor in your office. Your phone is ringing off the hook as you arrive at work. It seems that no one can log onto the network. You log on the server just fine, so it must be working properly. How can you begin troubleshooting the problem?

A. Cycle the power on the hub to reset the hub.

B. Isolate the network by dividing it up.

C. Check the integrity of the FDDI NIC in the server.

D. Verify that the user accounts are locked out.

## QUESTIONS AND ANSWERS

| | |
|---|---|
| None of the workstations on the network are able to communicate with each other. They use a thinwire coax Ethernet to connect to each other. | A bad cable or terminator. To isolate the problem, divide the cable in half and terminate each end. Determine which half is working. Continue this process until you have found the culprit. |
| Workstations on a twisted-pair network cannot communicate with each other. | A hub that is locked up. Reset the hub by turning the power on and off. |
| A workstation was just moved to a new location, and is no longer able to communicate on the network. There is nothing wrong with the workstation's configuration. | Cables have been damaged in the move. Replace each cable one at a time to find the problematic cable. |

**3.** ACME Media Format Specialists has a complicated network consisting of seven routers, 70 switches, 214 hubs, and 1,700 client computers spread throughout 22 buildings. Lately, network performance has been sluggish. What should you do to start resolving the network performance problem?

A. Use a time domain reflectometer to view network performance.

B. Use an oscilloscope to view network traffic.

C. Use a spectrum analyzer to view network performance.

D. Use a network monitor to view network traffic.

**4.** What type of tool uses the screen shown in the next illustration?

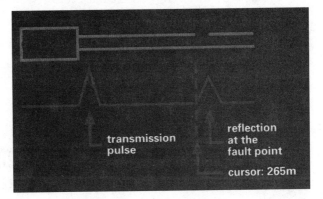

A. DVM

B. TDR

C. Protocol analyzer

D. Network monitor

**5.** ACME Interior Welders have decided to upgrade one of the servers on their network from 486DX2/66 system to DEC Alpha 500Mhz system. They are not sure how much of a performance gain it will be for their network, so they want to gather performance data on the DEC Alpha 500Mhz system to make sure that it will be sufficient for their needs. What tool can they use to gather the data?

A. Digital volt meter

B. Oscilloscope

C. Protocol analyzer

D. Signal generator

6. Your network resides on the second floor of a two-story building built in the 1950s. Management has hired contractors to renovate the building, starting with the second floor. The construction project will last several months and includes plumbing work as well as electrical work. What can you do to help ensure that the hubs and servers continue to work while the construction work is in progress?

   A. Use UPSs on the hubs and servers.
   B. Use MIBs on the hubs and servers.
   C. Use RAID on the hubs and servers.
   D. Use TDRs on the hubs and servers.

7. LED Blinkers Inc. has an extensive 10BaseT network located throughout their building. All hubs connect back to the switch located in the server room. Several users in room 24 have complained that they cannot log onto the network. Researching the network diagrams, you see that all the users connect to the network using the same hub. You have cycled power on the hub but it did not make a difference. No one else on the network is having any problem. What do you do next?

   A. Use a TDR to see if there is a short in the cable connecting the hub to the switch.
   B. Use a signal generator to see if there is an open in the cable connecting the hub to the switch.
   C. Use a TDR to see if there is an open in the cable connecting the hub to the switch.
   D. Use a signal generator to see if there is a short in the cable connecting the hub to the switch.

8. What tool do you use to detect whether an exposed part of a cable is touching another conductive surface?

A. Signal generator

B. TDR

C. DVM

D. Protocol analyzer

9. You have received a new server that you are going to use as a database server on your network. The server came with a 10Mbit network interface card, which you replaced because you want the server to have a 100Mbit network interface card, since it will be heavily utilized. You cannot get the 100Mbit card you purchased to work properly in the server. What can you do?

A. Replace the network cable from the switch to the router.

B. Change the media from 10BaseT to 10Base2.

C. Use a TDR to find the cable break.

D. Check the web site of the NIC card manufacturer.

10. Besides TechNet and manufacturers' web sites, what other support resource is available to help you when you have a problem with your Windows NT network?

A. Trade publications

B. Protocol analyzer

C. Resource kits

D. Network monitor

11. ACME Stocking Brokers has an extensive network located throughout their 72-building campus. Databases for the entire worldwide organization are operated from servers located at the campus. Management is very concerned that network problems be detected before any portion of the network has to be shut down, because of the money that would be lost during the downtime. What tool can you use to detect problems without having to shut any part of the network down?

A. Time domain reflectometer

B. Digital volt meter

C. Frequency counter

D. Protocol analyzer

**12.** What should you always do prior to performing an upgrade on your system?

  A. Run the protocol analyzer.
  B. Back up the entire system.
  C. Segment the affected area.
  D. Restart the system.

# Internet Technologies

**1.** General Jalopy Inc. has hired you to put their network on the Internet. The vice president is insistent upon using the IPX/SPX protocol, and no other. His reasoning is that IPX/SPX is small and fast and he doesn't want any other protocol slowing their network down. You try to convince him that they can't use IPX/SPX, but he does not budge on his position. What do you use to prove to him that they need to use another protocol to put their network on the Internet?

  A. DNS
  B. RFCs
  C. IRC
  D. FQDN

**2.** You have several UNIX client computers that do not use any type of X Window system. You would like to give the users of those clients access to the World Wide Web so that they can research data as needed. How can you do that?

  A. Install Netscape Navigator.
  B. Install Mosaic.
  C. Install Midas.
  D. Install Lynx.

**3.** Office Integrators Inc. has a direct connection to the Internet so that the 2,462 employees can search the World Wide Web looking for companies that need temp workers. Lately, it seems as though several hundred of the users are using the World Wide Web for non-job-related purposes. The CEO is mad because he pays the people to do work, not "surf". He has demanded that you revoke Internet access from the several hundred users immediately! After he calms down, you explain that if you revoke their Internet access they definitely won't be able to do their job. The CEO gets frustrated and tells you to fix the problem somehow and to get it done ASAP! What do you do?

A. Implement an IRC server.

B. Implement a proxy server.

C. Implement a FTP server.

D. Implement a telnet server.

**4.** What type of Internet service is in use with the software pictured in the next illustration?

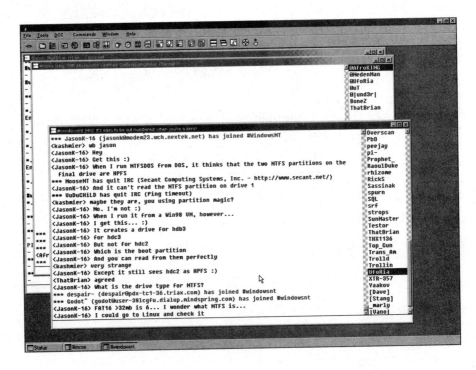

    A. FTP

    B. Telnet

    C. IRC

    D. Archie

**5.** What protocol is used for accessing web pages?

    A. HTML

    B. FTP

    C. HTTP

    D. STP

**6.** Max needs to retrieve a file from a site on the Internet. The only tool available on his computer is a web browser. Which of the following uniform resource locators allows him to retrieve the file name BOOKS.DOC?

    A. NEWS://NEWS.SYNGRESS.COM/BOOKS.DOC

    B. HTML://WWW.SYNGRESS.COM/BOOKS.DOC

    C. ARCHIE://ARCHIE.SYNGRESS.COM/BOOKS.DOC

    D. FTP://FTP.SYNGRESS.COM/BOOKS.DOC

**7.** David is in the military and stationed in Naples, Italy. He calls his family every week and tells them everything that happened during the week. The phone bills are starting to put a financial crunch on David, but he does not want to stop communicating with his family. What alternatives are available to David?

    A. Electronic mail

    B. Browsers

    C. IRC

    D. Gopher

**8.** Steven loves to work with his widgeteer. It is one of his favorite hobbies, but no one else in his community has one, so it is hard for him to find information for it. Where could Steven find information on his widgeteer, and possibly find others who have widgeteering for their hobby?

   A. Telnet

   B. Browsers

   C. Newsgroups

   D. Internet Relay Chat

**9.** Debra has her home computer set up to access the World Wide Web using Internet Explorer 4.0. She is concerned about some of the material available on the web that could be accessed by her young child. She has heard of RSAC and would like to use their ratings as a starting point for blocking some of this material. How can Debra implement RSAC ratings in IE4?

   A. From the Security tab of Internet Options

   B. From the Advanced tab of Internet Options

   C. From the Content tab of Internet Options

   D. From the General tab of Internet Options

**10.** _____ means that each packet entering and leaving the network through the firewall is analyzed.

**11.** Raymond is on a business trip when he discovers that he does not have the document he needs for a briefing he is giving to the client's Board of Directors first thing the next morning. The document is located in his home directory on the company server. No one else has access to his home directory, and even if they did, it is too late to get it e-mailed because it is 1:00 A.M. How can Raymond get access to his much needed document?

   A. He can't

   B. Squirrel

   C. Archie

   D. Telnet

**12.** What type of IP address changes every time you make a dialup connection to your ISP?

A. Static

B. Dynamic

C. Stationary

D. Active

**13.** What type of gateway is implemented when a TCP or UDP connection is established?

A. Application

B. Circuit-level

C. Performance

D. Domain-level

**14.** What do you need to set up a World Wide Web server on your Windows NT server?

A. Permanent Internet connection

B. Web server software

C. Fault tolerance

D. Static IP address

MICROSOFT CERTIFIED SYSTEMS ENGINEER

# Networking Essentials Answers

*Q & A*

# T

he answers, like the questions, are divided up by the applicable chapter. A brief explanation follows the correct answer.

# Answers: Networking Basics

1. **C.** The bus topology is best for this situation, as it is simple to install and maintain. Since the office space is rented for a limited time, and the only purpose of the network connectivity is to share a printer, there is no need to use any other topology for this situation.

2. **A.** The star topology uses more cable than the bus topology. This is because each computer must have its own connection back to the hub. For example, if there are five computers in an office that is located 50 feet away from the hub, then 250 feet of cable is necessary to hook up those five computers. In a bus topology it is possible that those same five computers could be hooked together with less than 25 feet of cable.

3. **D.** If the amount of broadcasts on a network exceeds the capacity of the network bandwidth, a broadcast storm will result. A broadcast storm can shut down a network. Routers do not pass broadcasts, so they can be used to stop broadcast storms.

4. **C.** A LAN is a network that has the computers geographically close to each other. Even though the office building has 17 stories, the computers are physically hooked into the same network and located geographically close enough to each other for it to be considered a LAN.

5. **B.** Data stays on the application server, whereas data transfers to the client from the file server. The application server does transfer results of an action but not the actual data.

**6.** **A, C.** Client/server networks are best described as networks where tasks are divided between the back end (server) and front end (client) and the back end answers the requests from the front end.

**7.** **A.** A server-based network is the best type of network to implement when security is a concern. Security needs to be a concern in this situation, since there is confidential customer information on the company's computers.

**8.** **D.** Peer-to-peer networks are best described as networks that allow each user the ability to administer his or her own resources. They can decide what files or directories they will share, and with whom they will share them. A peer-to-peer network is best when there are fewer than ten users, and security is not a major concern.

**9.** **A.** An example of client/server networking is when an application on a workstation accesses a database on a remote computer. In a client/server network the query is sent from the workstation application (front end) and processed by the remote computer that stores the database (back end).

**10.** **C.** The topology shown in the illustration is the star ring topology. Each computer hooks into a smaller hub, which in turn hooks into the single main hub.

**11.** **B.** Another name for a peer-to-peer network is workgroup. This is because the design is applicable to a network of no more than ten computers.

**12.** **D.** If the entire network has failed in a star ring topology, then the main hub has failed. If one of the office hubs had failed, then only that office would be down.

**13. D.** To alleviate network traffic, replace the hubs used in your star network with switched hubs. This will reduce the traffic by allowing two ports to communicate between themselves while also allowing the other ports to communicate if needed. If a switched hub is not used, all the other ports have to wait until the original two ports are finished communicating.

**14. B, C.** Frame Relay and X.25 are both options that are available from third-party providers of Public Data Networks.

# Answers: Network Models

**1. C.** 10Base2 can be used since the computers are located less than 185 meters from the wiring closet. However, 10BaseT can be used as well, since the computers are less than 100 meters away. Also, 10BaseT is cheaper to install and maintain, since 10Base2 cable is more expensive and harder to work with. In order to meet the required and optional results you should use 10BaseT cable.

**2. D.** The required result is not met because 10BaseT cable allows a maximum distance of 100 meters, and the computer is located 210 meters away from the network. In order to add the computer to the network you will need to look into a hardware solution.

**3. router.** The router operates at the network layer, which is also known as layer 3. The network layer is concerned with network addressing for larger networks that consist of many physical networks, often with multiple paths between them.

**4. D.** The proposed solution does not meet the required result because a repeater cannot be used to mix different frame types such as those used by 802.3 (which is Ethernet) and 802.5 (which is token ring). It is possible to use a router in this situation to join the networks.

**5. B.** Adding routers to your network meets the required result of opening up multiple paths for data flow and it also meets the optional result of allowing for future growth. Adding a router does not help with monitoring the data link layer, since the router works at the network layer.

**6. Connection-oriented.** Connection-oriented communication ensures reliable delivery of data from the sender to the receiver, without intervention required by the sender or receiver. Error correction and flow control are provided at various points from the source to the destination. Most network protocols have connection-oriented services. The TCP/IP protocol provides this capability with the transmission control protocol (TCP). In the IPX/SPX protocol, the sequenced packet exchange (SPX) protocol provides connection-oriented services.

**7. D.** Using 10BaseT cable will not produce the required results. The existing network uses the bus topology so you need to either use 10Base2 or 10Base5 cable to hook the five computers into the network. 10Base2 and 10Base5 are both used for the bus topology. Normally 10Base5 is used for the backbone and 10Base2 is used for the branch segments.

**8. B.** The 802.4 standard should not be adopted for the network, because it was designed for automating machinery. The 802.4 standard defines a physical bus topology that uses tokens for media access control. For this network the 802.3 standard would work fine. 802.3 is the standard for Ethernet networks in use today.

**9. C.** Replacing the repeaters with routers will eliminate the broadcast storms. Repeaters do not look at the frames they are forwarding, and pass along even damaged frames. This can be especially problematic if one segment malfunctions and begins a broadcast storm. All broadcasts are forwarded faithfully by the repeater. However, a router, by nature, does not forward broadcasts, so broadcast storms are eliminated.

NETWORKING
ANSWERS

**10. A.** A virtual circuit establishes formal communication between two computers on an internetwork using a well-defined path. The path the data takes while being exchanged between the two computers may vary, but the computers do not know this. They do not need to. Since the virtual circuit uses connection-oriented communication, all the points that make up the circuit ensure that the data gets through unharmed, even if those points change while the virtual circuit is in place.

**11. C, D.** The two sublayers of the Data Link layer are the Media Access Control sublayer and the Logical Link Control sublayer. The Media Access Control sublayer uses Carrier Sense Multiple Access with Collision Detection (CSMA/CD) for access to the physical medium. CSMA/CD keeps devices on the network from interfering with one another when trying to transmit. The Logical Link Control sublayer allows Network layer protocols to be designed separately from the low-level Physical layer and MAC sublayer protocols. The LLC adds header information that identifies the upper-layer protocols sending the frame.

**12. D.** The Network layer of the OSI model uses logical network addresses to route packets. As you know, routers operate on the Network layer.

# Answers: Protocols and Packets

**1. D.** The proposed solution of installing the NetBEUI protocol on all 180 computers does not meet the required result. NetBEUI is not a routable protocol, so communication would not occur with corporate headquarters. In order to communicate across the routers you must use a routable protocol, such as TCP/IP.

**2. C.** In order for each client machine to directly access the Internet you need to install the TCP/IP protocol. TCP/IP is the protocol that the Internet is built upon. TCP/IP, a routable protocol, is very robust and is commonly associated with UNIX systems.

**3. B.** The client machines will only be able to access the Windows NT servers but they will not be able to access the UNIX servers. This is because the UNIX servers do not use the NetBEUI protocol. In order for the client machines to be able to access the UNIX servers you will need to install the TCP/IP protocol.

**4. C.** You recommend that they use FTP since it is a connection-oriented protocol that checks that each packet successfully reaches its destination. You would not recommend TFTP since it does not verify that the packets of data have arrived at the destination.

**5. IPX/SPX.** IPX/SPX is the fastest routable protocol suite available today. It was developed by Novell for use in their NetWare operating system. NWLink is the Microsoft implementation of the IPX/SPX protocol.

**6. C, D.** TCP/IP and IPX/SPX are routable protocols. DLC and NetBEUI are not routable protocols. A routable protocol is one that can transfer packets of data across a router. Nonroutable protocols are normally faster than routable protocols because they have less overhead.

**7. D.** DLC is not a routable protocol so it will not work for the entire corporation. DLC is normally used to connect either to mainframes or printers. The DLC protocol works with either Ethernet or token-ring networks.

**8. D.** ATM uses the Demand Priority access method. Demand Priority is an access method primarily used with multimedia in a voice grade network. A central device controls which device can transmit on the network, ideally optimizing transmission on the network while eliminating collisions.

**9. C.** NetBEUI operates at the Transport layer of the OSI model. The Transport layer ensures that messages are delivered error-free, in sequence, and with no losses or duplication.

**10. D.** Telnet would allow the user to connect to the UNIX server just as if he were sitting in front of it. Telnet is useful for command-line-driven remote logons, since it is unable to use any form of graphics. Anything that is typed within a Telnet session is not secure in any form.

**11. C.** SMTP (Simple Mail Transport Protocol) is the protocol that defines the structure of Internet mail messages. SMTP uses a well-defined syntax for transferring messages. An SMTP session includes initializing the SMTP connection, sending the destination e-mail address, sending the sources e-mail address, sending the subject, and sending the body of the e-mail message.

**12. B.** CSMA/CD is defined by the IEEE 802.3 standard. The IEEE 802 standards define the way network adapter cards access and transfer data over physical media.

# Answers: Data Link Protocols

**1. D.** The proposed solution does not produce the required result because a single segment of thinnet can support a maximum of 30 computers. In order to network the 38 computers located on the second floor, you would need to use multiple segments of thinnet.

**2. D.** It is impossible for anyone to have experience with 802.5 Ethernet networks, since 802.5 defines token ring networks. The 802.5 standard was actually modeled after the IBM Token Ring network, which had been in use for many years before the standard was even developed. Ethernet networks are defined by 802.3.

**3. A.** Installing an FDDI topology produces the required result of connecting all 14 LANs on the campus. Both optional results are also produced, as FDDI operates at the high speed of 100 Mbps, and it has fault tolerance, since it uses dual counter rotating rings.

4. **C.** The thicknet network exceeds the 5-4-3 rule because it has six segments. The 5-4-3 rule states that there can be only five segments, separated by four repeaters, and only three of the five segments can be populated with computers.

5. **D.** The distance from the research and development building to the administration building exceeds the maximum cable length for FDDI. The distance between the buildings is 3000 meters, while FDDI cannot exceed 2000 meters.

6. **A.** The 16 Mbps token ring network will not function if one of the network interface cards is set to operate at 4 Mbps. This is because every device on the network must be configured to operate at one speed. If a network card is configured to run on a 16 Mbps network, but the network is deemed to be 4 Mbps, the network card reverts to the network speed of 4 Mbps. However, a 4 Mbps card can not revert to 16 Mbps if placed on a higher-speed network.

7. **C.** Copper Distributed Data Interface (CDDI) meets the needs for the network. It operates at 100 Mbps and is fault tolerant. Even though Fast Ethernet operates at 100 Mbps, it does not have any fault tolerant features so it would not meet the requirements for this network.

8. **C.** Installing 100BaseFX produces the required result by upgrading the network to 100 Mbps. However, it does not produce either of the optional results. Minimal costs are not obtained, because the Category 5 cable will need to be replaced with fiber optic cable, and there will have to be a complete replacement of all the network interface cards. Minimal installation time is not obtained, because all the cable will need to be reinstalled. Since Category 5 cable was already in place, using 100BaseTX would have been a better choice as the same cable could have been used.

9. **A.** 10Base2 networks use thin coaxial cable and have a maximum distance of 185 meters. Longer distances are possible if repeaters are used.

**10. B.** The most common Ethernet implementation used today is twisted pair (10BaseT). Studies show 90 percent of networks being installed today are using Category 5 twisted pair cable in a star topology. These networks use the star topology, but still behave as a standard Ethernet bus configuration. Hubs are used to connect the workstations and network devices to the network backbone. These hubs can act as repeaters to extend the 100-meter (328 feet) maximum distance for the workstations.

**11. B.** Each segment of a 10Base5 network can have a maximum of 100 nodes. 10Base2 segments can have 30 nodes and each ring of an FDDI can have 1000 nodes. 10BaseT can have a maximum of 1024 nodes.

**12. Token Ring.** Token ring networks use multistation access units (MSAUs). The physical star of a token ring network is made up of stations connected to their own port on an MSAU, much like a concentrator or hub is used with 10BaseT in the star topology.

# Answers: Network Operating Systems

**1. C.** Windows NT Server can be installed without using the floppies by using the /B switch with WINNT.EXE. The install routine will copy the files from the CD-ROM into a temporary directory and install from there.

**2. D.** LAN Manager 2.2c for MS-DOS clients cannot use the IPX/SPX protocol so there is no way for them to access the Novell NetWare network. If it is really critical that the users on those machines access data from the network, the systems they use need to be updated to an operating system that can use the IPX/SPX protocol.

**3. A.** Add them to a group and then give that group access to the directory. While it is entirely possible to grant each user access to the directory, it can become cumbersome when dealing with many users. If the team adds 20 people and then they need access to another resource in the future, it is much easier to add the group than to add 23 names to the resource.

**4. C.** The IP addresses are in the wrong location. The IP addresses must start in column 1 of the HOSTS file so that it can function correctly. It does not matter how many spaces are between the IP addresses and the names, as long as there is at least one space.

**5. C.** Remove him from the Sales group. The Sales group has No Access permissions to the directory that he is trying to gain access to, and No Access takes priority over other permissions. Since he is a member of the Sales group he cannot access the directory, even though he is a member of the Marketing group that has Full Control of the directory. Once he is removed from the Sales group he will be granted Full Control access based upon his membership in the Marketing group.

**6. C.** Add Raymond to the Account Operators group. Adding him to the Account Operators group allows him the permissions necessary to create the new user accounts but does not give him Administrator access.

**7. B.** Since her application is having problems communicating with the printing device, you need to reinstall the printer driver. Print drivers are the software utilities that allow an application to communicate with printing devices.

**8. A, C.** The Guests group should be used for one-time or temporary access to resources. A user account should be set up for people who need regular access to the resources.

**9. D.** The DLC protocol is not installed on the print server, so it cannot communicate with the Hewlett-Packard JetDirect card. The JetDirect card does not have to use DLC; it can also be configured to use the IPX/SPX or TCP/IP protocols.

**10. C.** The Administrator account cannot be deleted or disabled, but it can be renamed. Renaming the account makes it more difficult for someone to hack into your network. The would-be hacker is missing 50 percent of the information he needs to break in.

11. **B.** In Windows NT, applications controlled internally by the operating system are called services, in NetWare, they are referred to as NetWare loadable modules, and in UNIX, they are referred to as daemons. They all perform the same function, but just have different names.

12. **D.** \\demo1\*sharename* is the proper syntax for the Universal Naming Convention. The UNC name consists of the computer name, in this case demo1, and then the share name. The share name is created on the computer sharing the resources. The computer name is preceded by two backslashes, and the share name is preceded by one slash.

# Answers: Network Applications

1. **B.** Install a multi-vendor gateway. Multi-vendor gateways provide a translation method from one type of mailbox server to another type of mail client. The gateway allows clients such as Microsoft Outlook to read data from a variety of hosts.

2. **D.** Since there are so many users who need access to the application, it would be best to install it on your application server. It has low overhead, so it will not cause much stress on your application server. Licensing is not a concern, since you have more licenses than the amount of users needing access. While it is possible to install it on each system that needs it, it would be a huge waste of manpower, since you only need to install it once for everyone to be able to utilize it.

3. **C.** Internet Message Access Protocol (IMAP) in which the mail is kept in the mailbox on the server at all times. There is only one copy of each message stored on the server. The client only reads the messages from the server, and never stores them locally.

**4.** **B.** A WEB-based groupware product would be best in this situation because of the variety of operating systems in use. These products allow any platform to access it so long as they are able to use a Web browser. The biggest challenge that most groupware products face is that they are not extraordinarily multi-platform or mixed-environment-capable.

**5.** **C.** The computers shown in the illustration are using a centralized application. Centralized applications run entirely on the server. The client only displays the output of processing. Centralized applications are not as efficient as client/server applications.

**6.** **B, D.** Remote Procedure Calls (RPC) and Windows sockets are two examples of interprocess communications (IPCs). Other IPCs are OS/2 named pipes, Windows DDE, Server Message Blocks (SMB), and UNIX pipes.

**7.** **A.** You should use Post Office Protocol 3 on your mail server, because it is the most common standard for mail and is supported on nearly every platform available today. By using the Post Office Protocol 3 you can be assured that, no matter which notebook computer the user takes on his business trip, he will be able to access his mailbox.

**8.** **B.** Mailslots are exclusive to Microsoft products. Mailslots can be used for one-to-one or one-to-many communication. When a message is sent to a mailslot, the sending application specifies in the mailslot message structure whether the message is to be sent using first-class or second-class delivery. First-class delivery is a session-oriented, guaranteed data transfer for one-to-one or one-to-many communication. Second-class delivery is a datagram-based, unguaranteed data transfer for one-to-one and many-to-one communication. Windows 95 and Windows NT implement only second-class mailslots.

**9. B.** Windows NT uses named pipes for connection-oriented communication. Named pipes provide an easy-to-access conduit for a one-to-one, reliable data transfer between two processes. Another common use for named pipes is in client-server applications based on SQL.

**10. C.** Add the mapping for the word processing application to a logon script that the users run each time they log on. Doing this ensures that the users will be able to find the word processing application after logging on. If for some reason a user calls saying that he can't find the word processing application, then have him log off the system and back on so the logon script runs again, adding the mapping back again.

**11. mail routing.** An example of mail routing is if you send a message from the corporate offices in Chicago to a field office in Houston. The mail travels from Chicago through the WAN connections to Houston, going through any server in between.

**12. D.** Windows NT uses mailslots for connectionless-oriented communication. Windows NT implements only second-class mailslots, which are most useful for identifying other computers or services on a network, and for wide-scale identification of a service.

# Answers: Multi-Vendor Environments

**1. A, D.** There are two choices available for you to get Marissa access to the Novell NetWare servers. You can either install the Microsoft Client for NetWare Networks or you can install Novell's Client32 for Windows 95 and achieve a similar result. Client32 offers much of the same functionality as Microsoft's Client for NetWare Networks, but was developed by Novell rather than Microsoft.

2. **D.** File and Print Services for NetWare is an add-on product for Windows NT Server that allows Windows NT Server to function as a NetWare 3.12-compatible file and print server. This product provides users with the capability to use desktop machines with NetWare client software to access file and print resources and advanced server applications on the same multi-purpose Windows NT Server machine.

3. **B.** Windows NT Server 4.0 includes the Services for Macintosh product, which allows users of Apple Macintosh computers to use folders and printers shared by Windows NT domains. Install Services for Macintosh on the Windows NT server that houses the data that the Apple computers need to access.

4. **A.** The NetWare NOS has been around since the late 1980s, and has evolved through three generations: 2.*x*, 3.*x*, and 4.*x*. Only Version 4.*x* servers support NetWare Directory Services (NDS), which replaced the older bindery mode architecture of 2.*x* and 3.*x* servers.

5. **D.** To make the card catalog database available to the majority of computer owners in the community, they should install a web server. Web servers can connect to a variety of data sources utilizing database connectors like ODBC to pull data from a database and publish it to a Web browser. The users in the community could connect to the library web page and research the database for the information they need.

6. **Redirector.** In order for computers to communicate over a network to one or more network servers, they have to have one or more redirectors installed. Each redirector handles only the protocols or language that it can understand. When you decide which resource you want to access, implement the appropriate redirector for that resource, and it sends your requests to the appropriate destination.

7. **B, D.** Novell's VLM redirectors represent an older line of real-mode drivers designed to load at the DOS level and provide native access to NetWare servers. These drivers are compatible with DOS and Windows for Workgroups, but are not preferred for use with Win32-based systems such as Windows 95 and Windows NT.

8. **A.** UNIX laid the foundation for the Internet, as it was the primary operating system associated with the TCP/IP protocol. Until recently, UNIX-based systems were the dominant operating system on the Internet.

9. **B.** Gateway Service for NetWare (GSNW) is a Microsoft Windows NT Server utility that allows a Windows NT Server computer to act as a gateway to a Novell NetWare network. With GSNW, you can deploy Windows NT Server as a communications server and enable Microsoft Server Message Block (SMB) clients, such as MS-DOS-based clients, to have access to the NetWare LAN.

10. **A.** Novell provides redirectors, which they call requester software, for many different operating systems. The operating systems they support are MS-DOS, OS/2, all versions of Windows, and Apple Macintosh.

11. **C.** Dan needs to install the TCP/IP protocol on the system, since he plans on setting up an FTP server on the Internet. He also needs to get the system connectivity to the Internet, since the system is only local currently.

12. **D.** In 1974, UNIX became the first operating system written in the C language. UNIX has evolved over time with many extensions and new ideas provided in a variety of versions from many vendors. UNIX became the first open or standard operating system, partly because it is not a proprietary operating system (owned by one of the leading computer companies), and partly because it is written in a standard language and embraces many popular ideas.

# Answers: Transmission Media

1. **D.** Coaxial cable is resistant to the interference and signal weakening that other cabling, such as unshielded twisted-pair (UTP) cable, can experience. This is because it uses a solid-core wire down the middle of the cable, protected by insulation. Covering that insulation is braided wire and metal foil, which shields against electromagnetic interference. A final layer of insulation covers the braided wire. Fiber optic cable could also protect against the interference, but it's much more costly than the coaxial cable, and thus does not meet the requirements set forth in the scenario.

2. **D.** The terminator is missing, so the network will not work properly. A terminating resistor has to be used at each end of a coaxial cable, as shown in the next illustration, to ensure that signals do not reflect back and cause errors. RG-58 A/U coaxial cable requires a 50 ohm resistor in the terminator.

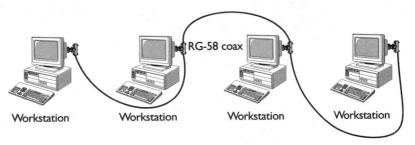

3. **A.** It is possible to upgrade the ACME Barrel Breakers token ring network to 16 Mbps, but the 16 Mbps transmission rate comes at a price. It requires IBM Type 1, 2, or 9 shielded cabling, and cannot use the inexpensive UTP.

4. **C.** Tell Jason that thicknet cable, also known as 10Base5, does not use RJ-45 connectors. If he needs to put a connector on the end of the 10Base5 cable, then he needs to use a BNC connector. Both thicknet and thinnet (10Base2) cables use BNC connectors.

**5. B.** Microwave technology is used is to interconnect LANs between buildings. This requires microwave dishes on both ends of the link. The dishes must be in line of sight to transmit and collect the microwave signals. Microwave technology is used to bypass the telephone company when connecting LANs between buildings. The data is not protected from unauthorized parties, because anyone with the right equipment in the line of site can intercept the signals for their own use.

**6. C.** The 10Base5 cable works fine as the backbone for connecting all the thinnet LANs together. However, it will not allow corporate headquarters to perform the desired functions, because the maximum distance for 10Base5 is approximately 500 meters, or 1640 feet. The corporate headquarters building is located 2 miles away from the research and development building.

**7. C.** You should recommend 10BaseT. Even though the number of nodes is 28, and 10Base2 would work because it supports 30 nodes, it will not support the future expansion that is planned. 10BaseT can support the future growth with no problem, as well as any more growth that may come later.

**8. C.** Fiber optic cable would prevent the trade secrets of the ACME Candle Corporation from being stolen by someone tapping into their network. Fiber optic cable uses modulated pulses of light—not electrical impulses—for data signals. This means that fiber optic cable cannot be tapped, as would be the case with copper-based cable carrying data in the form of electrical impulses.

**9. D.** The connector shown in the illustration is an AUI connector, and it is normally used with the 10Base5 networks. A transceiver is often connected directly to the 10Base5 cable by a connector known as a piercing tap. Connection from the transceiver to the network adapter card is made using a drop cable to connect to the adapter unit interface (AUI) port connector.

**10.** C. The maximum bandwidth of a Fast Ethernet network is 100 Mbps. Plain Ethernet has a maximum bandwidth of 10 Mbps, while token ring has a maximum bandwidth of 16 Mbps.

**11.** D. Debra forgot to add a media filter to her design. When Type 3 cable is connected to the MSAU, a Type 3 media filter is needed. This filter attaches directly to a data connector for IBM Type 1 and Type 3 cable. One end of the media filter connects to the data connector, while the other end has an outlet that allows the RJ-11 connector to be attached.

**12.** C. Broadband transmission uses analog signaling. Broadband transmission uses coaxial or fiber-optic cable to carry multiple channels of data. A single cable can carry five or six separate communications channels. A broadband network is analogous to cable TV: One cable brings in many TV channels.

# Answers: Network Interface Cards

**1.** C. The first thing you should do anytime you want to add new hardware to a Windows NT server is to check the Hardware Compatibility List to see if the hardware is on it. The HCL is a list of hardware that Microsoft has tested successfully with Windows NT. Microsoft releases an update to the list quarterly.

**2.** B. William forgot to load the software drivers for the NIC card when he installed it in his system. When a new hardware device is installed in a computer system, the corresponding software driver for that device must also be installed in order for it to function.

**3.** D. The sound card and network interface card are conflicting. Most sound cards use IRQ 5 when they are installed. You need to change the network interface card to another IRQ that is available to resolve the conflict.

**4. A.** The card shown in the illustration is a 16-bit card that fits in an ISA data bus. IBM developed the ISA (Industry Standard Architecture) bus for use on their PCs. Originally an 8-bit bus, it was later extended to 16 bits using a connector strategy that retained compatibility for the older 8-bit cards. This is still one of the most common buses in use, particularly for general purpose workstation PCs. Network cards for ISA buses are the least expensive but lowest performance cards due to the limitations of the 16-bit architecture.

**5. B.** The settings on the network interface card must be the same as those set for the driver in Windows 95 for it to work correctly. Setting parameters on a network adapter has traditionally been performed using jumpers on the card. However, in recent years, software-configurable adapters have become very common. Software-configurable adapters use a software configuration utility to set parameters, which allows them to be reconfigured without accessing or removing them from the system.

**6. C.** Performance can be increased by replacing the 16-bit ISA NICs with 32-bit PCI NICs. The 32-bit architecture of the PCI bus supports much faster transfer rates than the 16-bit ISA bus. More performance is gained if you use 32-bit PCI bus mastering cards. Bus mastering is a process by which the network card assumes temporary control of the data bus instead of the system processor.

**7. B.** Micro Channel Architecture (MCA) cards are very expensive and difficult to find today. IBM invented the 32-bit MCA architecture in 1988 and has since phased out MCA.

**8. A.** The Network Device Interface Specification (NDIS) is the Microsoft/3Com specification for the interface of network device drivers. All transport drivers call the NDIS interface to access network cards. All network drivers and protocol drivers shipped with Windows NT Workstation and Windows NT Server conform to NDIS.

9. **B.** He forgot to select the correct transceiver type. Since the network interface card has multiple connectors, it can support more than one type of media. Typical cards of this nature include Ethernet cards that have both twisted pair and coaxial connectors. This is one of the more common oversights in configuring a network interface card. The card is rendered nonfunctional if it is configured for the wrong media connection.

10. **A, D.** On-board transceivers are built onto the network interface card. With these types of transceivers, the media connector is built right on the back of the NIC. Common examples of this type include RJ-45 receptacles for twisted pairs, and BNC connectors for thinwire coaxial cable.

11. **B.** Network interface cards use each other's MAC addresses to communicate. The MAC address is hard-coded into the cards by the NIC's manufacturer.

12. **C.** LPT1 is conflicting with the network interface card, because LPT1 uses IRQ7 as its default. If LPT1 is not being used, you can disable it in BIOS and leave the network interface card on IRQ7. However, if you need to use LPT1, then you need to find an available IRQ and relocate the network interface card to it.

# Answers: Network Connectivity Devices

1. **D.** To allow users to connect to the mainframe from their desktop rather than going to a special mainframe terminal, a gateway should be installed. The gateway converts information from a format that the workstation understands to one that the mainframe understands, and vice versa.

2. **D.** The proposed solution does not meet the required result. Token ring networks use Multistation Access Units (MSAUs). Sometimes a MSAU is also referred to as a hub. But it is not the same type of hub as the UTP hub. UTP hubs are used on Ethernet networks, not token ring networks.

NETWORKING
ANSWERS

**3. B.** Installing a bridge on the network is a simple way to accomplish network segmentation. Use the bridge to create two separate networks. For example, make each floor its own network. The bridge will decrease the amount of traffic on each of the networks by filtering the local traffic, so the network will speed up for the users.

**4. A.** Segmenting a network by installing a router is the ultimate solution to a broadcast storm problem. Routers do not pass anything sent as a broadcast in the standard convention. Replacing a bridge with a router is a good start to lessening the impact of broadcast storms on your network.

**5. A.** A repeater resides within the Physical layer of the OSI model, meaning that it does not look within the packets; the repeater simply receives packets on one side, and sends them on another side. A repeater never filters packets; all packets are always repeated.

**6. D.** Replace the 10Base2 network with a 10BaseT network and then add a switch to it. Put each of the graphics designers on the switch, so that they have their own port. Implementing switching allows machines to communicate with each other with a full 10Mb of bandwidth on a 10Mb network. A switch provides a direct path from each port in the switch to each of its other ports. Switching should be implemented when machines will be creating a great deal of traffic among themselves.

**7. C.** Thickwire should be used because it reaches the length needed for between the administration building and the warehouse. Its maximum length is 500 meters. It is not unusual for thickwire to be used as a backbone. The major advantage of using something other than UTP for your backbone is that data can be transmitted a greater distance than the 100-meter length supported by UTP.

8. **D.** Bridges maintain their own bridge routing table dynamically, and do not require that the administrator manage it unless he or she wishes to make a manual change to the table. A bridge is constantly tracking the destination MAC addresses of all packets that it receives and adds the addresses to the bridge routing table.

9. **A, B, C, D.** A gateway is a device that enables two dissimilar systems that have similar functions to communicate with each other. A gateway can modify data at the Transport, Session, Presentation and Application Layers of the OSI model. These layers are collectively referred to as the OSI upper layers.

10. **B.** To keep the network usable with such heavy growth, they need to implement routing. Routing should be implemented when overall traffic on your network is becoming increasingly heavy. Ethernet routing is a popular solution for traffic problems today.

11. **D.** The easiest way for SDC Racing to extend their 10Base2 network is to add a repeater to the network. For a repeater to work, both segments that the repeater joins must have the same media access scheme, protocol, and transmission method. In this case, SDC Racing just needs to add the repeater and continue using coaxial cable, as well as the protocols they already are using on the network.

12. **C.** They need to replace the Category 3 cable with Category 5 cable. Category 5 cabling can run Fast Ethernet at a speed of 100 Mbps, whereas Category 3 will never be able to go any faster than 10 Mbps.

# Answers: Wide Area Networks (WANs)

**1.** **C.** Guitar Analyzers are wasting money because the leased line is being paid for all the time, whether or not data is flowing between the two sites, and whether or not full bandwidth is being utilized. Since they are only using it to transfer data once a month, they could save a lot of money by setting up a RAS server at the main office and having the office in Seattle send the information to it that way.

**2.** **B.** Replacing the asynchronous modems with synchronous modems would be cost effective and still meet their needs. Asynchronous modems have the disadvantage of having a high overhead, comprising between 1/5 and 1/3 of the bandwidth used. As a result, data transfers are slow. Also, asynchronous transmissions are subject to errors due to the nature of the legacy telephone wires that are typically used. Synchronous transmission is more efficient and much faster than asynchronous transmission.

**3.** **C.** The bandwidth of an OC-12 circuit is 622.08 Mbps. The lowest optical carrier rate is OC-1, which has a bandwidth of 51.84 Mbps. The highest optical carrier rate is OC-48, which has a bandwidth of 2488.32 Mbps.

**4.** **B.** You could access you machine by using Point to Point Tunneling Protocol. Since you have an Internet connection, you could connect to the PPTP server on the company network, and then access your machine for the document that you need, as shown in the next illustration. You are already running the correct protocols, TCP/IP for access to the Internet and NetBEUI for access to your machine. PPTP encapsulates packets of information (IP, IPX, or NetBEUI) within IP packets for transmission through the Internet. At the destination, the IP packet encapsulation is discarded, and the original packets are forwarded to their appropriate destinations. Both encryption and authentication are used in PPTP. Encryption of the transmitted data protects the data. Authentication is used to verify the identity of the user in order to grant access to network resources. Once connected via PPTP, you have a virtual connection to the network.

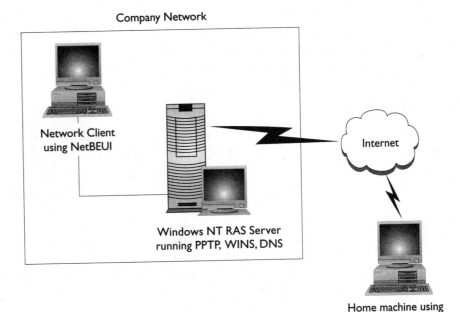

Company Network

Network Client
using NetBEUI

Windows NT RAS Server
running PPTP, WINS, DNS

Internet

Home machine using
NetBEUI and TCP/IP

**5. D.** The proposed solution does not meet the required result, because
Windows NT RAS cannot be configured as a Serial Line Internet Protocol
(SLIP) server. It must be configured as a PPP (Point to Point Protocol)
server. SLIP is a legacy UNIX communications standard. Windows NT can
be set up as a SLIP client if it needs to connect to a UNIX server that is
configured as a SLIP server.

**6. B.** The serial port in the 386 is using a 16450 UART. The 16450 UART
uses a one-byte buffer. Cones Unlimited needs to switch to an internal
modem that uses a 16550A UART because it has a 16-byte buffer, or use an
upgraded serial port card with a 16550A UART.

**7. D.** Jangle Coins Limited should switch from X.25 to Frame relay. Like
X.25, frame relay uses variable-length packets. However, frame relay nodes

do not check each frame for errors. Instead, the frame relay switch reads the header, then forwards the packet, at times without fully receiving a frame before forwarding it. ATM does not meet the criteria of Jangle Coins Limited, because it uses fixed cells. SONET is mainly used as the transport layer for ATM traffic. SMDS also uses cells.

8. **B, D.** RTS/CTS flow control, also known as hardware flow control, is faster and more reliable than XON/XOFF flow control, which is also known as software flow control. Hardware flow control bases its pause and resume features on whether the RTS or CTS wires in the modem cable send a bit of data.

9. **B.** Set up Hijinks Emporium with a fractional T1 that is equal to the 256 Kbps that they need. Since each channel of a T1 is 64 Kbps, you need to use four channels.

10. **B.** PPP improved on SLIP by functioning at both the Physical and Data Link layers, thereby providing error control, security, dynamic IP addressing, and support for multiple protocols. Within the Data Link Layer, the MAC portion handles the physical addressing of the device, and the LLC portion handles error control for connection services.

11. **Switched Megabit Data Service.** SMDS uses a line that terminates at a central location, where the data is then switched to the destination network. Instead of using circuits, SMDS uses connectionless datagram services. Each SMDS frame contains a source and a destination address. Any SMDS device may transmit to any other SMDS device simply by addressing the frame to it.

12. **A.** They need to use ISDN since they need increased speed and don't want to run any other lines. ISDN can take advantage of their existing telephone lines and give them 64 Kbps per B channel for a Basic Rate connection.

# Answers: Network Security and Reliability

1. **C.** The proposed solution meets the required results, because share-level security can be used to protect resources on the Windows 95 network. However, the proposed solution does not meet either of the optional results, because share-level security does not support auditing, nor does it support setting permissions on a per-user basis. Share-level security only supports two levels of resource password protection, Read-Only and Full Access.

2. **D.** The proposed solution does not meet the required results, because the RAID that is provided by Windows NT is software based. In order to provide the capability to swap a failed disk while the system still runs, you will need to get a hardware-based RAID solution from a third-party vendor.

3. **A.** Since the battery did not help in her computer retaining its CMOS settings, it is very possible that it has a virus. You need to run an antivirus program on the machine to eradicate it.

4. **B, D.** Both Iltgb0f and L8SeR=$h0W are good passwords. You may think that they would be impossible to remember, but they aren't really if you think about it. Iltgb0f can be broken out to the first letter of the sentence, "I Like To Go Bowling On Fridays." To make it even more difficult to crack, you can replace the letter O with the number 0. L8SeR=$h0W is a good password because it doesn't look like a phrase, but it suggests one: "laser show". The other two choices are not good passwords, because they could be cracked easily with any dictionary cracking program. Even though you might think a word like "meerschaum" is so uncommon that nobody would guess it, I am here to tell you that it can be found by a dictionary cracking program, because I discovered it being used on my network!

5. **C.** The network server is not in a secure location; anyone passing by the reception area could tamper with it. There is a good possibility that whoever

is tampering with it works in the Finance department, since the network goes down when a product is due from that department. Physical security for servers needs to be a high priority for anyone with a network because of the damage that can result, intentional or unintentional.

6. **B.** GBE took care of most of the reliability issues for their network, but they forgot to perform regular tape backups. Even though they are using RAID 5, they still need to perform regular tape backups and store the tapes off site. If the building catches fire, then the RAID 5 subsystem will not be able to recover their data. They will need to depend on the tapes they stored off site to recover the information.

7. **C.** The parity stripe block is used to reconstruct data for a failed physical disk. When a disk that is part of the stripe set fails, read operations for data are substantially slower than that of a single disk. Because a stripe set with parity works with the operating system, it requires more memory than a mirror set.

8. **A, B.** The Remoteboot service of Windows NT Server allows the client systems to start across the network, so there is no need for the contractors' machines to have hard disks. They can store the data they need on their home directory of your Windows NT server. Since they have a place to store their data on the server, there is no need for them to have floppy disk drives, so you can remove those from their machines also. This prevents them from taking data out of SBI on floppy disks.

9. **C.** If the FTDISK.SYS becomes corrupted or not initialized for any reason, then Windows NT is totally oblivious to any fault-tolerant service such as volume sets, stripe sets, or mirror sets.

10. **A.** The RAID shown in the illustration is RAID 5. Fault tolerance functionality is added to disk striping with the addition of parity information in one of the stripes. The parity strip is the exclusive OR

(XOR) of all the data values for the data strips in the stripe. If no disks in the stripe set with parity have failed, the new parity for a write can be calculated without having to read the corresponding strips from the other data disks.

11. **C.** The maximum amount of data that can be stored on the RAID 5 set is 16GB. For striping with parity, there is a parity block for each stripe of data, and parity stripes are distributed across all disks. Therefore, for a stripe set with parity consisting of five disks, one fifth of total disk capacity is used for storing parity information. In this case that means that 4GB of the 20GB will be used for parity information leaving 16GB for data storage.

12. **B, D.** Physical security is vital for the integrity of the company's servers. They need to be placed in a secure room with limited access. User training is also important, because if the users don't take security seriously, then it will be even more difficult to apply other successful security measures. C2 security is important to some organizations, but it does not need to be part of every organization's security plan. The security policy for GDS needs to be written and not verbal. A written security policy provides a clear and concise set of process guidelines for applying security safeguards.

# Answers:
# Network Monitoring and Management

1. **C.** Making the users change their passwords every 90 days is part of your User Account Policies portion of the administrative plan. It is important that you determine the policies that will be in effect for all user accounts that are on your network.

2. **C.** Preparing and maintaining network documentation pays great dividends when you need to troubleshoot a problem on the network, as evidenced by this situation. Now that you have fixed the problem, it is time to get to

work documenting every detail of the complete network, including the locations of every piece of hardware, and details about the cabling.

3. **D.** Performance Monitor is an outstanding tool to use to establish a baseline for your network server. A baseline needs to be developed before you can determine if the network server is performing below normal conditions.

4. **B.** You should have performed the upgrade on a test group of systems before rolling it out to the entire organization. Your test group should consist of at least one of each type of machine on your network, if feasible, so that compatibility problems could be observed prior to the big rollout.

5. **D.** %Processor Time is pegged at 100 percent, which is the cause of the system being sluggish. Now that you have a symptom, you need to further isolate the problem by finding what is causing the processor to stay so high.

6. **C.** Log files, which are in binary format, provide a way to save the counter information and then later run it through the Performance Monitor application. They enable you to track counters over a long time period, and provide a reliable method for documenting your system's performance.

7. **B.** Jimmy cannot change his password because he is trying to use one that he has used previously. As you can see from the illustration, the account policy is set to remember the last 10 passwords. This means that the last 10 passwords that Jimmy has used cannot be used again.

8. **B.** The security strategy of your administrative plan needs to plan for the access of corporate databases by users of the Internet. Without taking this into consideration, you put the entire survival of your business at risk. Imagine if somehow you opened up the employee database for Read/Write access to millions of unknown people because you had not considered it relevant enough to cover in the security strategy!

9. **B.** The Performance Monitor can help you to resolve bottlenecks that may be in your system. To resolve bottleneck problems, you must identify the device that has the high rate of use. Items that you should check are memory, processor, disk drives, network interface card, and the disk drive controller card.

10. **A.** The default size for each log file is 512KB, and the log file will get overwritten every seven days. The settings can be changed to reflect the needs of your network.

11. **A.** If the company standardizes on the software that is used throughout the company, incidents like this would not occur. A common problem in all companies is that some departments want to upgrade to the newest version of an application as soon as it is released, whereas some other departments do not want to move away from the version that they are used to.

12. **D.** Establishment of a baseline is the first action to perform with regard to monitoring your network. The establishment of the baseline needs to happen over time, but prior to anything going wrong.

# Answers: Network Troubleshooting

1. **C.** Cable testers test a cable for its usability. They do not determine *where* a problem exists, just *if* a problem exists. Cable testers are mostly used to test cables to verify their integrity prior to installation. Imagine running all 12,000 feet of Category 5 cable, only to find that some of it is not usable. You'd have no choice but to pull it and install good cable.

2. **B.** Since the network uses 10Base2, you should begin by dividing the network by removing the cable from the T-connector of a machine and replacing it with a terminator. This isolates the network, allowing you to troubleshoot a smaller section. In this situation you may want to place the

terminator at the last machine on the first floor so that the network is split in half, isolating the entire first floor. If the network still does not work, then you know that the problem exists on the first floor. Move the terminator to the halfway point of the client computers, in this case at computer number 7. If the network works after moving the terminator to computer number 7, move it back out to the halfway point between computers 14 and 7. Continue troubleshooting in this manner until you find the problem.

**3. D.** The first step in resolving network performance issues is to use a network monitor to view traffic. Using the network monitor gives you the opportunity to determine if the network traffic is the problem or if something else is causing the network performance degradation.

**4. B.** A time domain reflectometer (TDR) uses the screen shown in the illustration. The TDR sends a signal down the cable, where it is reflected at some point. The TDR then calculates the distance down the cable that the signal traveled before being reflected by measuring the amount of time it took for the signal to be returned. It is a very useful tool for locating the distance to a cable fault.

**5. C.** The protocol analyzer can be used to gather performance data for the new server so that ACME Interior Welders can see the effect the new server is having on their network.

**6. A.** Use uninterruptible power supplies (UPSs) on the hubs and servers. This will ensure that if there is a brownout or other power anomaly, it will not affect the hubs or servers. There is a very good chance that at some point during the construction power will be affected, intentionally or unintentionally, since the contractors will be doing electrical work. If possible, you should also purchase UPSs for the client systems on the network.

**7.** **C.** A TDR is a good tool to use for diagnosing cable problems. The TDR sends an electronic pulse down the network cable and measures the amount of time it takes for that pulse to be echoed back. If the pulse never echoes back, there is an open or break in the cable. The TDR can measure the length that the pulse traveled before it was reflected. If this length is less than the total length of the cable, the problem with the cable is at that distance from the TDR.

**8.** **C.** A digital voltage meter (DVM) measures the continuity of a cable and can determine if there is a short in a cable. If an exposed part of the cable is touching another conductive surface, then a short occurs. A DVM cannot tell you where the short is.

**9.** **D.** Check the web site of the NIC card manufacturer to help you get the NIC card working with your server. It may have troubleshooting information containing suggested steps to resolve your problem, the latest updated drivers, and if all else fails, it should have the phone numbers that you can use to contact their technical support.

**10.** **C.** Resource kits can be a very handy tool when you are having problems with your Windows NT network. Resource kits contain additional documentation on your operating system that was too comprehensive to cover in the standard documentation. Whenever you are faced with a problem that you cannot solve, check the resource kit; your problem may already have been solved. Trade publications can be a great source of information about what is currently happening in the industry, but in the event of actual network problems, these publications will probably be of little direct use to you.

**11.** **D.** The protocol analyzer can be used while the network is on and functioning. By properly analyzing the data that it produces, you can detect problems on your network that should be handled while they are small. When they become big, then your network may go down.

**12. B.** Make sure that you back up the entire system prior to any upgrade. That way, if something goes awry with the upgrade, you still have your data, safe and sound. It is smart to plan for problems to arise after a system upgrade, so monitor your system closely.

# Answers: Internet Technologies

**1. B.** The Internet and its development have been documented in documents called Requests for Comments (RFCs). Using RFCs you can prove to the vice president of General Jalopy Inc. that IPX/SPX is not supported, and that they must use TCP/IP, as it is the protocol that the Internet is built upon.

**2. D.** Since the UNIX clients are not running an X Window system, they cannot use a graphical browser like Netscape Navigator or Mosaic. Instead they have to have a text browser installed. Lynx is a text browser that is available for UNIX systems, as well as VAX and IBM systems.

**3. B.** Since the several hundred users need access to the Internet to perform their jobs, you need to implement a method of controlling where they go on the Internet. Implementing a proxy server can fulfill both needs of the CEO. It can restrict access to frivolous sites but still allow the employees the capability to do their job.

**4. C.** The software used in the illustration is for IRC, Internet Relay Chat. IRC offers Internet users the ability to communicate in real time with other Internet users. There are many different channels available that cover almost every subject. If you cannot find a suitable channel, then you are free to create your own.

**5. C.** Hypertext Transfer Protocol (HTTP) is the underlying protocol by which WWW clients and servers communicate. HTTP is an application-level protocol for distributed, collaborative, hypermedia information systems. It is a generic, stateless, object-oriented protocol. A feature of HTTP is the typing and negotiation of data representation, allowing systems to be built independently of the data being transferred.

6. **D.** File Transfer Protocol (FTP) is the protocol used to transfer files across the Internet to your computer. There are FTP-specific clients that can operate similarly to a DOS-like prompt, or they can be graphical in nature, similar to Windows NT Explorer. But since Max only has his web browser, he must let it know which protocol to use. The FTP:// tells the web browser that it needs to use the FTP protocol when accessing the host listed at the right of the //.

7. **A, C.** David can save on the long distance phone calls by utilizing electronic mail and the Internet Relay Chat. He can send electronic mail that his family can read at their convenience. If he wants to "talk" to them live then he can create his own channel on IRC for just him and his family to use.

8. **C, D.** Steven has two possibilities for finding information about his widgeteer, as well as other widgeteer hobbyists. He can see if there is a Usenet newsgroup for widgeteers. Usenet newsgroups are a centralized system of messages on a certain topic. Each newsgroup is devoted to a particular topic, such as widgeteers. Steven can also see if there is a channel for widgeteers on the Internet Relay Chat. If not, then he can create a channel and see if anyone else in the world wants to talk about widgeteers.

9. **C.** Within the Content tab of Internet Options, Debra can control what content is viewed by her browser. Debra can password-protect the settings to keep her child from seeing certain items and trying to change the settings. Even though this is a step in the right direction, Debra may need to take additional measures, as the only sites that will be blocked are those that are rated by RSAC.

10. **Packet filtering.** The packet is either accepted or rejected, depending on how the administrator has the firewall configured. The administrator needs to be very careful with the configuration because she may filter packets that she didn't intend to.

11. **D.** Raymond can get access to his document by using telnet. Telnet is a terminal emulation protocol for logging on to remote computers. Telnet is defined in RFC 854, among others. In order for Raymond to be able to telnet into the company server, a telnet server service must be running.

12. **B.** If your IP address changes each time you make a dialup connection to your ISP, then it is a dynamic IP address. Static IP addresses are addresses that never change. (Every time you make a dialup connection to your ISP, you use the same IP address.)

13. **B.** A circuit-level gateway is implemented when a TCP or UDP connection is established. Once the connection is made, information can enter and leave the network without further checking. (Another type of gateway is the application gateway. Application gateways secure specific applications such as FTP or telnet.)

14. **A, B, D.** To set up a World Wide Web server using Windows NT, you need to have a permanent connection to the Internet, web server software, and a static IP address. Fault tolerance is not a requirement, although it may be a wise investment depending on what you are using your web server for.

# Part 4

## Windows NT Server 4.0 in the Enterprise

## EXAM TOPICS

Planning Your Windows NT Server 4.0 Domain Strategy

Installing and Configuring Windows NT Server 4.0 Core Services

Managing Windows NT Server 4.0 Users and Groups

Planning Your Windows NT Server 4.0 Protocol Strategy

TCP/IP Installation and Configuration

NetWare Connectivity

Configuring Windows NT Server 4.0 Protocol Routing

Installing and Configuring NT Server 4.0 Remote Access Service

Internet Information Server

Monitoring and Performance Tuning

Troubleshooting Windows NT 4.0

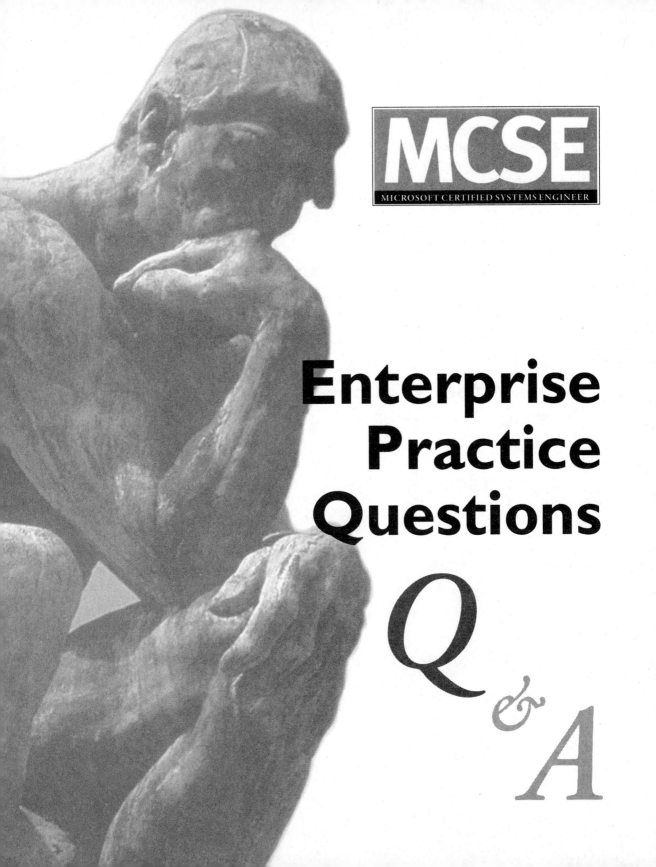

The following questions will test your knowledge of supporting Windows NT Server 4.0 in the Enterprise. Read all questions and choices carefully. There may be more than one correct answer for a question, and you must choose all correct answers. While the multiple choice format might seem easy, some questions will require considerable reasoning to select the correct answers.

You will find simple questions mixed in with difficult ones, in no particular order. This is the same approach used in the Microsoft tests. In addition, the Microsoft test questions won't be sorted by subject matter. The questions in this book are organized by chapter, but not by section within a chapter. This will give you some sense of the random order of the actual exam, but still make it easy for you to look up an answer in the right chapter, or to test your comprehension of a chapter after you've read it.

# Planning Your Windows NT Server 4.0 Domain Strategy

**1.** What does Microsoft call the partition containing NTLDR that is used to boot the system?

A. Boot partition

B. System partition

C. Bootstrap partition

D. NT load partition

**2.** What RAID options are supported by software in Windows NT Server?

A. Mirroring

B. Duplexing

C. Striping

D. Striping with parity

3. Your organization has 30,000 employees in one location, and about 200 servers. Each employee uses a Windows NT Workstation system. The resources provided by the servers logically break down into about 20 areas. Which of the following domain models would you implement?

   A. Single
   B. Master
   C. Multiple Master
   D. Complete Trust

4. Bob wants to control user accounts centrally in his company, but allow each department to manage its resources. His company has 1,000 employees. Which domain model should he use?

   A. Single
   B. Master
   C. Multiple Master
   D. Complete Trust

5. Jim and some other users are complaining that they can't change their domain password. Users are able to log on and authenticate against a domain controller. Your domain has two domain controllers, one of which has crashed. Which of the following could correct Jim's problem?

   A. Boot the PDC.
   B. Boot the BDC.
   C. Promote the BDC.
   D. Nothing. It's user error.

**exam**
**Watch**

*You may see one or two questions about Per Seat and Per Server licensing. Be sure to keep in mind that you can make that one-time switch only from Per Server to Per Seat. You cannot switch in the other direction.*

**6.** Tom wants to move his BDC from one domain to another. How can he accomplish this?

A. Go into Control Panel, choose Networking, change the domain name, and reboot.

B. Same as A, but add the server to the destination domain first as a standalone server.

C. Same as A, but add the server to the destination domain first as a backup domain controller.

D. It can't be done without completely reinstalling Windows NT Server on the system.

**7.** Jerry is planning on having two Windows NT servers (set up as PDC and BDC) and 200 client workstations, of which a maximum of 120 would be logged on at any given time. Which of the following would represent his licensing options?

A. 120 per seat client access licenses

B. 240 per server client access licenses, 120 per server

C. 200 per seat client access licenses

D. 400 per server client access licenses, 200 per server

**8.** Todd wants a coherent node naming scheme for all computers in his organization. He'd like to use a five-character alphabetic building code followed by a three-digit room number, followed by the username of the primary user. The usernames in his organization are restricted to eight characters to be compatible with usernames on their legacy systems. For servers, he'd name them by their primary function instead of username, and the longest function name has six characters. Which of the following are true about his plan?

A. It will provide a coherent scheme for all systems.

B. It will provide a coherent scheme for the servers.

C. It will provide a coherent scheme for the workstations.

D. It will not provide what he wants for any systems.

**9.** Bill is installing a new Windows NT server that will be used primarily as a SQL server. He's not sure about what to select for the server type, as it's one of the first in his environment. What should he choose?

A. Primary Domain Controller

B. Backup Domain Controller

C. Member or standalone server

D. Domain Master Server

**10.** Mary is the administrator over a Master Domain model network. Her master domain is called MOE. However, she can't administer one of her resource domains (called CURLY) unless she logs onto an account in that domain. What does she need to do?

A. Log on from an administrator account in MOE and add MOE\Domain Admins to the CURLY\Domain Admins group.

B. Log on from an administrator account in CURLY and add MOE\Domain Admins to the CURLY\Domain Admins group.

C. Log on from an administrator account in MOE and add MOE\Domain Admins to the Administrators group on CURLY's PDC.

D. Log on from an administrator account in CURLY and add MOE\Domain Admins to the Administrators group on CURLY's PDC.

**11.** When should a BDC be promoted?

A. If it's done a good job authenticating

B. If the PDC has crashed, and you're booting it

C. If you expect to shut down and reboot the BDC soon

D. If you expect to shut down the PDC and have it offline for a while

**12.** Stan is a manager and has a roaming profile in a shared directory on his server. He's got personnel evaluations in his Personal folder. Stan often logs onto his staff's computers as well as his own. Assuming he has eight staff members, how many copies of those personnel evaluations exist in his department? Hint: The Personal folder is stored in a user's profile.

A. One

B. Two

C. Nine

D. Ten

**13.** Your system has four disk drives. There's free space of 50MB, 30MB, 120MB, and 200MB on each disk. What's the biggest partition you can make with them?

A. 240MB by striping the two larger free spaces

B. 400MB by creating a volume set from all free spaces

C. 150MB, 100MB usable by creating a RAID5 set from the three larger areas

D. 400MB by striping all free spaces

**14.** Which of the following software RAID solutions available with Windows NT yields the best performance?

A. Mirroring (RAID 1)

B. Striped mirror sets (RAID 0+1)

C. Striping (RAID 0)

D. Striping with parity (RAID 5)

**15.** Martha's company is split into three major divisions. Each division has about 10,000 employees, and is fairly autonomous. Centralized account administration is not an issue. Each division would like to control accounts and access to resources as it sees fit. Also, certain departments in each division need regular access to resources in the other divisions. What domain model would make sense for Martha's company?

A. Single domain model

B. Master domain model

C. Multiple Master Domain model

D. Complete Trust Domain model

16. John has a roaming profile that is located on a share on the domain's sole BDC. John wishes to log on to a workstation in his domain that he's never used before. Which of the following are true, given the various states of the PDC and BDC?

A. If the BDC is down, a new profile will be created on the workstation.

B. If the PDC is down, his roaming profile will be used and copied to the workstation.

C. If the PDC and BDC are down, a new profile will be created on the workstation.

D. If the PDC and BDC are down, he will be unable to log on to the workstation.

17. Greg wants to get the highest performance partition he can create, and as big a stripe as possible within that. He has four disks with 120MB, 210MB, 150MB, and 500MB areas available on each. What option should he choose?

A. Make a volume set of 980MB from the free space on each drive.

B. Make a stripe set with parity with 360MB of usable space.

C. Make a stripe set without parity with 360MB of usable space.

D. Make a stripe set without parity with 480MB of usable space.

18. Jennifer has decided to set up a trust relationship between GOTHAM and METRO domains. GOTHAM will have accounts to utilize an HP printer in METRO. Which will be the trusted and trusting domains?

   A. GOTHAM will be trusted, METRO will be trusting.

   B. GOTHAM will be trusting, METRO will be trusted.

   C. Both will be trusted.

   D. Both will be trusting.

**19.** Archie has a server with only three identical disk drives. He'd like to place a single partition on each, and stripe them with software. What are his options?

   A. A stripe set without parity.

   B. A stripe set with parity.

   C. He can't stripe all the space on the disks into a single partition.

   D. A stripe set with even parity.

## QUESTIONS AND ANSWERS

| | |
|---|---|
| An NT Server has two disk drives and you need to provide fault tolerance... | Use Disk Administrator and configure a mirror set that will provide redundancy for the data. |
| You have four disk drives and want to set them up for RAID 5. The first drive has the system and boot partition on it. The second, third, and fourth drive have data from your mail server application... | The first drive cannot be included in the RAID 5 set since it has system and boot information. However, the other three disks can be set for RAID 5. |
| You have six disk drives. The free space available on each drive is 240MB, 418MB, 125MB, 413MB, 130MB, and 297MB. What is the maximum size of a stripe set without parity? | 125+125+125+125+125+125=750MB. A stripe set without parity consists of the same amount of free space from each drive that will make up the set. Since 125MB was the amount of free space that each drive could provide, that is the maximum size it can be. |

# Installing and Configuring Windows NT Server 4.0 Core Services

1. Your domain is contained on two subnetworks. What browser roles will be played by your PDC?

   A. Master Browser
   B. Domain Master Browser
   C. Backup Browser
   D. Non-browser

2. Users logging onto your domain sometimes have the logon script execute, and sometimes don't. Your PDC and BDCs are all available. You always log on to the PDC, and the script always executes for you. What should you check?

   A. Nothing. The users are just complaining as usual, and sometimes the script executes so fast they don't even notice it.
   B. Synchronization on the BDCs.
   C. Replication on the BDCs.
   D. Predestination on the BDCs.

3. George's workstation has MaintainServerList set to Auto. He is just learning about browsing, and asks you what determines whether his computer browses or not. What can you tell him?

   A. His computer always browses, and can automatically become a backup browser.
   B. His computer doesn't browse by default, but a master browser can request that it start so that it may act as a backup browser.
   C. His computer will automatically start browsing if an election is held.
   D. If IsDomainMaster is set to True, his computer will automatically become a master browser.

**4.** Terry is having problems with replication, and realizes he forgot to set the replication users' group memberships. Which groups must he choose to have replication work correctly?

   A. Replicator

   B. Replication Operators

   C. Backup Operators

   D. Server Operators

**5.** You have configured replication using the standard directories. Which of the following on the export system will be replicated on the import system(s)?

   A. Directories in %SYSTEMROOT%SYSTEM32\REPL\IMPORT

   B. Non-directory files in %SYSTEMROOT%SYSTEM32\REPL\ EXPORT

   C. Directories in %SYSTEMROOT%SYSTEM32\REPL\EXPORT

   D. Files and directories (folders) contained in the directories in answer C

   E. The directory and contents of %SYSTEMROOT%SYSTEM32\ REPL\EXPORT\SCRIPTS

**6.** The boot partition on your server occasionally fills up, causing problems. What is one way to keep potentially large files from consuming space on that partition?

   A. Move the PROGRAM FILES directory to another partition.

   B. Disable replication.

   C. Move the %SYSTEMROOT%SYSTEM32\PRINTERS directory to another partition.

   D. Create a print spool directory on another partition and set it as the value for HKEY_LOCAL_MACHINE\System\CurrentControlset\ Control\Print\Printers.

exam
ⓦatch   *Only computers that are running Windows NT Server can be configured as export servers. The Windows NT Server does not have to be a domain controller to be used in this configuration.*

**7.** Mike came into work in the morning only to find that printing had stopped working. On further investigation, he discovered that the print server had lost power and rebooted the previous night. What should Mike do to correct the problem?

    A. Remove and add back the printers on all systems that use the print server.

    B. Synchronize the domain.

    C. Stop and start the Spooler service.

    D. Set up a new print server for all the printers on the old one.

**8.** What effect does the ReplicationGovenor Registry setting have on a BDC?

    A. Affects how often replication occurs

    B. Affects how often synchronization occurs

    C. Affects the buffer size of replication data transferred

    D. Affects the buffer size of synchronization data transferred

**9.** How could increasing Pulse increase network traffic?

    A. Increasing Pulse causes the network heartbeat to race.

    B. The BDCs will check the PDC's pulse more often.

    C. The PDC will send out a pulse more often.

    D. As pulse increases, so does the likelihood of full synchronizations.

**10.** Barbie is looking for ways to control replication of scripts as she's editing them. What can she use to prevent or delay replication of scripts?

    A. Lock the EXPORT\SCRIPTS directory on the export server.

    B. Lock the IMPORT\SCRIPTS directory on the import server.

    C. Check the Wait Until Stabilized box for that directory on the export server.

    D. Check the Wait Until Stabilized box for that directory on the import server.

ENTERPRISE QUESTIONS

**11.** Which of the following are valid names for the user account used by the Directory Replicator service?

A. DReplicator

B. Replicator

C. ReplUser

D. DirectoryReplicatorUser

**12.** Billy has just increased the Randomize Registry value under NetLogon to 10 seconds on all his domain controllers. What else does he need to do?

A. Increase PulseTimeout1 on his BDCs to 15 seconds.

B. Increase PulseTimeout1 on his PDC to 15 seconds.

C. Increase PulseTimeout2 on his BDCs.

D. Increase PulseTimeout2 on his PDC.

**13.** Joshua knows a Windows NT workstation in his domain has been up all day, but he can't find it in the browse list. What could explain this?

A. The DoNotAdvertise Registry parameter is set to True.

B. The workstation has hidden shares.

C. The Server service was stopped or disabled.

D. The MaintainServerList Registry parameter is set to No.

**14.** Which of the following are true statements about user account database synchronization?

A. After a partial synchronization, the database is only partly synchronized with the PDC.

B. Full synchronization must occur before the database is identical on the PDC and BDCs.

C. When a BDC has been down for a long time, it's more likely to need a full synchronization.

D. BDCs issue all synchronization requests; PDCs issue all pulses.

**15.** The following computers share a subnet: a Windows NT Server 4.0 BDC, a Windows 95 system, a Windows for Workgroups 3.11 system, a Windows

NT Server 4.0 running WINS, and a Windows NT Workstation 4.0 that has IsDomainMaster set to True. What is the ranking order to be elected Master Browser for their subnet?

A. NT Server BDC, Windows NT Server WINS, Windows NT Workstation, Windows 95, WFW 3.11

B. NT Server WINS, Windows NT Server BDC, Windows NT Workstation, Windows 95, WFW 3.11

C. NT Workstation, Windows NT Server BDC, Windows NT Server WINS, Windows 95, WFW 3.11

D. Windows 95, WFW 3.11, Windows NT Server BDC, Windows NT Workstation, Windows NT Server WINS

16. There have been sporadic problems printing through your system. Where should you check for the cause of the problems?

A. The System Log on Event Viewer

B. The Print service in Services in Control Panel

C. The Registry under HKEY_LOCAL_MACHINE\ System\ CurrentControlset\Control\Print

D. The cache on the print device

17. During installation of Windows NT Server, you are unsure as to which type of licensing to choose. Which type of licensing will allow you to make a one-time switch?

A. Per server

B. Per seat

C. Per server and per seat

D. Neither per server nor per seat

exam Watch

*You can name the replicator service account by any name that you want, with the exception that it cannot have the same name as a group. That is the reason it is named dReplicator—not just Replicator—because a group by that name already exists.*

**18.** You are planning to implement fault tolerance before installing Windows NT Server. Which level of RAID can you use for the system and boot partitions of Windows NT Server?

A.  RAID 0

B.  RAID 1

C.  RAID 5

D.  You can't use RAID on a Windows NT system or boot partition.

**19.** A power outage causes your Windows NT server to crash while it has a print job in the spooler. After the server is rebooted, you realize the file has been corrupted and is still in the spooler. What will you do to solve this problem? (Choose all that apply.)

A.  Stop and restart the spooler service.

B.  Remove the printer from the network.

C.  Reboot the server.

D.  Delete all the files that won't print from the spooling directory.

E.  Delete the spooling file.

e x a m
ⓦ a t c h   *Be ready for questions regarding troubleshooting the printing process. Some of these questions talk about the spooler having a problem such as a corrupt file. If this is the case, it is a matter of stopping and restarting the spooler service. This is done under the Services option in Control Panel.*

# Managing Windows NT Server 4.0 Users and Groups

**1.** What mechanisms are provided for managing or establishing user environments?

    A. Account policies

    B. Logon scripts

    C. User profiles

    D. Home directories

    E. Group profiles

2. The Marketing domain and the Sales domain trust the Corporate domain. The Sales domain also trusts the Marketing domain. Which of the following statements are true?

    A. The Sales domain administrators can manage the Marketing domain.

    B. The Marketing domain administrators can automatically manage the Sales domain.

    C. This example follows the Multiple Master Domain model.

    D. Users from the Corporate domain can log on to the Marketing domain and the Sales domain.

    E. Users from the Marketing domain can log on to the Corporate domain and the Sales domain.

3. Which of the following, once set, cannot be changed?

    A. Password

    B. Profile filename

    C. Username

    D. Full Name

    E. Account Security ID

4. Gary is the manager of the Sales Department. Gary and his sales team need to be able to run their programs, print spreadsheets and reports, and access other computers' printers. Gary also needs to be able to manage the printers and shut down the server, if necessary. Without giving anyone any more rights than necessary, which course of action would be best?

ENTERPRISE QUESTIONS

A. Make Gary an administrator and make his sales team members of the Print Operators group.

B. Make the entire Sales department a global group called Sales. Then make the global group a member of the built-in local group Print Operators.

C. Make Gary a member of the Print Operators group and make sure the printers have permissions that allow the members of his sales team to print.

D. Use Account Policies to give only the rights necessary to each individual.

**5.** What utility is used to create trust relationships?

A. User Manager for Domains

B. Server Manager

C. Control Panel

D. User Manager

E. System Tools

**6.** Resources for the Sales, Accounting, Service, and Corporate domains are to be managed separately, but all the user definitions are going to be managed from the Support domain. What trust relationships must be established?

A. Support must trust Sales, Accounting, Service, and Corporate.

B. Sales, Accounting, Service, and Corporate must trust Support.

C. Sales, Accounting, Service, and Corporate must trust Support, and Support must trust Sales, Accounting, Service, and Corporate.

D. Sales trusts Accounting, Accounting trusts Service, Service trusts Corporate, and Corporate trusts Support. Support trusts no domains.

**7.** During the Christmas season, your shipping department employs three extra employees to help track orders and shipping. Your department has 15 workstations, but you do not want them to be able to use the manager's computer (named MGR). How do you achieve this arrangement?

A. Take the extras' accounts, select Logon To, set User May Logon Only To These Workstations, and list all of the workstations except the one named MGR.

B. Take the extras' accounts, select Logon To and set Logon To All Workstations Except MGR.

C. This arrangement is not possible.

D. On MGR, remove the Log On Locally right from the groups to which these employees belong, and grant the right to anyone who needs to use it.

8. You have set Julia's logon hours to allow logon from 7:30 A.M. to 5:00 P.M. The domain's account policy is set to automatically log off a user when his or her time expires. At 5:00 P.M. Julia is logged on to the PDC. What happens?

A. Julia is logged off, and then must log on as another user.

B. Julia is logged off and unable to log back on.

C. Julia cannot be logged off when logged onto a domain controller.

---

exam
ⓦatch

*On some exam questions you may be offered answers that suggest adding users to the administrators group to give them the appropriate permissions. The rule of the thumb on these questions is that you never want to give an end user administrator permissions. There should be a better answer. With exams questions, first discard answers you know are not correct, to give yourself better odds at choosing the right answer.*

---

9. Your company is setting up a new research and development department with a staff of 15 new employees. The new employees will all belong to the global group RND that you have already set up. These employees will all be allowed to log on during the same times. They all need access to the same resources, and they will all have the same group memberships. As the administrator, you wish to make this as easy as possible, so you:

A. Create a user account with all the information that will be the same from user to user. Pick a default password and make sure the User Must Change Password At Next Logon box is checked. Then select the Account Disabled box so that this account is never actually used to log on. Now copy this user like a template to create all the accounts.

B. Change the default user settings for this session with all the information that will be the same from user to user. Now you can create new user accounts with the default settings.

C. Log on as an administrator and open User Manager for Domains. Select the Create New User Account Template, and fill in all the information that will be the same from user to user. Click the Add button. Create each user from that Account Template.

**10.** Rick, an administrator, runs a backup from 2:00 A.M. to 4:00 A.M. every morning. Sometimes, files do not appear to be backed up. Rick suspects that users may periodically be using files during that time frame. What can he do to automatically ensure that no users are logged on during the backup period?

A. Rick can run Server Manager and forcibly disconnect users at 2:00 A.M. Then all files will be automatically backed up.

B. Rick can send a memo to all users requesting that they not be logged onto the system from 2:00 A.M. to 4:00 A.M.

C. Rick can create a global group that disallows logons during the 2:00 A.M. to 4:00 A.M. timeframe, and add all users to this group. Then he can check the Forcibly Disconnect Remote Users From Server When Logon Hours Expire box in User Manager for Domains.

D. Rick must set the logon hours for all users to disallow logons during the 2:00 A.M. to 4:00 A.M. timeframe. Then he must check the Forcibly Disconnect Remote Users From Server When Logon Hours Expire box in Account Policies.

exam
Ⓦatch   *Be sure that you understand trust relationships and the different trust models for the exam. These are key to passing the Enterprise exam.*

# QUESTIONS AND ANSWERS

| | |
|---|---|
| Which utility allows you to manage your account information and set up new users on the network? | User Manager for Domains |
| Which default user is the main account to manage the network? | Administrator |
| Doing this will make it harder for hackers to log on with your Administrator account. | Rename the account |
| True or False: It is a good idea to add a user to the Administrators group, to give the user appropriate permissions. | False |
| These groups are specific to a machine. | Local groups |
| True or False: It is a good idea to make a backup copy of your Administrator account. | True |
| When setting up a new user, you try to use the password Frederick21BKF74 and the system will not accept it. What problem are you encountering? | The password is too long. The maximum password length is 14 characters. |
| You want to add the local Users group to the Global Domain Users group. What do you have to do? | You can't add local groups to global groups. |
| As an administrator, you have user Joe all set up with permissions and group memberships. Joe leaves the company, and you delete his account. Two months later, Joe returns to the company. You re-add Joe to the domain. When he logs on, he finds that he cannot access the directories he could access before. Why is this? | Since Joe's account was deleted and re-added, the SID changed. Permissions and group memberships are saved with the SID. If the account is deleted, so are the permissions and group memberships. When the new account is created, the permissions and group memberships have to be reassigned. |
| To rename an account, you select the Option menu and Rename. True or False? | False. The User menu and Rename is correct. |
| These groups are specific to the domain. | Global group |

**11.** You want to set a standard account creation policy that uses the same value for username, initial password, and home directory. Using this policy, what is the maximum length for the username?

A. 8 characters

B. 14 characters

C. 20 characters

D. 32 characters

**12.** Jessie wants all the domain administrators of the TIGER domain to be domain administrators of a trusting domain, CUBS. How can she accomplish this most easily?

A. Add TIGER\Domain Admins to the CUBS\Domain Admins group.

B. Add TIGER\Domain Admins to the Administrators group on the CUBS PDC.

C. Add each member of TIGER\Domain Admins to CUBS\Domain Admins.

D. Add CUBS\Domain Users to the TIGER\Domain Users group.

E. There's no way to give domain administrators in the TIGER domain the same access they'd have as domain administrators of the CUBS domain.

**13.** Which of the following must be done to make a system policy (created with the System Policy Editor) apply for every user in a domain?

A. It must be called NTUSER.MAN.

B. It must be called NTCONFIG.POL.

C. It must be in the directory share for roaming profiles.

D. It must be in the NETLOGON share directory on all domain controllers.

**14.** Pete is trying to set an audit policy that will allow him to track down possible security problems after the fact. He doesn't want to audit so many events that they get to "noise" level, though. He's going to turn on success and failure audits for everything, except for setting only failure audits on which of the following?

A. Logon and Logoff
B. Process Tracking
C. File and Object Access
D. Use of User Rights
E. Security Policy Changes

**15.** A local group may have which of the following as members?

A. Local and domain users
B. Local groups
C. Global groups
D. Domain users from a trusted domain
E. Global groups from a trusted domain

**16.** The network you are planning is moderately sized, but requires centralized administration of accounts. In addition, you are required to have resources controlled by the domains that host them. What kind of domain model will you use in this situation?

A. Single Domain
B. Master Domain
C. Multiple Master Domain
D. Complete Trust

**17.** After problems with a user in your domain, you've decided to implement a User Rights Policy in User Manager for Domains on your PDC. Who will be affected by this policy?

A. Only the local machine will be affected.
B. Only the local groups will be affected.
C. The entire domain will be affected.
D. Only the account of the user in question will be affected.

exam
ⓦatch  *Be sure to understand the difference between the trusted and the trusting domains—which one has the resources and which one has the users!*

**18.** Jennifer is a member of three groups: Graphics, Marketing, and SQLUser. The Graphics group has Read access to an object, Marketing has no access, while SQLUser has Read and Write. What group permissions does Jennifer have?

    A. Read

    B. Write

    C. Read and Write

    D. No Access

*Remember the acronym AGLP for the exam. This will help you remember that accounts are added to global groups, which are added to local groups, which are assigned permissions.*

# Planning Your Windows NT Server 4.0 Protocol Strategy

**1.** Your domain will span two subnets. Assuming that the router will support them, what protocols can be set up as the only protocol on each Windows system?

    A. TCP/IP

    B. IPX/SPX (NWLink)

    C. NetBEUI

    D. AppleTalk

**2.** Bob wants to set up his site so that it can be connected to the Internet. Which protocol should he use?

    A. Internetwork Protocol eXtended (IPX)

    B. Transmission Control Protocol/Internet Protocol (TCP/IP)

    C. Inter-NetBEUI (Binary Extensions Under Internetworking)

    D. Distributed Link for Computers (DLC)

**3.** Which protocol would you use if you wished to ease migration from a NetWare environment?

A. TCP/IP

B. IPX/SPX

C. NetBEUI

D. AppleTalk

**4.** Harry is setting up a small network, but wants to avoid having to change network protocols in the future. Which protocol should he choose?

A. TCP/IP

B. IPX/SPX

C. NetBEUI

D. AppleTalk

**5.** What three things must be bound together to enable Windows networking on a system?

A. Network adapter

B. Network protocol

C. Network service

D. Network class

E. Network routing

**6.** Which of the following are true about Services for Macintosh?

A. It allows Macintosh clients to print to non-Postscript printers.

B. It may be configured on any Windows NT workstation or server.

C. It requires an NTFS partition.

D. It can act as a seed router in an AppleTalk network.

E. It allows Windows systems to print to AppleTalk Postscript printers.

**7.** Vicki wants to set up a Macintosh volume share with full access for her group to manage, and to set up Macintosh volume shares in subdirectories under this, with access restricted to particular user groups. What's the best way to set this up?

A. Do just as she's planned.

B. Since she can't nest Macintosh volumes, she should just set up volume shares for each subdirectory, and belong to all groups that may access one of the shares.

C. As in answer B, but Vicki should use a separate user account for each group that may access one of the shares.

D. Set up the single volume and password-protect it rather than using group access.

8. You have just mixed your Windows NT network with a Macintosh network. You want to install a Macintosh print processor for a Postscript printer on Windows NT Workstation. What must you install to have this print processor on your Workstation?

A. AppleTalk

B. Services for Macintosh

C. Print Services for Macintosh

D. Client Services for Macintosh

---

exam
Ⓦatch

*Be careful when setting the lease duration. You should set a lease duration that best meets your needs. If you have a lot of IP addresses but relatively few computers, you can set a long lease duration. Conversely, if you have only a few IP addresses and many computers you should set a short lease. If you have many IP addresses you may be tempted to choose Unlimited. That isn't recommended, because DHCP not only assigns IP addresses, but also client configuration information. If you set the lease duration to Unlimited, your clients won't ever update their configuration information, if it changes, unless you manually update DHCP at each client.*

---

9. A new Hewlett Packard laser printer has been added to the network, but no one can print to it. You check that it is properly attached to the network, and find it is running and correctly attached. What is most likely the reason no one can print to this printer?

A. The default protocol of Windows NT is TCP/IP, which obviously hasn't been installed.

B. HP printers require AppleTalk to communicate with the network.

C. The cable connection to the printer is faulty.

D. DLC hasn't been installed on the network.

**10.** Your network has recently gotten Internet connections, but uses NetBEUI as its network protocol. You install TCP/IP, but users complain that access time to the Internet is slow. You believe the problem to be the binding order of these protocols. What can you do to the binding order to increase access time?

A. Lower TCP/IP in the binding order.

B. Raise TCP/IP in the binding order.

C. Leave TCP/IP where it is in the binding order, and raise NetBEUI.

D. Raise the adapter card in the binding order.

**11.** You are running the NWLink protocol on your Windows NT server, and wish to view its configuration information from the command prompt. Which command will provide this information?

A. IPXSPX

B. IPXROUTE

C. IPXROUTE CONFIG

D. NWLINK CONFIG

**12.** You have installed TCP/IP on your network, but don't want to take the chance that users will change the IP addresses on their computers. What will you do to solve this problem?

A. Implement DLC on your network.

B. Implement DHCP, and specify a range of addresses to issue to hosts.

C. Implement DNS, and set the IP address on each computer on the network.

D. Implement WINS on your network.

e x a m
ⓦa t c h
*When using DHCP and WINS, your WINS renewal interval must be at least one-half the time of the DHCP lease. This ensures that the registered computer names have the proper IP addresses assigned to them.*

**13.** Of the following, which are serial protocols? (Choose all that apply.)

A. TCP/IP

B. DLC

C. SLIP

D. PPP

E. AppleTalk

**14.** You have set up a multihomed computer to act as a router between two subnets. You have installed everything properly, but it still doesn't route TCP/IP packets. What must you enable for the Windows NT server to act as a router?

A. Routing in the DHCP Relay tab of TCP/IP Properties

B. IP Forwarding in the Services applet in Control Panel

C. IP Forwarding in the Routing tab of TCP/IP Properties

D. Routing in the Routing tab of TCP/IP Properties

**15.** You have two ISDN adapters connected to your Windows NT server, and you want the bandwidth of both combined, thereby increasing the bandwidth and throughput. Which protocol makes this possible?

A. PPTP

B. PPP-MP

C. SLIP

D. PPP

**16.** Which of the following protocols require configuration? (Choose all that apply.)

A. TCP/IP

B. NetBEUI

C. NWLink

D. DLC

17. You are connecting your Microsoft network to a Novell NetWare network. Assuming that the NetWare network is using its default protocol, which protocol should you install on your Windows NT server, if you want to integrate the two networks?

A. TCP/IP

B. IPX/SPX

C. NWLink

D. NetBEUI

18. You want to separate a small group of computers from a network that only uses NetBEUI. You want to avoid physically separating them. You require these computers to communicate with each other, but they cannot interact with the rest of the network. What can you do?

A. Use the same Scope ID on each computer on the entire network.

B. Use a different Scope ID on each computer on the entire network.

C. Use the same Scope ID on each computer in this group.

D. Use a different Scope ID on each computer in this group.

## QUESTIONS AND ANSWERS

| | |
|---|---|
| An NT Server cannot communicate outside of its own subnet... | Make sure that a valid default gateway has been configured in the IP Address tab. |
| You have two NICs installed in a single server, and data fails to pass between the two different networks... | Make sure that Enable IP Forwarding is checked on the Routing tab. |
| IP address to NetBIOS name resolution is failing... | Make sure that you have a valid WINS server configured in the WINS tab. |

**19.** Your network has incorporated DHCP. A user on a different subnet would like to use DHCP, but complains that it doesn't seem to work. What is the problem, and how can you fix it?

A. Broadcasts to the DHCP server aren't being routed. Implement a DHCP relay agent.

B. Broadcasts to the DHCP server are being routed, but the DHCP server doesn't have DHCP relay agent enabled.

C. DHCP can only be configured with addresses for one subnet. Install a new DHCP server on each subnet.

D. DHCP can only be routed on a network that uses a routable protocol. Install such a protocol.

---

**e x a m**
**Ⓦ a t c h**

*One or more seed routers are required on each physical network so that the routing information for that network can be broadcast.*

---

# TCP/IP Installation and Configuration

**1.** Which of the following are transport layer protocols that run over the IP network layer?

A. FTP

B. TCP

C. UDP

D. HTTP

E. SMTP

**2.** According to the network class system, which of the following could be valid networks?

A. 129.0.0.0

B. 196.43.0.0

C. 16.0.0.0

D. 203.89.4.0

E. 190.5.0.0

**3.** Which of the following map NetBIOS names to IP addresses?

A. HOSTS file

B. LMHOSTS file

C. DNS

D. WINS

**4.** Stan wants his network to be easy to manage. What can he set up to make it easy to configure systems with their IP address, subnet mask, and default gateway?

A. DNS

B. WINS

C. DHCP

D. ARP

**5.** Which protocol allows translation of IP addresses to MAC addresses?

A. WINS

B. DNS

C. UDP

D. ARP

**6.** What protocol is used by the PING and TRACERT utilities?

A. TCP

B. UDP

C. ARP

D. ICMP

**7.** Which of the following are necessary to use TCP/IP on a LAN?

A. A unique TCP/IP address for each system

B. An appropriate subnet mask

C. A default gateway

D. A WINS server

E. A DNS server

**8.** If the subnet mask is 255.255.255.0 and a network address on that subnet is 10.53.49.136, what is the network address of that subnet?

A. 10.0.0.0

B. 10.53.0.0

C. 10.53.49.0

D. 255.255.255.136

## QUESTIONS AND ANSWERS

| | |
|---|---|
| Can I use TCP/IP as my only network protocol without a router? | Yes. You only need a router to reach nodes outside a local area network. |
| Does it really matter which subnet mask I use on a local area network? | Yes. The mask needs to indicate that the other addresses are on the same network. |
| Do I need a WINS server to use TCP/IP on my local area network? | No, and it's probably not worth implementing on a network of this size. NetBIOS names can be resolved with broadcasts. |
| Do I need a DHCP server to use TCP/IP on my network? | No, but if you're closer to 50 systems, it will help in their configuration. |
| Do I need a DNS server to use TCP/IP on my local area network? | No, you don't have to use domain names at all, or you could enter the names in the HOSTS files if you need DNS naming for some reason. |
| Do I need to apply for range of Internet addresses? | No, you can use pretty much any network address range you choose, though it's good practice to use one of the reserved ones, like 10.1.1.* for your LAN. If you decide to connect to the Internet in the future, you usually work out the address assignments with your service provider. You'll probably need only a 30- or 62-node range, subnetted from one of your provider's Class C licenses. |

**9.** You decide to send a message to a user in a different domain. TCP/IP looks at the IP address of the destination and realizes it must be routed. Where will the message be sent?

A. The DNS server

B. The default gateway

C. The default router

D. Directly to the computer the message is for

**10.** You have installed WINS and DNS on your network. Your boss knows a little about the process but asks you what the difference is between the LMHOST and HOST files? What will you tell her?

A. The HOST file maps host names to IP addresses, while LMHOSTS maps IP addresses to NetBIOS names

B. The HOST file maps IP addresses to NetBIOS names, while LMHOSTS maps host names to IP addresses)

C. The HOST file maps host names to NetBIOS names, while LMHOSTS maps NetBIOS names to host names

D. The HOST file maps host names to WINS, while LMHOSTS maps host names to IP addresses

## QUESTIONS AND ANSWERS

| | |
|---|---|
| Do I need a WINS server on my network? | No, but it would cut down dramatically on broadcast traffic. |
| Do I need a DHCP server on my network? | No, but you definitely want at least one. Configuring that many nodes manually is not easily maintainable. |
| Do I need a DNS server? | Yes, either you or your ISP need to provide a DNS server. Preferably, you'd set up a primary and secondary, and have your ISP set up another secondary name server. |
| What is the subnet mask for systems on this network? | The subnet mask is 255.255.0.0, since it's a non-subnetworked Class B network. |

ENTERPRISE
QUESTIONS

**11.** Packets are getting lost somewhere in route between your host and the destination host. Which utility will you use to view the route a packet is taking on a TCP/IP network?

A. ARP

B. TRACERT

C. PING

D. FINGER

**12.** Jennifer will not be using her computer for quite some time, and has decided to release the lease on her IP address. How can she do this?

A. Use the IPRELEASE utility.

B. Use the IPROUTE utility.

C. Use the IPCONFIG utility.

D. She can't. IP addresses are issued for a set period of time.

**13.** You have just installed TCP/IP on your network, and you give your Windows NT server the IP address of 127.0.0.1. You enter the other configuration information, and then go to test the connection with a command line-based utility. You see that this address is responding. However, when users attempt to connect to the server using this IP address, they can't interact with your computer. What is the problem?

A. DNS hasn't been enabled.

B. The subnet mask needs to be changed on the server.

C. The IP address needs to be changed on the server.

D. You haven't set up reverse lookup, so users need to type in an FQDN.

**14.** You are setting up an Internet domain for a charity, and have decided to register for a domain name. Which domain would you register with?

A. .COM

B. .EDU

C. .NET

D. .ORG

**15.** You are using the Internet to access a web site and view web pages. Which protocol of the TCP/IP suite is being used to transfer these HTML documents?

A. HTTP

B. FTP

C. IP

D. TCP

**16.** Which of the following command line utilities allow you to view the connections to your TCP/IP server, and the ports being used?

A. NETSTAT

B. IPCONFIG

C. NSLOOKUP

D. TRACERT

**17.** Your IP address is 199.128.244.1. Based on that IP address, what would your default subnet mask be?

A. 255.0.0.0

B. 255.255.0.0

C. 255.255.255.0

D. 255.255.255.255

**18.** Your network has obtained a pool of Class B addresses. How many host addresses is it capable of having?

A. 254

B. 32,000

C. 65,534

D. 16,777,214

**19.** Of the following, which addresses can't be used for the host's IP address on a TCP/IP network? (Choose all that apply.)

ENTERPRISE QUESTIONS

    A. 127.0.0.1

    B. 224.0.0.1

    C. 223.128.48.255

    D. 0.128.56.1

# QUESTIONS AND ANSWERS

| | |
|---|---|
| How should I set up DNS servers? | It would probably be simplest to set up one site as the primary, and set up a secondary at each of the other sites. You can also set up nameserver records for sub-domains at each site if you wish each to maintain its own information. For example, *.london.example.com nodes could have a different nameserver from *.rome.example.com nodes, and *.example.com could be yet another. |
| How will the routing work with a single domain and nameserver, but with multiple address ranges? | It's a common mistake to confuse name resolution with address routes. The name is resolved to a number before any path to the target is required. The nameserver that has authority over a domain doesn't even have to be located in any of the address ranges for the network or networks in question. |
| Do I need a WINS server? | A WINS server would be the best way to provide connectivity across your networks to create a single NetBIOS network name space. You might want one in each network for availability, but you should balance that against the simplicity of having few to keep synchronized. |
| Do I need a DHCP server? | It depends on the size of each local area network. You'd set up a DHCP server at each site that was big enough to benefit from it. It wouldn't really make sense to try DHCP Relay Agents in this scenario; they're more for when your local networks are adjacent. |

# NetWare Connectivity

1. You are mixing your Microsoft network with a NetWare network. You want to use the best protocol possible on the Windows NT domain for communicating with the NetWare network. The NetWare network uses its default protocol. Which protocol will you install on the Windows NT machines?

   A. IPX/SPX
   B. TCP/IP
   C. NWLink
   D. NetBEUI

2. An office with a NetWare 3.12 server has just been incorporated into a division that uses Microsoft Windows NT networking. Until the NetWare resources have been migrated, what's the easiest way to give access to the resources on that server to the rest of the division?

   A. Install CSNW on all the Windows NT workstations.
   B. Install GSNW on all the Windows NT servers.
   C. Install GSNW on a Windows NT server.
   D. Install FPNW on all the Windows NT servers.

3. Donnie is running a mixed network of NetWare 4.x (with NDS), and Windows NT. He wants to enable Windows NT Server to access files on the NetWare server. He installs GSNW on the Windows NT server. What else must he do?

   A. Nothing. GSNW will work as is.
   B. Nothing. NDS isn't supported, so he can't do anything.
   C. He must install Directory Service Manager for NetWare.
   D. He must supply GSNW with the default tree and context.

**4.** Dan is using the Migration Tool to migrate users from a NetWare server to a Windows NT domain controller. He wants to preserve as much information as possible. Which of the following may he copy?

A. Username

B. Password

C. Groups

D. Files and Directories

**5.** A GSNW share for a NetWare share is created with the default permissions on a Windows NT server. What access permissions would a user in the Windows NT domain have on the NetWare server share?

A. Whatever permissions his account on the NetWare server has

B. Whatever permissions the Administrator account has

C. Whatever permissions the Supervisor account has

D. Whatever default permissions a NetWare user has

**6.** Jennifer is using the Migration Tool for NetWare to migrate a small group of users on a NetWare server to a Windows NT server. Their usernames are common knowledge, and she wants to do the best she can to ensure that users outside the group won't play with these accounts before the users can get on and change their passwords. What's her best option for passwords?

A. Retain the NetWare password.

B. Set the password to be the same as the username.

C. All accounts have no password.

D. Set all the passwords to a specific character string.

**7.** You want to migrate a NetWare server to a Windows NT server. What will you use?

A. NWCONV

B. CONVERT

C. NTCONV

D. NDSCONV

**8.** You are preparing a migration. What file system must you use on Windows NT to preserve file and directory permissions?

A. FAT

B. NTFS

C. NWFS

D. It doesn't matter. File and directory permissions will go into the SAM.

**9.** Your network consists of three Windows NT servers, and 50 Windows NT workstations. You are in the process of connecting this network to another that runs Novell NetWare. You don't want to install anything on your workstations to connect to the NetWare network. Which of the following can you use under these circumstances?

A. GSNW

B. CSNW

C. FSNW

D. DSNW

**10.** Which application would you use to manage NetWare shares and their permissions from Windows NT Server?

A. GSNW

B. CSNW

C. FSNW

D. DSNW

exam
ⓦatch

*Although the majority of the Enterprise exam focuses on Directory Services (Domains and Trusts), there are several NetWare-related questions. Be prepared to see such questions, and be confident that you are familiar with the topic.*

**11.** Your network is a mix of NetWare and Windows NT. NetWare clients have been coming to you, needing access to files located on a Windows NT server. What can you do to enable NetWare users to access files on the Windows NT server?

    A. Implement GSNW, and set up a gateway for NetWare users to access the Windows NT server.

    B. Implement CSNW on the NetWare client computers.

    C. Implement FSNW.

    D. Implement DSNW.

**12.** What information must you provide to Windows NT in order to connect for the first time to a NetWare 3.12 server?

    A. Default Tree

    B. Context

    C. Preferred Server

    D. Network ID

**13.** You have just set up your Windows NT server to work with a Novell NetWare network. What information must you provide Windows NT Server to connect to a NetWare 4.*x* server? (Choose all that apply.)

    A. Default Tree

    B. Context

    C. Preferred Server

    D. Server name

**14.** You have installed GSNW on a Windows NT server that isn't running NWLink protocol. What will happen?

    A. You will receive an error and have to install NWLink, then reinstall GSNW.

    B. GSNW will use the protocols already installed on the Windows NT server.

    C. GSNW will appear to load properly, but log an error to the system log.

    D. Nothing. If NWLink isn't present when GSNW is installed, it will automatically be installed.

**15.** You have decided to use Migration Tool for NetWare to migrate a NetWare server to a Windows NT server. What versions of NetWare can you migrate using this tool?

    A. 2.*x*

    B. 3.*x*

    C. 4.*x*

    D. All of the above

    E. Only 3.*x* and 4.*x*

**16.** You want to slowly migrate a NetWare network to Windows NT Server. Windows NT comes with services and tools to make this migration possible. Which of the following aren't included with Windows NT, and must be purchased separately?

    A. GSNW

    B. CSNW

    C. FSNW

    D. DSNW

    E. Migration Tool for NetWare

**17.** You suspect that an invalid frame type is being used by your Windows NT server. Which application would you use to change the frame type?

    A. Network

    B. Services

    C. NWLink IPX/SPX Properties

    D. Server Manager

**18.** Your Windows NT server is having problems communicating with a NetWare network. You suspect that the problem may be an invalid frame type. What utility can you use to see what frame type your server is using?

    A. FRAME /SHOW

    B. ROUTE CONFIG

    C. NWLINK CONFIG

    D. IPXROUTE CONFIG

**19.** The NetWare clients on your network are feeling a little jealous of Microsoft users' being able to enjoy a single logon. At present, the NetWare users have to log on to each and every NetWare server they need access to. What can you do to solve this problem?

    A. Set up a gateway to PDC using GSNW, so the NetWare clients can use NT's logon.

    B. Implement CSNW on each of the NetWare clients.

    C. Implement FSNW.

    D. Implement DSMN.

exam
ⓦatch
*Plan on arriving to the exam site 30 minutes early so that you have ample time to get composed and ready. Utilize the scratch paper to help you visualize the questions.*

# Configuring Windows NT Server 4.0 Protocol Routing

1. Bobby has two network cards in his Windows NT server, and has enabled routing. The TCP/IP bindings look right. Unfortunately, it still doesn't seem to be working. What should he do?

   A. Remove the Rest-In-Peace (RIP) route-blocking service.
   B. Install Routing Information Protocol (RIP) for TCP/IP and reboot.
   C. Unbind all other protocols from the NIC.
   D. Install OSPF for TCP/IP and reboot.

2. You want to enable routing over an IPX network. You have both NWLink and TCP/IP installed on your Windows NT server. What else must you do to your Windows NT server to enable RIP for NWLink?

   A. Add the RIP for NWLink service to the Windows NT server.
   B. Add the RIP for IPX service to the Windows NT server.
   C. Add the RIP for IPX service to the NetWare server you're connecting to.
   D. Check Enable RIP Routing from the Routing tab of the protocol.

3. Which of the following protocols can Windows NT Server 4.0 route on a network? (Choose all that apply.)

   A. IPX/SPX
   B. NetBEUI
   C. InterNIC
   D. TCP/IP

**4.** You have set up your PDC as a router between two segments using different protocols. During peak hours, when users are logging onto the network, the network's performance slows to a crawl. Users are complaining. What can you do to fix this situation?

A. Quit using the PDC as a router, and make a BDC a router.

B. Quit using the PDC as a router, and create a dedicated server to act as a router.

C. Disable IP Forwarding, which will make logons quicker and simplify routing.

D. Disable the router service from the PDC, and enable it on another computer.

**5.** Which of the following best defines a routing table?

A. It dynamically exchanges information with other routers.

B. It stores computer and network addresses.

C. It statically stores and then exchanges information with other routers.

D. It statically stores and assigns IP addresses.

**6.** Your WAN consists of Windows NT in one domain, and Macintosh computers in another. They don't use the same protocols. What will you use to enable these two networks to communicate?

A. Bridge

B. Router

C. BOOTP Relay Agent

D. Gateway

**7.** You have decided to connect your network to the Internet. Your network already uses TCP/IP as its transport protocol. Which of the following would you use?

A. Router

B. Bridge

C. BOOTP Relay Agent

D. Gateway

**8.** You have been experiencing problems with broadcast traffic bogging down the network. At present, when someone broadcasts a message, it is transmitted across the entire network. You find that these broadcasts are primarily coming from one small group. How can you solve this problem?

A. Segment the problem area of the network, and set up Windows NT Server as a bridge between the two segments.

B. Segment the problem area of the network, and set up Windows NT Server as a BOOTP Relay Agent.

C. Segment the problem area of the network, and set up Windows NT Server as a Proxy Server.

D. Segment the problem area of the network, and set up Windows NT Server as a gateway.

**9.** Which of the following best defines RIP?

A. It dynamically exchanges information with other routers.

B. It dynamically stores computer and network addresses.

C. It statically stores and then exchanges information with other routers.

D. It statically stores and assigns IP addresses.

**10.** Your WAN consists of three T1 lines, connecting Detroit, Toronto, and New York. Which should you use to connect your Local Area Network to the Wide Area Network?

A. Router

B. Bridge

C. RIP

D. RAS

exam
ⓦatch

*Make sure that you know that if you have installed the IPX/SPX protocol on your network and you still cannot communicate with other computers using the IPX/SPX protocol you will need to check your Frame Type.*

## QUESTIONS AND ANSWERS

| | |
|---|---|
| You are connecting two separate LAN segments. Which network device (bridge or router) would you use? | Bridge |
| You have to connect your LAN segment to the Internet. What needs to be in place so that the computers on your network can get there? | Router |

**11.** A company merger has forced you to add a subnet of Macintosh computers. What will you use to route AppleTalk over Windows NT Server? (Choose all that apply.)

A. Add Services for Macintosh to the Windows NT server you're going to use for routing.

B. Add the Macintosh Routing Service to the Windows NT server you're going to use for routing.

C. Add CSNT to each of the Macintosh client computers.

D. Check Enable Routing from the Routing tab of Service for Macintosh's Properties.

**12.** You have several subnets but only one DHCP server. You want to have IP addresses issued to everyone on the network, but broadcasted requests for IP addresses are being filtered out, and not making it to the DHCP server. What will you do to remedy this problem?

A. Set up a DHCP Relay Agent on each subnet.

B. Set up NetBEUI as your protocol so you don't have to worry about this problem.

C. Configure your Windows NT server to enable IP Routing.

D. Set up a DHCP Proxy Server on each subnet.

**13.** Your network uses NetBEUI as its protocol. Due to expansion, you add several segments to the network, but you know NetBEUI isn't routable. What can you do?

    A. Use a router.

    B. Use a bridge.

    C. Enable NetBEUI routing.

    D. Use NetBIOS extensions.

**14.** You have decided to use a Windows NT Server 4.0 computer as a dedicated router. This computer has both NWLink and TCP/IP bound to the network card installed in it. Based on this information about the computer, why can't it be used as a dedicated router?

    A. Windows NT Server 4.0 can't be used as a dedicated router.

    B. NWLink isn't routable.

    C. TCP/IP isn't routable.

    D. You need to install more network cards.

**15.** Which of the following will periodically broadcast changes on the network?

    A. Dedicated Router

    B. Dynamic Router

    C. Static Router

    D. Bridge

**16.** The Multiprotocol Router is comprised of which of the following? (Choose all that apply.)

    A. RIP for IPX

    B. OSI

    C. RIP for TCP/IP

    D. DHCP Relay Agent

ENTERPRISE QUESTIONS

**17.** Your network uses both TCP/IP and IPX/SPX. You want to enable routing of both these protocols on a Windows NT Server 4.0 computer that you plan to use as a router. You decide to implement RIP for NWLink and RIP for TCP/IP on your server. Will this solution work?

    A. Yes, you can use both RIP for TCP/IP and RIP for NWLink, and route protocols simultaneously.

    B. Yes, but you must install two network cards for RIP for TCP/IP, and two network cards for RIP for NWLink.

    C. No, you must use RIP for NWLink on the NetWare server, and RIP for TCP/IP on the Windows NT server.

    D. No, only RIP for TCP/IP or RIP for NWLink can be used on a router—not both.

**18.** You have decided to use IP RIP to route packets on a TCP/IP network. You decide to use a Windows NT Server 4.0 computer, and a Windows NT Server 3.51 computer as dynamic routers. Will this solution work?

    A. Yes, you can use both computers to route packets using IP RIP.

    B. Yes, but you must use the ROUTE ADD command to configure the routing table in Windows NT Server 3.51 to use dynamic routing.

    C. No, Windows NT Server 3.51 can only use static routing.

    D. No, Windows NT Server 4.0 can't route with a Windows NT Server 3.51 computer.

**19.** You have decided to implement routing through a Windows NT server. How many network cards must be installed on the Windows NT server if it is to be used as a router? (Choose the minimum required.)

    A. One

    B. Two

    C. Three

    D. Four

# Installing and Configuring NT Server 4.0 Remote Access Service

1. Which protocols may be used on a Windows NT workstation dialing into a Windows NT server using RAS?

   A. SLIP

   B. PPP

   C. TCP/IP

   D. IPX/SPX

   E. NetBEUI

2. You want to use Multilink, but ISDN isn't available in your area. What options do you have?

   A. Install a multilink adapter, and get multiple phone lines.

   B. Install multiple modems, and get multiple phone lines.

   C. Install multiple ISDN adapters, and get multiple phone lines.

   D. Just use Multilink. It will automatically configure itself for this problem.

ENTERPRISE QUESTIONS

**3.** Timothy wants to use RAS to connect remote computers with his network. Which connection media may he use?

A. PSTN

B. ISDN

C. X.25

D. X.400

E. Internet

**4.** You have chosen Require Encrypted Authentication for your RAS server connections. What authentication protocols will it support?

A. PAP

B. SPAP

C. MD5

D. MS-CHAP

**5.** Rick wishes to keep to a single protocol on workstations dialing into his RAS server. The workstations need to access the Internet through the router at work, and also get to a particular share on a NetWare server. Which of the following are true about Rick's options?

A. He must install both TCP/IP and IPX protocols on the workstations.

B. He can install just TCP/IP on the workstations and use GSNW to access the NetWare share.

C. He must configure RAS to support both TCP/IP and IPX.

D. He can install just IPX on the workstations and use GSIP to access the Internet.

**6.** In order to set up a VPN through the Internet, which of the following are needed?

A. PPP

B. PPTP

C. A dial-up connection to the RAS server

D. Internet access for the RAS server and clients

E. Global Remote Access Secure Server (GRASS)

**7.** You have installed RAS on your Windows NT server, and want to view the device, error, and connection statistics. Which program will enable you to view all of this information?

A. RAS Monitor

B. DUN Monitor

C. TAPI

D. Remote Services

**8.** You set up RAS on a Windows NT server, and attempt to test whether it works. You don't want to risk making more changes than you have to, so you don't make any changes, except those made to RAS. You attempt connecting, but the session fails. What is most likely the reason for this?

A. You forgot to enable IP routing.

B. You attempted logging on locally.

C. You forgot to enable IP Forwarding.

D. You don't have the dial-in permission set on your account.

**9.** You are concerned about whether you are actually connected to a RAS server. Which utility will you use to test the connection?

A. PING

B. IPCONFIG

C. RASTEST

D. FINGER

**10.** You receive a complaint from a user that he cannot access the network via RAS. You check the number of connections, and find that there are 256 connections. You also find that the user is trying to connect to the RAS server using PPP. What is the problem?

A. RAS only supports 255 connections.

B. RAS only supports 256 connections.

C. RAS cannot accept incoming sessions using PPP.

D. RAS cannot accept outgoing sessions using PPP.

**11.** A user connects from a Windows NT workstation to a Windows NT server through RAS. Which authentication protocol will RAS use to authenticate this user?

A. SPAP

B. Clear Text

C. PAP

D. MS-CHAP

**12.** A Windows 95 user is having trouble connecting to a RAS server. She tells you that she keeps getting messages that a compatible set of protocols couldn't be negotiated. What is the problem, and how can you fix it?

A. You can't. RAS doesn't support Windows 95 users.

B. Change the protocols in the RAS server to match the configuration of the Windows 95 client.

C. Change the protocols in the RAS client to match a protocol in the RAS server.

D. You must install new protocols in the Windows 95 computer. They use different protocols than Windows NT Server does.

**13.** You decide to set up RAS on your Windows NT server, but have yet to install either a modem or a network adapter. What can you do so that you can configure RAS before installing the necessary hardware?

A. Choose the No Adapter option during installation.

B. Install MS Loopback adapter.

C. You don't need a modem or NIC to install RAS.

D. You can't install RAS without a modem or NIC.

exam

ⓦatch

*You will find that most questions concerning registry entries and where they should be placed will most likely find their way into the HKEY_LOCAL_MACHINE subtree. HKEY_LOCAL_MACHINE contains configuration information about the local computer system, including hardware and operating system data.*

**14.** You have installed RAS on a Windows NT server using TCP/IP, and now want to test it. You connect your laptop to the server with a null modem cable, and install NWLink on the laptop. You attempt making a connection to RAS and fail. What is the problem?

A. RAS doesn't support null modems.

B. RAS doesn't support TCP/IP.

C. RAS doesn't support NWLink.

D. The protocols must be the same on both the client and the server.

**15.** PPP clients want to run applications over RAS. What kinds of applications will be supported on a Windows NT server running RAS? (Choose all that apply.)

A. WinSock API applications that use IPX/SPX

B. WinSock API applications that use TCP/IP

C. Named pipes

D. Remote Procedure Calls

## QUESTIONS AND ANSWERS

| | |
|---|---|
| ISDN is not available in our locality. What can we do to increase our bandwidth to those kinds of speeds without spending lots of money? | Install additional modems on your clients and servers and take advantage of Multilink which will allow you to bundle together multiple modems into one connection. |
| I want to have users connect through an ISP and then establish a connection to my network through the Internet. | Use PPTP. Configure a RAS PPTP server and enable PPTP on your DUN client computers. |
| I have a Windows NT Workstation that I want to install a RAS server on. I expect to have up to ten simultaneous users connecting to it. What are my options? | Windows NT Workstation only supports one inbound RAS connection. You will need to install a RAS server on a Windows NT Server or reinstall Windows NT Server on your NT Workstation. |

**16.** Which of the following are serial protocols that RAS supports?

A. NWLink

B. PPP

C. TCP/IP

D. SLIP

**17.** You receive complaints that users are receiving the following message when trying to connect to the network through RAS: "Unable to connect. No more connections can be made to this remote computer because the computer has exceeded its client license limit." How can you solve this problem?

A. In RAS Manager, increase the number of incoming callers allowed to connect.

B. In License Manager, change Windows NT Server's licensing mode from per server to per seat.

C. In License Manager, change RAS licensing to a higher number.

D. In the Registry, change the value of the licensing in the RAS subtree to 5.

**18.** You attempt using RAS's autodial feature to connect to the Internet using SLIP. No matter how many times you try, you are unable to connect. What is the problem, and how can you fix it?

A. RAS doesn't support SLIP. Use PPP.

B. RAS's autodial doesn't work with SLIP accounts. Have your ISP switch you to a PPP account.

C. RAS deals with direct connections, not with connections to the Internet. Use Internet Explorer.

D. RAS is capturing the port, and not allowing anything else to use it.

exam
Ⓦatch   *Although Windows NT Workstation and Server have identical implementations of the RAS, Windows NT Server allows a whopping 256 simultaneous inbound connections while Windows NT Workstation allows only one.*

## QUESTIONS AND ANSWERS

| | |
|---|---|
| My users are currently using third-party SLIP client software to connect to an existing UNIX server at my site. I want to replace the UNIX dial-up server with a Windows NT RAS server. Are there any additional considerations I should make? | If you implement a Windows NT Server as your dial-up server, you will need to install PPP client software on your users' workstations. RAS does not provide a SLIP server component. If your users are using Windows 95 or Windows NT Workstation, consider installing DUN on those machines. |
| Users on my network currently connect to my RAS server using the NetBEUI protocol. I want these users to be able to browse Internet web sites through my network's current Internet gateway. | Install TCP/IP on the users' workstations. TCP/IP is the language we speak on the Internet and users will need it if they want to browse Internet resources. |

19. A Windows NT Workstation user finds out that you are using RAS on the Windows NT server. He is using RAS on his computer, but needs to support 13 simultaneous inbound sessions. How can you help this user?

A. Tell him that more client licenses must be purchased before he can accept that many incoming sessions.

B. Tell him that Windows NT Workstation doesn't allow more than one incoming session at a time, and that Windows NT Server must be installed.

C. Tell him to use RAS Manager to increase the number of incoming sessions allowed.

D. Tell him to use RAS Administrator to increase the number of incoming sessions allowed.

exam
ⓦatch

*Gateway Services For NetWare (GSNW) is a Windows NT Server network service that attaches to NetWare servers. Files, print queues, and some NetWare utilities on NetWare servers are then available to all clients, even though they may not be running a NetWare-compatible protocol or client. This applies as well to DUN clients dialing in to a RAS server.*

ENTERPRISE
QUESTIONS

## QUESTIONS AND ANSWERS

| | |
|---|---|
| What methods can I implement to make my RAS server more secure? | A secure physical facility with a locked door is a basic necessity. You can also implement callback so you can confirm where calls are being made from, monitor Windows NT auditing, apply PPTP filtering if required and implement a third-party intermediary device if you want more security than RAS itself provides. |
| If MS-CHAP is the best encryption method available to me in RAS, why wouldn't I always use it? | MS-CHAP is supported by Microsoft Windows clients but is not widely adopted by many other types of clients. Therefore, if you have UNIX hosts on your network or third-party dial-up clients, you will need to select another encryption method for those clients. |

# Internet Information Server

1. IIS provides an HTTP server. What does HTTP stand for?

   A. Holerithic TeleType Printer

   B. Hypertext Telemarketing Transmission Protocol

   C. HTML Transparent Transfer Protocol

   D. HyperText Transfer Protocol

2. You want to browse the intranet that you have installed on your network. Which of the following can you use to perform this action? (Choose all that apply.)

   A. Internet Explorer

   B. IIS

   C. Gopher

   D. Netscape Navigator

**3.** David created a virtual directory for IIS on an NTFS partition on FRED, his Windows NT server. He wants to allow anyone to access the files there through the web server, but he can't seem to get to the files there through the web. What does he need to do?

A. Allow Read access for IUSR_FRED.

B. Allow Read access for IUSR_DAVID.

C. Make sure his account has Read access.

D. Make sure Everyone has Full Control access.

**4.** Anita wants to use Active Server Pages (ASP) on her Windows NT server running 4.0 SP3. She installed IIS with Windows NT Server. Can she do what she wants?

A. Yes, she's ready to go.

B. No, she needs to upgrade IIS to at least version 3.

C. No, she needs to upgrade IIS to at least version 4.

D. No, she needs to be at SP4.

**5.** You have installed IIS, and have a direct connection to the Internet. Aside from IIS, what else must you configure to publish on the Web? (Choose all that apply.)

A. DNS

B. WINS

C. INS

D. Registered IP address

**6.** Jim wants to create an intranet at his site. What does he need?

A. He must have the Internet protocol on his computers.

B. He must have the intranet protocol on his computers.

C. He must install a firewall.

D. He must hire a consultant.

E. He must make the information he wants to share accessible via the network to users at his site.

ENTERPRISE
QUESTIONS

7. You have just installed IIS on a Windows NT server. Your boss likes what you have done with the company's Internet site. Now he would like to register a second domain name and IP address, and have his own personal site on the same server. How can you create two different servers on one physical server?

   A. Create a directory called WWWROOT2, and place it in the IIS directory.
   B. Create a virtual server through Internet Service Manager.
   C. Run a second instance of IIS.
   D. It can't be done.

8. Internet Information Server is made up of which services?

   A. World Wide Web (HTTP)
   B. Internet Relay Chat
   C. Bulletin Board Service
   D. FTP
   E. Gopher

9. When Internet Information Server is installed, it creates an account that is used for anonymous access. You decide to change the password of this account. What is the name of this account, and where must you change the password?

   A. IUSR_COMPUTERNAME. You must change the password in User Manager.
   B. IUSR_COMPUTERNAME. You must change the password in Internet Service Manager.
   C. GUEST. You must change the password in User Manager.
   D. IUSR_GUEST. You must change the password in User Manager and Internet Service Manager.
   E. IUSR_COMPUTERNAME. You must change the password in both User Manager and Internet Service Manager.

**10.** Jennifer wants to publish web pages through IIS. What language should she use to create these documents?

    A. Use Frontpage 98 to create HTTP documents.

    B. Use Frontpage 98 to create HTML documents.

    C. Use FTP as a means to create web pages.

    D. Write the web page in Interlac.

**11.** Anonymous users are complaining that they can't connect to IIS. You recently changed the password for the anonymous account in User Manager. What did you forget to do?

    A. Inform users of the password change.

    B. Change the password in Internet Service Manager.

    C. Delete the old anonymous account.

    D. Enable the account after the change was saved.

**12.** You are using IIS to publish on an intranet. Which of the following must you also install and configure if you're going to do this? (Choose all that apply.)

    A. DNS

    B. InterNIC

    C. BOOTP Relay Agent

    D. WINS

**13.** Julie wants to be a webmaster, and install IIS on her network. She is concerned about security. What can you tell her?

    A. IIS has no security.

    B. IIS's security features are integrated with Windows NT Server.

    C. You need to implement security through an ISP.

    D. You need to implement security with a special add-on program.

**14.** You've noticed that a particular user is causing major problems on your web site. What will IIS 2.0 allow you to do to solve this problem?

A. Restrict access by hostname.
B. Restrict access by subnet.
C. Restrict access by IP address.
D. Restrict access by infecting the bad user with a nasty virus.

**15.** You have made security changes in IIS to restrict users of the FTP service. You notice that, even though these changes have been made, users are still unaffected. What did you forget to do?

A. Reboot Windows NT Server.
B. Stop and Restart the FTP service.
C. Changes cannot be made while users are using the service.
D. Changes cannot be made while you are online.

**16.** You are administering IIS with the HTML version of the Internet Service Manager. You make certain changes to permissions that deal with a particular service, but nothing happens. Why?

A. You don't have the ability to reboot the server.
B. Such changes can't be made through the HTML version.
C. You can't stop, pause, or start the service.
D. The changes won't take effect until after you've logged off.

**17.** You are experiencing bandwidth problems due to the number of people using the FTP service of IIS. What can you do to lower the bandwidth used for this service?

A. Lower the bandwidth allowed to the FTP service.
B. Raise the bandwidth allowed to HTTP and Gopher.
C. You can't lower the bandwidth used by IIS services.
D. You must lower the bandwidth of all services provided by IIS.

*If you are connecting to the Internet directly, you don't need DNS or WINS for name resolution. Your ISP can take care of this for you. If you are using IIS for an intranet, you need either DNS or WINS for name resolution.*

**18.** Which of the following is a Uniform Resource Locator? (Choose all that apply.)

A. Server1

B. www.odyssey.on.ca/~mcross/welcome.html

C. www.microsoft.com

D. 198.0.23.1

**19.** You have IIS on a Windows NT server that you've connected to the web using RAS. You have always been issued an IP address from your ISP when connecting. Now that you have IIS installed on your server, you feel you're ready to publish to the Internet. You use IPCONFIG to check what IP address you have, and give it to potential customers. Users are now complaining that they can't connect using the IP address you've given them. Why?

A. You haven't set up DNS on your Windows NT server to perform name resolution.

B. IIS doesn't create anonymous accounts, so they can't connect.

C. You don't have a registered IP address, and the lease on the one you had before has expired.

D. You need the ISP to release a new IP address to you. The one you had before has expired.

# Monitoring and Performance Tuning

**1.** The network has been sluggish during peak hours, when one department is going through a shift change, and another is downloading reports. What tool will allow you to log the activities of components on the network, and monitor where potential bottlenecks may exist?

    A. Network Monitor

    B. Task Manager

    C. Performance Monitor

    D. System Monitor

**2.** You check your PDC and find that Pages/sec is above 20, and that %Disk time is over 90 percent. What does this indicate?

    A. Everything is normal.

    B. Disk thrashing. Upgrade the CPU.

    C. Disk thrashing. Upgrade the memory.

    D. Disk thrashing. Upgrade the hard disk.

**3.** You notice that performance on a stripe set with parity has slowed tremendously. While there appears to be plenty of space left on the set, you notice that the memory on this Windows NT server is being filled up. What is most likely the problem?

    A. The entire stripe set with parity has failed.

    B. The server needs more memory.

    C. A disk in the stripe set with parity has failed.

    D. One of the disks in the stripe set with parity is full.

**4.** Your Windows NT server is experiencing disk thrashing. Excessive paging of information from RAM to the swap file is occurring. What can be done to improve performance? (Choose all that apply.)

    A. Add more memory.

    B. Create more pagefiles, and distribute them across other disks on the server.

    C. Buy a new hard disk.

    D. Remove the pagefile from the boot partition, and place it on another partition.

*A program might not work correctly when you use Run Program on Alert because Performance Monitor passes the Alert condition as a parameter to the program. If it does not work correctly, you should create a batch file to run the program and call the batch file from Performance Monitor.*

**5.** You want to create a baseline that you can refer to for future reference. Which view in Performance Monitor should you use to create a baseline?

A. Chart

B. Log

C. Report

D. Alert

**6.** You are unsure as to the processor in use on your domain's BDC. You want to view an inventory of the computer's components, and view its current configuration of hardware. Which application will you choose?

A. Server Manager

B. Performance Monitor

C. Task Manager

D. NT Diagnostics

**7.** You want to check the counters on your hard disk, but they don't rise any higher than a value of zero in Performance Monitor. What must you do for them to appear?

A. Run DISKPERF –Y from the command prompt.

B. Run DISKPERF –YE from the command prompt.

C. Run DISKPERF –N from the command prompt.

D. Activate the counters from Performance Monitor.

**8.** You want to check the counters on a particular disk in a stripe set, but they don't rise any higher than a value of zero in Performance Monitor. What must you do for them to be enabled?

   A. Run DISKPERF –Y from the command prompt.

   B. Run DISKPERF –YE from the command prompt.

   C. Run DISKPERF –N from the command prompt.

   D. Activate the counters from Performance Monitor.

**9.** You want to start an application with a thread priority of 13. Which command would cause an application to start with this priority level?

   A. START *<application name>* /LOW

   B. START *<application name>* /NORMAL

   C. START *<application name>* /HIGH

   D. START *<application name>* /REALTIME

**10.** You notice that network traffic is quite high over the slow WAN link that connects your London office to Memphis. To increase performance, you want to decrease network traffic while synchronization takes place. Which of the following must you modify for this to happen?

   A. Synch Pulse Rate

   B. Replication Governor REG_DWORD value

   C. Replication Governor FWord value

   D. NetLogon idle value

**11.** You are trying to determine a bottleneck on the network. You decide to analyze the frames that are being sent to and from the PDC. Which application will you use?

   A. Network Administrator

   B. Network Monitor

   C. Framer

   D. Performance Monitor

**12.** You want to optimize virtual memory by distributing the pagefiles across several disks. Where will you configure this?

A. Server Manager

B. Virtual Memory on the Disk menu of Disk Administrator

C. Virtual Memory, accessed from the Performance tab of System Properties

D. Virtual Memory applet in Control Panel

**13.** You check the %Processor time on your PDC in Performance Monitor, and find that it is constantly running at more than 80 percent. What does this indicate?

A. The network is a bottleneck.

B. The CPU is a bottleneck.

C. Memory is a bottleneck.

D. Virtual memory is a bottleneck.

**14.** You want to be informed when the Available Bytes counter, for Virtual Memory, drops below 7MB. Where can you configure this to happen?

A. Performance Monitor | Alert View.

B. Alerter applet in Control Panel.

C. Server Manager.

D. Disk Administrator.

**15.** You want to set up an alert that will tell you when a certain counter is below 50 percent or above 90 percent. How would you do this?

A. Use the Services applet in Control Panel.

B. Set the alerts in Server Manager.

C. Set the alerts in Performance Monitor.

D. You can only set one alert per counter. The alert is sent if a counter is over a value, under a value, or equal to a value.

**16.** You check the Disk Queue Length counters in Performance Monitor, and notice that it has a constant value of two or more. What is the bottleneck?

A. Nothing. The value is good.

B. Disk drive

C. Memory

D. CPU

**17.** The computer you're planning to use as a BDC has a PCI bus. What kind of network card should be installed on this computer?

A. 8-bit

B. 16-bit

C. 32-bit

D. 64-bit

**18.** By what value can you adjust an application's priority while it's still running?

A. 2

B. 4

C. 8

D. 16

exam
ⓦatch
*You must use DISKPERF –YE to monitor a physical drive in a RAID set. Using DISKPERF –YE installs the Disk Drive Performance Statistics Driver low in the disk driver stack so that it can see individual physical disks before they are logically combined.*

**19.** Your company merged with another company that has always liked Novell. Since you'll be interacting with the NetWare network over a WAN link, you add NWLink to all the Windows NT workstations and servers that currently use TCP/IP. Now users who also access the Internet from their workstations are complaining that performance of the protocols has decreased. These same computers will almost never use the WAN link. What should you do to optimize performance on these computers?

A. Change the binding order of the protocols, so the most used are highest on the list.

B. Remove TCP/IP from the computers, and just use NWLink.

C. Change the frame type currently being used.

D. Add the NetBEUI protocol, since it's faster than the other two currently used on the network.

*Many people taking the exam get confused by the number of processors that are supported by Windows NT Server and Windows NT Workstation. Be sure to recognize that NT Workstation, as shipped, supports only two processors, while NT Server supports four.*

# Troubleshooting Windows NT 4.0

**1.** Your WAN connects a Windows NT network to an IBM mainframe. You attempt connecting to the mainframe, but fail. What will you need to install for your Windows NT server to communicate with the mainframe?

A. TCP/IP

B. Services for IBM

C. DLC

D. RAS

**2.** A driver encountered a fatal error. What can you use to view information about the failure?

A. Performance Monitor | Log View

B. Event Viewer

C. Network Monitor

D. PERFMON

**3.** You want to improve the speed at which data is accessed on a set of hard disks. Fault tolerance is not an issue. Which level of RAID should you choose?

A. RAID 0
B. RAID 1
C. RAID 3
D. RAID 5

4. You have implemented disk striping with parity on a set of disks. One of these disks fails. You replace the failed disk with a new one, and create a partition equal to those on the other disks. How will you regenerate the stripe set?

A. In Disk Administrator, select the set and the free space on the new disk. Choose Regenerate from the Fault Tolerance menu.
B. Use RDISK to regenerate the disk.
C. Use Windows NT Explorer to select the set and the free space on the new disk. Choose Regenerate from the File menu.
D. The disk will automatically regenerate now that the failed disk has been replaced.

5. Your Registry has become corrupted. Which is the easiest way to restore the Registry?

A. Boot the system from a startup disk. Restore the files from backup.
B. Boot the system from a startup disk. Invoke the LastKnownGood configuration when prompted.
C. Boot the system from the hard disk. Invoke the LastKnownGood configuration when prompted.
D. Boot from the installation disk. Use the emergency repair disk when prompted.

6. While running an application, a general protection fault occurs. Which tool would you use to troubleshoot the problem?

A. Performance Monitor
B. Task Manager
C. Dr. Watson
D. Kernel Debugger

**7.** What causes the LastKnownGood configuration to be invoked?

    A. A power outage is occurring.

    B. The LastKnownGood configuration is selected.

    C. The system is recovering from a critical error.

    D. The NTLDR file is missing.

**8.** You are having problems with a backoffice application, and have decided to use the Registry to troubleshoot it. Which Registry subtree will you investigate?

    A. HKEY_CURRENT_SERVER

    B. HKEY_LOCAL_MACHINE

    C. HKEY_CURRENT_CONFIG

    D. HKEY_USERS

**9.** Your boss wants you to implement a level of RAID, so that if a disk fails it can be regenerated by parity information stored on the other disks. Which level of RAID is your boss talking about?

    A. RAID 0

    B. RAID 1

    C. RAID 3

    D. RAID 5

**10.** A user on your network has been complaining that every time he tries to print to a specific printer, the output is garbled. What is most likely the problem?

    A. User doesn't have the proper rights.

    B. Incorrect printer driver.

    C. User isn't connected to the network.

    D. ACL on the printer has affected the spooler.

exam
**W**atch

*The Security Accounts Manager (SAM) and Security files are not automatically updated by RDISK. To update those files you need to use the /S switch in conjunction with RDISK.*

11. You have a SCSI disk with the BIOS not enabled that is the primary master. You want to define the first partition on the first controller. Which of the following would be the ARC path?

    A. MULTI(0)DISK(0)RDISK(0)PARTITION(2)
    B. SCSI(0)DISK(0)RDISK(0)PARTITION(2)
    C. MULTI(0)DISK(0)RDISK(0)PARTITION(1)
    D. SCSI(0)DISK(0)RDISK(0)PARTITION(1)

---

exam
ⓦatch     *If your BOOT.INI does not list the SCSI ARC name, then NTBOOTDD.SYS is not used.*

---

12. You want to implement fault tolerance on your Windows NT server, which has two hard disks. Which of the following can you implement? (Choose all that apply.)

    A. RAID 0
    B. RAID 1
    C. RAID 3
    D. RAID 5

13. You have implemented disk striping with parity. Two of the disks fail. After replacing the two disks, and creating partitions equal to those on the other disks, what can you do to restore the information?

    A. Use Disk Administrator to regenerate the stripe set from parity information on the other disks.
    B. Use RDISK to regenerate the information stripe set from parity information on the other disks.
    C. Regenerate the stripe set through Windows NT Explorer from parity information on the other disks.
    D. Nothing. Everything is lost.

**14.** You have a non-SCSI disk that is the primary master. You want to define the second partition on the first controller. Which of the following would be the ARC path?

   A. MULTI(0)DISK(0)RDISK(0)PARTITION(2)

   B. SCSI(0)DISK(0)RDISK(0)PARTITION(2)

   C. MULTI(0)DISK(0)RDISK(0)PARTITION(1)

   D. SCSI(0)DISK(0)RDISK(0)PARTITION(1)

**15.** What utility ships with Windows NT Server 4.0, and allows you to check whether your computer has the requirements to install the operating system? (Choose all that apply.)

   A. NTHQ

   B. HQL

   C. SCSITOOL

   D. NTCHECK

**16.** Which of the following comes with Windows NT Server 4.0, and can be used to identify external network problems?

   A. Network Monitor

   B. PING

   C. Protocol Analyzer

   D. NETCHCK

**17.** You are using disk mirroring on your PDC. One disk fails, and you now want Windows NT Server to boot from the mirrored copy. What must you do?

   A. Nothing. Everything is mirrored, so it will boot normally.

   B. Nothing. You must replace the disk before it can boot.

   C. Use a boot floppy. Modify the BOOT.INI so Windows NT starts from the mirror partition.

   D. Just create a boot floppy to boot the system.

ENTERPRISE QUESTIONS

exam
ⓦatch

*If you encounter a permission problem with a network share, be sure to verify the effective permissions for the user.*

**18.** A service failed to start on your BDC. Where can you view more information on the failure?

A. Performance Monitor | Log View.

B. Use Event Viewer to view the server's SERVICE.LOG.

C. Use Event Viewer to view the server's SECURITY.LOG.

D. Use Event Viewer to view the server's SYSTEM.LOG.

**19.** Your PDC is running on an Intel Pentium II processor. Which file will be used to load the Windows NT operating system?

A. BOOTSECT.DOS

B. BOOT.INI

C. NTLDR

D. NTDETECT

A nswers to questions that just test your knowledge of a topic typically have short answers. Questions that require you to apply that knowledge typically are longer, taking you through the reasoning process used to select the correct answers. Just as in the actual Microsoft tests, there are more of the latter type of questions than the former.

# Answers: Planning Your Windows NT Server 4.0 Domain Strategy

**1. B.** Microsoft refers to the partition used to boot as the "system partition", while the partition with the Windows NT operating system on it is called the "boot partition". It's logically backwards from what most people would think. Because of this, it's best to clarify what you mean if you use these terms, and stick to Microsoft's definitions if they appear on the test. Microsoft's usage is probably historical, since the "system partition" contained all the system files, including those needed to boot. They attached more importance to the bootable nature of the system partition than to the matter of holding whatever operating system files that would eventually be loaded by the boot process. This interpretation makes their choice of terminology seem more reasonable, and may help you remember it for the test.

**2. A, B, C, D.** Windows NT Server provides all of these options. Windows NT Workstation provides only option C, striping without parity (RAID 0). Mirroring provides a "mirror copy" of a partition on a different disk on the same disk controller. Duplexing is like mirroring, but across disk controllers, removing the controller as a single point of failure. Mirroring and duplexing are both RAID 1 implementations. The type of striping with parity that Windows NT provides is RAID 5.

3. **C.** Since the accounts database size limit is 40MB, you should use the Multiple Master Domain model. Providing 30,000 user accounts (30,000 x 1KB/user = 30MB), 30,000 computer accounts for their workstations (30,000 x 512B/computer = 15MB), and another 200 computer accounts for servers (200 x 512B/computer = 100KB), we're already up to 45.1MB without creating any groups (which take 4KB/group). This eliminates the possibility of having a single domain with all the accounts. Both the Single Domain and Master Domain models have all accounts in one domain, so they're ruled out.

Since it looks likely that there will be 20 domains with resources, that would mean you'd have to maintain 380 trust relationships [n x (n-1) is 20 x 19 = 380] if you went with the Complete Trust model. Since you wouldn't want to create such a nightmare for yourself, you'd choose the Multiple Master Domain model. If you implemented it with two master domains and twenty resource domains, you'd still have 42 trust relationships to maintain (one-way trusts from the 20 resource domains to each of the two master domains, plus a two-way trust between the two master domains). You'd also only have two places to maintain accounts instead of twenty. In summary, the Complete Trust model would take about nine times the number of trust relationships and ten times the number of user account servers to administer over the Multiple Master model, even though you'd have two fewer domains!

4. **B.** The Master Domain model allows Bob to manage the user accounts in the master domain, while allowing the departments to use resource domains. Since Bob only has 1,000 users, the Multiple Master model isn't anywhere close to being needed. While the Single Domain model would easily hold his users, it wouldn't give the distributed control over resources that the resource domains provide. The Complete Trust model doesn't give him the central administration of user accounts.

**5. A, C.** It's obvious from the scenario that the Primary Domain Controller (PDC) has crashed. Backup Domain Controllers have read-only copies of the account database, so they can authenticate, but not change any information. In order to provide a writable database, you need to provide a PDC. You can either boot the one that crashed or promote the BDC to a PDC. Answer A is preferable, because the copy of the database the BDC has may not be current, and changes since the last synchronization would be lost.

**6. D.** Domain controllers can't change domains or change their roles to that of member server without completely reinstalling Windows NT Server. This is one reason you should plan your domain structure carefully. Note that answer B would have worked if the server had been a member (or standalone) server instead of a domain controller. Expect to see this type of question on the Microsoft test.

**7. B, C.** For per server licensing, he'd need the maximum number of concurrent users for each server. For per seat licensing, it's the number of workstation clients. While per server licensing works fairly well for a single server, per seat quickly becomes more cost effective as you add servers.

**8. B.** The maximum length for a NetBIOS node name is 15 characters. His scheme would allow for workstation names of 16 characters, which won't work. Servers would have up to 14-character names, so it would work for them, and even allow for one additional character if he has two servers in the same room performing the same function, though he apparently hadn't thought of that problem. There are sure to be questions on the Microsoft test that will hinge on the maximum lengths for node and user names, so make sure you read questions carefully to make sure the maximums aren't violated.

9. **C.** If he's not joining an existing domain, he doesn't have the choice of answer B. Since answer D is fictitious, he could start a domain or create a standalone server. There are several reasons he should choose the latter:

   ■ He shouldn't start a domain without planning it first.

   ■ A SQL server is better off doing that job and not providing logon services.

   ■ He can always have the standalone server join a domain later, though it can't be a domain controller. This is better than having to set up a trust relationship later just because he made it a domain controller.

10. **D.** She obviously can't log on from an administrator's account in MOE to administer CURLY, because that was the problem she wanted to fix. Adding the global MOE\Domain Admins group to the local Administrators group on CURLY's PDC is the way she can allow all domain administrators in MOE to administer the domain controllers in CURLY. She can't add the global group in MOE to the global group in CURLY, because global groups can't have other global groups as members. If she wanted to administer the member servers in CURLY from a MOE administrator account, she'd have to do the same for each one; sometimes it's just easier to log on as an administrator in the resource domain to administer systems in that domain.

11. **D.** You don't promote BDCs just because they've done a good job, though you might consider it if the PDC has been unstable. You also don't want to promote a BDC that may have a stale copy of the authorization database if the PDC will be up soon. If you're expecting to shut down a BDC, it has no effect on the PDC. The PDC will continue to authenticate logons, and do its other work. It may just be slowed down a little while the BDC is offline. It's especially important if you plan to have the PDC offline for some time.

12. **D.** There's one copy on the server, and one copy on his and each of his staff's computers. Remember, a roaming profile is copied to each system to which someone logs on. So, each of his staff members has a copy of the personnel evaluations he's done on their systems. This is something to consider before implementing roaming profiles.

13. **B.** In general, creating a volume set will yield the most space. Unless all free spaces are identical in size, striping will have to use only part of the larger spaces, since all stripe areas must be the same size. Striping with parity (RAID 5) yields less usable space by the size of one of the areas.

14. **C.** Stripe sets have the best performance, but the lowest availability of the options listed. Stripe sets with parity (RAID 5) have the poorest write performance, and are a compromise between space and availability of RAID 1 mirrored sets. Striped mirror sets (RAID 0+1) aren't available in Windows NT software, although hardware implementations are available for Windows NT systems.

15. **D.** This is one of the few times the Complete Trust model makes the most sense. First, each division would need only a single domain. If the divisions were completely autonomous, three Single Domain models would be fine. With Complete Trust, each division can manage the authentication and resources as it sees fit, while allowing some resource sharing with the other two divisions as needed. Since there are only three domains, only six trust relationships need to be maintained, which is manageable. If the company had central administration, the Master Domain model would probably have worked better, with resource domains in the three divisions.

16. **A, B, D.** Since his roaming profile is on the BDC, it must be available to be used. The BDC can authenticate him if the PDC is down, but if both are down, he cannot be authenticated on a workstation to which he's never logged on, because there's no chance that his username and password have been cached there.

**17.** **D.** A stripe set without parity is the highest performance option. The biggest stripe set Greg can make under these circumstances is to use 120MB areas of free space from each of the four disks, for a total of 480MB of usable space. While Disk Administrator may let you place more than one stripe area on a single disk (like the one with 500MB free area), it's not the highest-performance solution. On the Microsoft tests, you should rule out that possibility, even if they ask strictly in terms of maximum space for the stripe set.

**18.** **A.** GOTHAM will be the trusted domain. The domain with resources to be used is trusting, while the domain with the accounts to utilize them is trusted.
Here's an easy method for keeping this straight in your head: *Ed* wants to use some *thing* in another domain. Ed is trustED, while the domain with the thing (resource) to be used is trusTHING! On the Microsoft exam, just rename the domains Ed and Thing, and you should get the answer with no problem.

**19.** **C.** Archie can't make one stripe set with his disks, because the system partition can't be software striped. He could use either striping or striping with parity across areas of the three drives. He could do as he wished if he installed another drive to hold the system and boot partitions. The reference to "even parity" comes from the world of asynchronous serial communications, and has nothing to do with disk striping.

# Answers: Installing and Configuring Windows NT Server 4.0 Core Services

**1.** **A, B.** The PDC is always the Domain Master Browser, and is the Master Browser for the subnet if it is available. A system in the other subnet would also have the role of Master Browser for that subnet.

**2. C.** The problem is probably that the logon scripts aren't being replicated to one or more BDCs. Synchronization deals with the user accounts database, not files and directories. Ignoring user complaints because you aren't having the same problem is a sure way to lose control of your network.

**3. B.** The Auto setting of MaintainServerList allows a master browser to designate the computer as a backup browser if another is needed. If it were the only computer available in a workgroup, it would be the master browser. If it were the only computer in its domain on a particular subnet, it would also be a master browser.

**4. A, C.** The user account created for replication services must belong to the Replicator and Backup Operators groups. After Terry adds the user to these groups, he can try again to start the service. Any errors should be checked with the Event Viewer.

**5. C, D, E.** Only sub-directories (or sub-folders) of %SYSTEMROOT% SYSTEM32\REPL\EXPORT are exported, including any files they contain. Files in the EXPORT directory aren't themselves replicated. There is already one such directory there by default, the Scripts folder.

**6. D.** Moving the PROGRAM FILES or SPOOL directories has the same basic problem; the Registry still has the old path information. The files being replicated shouldn't be that big, and must stay where they are unless you want to change replication settings on all your servers. Large print jobs may take a lot of space, so it's a good idea to create a directory on another partition and set the Registry to spool there.

**7. C.** Stopping and starting the Spooler service should take care of the problem if it was caused by a corrupted print file. If the Spooler is having trouble, answer A won't help clear it, and would be a lot of futile work.

Domain synchronization has nothing to do with the problem. Answer D would also require performing the work in answer A to point the workstations to the printer on the new print server, so should be left only as a final recourse.

8. **B, D.** In another unfortunate choice of terms, ReplicationGovernor controls the domain accounts database synchronization, and has nothing to do with directory replication. The ReplicationGovernor is set on BDCs. It's created in the PARAMETERS key of the NetLogon service area of the Registry. It's a percentage, and represents both the maximum time that may be spent synchronizing, and the buffer size of the transfer. So a setting of 50 would mean half the time with half the buffer size. It should only be used over slow WAN links.

9. **D.** If there are more changes than can be stored in the change log between synchronizations, which are requested by a pulse, a partial synchronization cannot be performed. A full synchronization must be performed, where the full database must be copied (up to 40MB of data). This is potentially a lot more data than whatever caused the change log to overwrite at 64KB, so bandwidth utilization could actually increase.
The pulse has nothing to do with network heartbeat (for those of you who've been dealing with Ethernet protocols long enough to remember them), and the pulse is a signal sent by a PDC, not something the BDC checks. Increasing the pulse increases the time between pulses because it's a time interval in seconds, not a frequency per unit of time.

10. **A, B, C.** She'd probably wish to do answer A, putting the lock on the export server, to prevent replication until she was finished. Answer B is also a possibility, but a less likely choice than answer A or answer C, because it would need to be done on all import servers, and she's already using the export server. Answer C will delay replication, but it may still occur before she's ready. Answer D isn't an option because there is no such check box in the Manage Imported Directories window.

11. **A, C.** You can't use the name of a group, which "Replicator" is, as the name of a user, and the username has to follow the other standard restrictions; "DirectoryReplicatorUser" is too long for a username. The most common names for the replication account are "ReplUser" or "Repl", but it could really be any valid username. You wouldn't want to use the same account for anything else, though, since this user will be in the Replicator group.

12. **A, B.** The Pulse parameters modify the PDC's behavior. If you just said answer B, you should get partial credit. The only reason to do answer A is that you might end up promoting one of those BDCs to PDC, and you don't want to have to figure out what is wrong with synchronization, in addition to whatever made you have to promote a BDC in the first place. As for answer B, which is the real issue, letting a BDC delay responding up to 10 seconds to a pulse will cause a timeout over half the time if PulseTimeout1 is still set to its default value of 5 seconds. It needs to be something over Randomize, and 15 seconds gives a 5-second grace period. While you could increase PulseTimeout2, the default of 5 minutes isn't going to be affected much by a 10-second change in PulseTimeout1.

13. **C.** The Server service must be running on a system for it to advertise shared resources or share them. As far as I know, there is no DoNotAdvertise Registry parameter. While hidden shares (those whose names end in $) won't show up in the browse list, the workstation and any non-hidden shares would. Having MaintainServerList set to No just means that this system won't browse, not that it won't be browsable. Disabling the Server service on workstations that don't intend to share any resources is common, and recommended for security reasons. Of course, if you do that, access to partitions through the hidden administrative partition$ shares is also disabled.

   (One choice that isn't listed here, but could appear on your Enterprise exam, is the NET CONFIG command. This command will allow you to share resources, but won't advertise them.)

**14. C, D.** Partial synchronization can take place when all the changes since the last synchronization fit in the change log. The database on a BDC is fully synchronized with the PDC after either a partial or full synchronization. If a BDC has been offline for an extended period, it's more likely that there have been more changes than will fit into the change log, and a full synchronization is required. BDCs are always the ones to request synchronization, and will do so when they start the NetLogon service if Update is Yes or they receive a pulse from the PDC. The pulse can be seen as a request from the PDC for the BDC to request synchronization.

**15. B.** The major factor is the operating system, and within that, the version. So, the two Windows NT Server systems have priority, then Windows NT Workstation, then Windows 95, then WFW 3.11. Since we have two Windows NT Server systems, we have to go to the bonuses. The bonuses, in order from greatest to least, are: (1) PDC, (2) Running WINS, (3) Preferred Master Browser, (4) currently the Master Browser, (5) MaintainServerList is Yes instead of Auto, and (6) currently a Backup Browser. As you can see, BDCs get no preference over other Windows NT servers, but running a WINS server is second only to being the PDC. Having IsDomainMaster set on the Windows NT Workstation isn't enough to overcome the fact that it's not running Windows NT Server, and would only give it priority over other Windows NT Workstation systems.

**16. A.** Errors from the Spooler will be logged to the System Log, which you view with Event Viewer. The service is Spooler, not Print, so answer B isn't correct, even if you wanted to see if the service was currently running. Checking the Registry probably wouldn't be helpful, and the cache on the print device even less so, assuming it were even possible.

**17. A.** During installation of Windows NT Server, you are given the licensing option of per server or per seat (as is shown in the next illustration). If you're unsure as to which to choose, pick per server. If you change your mind later, Windows NT Server will allow you to make a one-time switch from per server licensing to per seat licensing.

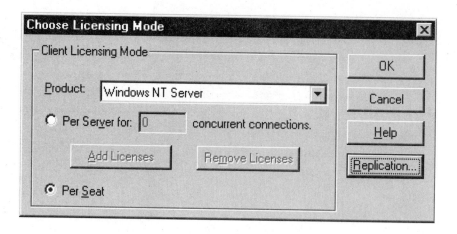

18. **B.** RAID level 1 is disk mirroring, and the only fault-tolerant scheme you can use on a system or boot partition. Information is duplicated from one disk to another, and doesn't adversely affect these partitions. RAID 0 is a stripe set without parity, and RAID 5 is a stripe set with parity. Because information is spread across several disks with these last two methods, you can't use either as a system or boot partition.

19. **A, D.** When files in the spooler have been corrupted due to a system crash, you need to stop the spooler service, delete each of the files that won't print from the spooler directory, and then restart the spooler service.

# Answers: Managing Windows NT Server 4.0 Users and Groups

1. **A, B, C, D.** Account policies affect all accounts, and the logon scripts, user profiles, and home directories are set individually. There are no group policies.

**2. D.** The trusts being used don't support answer A, and additional steps must be taken to allow answer B (primarily, adding Marketing\Domain Admins to the Administrators group on the Sales domain controller). This example doesn't follow any of the domain models. (Perhaps there should be a "Chaos" model to fit the creation of trusts as they're needed!) Since the Corporate domain is trusted by both Sales and Marketing, its users may log onto any of the three domains. While Sales does trust Marketing, Marketing isn't trusted by Corporate, so Marketing users can't log onto the Corporate domain.

**3. E.** Only the Security ID (SID) cannot be changed. It also cannot be set manually, so deleting an account and adding it back with the same information will result in a new SID, and prior permissions for that user will be lost.

**4. C.** Print Operators can manage printers and shut down the system, so making Gary a member of that group will satisfy the requirements, and it matches the intended purpose of the group. The members of his sales team should need no extraordinary rights if the printer shares are properly set up. Both answer A and answer B give more rights than needed, and you don't set user rights from the Account Policies window, so answer D is wrong.

**5. A.** User Manager for Domains (under Policies | Trust Relationships) is used to create trust relationships. You should be familiar with what options are available within User Manager for Domains and Server Manager, especially, because Microsoft tends to include at least a few questions of this type.

**6. B.** This is the standard Master Domain model, where all the resource domains trust the single accounts domain.

**7. D.** You can only restrict a user to log onto eight named workstations, so you can't restrict to fifteen that way. There is no mechanism to block a particular workstation, either. While you can't use that strategy to block the user, attacking the problem from the MGR workstation itself will work, as described in answer D.

**8. C.** The actual wording of the account policy check box is "Forcibly disconnect remote users from server when logon hours expire". Julia on the PDC is a local, not remote user, and won't be logged off.

**9. A.** While answer B and answer C functionality would be nice, it's not there. You have to create a regular user that you'll never use and copy it, changing the username, owner, and whatever other information is not the same from user to user.

**10. D.** Even if Rick were present at 2:00 A.M. every morning, simply disconnecting the users would allow them (more likely their applications) to reconnect. Even if all the users paid attention to his memo (which is not likely in most environments), there would often be someone who honestly forgot to log off. Forcibly disconnecting the users is the only sure way to know that they'll be logged off, and will encourage users to log off before they leave. Logon hours are not something you can set up for a group; they're strictly for user accounts.

**11. B.** The limiting factor is the password, which can be no longer than 14 characters. If you were willing to use the first 14 characters of the username for passwords over 14 characters, you could go up to the username maximum of 20 characters.

**12. E.** Unfortunately, there's no way to accomplish this without an administrative account in each domain, or by manually adding the TIGERS\Domain Admins group to each workstation and maintaining that (which would be more difficult in most cases). Jessie can gain most of the functionality of this move by following answer B, at least regarding user account management. However, this doesn't give those users administrative access to the workstations in the domain like a CUBS\Domain Admins member has (being in the Administrators group on every system). While it would be great to be able to do answer A, you can't have a global group be a member of another global group. Answer C isn't possible, because you can't have accounts in one domain as members of a global group in another domain, regardless of trust relationships. Answer D isn't possible, because of the global group membership nesting and because the one-way trust relationship wouldn't support it. It wouldn't help solve the problem, anyway.

13. **B, D.** Don't confuse user profiles, mandatory profiles, or roaming profiles with system policies. The System Policy Editor can create the NTCONFIG.POL file, which must be placed in the NETLOGON share directory on all domain controllers. Copying the files in the NETLOGON directory to all domain controllers is typically done with replication.

14. **B, C, D.** The failures of File and Object Accesses, Use of User Rights, and Process Tracking are more interesting than the successes, and the sheer number of successes on these categories will severely limit how much useful information you could store. Logon and Logoff information, both successes and failures, is extremely valuable in tracking down possible security incidents. User and Group Management, Security Policy Changes, and Restart, Shutdown, and System should all be logged for success and failure; both should be infrequent enough to not be overwhelming.

15. **A, C, D, E.** A local group can contain any user or group that is visible to that system, except for other local groups. This includes local users, domain users from this or a trusted domain, and global groups from this or a trusted domain. Local groups can contain any accounts, except local groups.

16. **B.** The Master Domain model is used when centralized account administration is required, and resources must be maintained by the domain that has them. This allows the network to have centralized control of accounts, while still allowing areas of the network to control their own resources. Accounts are maintained by the master domain, while resources are controlled by the resource domain.

**17.** C. On a domain controller, the entire domain is affected by the User Rights Policy. If rights are set up on a standalone server, only that machine is affected.

**18.** D. When a user belongs to several groups, the user's access to an object is a combination of the each group's permissions. The only exception to this is when a group has No Access assigned. In all cases, No Access will override the cumulative rights of the user.

# Answers: Planning Your Windows NT Server 4.0 Protocol Strategy

**1.** A, B. NetBEUI can't be used because it's not routable. AppleTalk is for Macintosh support, and can't be used as the sole protocol for Windows systems. Both TCP/IP and IPX/SPX (NWLink) would work.

**2.** B. TCP/IP is the common name for the protocol in use on the Internet. The other answers had fictitious acronym definitions. IPX, really the Internetwork Packet eXchange protocol, is sometimes confused with IP, the Internet Protocol, by those without network protocol knowledge.

**3.** B. IPX/SPX is used by Novell's NetWare servers and clients. If you install NWLink (IPX/SPX) on your computer, you may install the client or gateway for NetWare so that you can still access resources on NetWare servers. It's also required to install FPNW, to allow NetWare clients to access resources on a Windows NT server.

**4.** A. Most of the growth possibilities are in the TCP/IP area, whether he wishes to connect to the Internet or just use Internet server technologies for an intranet. Today, anyone should think twice before choosing another networking protocol. Again, AppleTalk isn't really an option because it's not supported for Windows networking, just for Macintosh.

5. **A, B, C.** A network service such as the Client Services for NetWare must be bound to a network protocol such as IPX, which must in turn be bound to a network adapter (or interface card) such as an Ethernet card.

6. **A, C, D, E.** Services for Macintosh is only available on Windows NT Server, although the AppleTalk protocol itself is available on Workstation to support Windows printing only. Services for Macintosh does support Macintoshes printing to printers on Windows NT Server (whether or not they're Postscript), as well as creating a printer on Windows NT Server for AppleTalk printers. It does require NTFS for the Macintosh volumes. It can act as a seed or non-seed router for an AppleTalk network as well.

7. **C.** Since Macintosh volumes can't be nested and a user can have only one primary group, there's really no good way to do this. Answer C comes closest to matching the functionality. Vicki will need separate user accounts for each group, because each will need to have that as its primary group. Setting passwords on the volumes instead of group access might be an alternative she'd consider (depending on the environment), but answer D used only one volume and so couldn't restrict access per subdirectory. She might also consider setting up just one user account set as the owner on all volumes; members of her group may log on with that account to manage these volumes.

8. **B.** When Services for Macintosh is installed, the print processor for printers using the PScript1 data type is also installed. Nothing else needs to be installed.

9. **D.** DLC is a protocol used for communicating with HP printers and mainframes. Since the printer has already been established as properly attached, this rules out the connection choice.

10. **B.** When a protocol is raised in the binding order, access to the protocol increases. The protocol highest in this list is used first. Therefore, the higher TCP/IP is in the binding order, the faster a computer can access it.

**ENTERPRISE ANSWERS**

**11. C.** NWLink configuration information can be viewed from the command prompt by typing IPXROUTE CONFIG.

**12. B.** Implementing DHCP will solve this problem. You can set a pool of IP addresses that will be issued to hosts for a period of time.

**13. C, D.** Only SLIP (Serial Line Internet Protocol) and PPP (Point to Point Protocol) are serial protocols. None of the others listed fall into this category.

**14. C.** You must enable IP Routing from the Routing tab of TCP/IP Properties (as shown in the next illustration) before you can use a Windows NT server as a router.

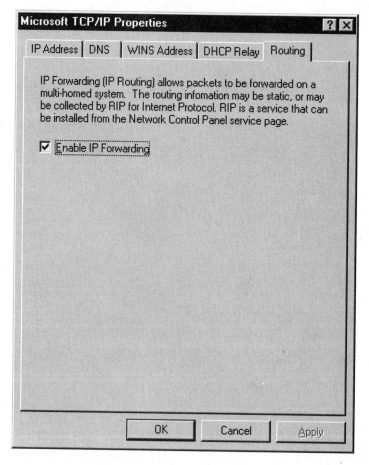

**15.** **B.** PPP-MP (Multilink) lets you combine the bandwidth of multiple modems (with separate telephone lines), ISDN channels, or multiple ISDN adapters and lines into a single bundle, thereby increasing the throughput and bandwidth.

**16.** **A, C.** TCP/IP requires configuration. The only time this is not the case is if a DHCP server is providing all the necessary configuration information to your computer. NWLink might require some configuration, while NetBEUI and DLC do not.

**17.** **C.** The default protocol of NetWare is IPX/SPX. However, Windows NT uses NWLink IPX/SPX-compatible transport, not IPX/SPX. NWLink is Microsoft's implementation of the IPX/SPX protocol.

**18.** **C.** Using Scope IDs can separate a group of computers from the rest of the network. Only computers with the same Scope ID will be able to see NetBIOS traffic, so they won't be able to communicate with computers that have a different Scope ID, or none at all.

**19.** **A.** TCP/IP is a routable protocol, so that eliminates one of the answers. You can configure a pool of IP addresses for multiple subnets on a DHCP server. Since clients broadcast their requests for IP addresses, the routers will generally filter out the request, so it never gets passed off that segment. If you implement a DHCP relay agent, the agent can forward the request to the DHCP server, and then pass back the results to the client computer. DHCP relay agents can be configured from the DHCP Relay tab of TCP/IP properties, shown in the next illustration.

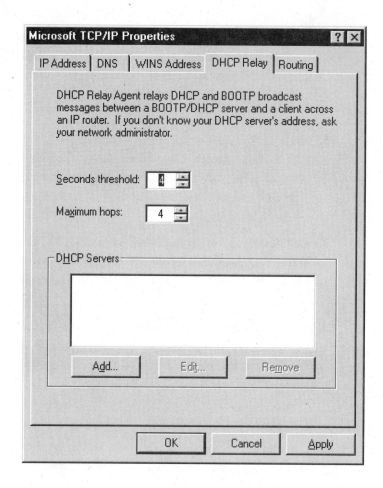

# Answers:
# TCP/IP Installation and Configuration

1. **B, C.** The Transmission Control Protocol (TCP) and User Datagram Protocol (UDP) are both transport layer protocols. The File Transfer Protocol (FTP), HyperText Transfer Protocol (HTTP), and Simple Mail Transfer Protocol (SMTP) are application protocols for transferring files, web pages, and mail, respectively. These application protocols all use TCP for their transport layer.

2. **C, D, E.** 16.0.0.0 could be a valid Class A network, 203.89.4.0 could be a valid Class C network, and 190.5.0.0 could be a valid Class B network. 129.0.0.0 isn't valid because 129 falls in the Class B range, and can't be a valid Class A network. 196.43.0.0 falls in the Class C range, and can't be a valid Class B network.

3. **B, D.** The LMHOSTS file can be used to statically map NetBIOS names to IP addresses, while a Windows Internet Name Service (WINS) server will dynamically map them. The hosts file and Domain Name System (DNS) server map Internet domain names to IP addresses.

4. **C.** A DHCP server will allow the clients to select the option to get their configuration automatically, without typing in the information. Stan can also include the DNS and WINS server configuration information in DHCP, if he wishes.

5. **D.** The Address Resolution Protocol (ARP) is used to discover the Media Access Control (MAC) address for a given IP address on a subnet.

6. **D.** The Internet Control Message Protocol (ICMP) is used by diagnostic utilities like PING and TRACERT.

7. **A, B.** All you need are IP addresses and a valid subnet mask. On a Local Area Network (LAN), you don't have a router, so there's no default gateway. It's unlikely you'd have a DNS or WINS server, either, unless it was a large LAN.

8. **C.** Again, we have a Class C size subnet (which we can tell from the network mask). So, the first 24 bits (3 octets) of the address is the network, the last octet determines the node on that network. Using the reserved Class A network 10.0.0.0 is common for networks behind firewalls or not connected to the Internet. Keeping the networks on octet boundaries means you don't have to calculate anything, and you shouldn't expect to have to on the enterprise exam; the TCP/IP elective exam is another matter.

ENTERPRISE ANSWERS

9. **B.** When the destination IP address is compared to the subnet mask, the computer realizes that this message is for another subnet, and sends it to the default gateway, which then takes over the role of sending it to the true destination.

10. **A.** The HOST file maps host names to IP addresses, while LMHOSTS maps IP addresses to NetBIOS names.

11. **B.** TRACERT is a utility that comes with Windows NT Server, and will display the route a packet has taken between a source and destination host.

12. **C.** The IPCONFIG utility displays information regarding TCP/IP configurations. It also has switches that can be used to renew (IPCONFIG /RENEW) or release (IPCONFIG /RELEASE) DHCP leases of IP addresses.

13. **C.** 127.0.0.1 is the loopback address, and always reflects the host you are using. When users are trying to connect with this address, it is being reflected back onto their own computer. This address is a reserved address, and can't be used for the IP address of a host on a TCP/IP network.

14. **D.** Organizations that don't fall into other categories of domains (such as non-profits), are made part of the .ORG domain. The categories are listed in the next table.

| .COM | Commercial organizations |
|------|--------------------------|
| .MIL | Military organizations |
| .EDU | Educational institutions |
| .GOV | Government institutions |
| .NET | Network providers |

| .ORG | Organizations that don't fall into the other categories (like non-profit charities) |
|---|---|
| .CA (Canada) .NL (The Netherlands) .UK (United Kingdom) | Examples of country codes applied to most domain names that are outside of the U.S. |

**15.** A. HTTP is the Hypertext Transfer Protocol, used for the transfer of HTML documents (web pages) from one host to another.

**16.** A. NETSTAT is a utility used to display current connections, and the ports they're using.

**17.** C. The IP address listed here is a Class C address, which is capable of up to 254 hosts addresses per network. Because of that, your default subnet mask would be 255.255.255.0

**18.** D. A Class B address is capable of having up to 16,777,214 host addresses per network. However, if you did have such an address, you probably would have known this for some time, as they haven't been offered in a while. Class A and B addresses have all been used up.

**19.** A, B, C, D. All of the addresses listed are invalid IP addresses for a network host. 127.0.0.1 is the loopback address. Addresses that begin with 224-254 are reserved for special protocols. Addresses ending in 255 are used for broadcasting. Addresses beginning with 0 just don't exist!

# Answers: NetWare Connectivity

**1.** C. Though NetWare can use many different protocols, the one it uses by default is IPX/SPX. The Microsoft implementation of this is NWLink, an IPX/SPX-compatible transport protocol. It is the best choice of protocol to use when interacting with a NetWare network.

**2.** **C.** If you install GSNW on an existing Windows NT server, it can act as a gateway between the Microsoft Networking and Novell Networking on the new server. Installing CSNW on all the workstations isn't necessary, and requires a lot of extra work and support. (Had the situation been reversed—one Windows NT server, many NetWare servers—installing CSNW might have been a good option.) Installing GSNW on all the servers would also be excessive to gateway to a single NetWare server. File and Print Services for NetWare wouldn't help at all, except to offer services to the office users without using Microsoft Networking on their systems. In this case, they should use Microsoft Networking to natively take advantage of the Windows NT server environment.

**3.** **D.** Since the NetWare server is version 4.*x*, you must supply GSNW with the default tree and context. NetWare Directory Services (NDS) has a hierarchical, tree-like structure that contains information on such things as user accounts. Because of this, you must provide GSNW with the tree and context that will be used when connecting to NDS. The default tree is the NDS name that will be used when logging on. The context is where the user account resides in the NDS tree.

**4.** **A, C, D.** Passwords are stored in an encrypted form, and cannot be migrated. Usernames, groups, files, and directories may all be migrated, retaining their original attributes.

**5.** **C.** All accesses through the gateway use the account with Supervisor access. If access isn't restricted on the GSNW share (which, by default, gives Everyone Full Control), the user might as well be logged onto the NetWare share as Supervisor. Because of this, and the fact that the granularity of access permissions is so much lower on a Windows NT share than a NetWare directory, security is a major concern when using GSNW.

6. **D.** While answer A would be nice, she can't migrate the NetWare password. Both answer B and answer C would allow someone who knew a username to use their account with no further information. Answer D will allow all the accounts to have the same password that is unknown to others. Of course, users within the group would know the "password", so it's still not ideal.

7. **A.** NWCONV is a tool used to migrate a NetWare server to a Windows NT server. It is the program name for Migration Tool for NetWare.

8. **B.** NTFS must be used on the Windows NT machine during a migration. If it is not used, file and directory permissions will be lost. You can't use another file system, because other file systems supported by Windows NT (FAT, VFAT) simply don't have the capabilities of preserving the permissions.

9. **A.** Gateway Services for NetWare allows client computers on a Microsoft network to access resources on a NetWare network. All requests are passed through the gateway, so no additional software is needed on the Windows NT workstations to connect.

10. **A.** GSNW is used to manage NetWare shares and permissions (for Microsoft network users) from a Windows NT server. This is the only place you can provide this management from the Windows NT server.

11. **C.** FSNW is an add-on utility that isn't supplied with Windows NT Server. You can purchase it separately, and upon implementing it, allow NetWare clients to access a Windows NT server's printers and files.

12. **C.** When you connect to a NetWare 3.x server for the first time, you have to provide the name of the Preferred Server that you wish to connect to. If you don't provide this information, your logon information will go to the first NetWare server, rather than the server you prefer to use.

**13.** **A, B.** In NetWare 4.*x*, Novell replaced the bindery with NetWare Directory Services. NDS is a hierarchical database containing locations of resources and account information. Because it stores the information in a hierarchical fashion, it must be provided with the default tree the user will use, and the context of that tree. Without this, GSNW cannot use its account to log onto the NetWare 4.*x* server.

**14.** **D.** If NWLink isn't already installed when you install GSNW or CSNW, it automatically will be installed and bound for you.

**15.** **D.** Migration Tool for NetWare can be used to migrate NetWare versions 2.*x*, 3.*x*, and 4.*x* to a Windows NT server.

**16.** **C, D.** File and Print Services, and Directory Services for NetWare aren't included with Windows NT. These are services for the NetWare side of a mixed network, and as such, aren't provided with Windows NT Server or Windows NT Workstation. They are available as a separate package.

**17.** **C.** NWLink IPX/SPX Properties is the only place where you can change the frame type in Windows NT Server.

**18.** **D.** The IPXROUTE CONFIG command will allow you to view the frame type being used by NWLink. If you suspect frame type conflicts, use this command to view the frame type being used on your computer.

**19.** **D.** DSMN is Directory Service Manager for NetWare. This add-on utility isn't provided with Windows NT Server, and must be purchased separately. By implementing this utility, user accounts on NetWare servers are merged into a single database. This database is then distributed to each of the NetWare servers, allowing users to enjoy a single logon to the network.

# Answers: Configuring Windows NT Server 4.0 Protocol Routing

1. **B.** The Routing Information Protocol (RIP) for TCP/IP needs to be installed so that the router can discover the correct routes. Otherwise, Bobby would have to enter static routes to get things going.

2. **B, D.** To have RIP for IPX running on your network, add the RIP for IPX service (from the Service tab of the Network applet in Control Panel). After this, check the "Enable RIP Routing" checkbox from the Routing tab of the NWLink property dialog box.

3. **A, D.** TCP/IP and IPX/SPX are both routable protocols that are supported for routing by a Windows NT Server 4.0. InterNIC isn't a protocol but an agency where you can get a registered IP address. NetBEUI is a fast but unroutable protocol.

4. **B.** If a Windows NT server acting as a domain controller is being used as a router as well, you may experience serious performance issues. In such a case, if you can't afford a third-party routing device, create a dedicated server to act as a router.

5. **B.** A routing table stores computer and network addresses, which are then referred to by the router to route packets to their proper destination.

6. **D.** A gateway allows two networks using dissimilar protocols to communicate.

7. **A.** A router is used to connect two networks (such as a LAN and the Internet), and to route packets between them.

8. **A.** When broadcast traffic is bogging down the network, you can segment the network and use Windows NT Server as a bridge between the segments. A bridge won't pass broadcasts across segments. It will filter messages for one segment, and keep them from being passed to the other.

9. **A.** Routing Information Protocol (RIP) dynamically exchanges routing information with other routers. It solves the problem of statically creating routing tables.

10. **A.** A router is the best choice for connecting a LAN to a WAN, as it can choose from the different possible paths and select the best route. If one of the T1 lines go down, the router can use an alternate path.

11. **A, D.** To enable routing AppleTalk over Windows NT Server, install Services for Macintosh (SFM) on the Windows NT server, then check the Enable Routing check box on the Routing tab of SFM.

12. **A.** DHCP Relay Agents "listen" to the network for DHCP request broadcasts. A DHCP Relay Agent will then take this message and send it to the DHCP server on another subnet. The DHCP server then works with the Relay Agent, passing information to it, which is then transferred to the requesting computer. The computer is unaware of the entire process.

13. **B.** NetBEUI is a fast, efficient, but non-routable protocol. To allow NetBEUI to span across network segments, implement a bridge. A bridge only looks at the network address, and allows these packets to pass across networks.

14. **D.** Windows NT Server 4.0 can be used as a router, using both TCP/IP and NWLink as protocols. However, for such a computer to be used as a router, you must have two network cards installed. Each network card will connect to each segment you want to route.

**15.** **B.** A dynamic router will share routing tables with other dynamic routers. It will also periodically broadcast changes about itself or changes on the network. By doing so, the most effective (or available) route can be used to route a packet to its destination.

**16.** **A, C, D.** The Multiprotocol Router (MPR) is a service of Windows NT Server 4.0 that allows dynamic routing of packets among different subnets. It is made up of RIP for IPX, RIP for TCP/IP (also known as IP RIP), and DHCP Relay Agent (also known as BOOTP Relay agent for DHCP).

**17.** **A.** If you are using TCP/IP and IPX/SPX (NWLink) on your network, you can use both RIP for TCP/IP and RIP for NWLink. By doing so, you will be able to route both protocols.

**18.** **C.** Before Windows NT Server 4.0, you had to manually enter information into static routing tables. RIP is new to Windows NT Server 4.0, and allows dynamic routing. While Windows NT Server 4.0 and 3.51 can route packets to each other, Windows NT Server 3.51 is only able to use static routing.

**19.** **B.** To implement routing on a Windows NT server, you require a minimum of two network cards installed. One card will be connected to one segment of the network, and the other card will be connected to another segment. While you can have more than two installed, you can't have fewer than two network cards, if you're going to implement routing.

# Answers: Installing and Configuring NT Server 4.0 Remote Access Service

**ENTERPRISE ANSWERS**

**1.** **B, C, D, E.** Serial Line Internet Protocol (SLIP) and Point-to-Point Protocol (PPP) are more basic protocols than the others listed. While Windows NT supports SLIP as a client, it's not supported on the server side, so it can only be used for connecting to other servers that support SLIP. PPP is supported, and TCP/IP, IPX/SPX, and NetBEUI may all be run over PPP.

**2. B.** By installing multiple phone lines into your building, and multiple modems into your computer (not the other way around!), you'll be able to use Multilink. The Multilink protocol will combine the bandwidth of the modems you've installed, which will increase your throughput and bandwidth.

**3. A, B, C, E.** RAS will work over the Public Switched Telephone Network (PSTN), Integrated Services Digital Network (ISDN), and X.25 (a packet-switched network protocol particularly popular in Europe). RAS also supports Internet connections, providing PPTP for secure connections. X.400 is a directory service standard, and has nothing to do with access media.

**4. B, D.** Although RAS supports the Password Authentication Protocol, PAP doesn't encrypt passwords. The Shiva PAP (SPAP) does, and is supported. MD5 isn't supported on RAS servers, though it is on Dial-Up Networking (DUN) clients. The best encryption to use is Microsoft Challenge Handshake Authentication Protocol (MS-CHAP), but it can only be used with Microsoft clients.

**5. B.** If Rick can serve the NetWare share with GSNW, he only needs TCP/IP on his client workstations. He could, of course, run both TCP/IP and IPX over the RAS connection, but the question stipulates that he wants to run a single protocol. There is no GSIP, so that's not an option.

**6. B, D.** With Internet access, PPTP provides a Virtual Private Network (VPN). No dial-up access or PPP is needed for such access. There is no such thing as GRASS. (Although it's a catchy enough name that someone will probably develop it and market the security features with the slogan, "Keep off the GRASS!".)

**7. B.** DUN (Dial Up Networking) Monitor presents real-time statistical information on errors, connections, and devices.

**8. D.** Dial-in permissions allow a user to access the network via a dial-in connection. Although everything else in RAS may be configured properly, the lack of dial-in permission prevents a user from connecting to the network through RAS.

**9. A.** When concerned about a connection to a RAS server, PING can be used to test the connection.

**10. B.** RAS can only support 256 connections. (As for answer A, if 256 users are already connected, how could RAS only support 255 sessions? Be sure to read the questions carefully.) RAS can dial out or support dial-in sessions using PPP.

**11. D.** When an Microsoft client computer connects to a Windows NT computer running RAS, MS-CHAP will be used to authenticate the user. It will always default to this protocol, as it is the safest protocol offered through RAS for authentication.

**12. C.** When RAS can't negotiate a compatible set of protocols, have the client install a protocol that's being used by the server. The reason for this problem is that the client isn't using a protocol supported or installed on the RAS server.

**13. B.** You must have something that the protocols can be bound to, if RAS is to run. The MS Loopback adapter solves this dilemma if neither a modem nor a NIC is installed on the computer.

**14. D.** Both the RAS server and the RAS client must use the same transport protocol (for example, TCP/IP, NWLink, or NetBEUI) if a connection between the two is to be made. While RAS supports many different transport protocols, the two being used between the client and server must match. Otherwise, the client and server can't understand each other.

**15. A, B, C, D.** Users who connect to RAS with PPP can run applications that use named pipes, remote procedure calls, and the WinSock API with either IPX/SPX or TCP/IP.

**16. B, D.** Both PPP and SLIP are serial protocols. RAS can dial out using PPP or SLIP, but will only accept incoming sessions with PPP. TCP/IP and NWLink are both transport protocols, not serial protocols.

**17. B.** This error occurs in RAS when the licensing service isn't releasing the licenses of RAS users who have hung up. By changing the licensing mode of the server from per server to per seat, this problem is remedied.

**18. B.** RAS's autodial feature doesn't work with SLIP accounts. You must use a PPP account.

**19. B.** RAS on a Windows NT server will accept up to 256 incoming sessions, while Windows NT Workstation accepts only one. Upgrading the workstation to Windows NT Server 4.0 will allow for more incoming sessions.

# Answers: Internet Information Server

**1. D.** HTTP is the HyperText Transfer Protocol used by World Wide Web (WWW) servers. HTML is the HyperText Markup Language, which is the language in which web pages are written.

**2. A, D.** Of those listed, only Internet Explorer and Netscape Navigator are browsers. You browse an intranet the same way you browse the Internet. An intranet is a network that uses the same technology and protocols (such as TCP/IP, HTTP, FTP) that the Internet does. The only difference is that an intranet resides on a LAN or WAN. (Note that this means a WAN that is considerably smaller than the Internet.)

3. **A.** The IUSR_FRED account was created when IIS was installed, and is the account the web server uses to access the files. If IUSR_FRED doesn't have Read access, then access to the files isn't possible without further authentication. While answer D would allow IUSR_FRED access to the files, it would also open up Full Control access for anyone connected to the server.

4. **B.** She needs to upgrade IIS to version 3 by adding support for active server pages. While the ASP support was distributed with SP3, it isn't a part of SP3 itself or automatically applied when you apply SP3. If she can, she should probably go on to the latest version available; IIS 4 has much better functionality than IIS 3. As of this writing, SP4 is not available, but it probably won't be upgrading IIS, because of compatibility problems with other Windows NT 4.0-layered products (like Exchange 5.0, which requires IIS v3 specifically).

5. **D.** If you're connecting directly to the Internet, you don't need any name resolution set up on your network, or on the server where you're using IIS. This is because the Internet has its own DNS servers for name resolution. What you do need is a registered IP address. Without this, any domain name you've given your site will be invalid. For example, if you've given your domain the name of www.booboo.com and used an unregistered IP address, people won't be able to connect to your site. You must register your domain name with InterNIC.

6. **E.** Okay, this was a trick question, but it brings up some valuable points. An intranet is simply a network that facilitates sharing information among whomever you consider "internal" users. Most organizations with any network at all are already using it as an intranet. If they think they need an intranet, that probably really means that they need to overhaul their existing network to improve its functionality. "Intranet" is a new word for an old concept, rejuvenated by the ease of Internet networking.
A firewall may help ensure that Jim's internal data stays that way, but it isn't required, especially if Jim's organization isn't also on the Internet.

**7.** **B.** By creating a virtual server in Internet Service Manager, you can appear to have two servers on the Internet, even though IIS is running on one physical server.

**8.** **A, D, E.** Internet Information Server is made up of three services: World Wide Web (HTTP), FTP, and Gopher. It does not offer Internet Relay Chat, nor does it offer Bulletin Board Services (which is something different from the Internet).

**9.** **E.** IUSR_COMPUTERNAME is an account created by IIS during installation, and used for allowing anonymous access. When created, a random password is generated for it. If you change the password, you must do it in both User Manager and Internet Service Manager.

**10.** **B.** HTML is used to create web pages. For those who choose answer D, Interlac is an alien language used in comic books (gotcha!).

**11.** **B.** When a password is changed for the IUSR_COMPUTERNAME account in User Manager for Domains, you must also change it in Internet Service Manager. If you do not, anonymous users won't be able to connect to IIS.

**12.** **A, D.** If you're going to use IIS to publish on an intranet, you'll also need to install WINS and DNS on your network for name resolution. This isn't required if you're using IIS to connect directly to the Internet, because the Internet has its own DNS servers for name resolution.

**13.** **B.** IIS security features are integrated with Windows NT Server. The level of security you've placed on accounts, files and directories through

Windows NT is the level of security that will appear when people connect to your web site.

14. **C.** Though webmasters sometimes wish they could zap a rotten user with a nasty virus, that obviously isn't an option. You can restrict user access by IP address. If you know a user is connecting from a certain IP address, you can restrict his access by configuring IIS.

15. **B.** When any changes are made to security, permissions or use of log files, you must stop and restart the IIS service. Until this happens, the changes will not take effect.

16. **C.** When making changes over the web to IIS, you're using the HTML version of Internet Service Manager. The Internet Service Manager (HTML) won't allow you to stop, pause or restart a service. Because of that, any changes that require a restart of a service won't take effect.

17. **D.** While you can lower the bandwidth used by IIS, you can not change the bandwidth used by each individual service. If you want to lower the bandwidth of one, the bandwidth of the others will also be lowered. Lowering the bandwidth used by IIS is done through the Internet Service Manager. This application allows you to manage security, authentication, logging, and bandwidth. To adjust the bandwidth, simply double-click an Internet service shown in Internet Service Manager. In the Properties dialog box that appears, click the Advanced tab, and then check the box labeled Limit Network Use By All Internet Services On This Computer, as shown in the next illustration. You are then able to specify the bandwidth (in KB per second) that will be used by all Internet services.

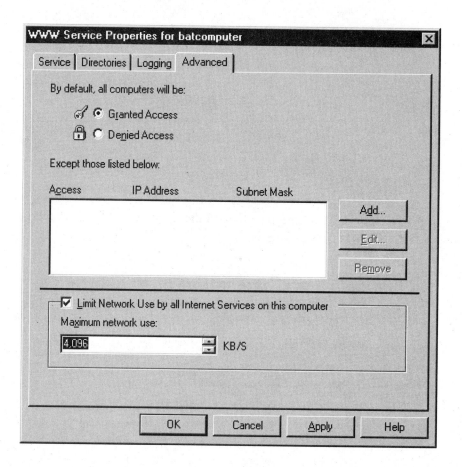

**18. B, C.** Uniform Resource Locators (URLs) contain the domain name of an Internet host, and can include the subdomain name and path to a resource.

**19. C.** DHCP issues IP addresses for a limited time. When you get a full-time connection to the web, and want to publish to it, you need to register with InterNIC. Doing so will register your domain name, and you'll also be issued an IP address for your site. If you don't want the hassle of doing this, you can also ask your ISP to do it for you. (There will no doubt be a fee charged by the ISP, on top of what you'll be charged for the registration.)

# Answers: Monitoring and Performance Tuning

1. **C.** Performance Monitor allows you to log information about individual components, and monitor potential bottlenecks.

2. **C.** Disk thrashing means that memory is being swapped to the disk excessively. The Pages/sec counter and the disk use are excessively high. In such a case, upgrading the memory will solve the problem.

3. **C.** When performance of a stripe set with parity is very poor, and memory on the computer that contains the set is being filled up, the problem is probably that one of the disks in the set has failed. The information from the failed disk is being regenerated in RAM from the parity information stored on the other disks in the set. This is causing slowed performance.

4. **A.** When excessive paging occurs, information in memory is being swapped at a high rate from RAM to the disk. When this occurs, add more RAM. Creating new pagefiles and distributing them across other disks on the server will help performance, but not in cases where there isn't enough memory to begin with. The same is true when the page file is on the boot partition. If the pagefile is on the boot partition (the one with the system files), then performance may improve by simply moving the pagefile to a different disk. In such cases, the pagefile and the system are contending for writes and reads from the same disk. However, it is important to remember that if there isn't enough RAM, information will continue to be swapped to the pagefiles.

5. **B.** Log view in Performance Monitor is used to create baselines, which can be used for future reference. The other view modes display the information, but don't record the results to a file.

6. **D.** Windows NT Diagnostics displays an inventory of all components (such as processor, hard disk, and memory) currently on your computer.

7. **A.** To activate the counters of a physical disk, you must run DISKPERF –Y from the command prompt. Unless you do this, the counters won't be enabled, and will not rise above the value of zero in Performance Monitor, as shown in the next illustration. To turn the counters off, run DISKPERF –N from the command prompt.

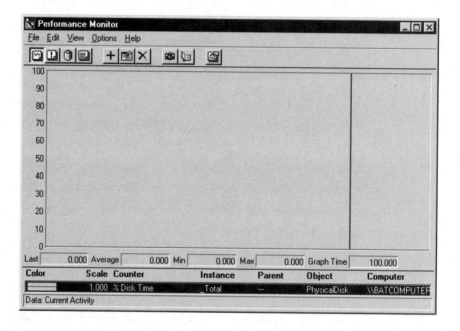

8. **B.** If you want to check the counters of a single physical disk in a strip set, you must go to the command prompt and run DISKPERF –YE. Until you do this, the counters won't be enabled, and will not change from the value of zero in Performance Monitor.

9. **C.** To specify the thread priority of a program when you start it, you use the START <application name> command followed by the proper switch. /LOW will start an application with a priority level of 4, /NORMAL will start it with a priority level of 8, and /HIGH will start it with a priority level of 13. /REALTIME starts an application with a thread priority of 24. Previous to Windows NT 4.0, the normal setting of a thread's priority was 7, but this was changed to 8 in Windows NT 4.0.

10. **B.** The Replication Governor REG_DWORD value needs to be changed to decrease the amount of traffic while synchronizing over a slow link. Decreasing this value to 50 will improve the performance.

11. **B.** Network Monitor is a tool for monitoring network performance. It can capture frames sent to and from your computer, and display information about these frames.

12. **C.** Virtual memory can be configured by clicking the Virtual Memory button on the Performance tab of System Properties. Here you can configure pagefile size, and have pagefiles distributed across several disks.

13. **B.** If the %Processor time is showing constant rates of 80 percent or more, then it is an indication that the CPU is a bottleneck, and should be upgraded.

14. **A.** The Alert View will allow you to set an alert to inform you when certain counters dip below or exceed a specific value.

15. **D.** You can only set an alert in Performance Monitor for one event. If the value is equal to, over, or below a specified value, an alert is sent. You can't set alerts for two or more things happening to one counter.

**16. B.** Disk Queue Length shows how much data is waiting to be written to the hard disk. It shows the number of requests waiting, and the number of requests being serviced, combined. If the value is greater than two, there may be a bottleneck.

**17. C.** A 32-bit card is the optimum card to use on a computer with a PCI bus. This means that the card transfers data in increments of 32 bits at a time.

**18. A.** You can adjust a running application's priority by a level of 2 with the Application Performance Boost slider bar in system properties. If the priority is normal (8), then moving the slider bar to maximum will make the new priority 10.

**19. A.** When performance of the network degrades after installing a new protocol, you may need to change the binding order of the protocols. Put the most used protocol at the top of the list, and Windows NT will attempt to use it first.

# Answers: Troubleshooting Windows NT 4.0

**1. C.** DLC is necessary to communicate with mainframes and HP printers.

**2. B.** Event Viewer allows you to view logs (such as the system and security logs), which contain information regarding events that occurred on the system.

**3. A.** RAID 0 can be used to increase the speed at which data is accessed. Because data is spread across several disks, several disks are reading different parts of the information you are loading into memory. However, it is not fault tolerant. If one disk fails, all information on all disks in the set is lost.

4. **A.** After a failed disk has been replaced and partitioned to the same size as the others in the set, you need to regenerate the data. In Disk Administrator, select the set and the free space on the new disk. Choose Regenerate from the Fault Tolerance menu.

5. **D.** Because the LastKnownGood configuration is stored in the Registry, and that's what got us into this fine mess, you can't use it to restore the system. While you can restore the system from a backup, that is more time consuming and more difficult (especially if you can't get into the system to use the restore feature of backup on your computer!) Booting from an installation disk and using an emergency repair disk is the easiest, and most effective, option.

6. **C.** Dr. Watson detects application errors, analyses them, and logs the information dealing with it to a file. This information can be used by technical support groups for diagnosis.

7. **B, C.** The LastKnownGood configuration will start when the system is recovering from a critical device-loading error, or when it has been invoked by the user pressing the space bar when prompted during startup.

8. **B.** The HKEY_LOCAL_MACHINE is the subtree in the Registry that you'll use for solving most problems. It is in this subtree that you'll be able to troubleshoot software problems.

9. **D.** RAID 5 is disk striping with parity and is an excellent, fault tolerance scheme. Parity information is spread across all disks in the stripe set, so that if one fails, the information can be regenerated. By replacing the disk and creating a partition equal to that used by the other disks, you're able to regenerate the set.

**10.** **B.** An incorrect printer driver will cause printed material to come out as gibberish. This is true whether the printer is attached to the local computer or the network.

**11.** **D.** The correct path would be SCSI(0)DISK(0)RDISK(0)PARTITION(1). The next table defines what each part of the path name means.

| Path Name | Meaning |
|---|---|
| MULTI(0) OR SCSI(0) | Defines which disk controller your hard disk is on. If the SCSI BIOS isn't enabled on a SCSI drive, then the first entry is scsi(x). The first controller starts at 0. |
| DISK(0) | Defines the SCSI number. It starts at 0, but is always 0 if the first entry is multi(x). |
| RDISK(0) | Defines the physical drive number for the disk. This starts at 0, but is always 0 if the disk is SCSI. |
| PARTITION(1) | This is the partition number. Unlike the other entries, this one always starts at 1. |

**12.** **B.** RAID level 1 is disk mirroring. Disk mirroring requires two hard disks. Information from one disk is duplicated onto the other, meaning that if one disk fails, the redundant data on the other disk can still be used.

**13.** **D.** When two or more disks in a stripe set with parity fail, all information on all disks in the stripe set is lost.

**14.** **A.** MULTI(0)DISK(0)RDISK(0)PARTITION(2) would be the ARC path for a non-SCSI disk that is the primary master, where the second partition on the first controller is defined.

**15.** **A, C.** NTHQ will check your system to make sure it has the minimum requirements to install Windows NT Server. SCSITOOL reports information on Adaptec and Buslogic SCSI adapters, and can also be used to check for hardware incompatibilities.

16. **B.** PING can help locate a problem on an external network. You can PING at greater distances from your local computer, and identify where the problem on the network resides.

17. **C.** Because everything has been mirrored, so has the original BOOT.INI. By using a boot floppy, and modifying the ARC path to point to the mirror partition, you'll be able to start Windows NT Server.

18. **D.** The SYSTEM.LOG contains information regarding services and drivers that have failed or experienced some sort of fatal error. This log can be viewed with the Event Viewer application.

19. **C.** NTLDR loads Windows NT Server on a computer that uses an Intel processor. This is a hidden, Read Only file that, after being loaded by the boot sector routine, finds and loads the Windows NT operating system.

# Part 5

## Test Yourself:
## Practice Exams

MICROSOFT CERTIFIED SYSTEMS ENGINEER

# Test Yourself: Windows NT Workstation 4.0

Q&A

# Workstation Practice Exam 1

Before you call to register for the actual exam, take the following test and see how you make out. Set a timer for 75 minutes—the time you'll have to take the live Workstation exam—and answer the following 51 questions in the time allotted. Once you're through, turn to the end of the module and check your score to see if you passed! Good luck!

1. You are preparing to upgrade a computer in your office to Windows NT Workstation 4.0. You are unsure if the hardware on this computer is compatible with the new operating system. What software can you use to determine if there are any hardware incompatibilities before upgrading to Windows NT Workstation 4.0?

    A. HCL
    B. Windows NTHQ
    C. HAL
    D. HQTOOL

2. Your network consists of 15 Windows NT workstations using the NetBEUI protocol. Your boss has informed you that he wants workstations on the network to be able to connect to another network. After installing several routers to connect the networks, you find that none of the workstations is able to connect. What is the most likely reason?

    A. The routers aren't initialized.
    B. You forgot to specify a subnet mask.
    C. The protocol isn't routable.
    D. The network has exceeded the size supported by Windows NT.

3. Which of the following is a part of the NT Executive?

    A. Password
    B. Logon Process
    C. Security Subsystem
    D. Security Reference Monitor

**4.** You are running three 16-bit applications designed for Windows 3.1, a DOS application, and a 32-bit Windows NT application on your Windows NT workstation. A 16-bit Windows application locks up. What will happen to the remaining applications running on your computer?

A. All applications will lock up on the workstation.

B. All 16-bit applications will lock up.

C. Only the DOS application will lock up.

D. The entire workstation will lock up.

**5.** You are doing an upgrade from a previous version of Windows NT to Windows NT Workstation 4.0. The workstation has a CD-ROM, but no floppy drive. What command will you use to start this upgrade? (Choose the best answer.)

A. WINNT32.EXE /B

B. WINNT.EXE /B

C. WINNT32.EXE /X

D. WINNT.EXE /X

**6.** You have decided to convert an existing FAT partition to NTFS. What must you do to convert the partition over, without destroying the existing data?

A. Use FDISK to remove the existing partition, then use the CONVERT *<drive letter>* /FS:NTFS command to create an NTFS file system.

B. Use FDISK to remove the existing partition, use the CONVERT *<drive letter>* /FS:NTFS command to create an NTFS file system, then restore your files from an existing backup.

C. Use the CONVERT *<drive letter>* /FS:NTFS command to convert the existing file system to NTFS.

D. Use the FORMAT *<drive letter>* /FS:NTFS command to convert the existing file system to NTFS.

**7.** During installation, you decided not to create an emergency repair disk. Since then, you've decided that safe is better than sorry. What can you do now that the installation is complete to create an emergency repair disk?

A. Run the ERD.EXE utility.

B. Run the RDISK utility.

C. Run the FDISK utility.

D. Run WINNT or WINNT32 again.

**8.** Your Windows NT Workstation has 32MB of memory. What is the recommended initial size of the paging file?

A. 12MB

B. 20MB

C. 44MB

D. 64MB

**9.** You are concerned that the Registry is reaching its maximum size. You know you will be installing new applications in the near future, which will cause the Registry's maximum size will be exceeded. What can you do to increase the maximum size allowed to the Registry? (Choose the best answer.)

A. Increase the size on the Registry tab of the System applet in Control Panel.

B. Increase the size in the Server applet in Control Panel.

C. Increase the size on the Performance tab of System Properties.

D. Increase the size in the Virtual Memory Window.

**10.** Rosa wishes to make changes to the Registry. She wants to use the easiest method of making these changes. What front-end application will you suggest she use?

A. Regedt32

B. Regedit

C. System Editor

D. Control Panel

11. You want to search the Registry for a particular value. Which of the following tools can you use to find this information? (Choose all that apply.)

    A. Regedit
    B. Regedt32
    C. System Editor
    D. System Administrator

12. Which of the following groups in the utility shown in the next illustration can automatically update files from servers to workstations in a network? (Choose all that apply.)

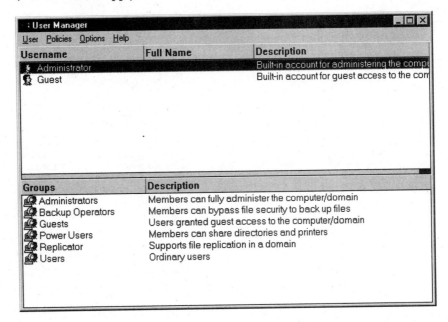

    A. Replicator
    B. Backup Operators
    C. Administrator
    D. Power Users

**13.** Harold has just retired from the Marketing department, and Wayne has just been hired to replace him. What is the best method of removing Harold from the network, and giving Wayne the same access to the domain that Harold enjoyed? Your solution must retain permissions and description information.

    A. Delete Harold's account, and create a new account for Wayne.

    B. Rename Harold's account for Wayne, then have Wayne change his password the next time he logs on.

    C. Make a copy of Harold's account, rename the copy for Wayne, then delete the original.

    D. Use Harold's account as a template for creating Wayne's account. Delete Harold's account.

**14.** You try to access your Windows NT workstation at work from home. After calling into the system and attempting to log on, you are disconnected by the computer. What is most likely the reason for this problem?

    A. You forgot to install a modem on the workstation.

    B. You forgot to install RAS on the workstation.

    C. You don't have a valid account.

    D. You don't have the Dial-In Permission set on your account.

**15.** Darren wants to create either a stripe set or a volume set. Darren knows the two are similar, but is unsure which one to choose. He uses NTFS, and plans to increase the set's capacity later. Which should he choose?

    A. The stripe set, as he can increase its capacity later.

    B. The stripe set, as NTFS can't be used on a volume set.

    C. The volume set, as he can increase its capacity later.

    D. The volume set, as NTFS can't be used on a stripe set.

**16.** You save a file in Windows NT Workstation which is called Michael Resume. When you look at this filename from DOS 6.22, how will the filename appear?

A. MICHAE~1

B. MICHAEL RESUME

C. MICHAE!1

D. You won't be able to view the filename, as it doesn't meet the naming convention.

17. Susan is upgrading from Windows NT Workstation 3.5 to version 4.0. The file system she is using is High Performance File System. What must she do before performing the upgrade to version 4.0?

A. Convert HPFS to NTFS.

B. Format the hard disk to a different file system.

C. Install Windows NT 4.0-compatible drivers to recognize the file system.

D. Nothing. Do the upgrade.

18. You grant Larry permission to access a shared folder called Finance on a server called FinServ. Larry tries to access the shared folder from his Windows NT workstation, but he can't. What is the most likely reason?

A. These permissions will not take effect until the next time he logs onto the domain.

B. The permissions won't take effect until FinServ is rebooted.

C. The permissions won't take effect until the Windows NT workstation is rebooted.

D. The changes in permissions have corrupted the access token.

19. Which of the following creates access tokens, authenticates users, and manages the local security policy?

A. SAM

B. ACL

C. LSA

D. ACE

**20.** You are a member of the Administrators group, and decide to take ownership of a file. When you do this, who actually holds ownership of the file?

A. Your account

B. The Administrator group

C. The User Group

D. The Replicator Group

**21.** What determines the level of file security you can use on Windows NT Workstation?

A. The operating system

B. The file system used

C. Security IDs

D. Security Reference Monitor

**22.** Which of the following protocols are routable? (Choose all that apply.)

A. NWLink

B. DLC

C. NetBEUI

D. TCP/IP

**23.** A Windows NT workstation is regularly accessing the Internet. You want to change the binding order of the protocol used for this, so that the protocol is accessed faster. Where would you do this?

A. Network in Control Panel

B. Protocols in Control Panel

C. Internet in Control Panel

D. Modems

24. You want to share a folder on your Windows NT workstation, so that other computers on the network can access the files contained within it. Which applications can you use to perform this action? (Choose all that apply.)

    A. Disk Administrator
    B. Network applet in Control Panel
    C. CSNW
    D. Windows NT Explorer

25. You have installed TCP/IP on your Windows NT network, and decided to have IP addresses assigned to all of the workstations. What will you use to accomplish this task?

    A. WINS
    B. DNS
    C. DHCP
    D. DCHP

26. You have decided to publish electronic information on your company's intranet, but don't want to do this from a server. Instead, you decide to use your Windows NT Workstation 4.0 computer. You don't want to purchase additional software. What will you use?

    A. Internet Information Server
    B. UNIX Services
    C. Internet Explorer
    D. Peer Web Services

27. Which of the following is true?

    A. LMHOSTS maps IP addresses to NetBIOS names, and HOST maps hostnames to IP addresses.
    B. LMHOSTS maps hostnames to IP addresses, and HOST maps IP addresses to NetBIOS names.
    C. LMHOSTS maps NetBIOS names to hostnames, and HOST maps hostnames to NetBIOS names.
    D. LMHOSTS maps hostnames to DHCP, and HOST maps hostnames to WINS.

28. You want to provide Internet services, but you're unsure whether to use Internet Information Server or Peer Web Services. Which of the following is provided by both packages?

    A. WWW Browsing

    B. FTP

    C. Gopher

    D. Virtual Servers

29. You want to use a share on a NetWare 3.12 server. What will you use to access this share from your Windows NT 4.0 workstation? (Choose all that apply.)

    A. Network Neighborhood

    B. NetWare Explorer

    C. NET SHARE

    D. Network Explorer

30. You are configuring the frame type settings, and want to choose the one that's best suited for most NICs. Which will you choose?

    A. Auto

    B. Ethernet_802.2

    C. Ethernet_802.3

    D. Ethernet_802.5

31. You want to run CSNW on your Windows NT workstation. What else must be running for CSNW to function?

    A. GSNW

    B. NWLink

    C. NetWare requestor

    D. NetWare compatible redirector

**32.** You work for a large company with various branch offices throughout the country, and a main office in London, Ontario. You want to configure RAS at the branch offices to access classified files located at the London office through the Internet. Your solution must provide security, and low transmission, administration, and hardware costs. What will you do?

A. Use PPP.
B. Use Point to Point Tunneling Protocol.
C. Use SLIP.
D. Use a T3 connection.

**33.** Workstations are attaching to your server through RAS. You want to enable these RAS clients to have access to the entire routed network. What will you need to do?

A. Attach a router to the RAS server.
B. Install Services for RAS Routers.
C. Enable Routing in RAS.
D. Nothing. RAS does it already.

**34.** You connect to a RAS server with a Windows NT workstation. Both the RAS server and the Windows NT workstation use NetBEUI and TCP/IP protocols. The binding order on both of these machines is the same, with NetBEUI first on the list. Which of the following will RAS not be able to support?

A. Running Windows Sockets applications
B. Routing
C. Running NetBIOS applications
D. Remote Access to the server

**35.** You have been a member of a workgroup, but now your Windows NT workstation has been added to a domain. You want to be part of the domain, but don't want to lose administrative control over your workstation. What can you do?

    A. Add your domain account to the Domain Administrators account.

    B. Add your domain account to the Local Administrators group.

    C. Add your computer account to the Local Administrators group.

    D. Do not join the domain. There is nothing that can be done.

**36.** Which of the following does a network browser include in its list of network resources?

    A. Domains

    B. Workgroups

    C. Computers

    D. Users

**37.** You have just installed a Windows NT workstation. You reach the point in the installation that requires you to join either a workgroup or domain. You don't want to join either. What can you do?

    A. Leave both workgroup and domain blank.

    B. Choose None.

    C. Choose Stand Alone Server.

    D. Choose Workgroup, and specify one that isn't in use.

**38.** The Windows NT server that is acting as Master Browser is shut off. What will happen now?

    A. An election datagram will be sent, calling an election.

    B. The Backup Browser will be promoted to Master Browser.

    C. The Backup Domain Controller will become a PDC.

    D. Nothing. Since the Backup Browser has a copy of the browse list, no election is needed.

**39.** One of your Windows NT workstations needs to print to a NetWare Print Server. What protocol will you install on your workstation so that it can use this printer?

A. DLC

B. IPX/SPX

C. NWLink

D. NetBEUI

**40.** Users are complaining that they can't print to the shared printer on your Windows NT workstation. In addition, you have found that these users can't delete the print jobs that were sent. How is this problem fixed? (Choose the most appropriate answer.)

A. Stop the spooler service, and then restart it.

B. Delete the print jobs from your computer.

C. Create a new printer, then delete the old one that has stalled.

D. Restart each user's workstation.

**41.** What can you do to start and stop the spooler service? (Choose all that apply.)

A. Use Printers in Control Panel.

B. User Services in Control Panel.

C. Use the NET START SPOOLER and NET STOP SPOOLER command from the command line.

D. Use the NET USE SPOOLER and NET STOP SPOOLER command from the command line.

**42.** Which of the following is responsible for the creation and management of objects in Windows NT Workstation?

A. The application

B. Object Manager

C. Object Packager

D. Performance Monitor

**43.** 16-bit programs need to load certain files to run. What files are required on Windows NT to load these files?

A. AUTOEXEC.NT

B. CONFIG.NT

C. DOS.NT

D. SHELL.NT

**44.** Pat is using Windows NT Workstation, and wants to edit the Program Information File (PIF) of a DOS application. How would you suggest she do this?

A. Use PIF Editor.

B. Use the Properties dialog box for the program she wants to configure.

C. Use the Properties dialog box of the VDM.

D. She can't. Windows NT Workstation doesn't use PIFs anymore.

**45.** Rosa wants to run a 16-bit program. There are other 16-bit programs running on her Windows NT workstation, but she doesn't want to run the risk of the other applications crashing this one. What can she do to keep the other applications from interfering with the important one that must be run?

A. Run the important 16-bit application in its own memory space.

B. Run the 16-bit applications in their own memory space.

C. Run the 16-bit application in a memory space that's shared with the others.

D. Don't run the 16-bit application.

**46.** Which of the following is a tool provided by Windows NT to optimize performance? (Choose all that apply.)

A. MSD

B. Windows NT Diagnostics

C. Task Manager

D. Performance Monitor

**47.** Your Windows NT workstation is acting sluggish, and you're noticing a high degree of activity from your hard disk. You start Performance Monitor and check the Memory. Page Faults/sec is showing a high number. What does this mean, and how can you fix the problem?

A. It means memory is low, and the computer is swapping to the page file at a high rate. Install more memory.

B. It means memory is low, and the computer is swapping to the page file at a high rate. Install a higher-capacity hard disk.

C. It means memory is high, so there are errors on the disk. Install a new hard disk.

D. It means that you haven't installed the counters for Memory. Do so immediately.

48. Windows NT divides memory into pages. What is the size of these pages?

A. 4KB

B. 8KB

C. 16KB

D. 32KB

49. Tom is having trouble with his computer, which dual boots between Windows NT Workstation and Windows 95. When he starts the machine, it jumps immediately into Windows NT without giving him the chance to decide which operating system he wants to use. What is the problem?

A. The BOOT.INI file is missing.

B. The NTLDR file is missing.

C. The Timeout entry in the BOOT.INI is set to 0.

D. The Default entry in the BOOT.INI is set to Windows NT Workstation.

50. What are the conditions that will cause the system to load the LastKnownGood configuration?

A. The system is recovering from a critical error.

B. The LastKnownGood configuration is selected.

C. The BOOT.INI file is configured to load the LastKnownGood.

D. The NTLDR file is missing.

51. Which file loads the Windows NT operating system on a computer with an Intel processor?

   A. NTDETECT
   B. NTLDR
   C. BOOTSECT.DOS
   D. BOOT.INI

# Workstation Practice Exam 2

Before you call to register for the actual exam, take the following test and see how you make out. Set a timer for 75 minutes—the time you'll have to take the live Workstation exam—and answer the following 51 questions in the time allotted. Once you're through, turn to the end of the module and check your score to see if you passed! Good luck!

1. Your processor is executing a process when a task with a higher priority needs to be executed. Windows NT Workstation takes control of the processor without the consent of the application currently using the processor. What kind of multitasking is being used?

   A. Asymmetric

   B. Symmetric

   C. Cooperative

   D. Preemptive

2. Your network is as shown in the next illustration. What kind of network model is being used?

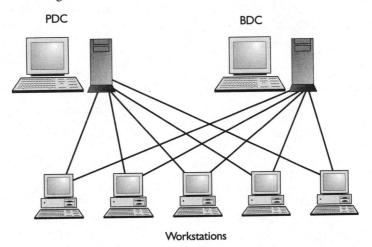

PDC     BDC

Workstations

   A. Workgroup Model

   B. Workstation Model

   C. Domain Model

   D. Multiple Master Domain Model

**3.** Which of the following is responsible for using the hard disk to simulate RAM?

   A. VMM

   B. Demand Paging

   C. Object Manager

   D. I/O Manager

**4.** Marni wants to install Windows NT Workstation 4.0 on her 386 computer, which has 12MB of memory, 120MB of free hard disk space, and a CD-ROM. Her attempts at installing the operating system fail. Why?

   A. Windows NT Workstation 4.0 requires 16MB of memory.

   B. Windows NT Workstation 4.0 requires 160MB of free hard disk space.

   C. Windows NT Workstation 4.0 requires a minimum Pentium processor.

   D. Windows NT Workstation 4.0 requires a minimum 486/33Mhz processor.

**5.** You are preparing to install Windows NT Workstation 4.0 on your computer. Which file systems will Windows NT support? (Choose all that apply.)

   A. HPFS

   B. NTFS

   C. OS/2 File System

   D. FAT

**6.** Which utility would you use to record the differences between a normal Windows NT installation, and one in which you have added files?

A. SYSDIFF

B. UDF

C. SETUPMGR

D. SNAP

7. Jennifer's computer dual boots between Windows NT Workstation 4.0 and Windows 95. She complains that when the computer starts, there is too short of a delay before automatically booting into Workstation. Which file can you edit to increase the delay time?

A. BOOT.INI

B. NTLDR

C. BOOTSEC.DOS

D. PAGEFILE.SYS

8. Harold opens the Display Properties sheet to change his icon size and wallpaper. He does so with no problem. Since he finds the desktop size too big, and finds it a little difficult to view the icons, he decides to change the display driver. He finds he cannot. What is most likely the reason for this?

A. Display drivers must be changed through Accessibility Options.

B. Display drivers must be changed through the System applet.

C. Display drivers must be changed through the Multimedia applet.

D. Harold doesn't have administrator privileges.

9. Your computer has had the following operating systems loaded in the following order: Windows 95, Windows NT Workstation, Windows NT Server. You are in Windows NT Workstation, and change your display driver. When you reboot your computer into Workstation, all you can see is a black screen. Which of the other options listed in your system startup, in the Startup/Shutdown, and BOOT.INI file will allow you to fix this problem?

A. Windows NT Server

B. Windows 95

C. Windows NT Workstation version 4.0 (VGA)

D. Windows NT Workstation version 4.0

**10.** You have just installed a device that will keep the your Windows NT workstation from shutting down in the event of a blackout or brownout. What applet on the Control Panel (shown in the next illustration) will you use to configure this device?

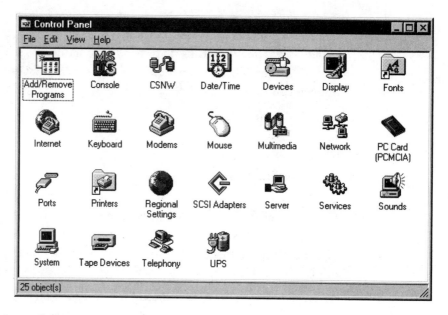

A. UPS

B. Devices

C. SCSI

D. Recovery section of Startup/Shutdown in System Properties

**11.** A user attempts to gain access to a new installation of Windows NT, using the Guest account. The attempt fails. You check Windows NT, and find that the Guest account still has all of its default settings. Why can't the user log on? (Choose the most likely reason.)

A. The Guest account is disabled by default.

B. The Guest group is disabled by default.

C. The Everyone group is disabled by default.

D. The Guest account requires a valid e-mail address as a password, which this user obviously doesn't have.

**12.** During a new installation of Windows NT, a user chooses his cat's name, Junior, as his password for the Administrator account. When he logs back on to the system, he types in "junior", and finds that the password will not work. Why?

A. The length of the password is too short, and hasn't been accepted by the system.

B. The length of the password is too long, and hasn't been accepted by the system.

C. Passwords for the Administrator account must be alphanumeric.

D. Passwords are case sensitive in Windows NT.

**13.** To what log file are audited events recorded?

A. User Log

B. System Log

C. Security Log

D. Event Log

**14.** What is the difference between User Rights and User Permissions?

A. Rights apply to the entire computer. Permissions apply to specific objects.

B. Permissions apply to the entire computer. Rights apply to specific objects.

C. Permissions apply to the entire domain. Rights apply to a specific computer.

D. Rights apply to the entire domain. Permissions apply to a specific computer.

**15.** You decide to create a volume set on a computer running Windows NT. One of the disks in the set fails. How can you recover the information?

A. Replace the failed disk. The lost information will regenerate and be restored.

B. Replace the failed disk. Force the set to restore itself through Disk Administrator.

C. Replace the disk. Recreate the set, and restore the information from a backup.

D. Nothing. The information is lost permanently.

**16.** You are naming a blank document that you plan to use later. The file is to be used by both Windows NT and DOS 6.22 users. You want to use a file naming convention that is supported by both. What will you name the file?

    A. NUL

    B. THIS_IS_BLANK

    C. EMPT/1

    D. BLANK.TXT

**17.** You are deciding which file system to use on your Windows NT workstation. The file system you choose must support compression, long filenames, and security attributes. Which file system will you choose?

    A. Use FAT with DriveSpace 3 to support compression.

    B. Use VFAT with DriveSpace 3 to support compression.

    C. Use HPFS, as it supports all these requirements.

    D. Use NTFS, as it supports all these requirements.

**18.** Which of the following maintains all user, group, and computer accounts in a database?

    A. ACL

    B. SAM

    C. LSA

    D. ACE

**19.** Which security feature of the mandatory logon prevents running User mode programs until after a valid logon occurs? (Choose the best answer.)

    A. Physical logon

    B. User Preferences

    C. Restricted User Mode

    D. Password

**20.** By default, any user with a valid account can press CTRL-ALT-DEL and shut down the Windows NT workstation they are working on. You want a particular workstation never to be shut down. What can you change to disable this default of a user being able to shut down the system?

A. Change the ShutdownWithoutLogon value of Winlogon in the Registry to 0.

B. Change the ShutdownWithoutLogon value of Winlogon in the Registry to 1.

C. Disable the System Shutdown option in System Properties.

D. Disable the System Shutdown option in Server.

**21.** What are the seven layers of the OSI model?

A. Application, Providers, Session, Transport, Network, Data Link, Physical

B. Providers, Presentation, Transport Driver Interface, Network, Data Link, Physical

C. Application, Presentation, Transport Driver Interface, Network, Data Link, Physical

D. Application, Presentation, Session, Transport, Network, Data Link, Physical

**22.** Your network is spread across two buildings and connected with several routers. You install Windows NT Workstation and the DLC protocol, so you can communicate with an HP printer located in the other building. You find that you are unable to print to this printer. Why?

A. DLC isn't routable.

B. TCP/IP is used to communicate with HP printers.

C. AFP is used to communicate with HP printers.

D. DLC routing is not enabled on the router.

**23.** You want to connect to a hidden share on another Windows NT workstation. You use Windows NT Explorer to browse the computer the share is on, but since it's hidden, you can't see it. What do you need to connect to this share? (Choose all that apply.)

A. The share's name, and the name of the computer that this share resides on.

B. The name of the user who created the hidden share.

C. Password for the share.

D. The proper permissions.

24. Network traffic has increased at various times throughout the network. You believe the cause for the increased traffic is elections for the Master Browser. What can you do to decrease the traffic?

A. Configure Windows NT workstations on each subnet not to hold elections.

B. Configure a computer on each subnet as a preferred master browser.

C. Configure Server service not to hold elections.

D. Nothing. It is required by a Windows NT network, and must occur for the network to function.

25. You have decided to download a new printer driver from the Internet. You get to the website, and click on a hyperlink to start the download. What protocol will transfer the driver to you?

A. HTTP

B. FTP

C. TCP

D. DLC

26. You have implemented Internet services on your Windows NT workstation. You decide you want to stop and configure some of these services. What tool will you use?

A. Internet Information Server

B. Internet Services Manager

C. Peer Web Services

D. Peer Web Services Install

**27.** You have decided to manually enter the IP address you will use on your Windows NT workstation. The items in your Control Panel are as shown in the next illustration. You require this IP address for connecting to the Internet via modem. Where will you go in Control Panel to enter this information?

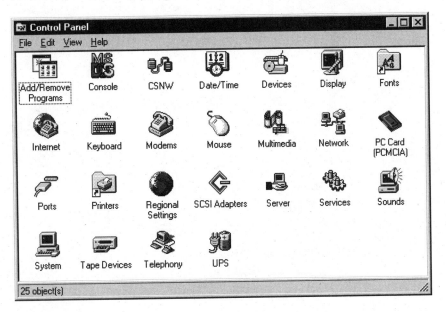

A. Modems

B. Internet

C. Network

D. CSNW

**28.** Jennifer wants to use network resources on a NetWare server. What must she install to do this?

A. CSNW

B. GSNW

C. NetWare Redirector

D. NetWare Requestor

**29.** You want to enable access to a NetWare server for a large group of Windows NT workstations. What is the easiest way to implement this?

A. GSNW

B. CSNW

C. NWLink

D. NetWare Lite

**30.** You want to view the frame type a particular Windows NT workstation is using. What can you type from the command prompt to view this information?

A. IPXROUTE

B. IPXROUTE CONFIG

C. IPCONFIG

D. IPXINFO

**31.** You want NetWare clients to have the ability to access files from your Windows NT workstation. Which will you need to install to enable this?

A. GSNW

B. FPNW

C. CSNW

D. DSMN

**32.** Which of the following does RAS support when dialing out? (Choose all that apply.)

A. PPP

B. API

C. SLIP

D. X.25

**33.** You try to connect through RAS to a server, but the connection is dropped. You try again, and the same thing happens. What tool can you use to view information about the RAS connection? (Choose all that apply.)

A. Device Log

B. RAS Monitor

C. Dial Up Networking Monitor

D. Event Viewer

**34.** Which of the following encryption methods provides the best security for authentication?

A. CHAP

B. PAP

C. MS-CRAP

D. MS-CHAP

**35.** You have just purchased SQL Server. All of your servers have basically the same hardware, but they have different roles on the network. Where is the best place to install this program?

A. Member Server

B. Primary Domain Controller

C. Backup Domain Controller

D. Router

**36.** Your network consists of a Windows NT server acting as master browser, five Windows NT workstations, 10 Windows 95 machines, and 15 Windows for Workgroups computers. The master browser becomes unavailable. Which machine will become the master browser?

A. A Windows NT workstation.

B. A Windows for Workgroups machine.

C. A Windows 95 machine.

D. None, the master browser has to be a server.

**37.** The PDC maintains a database. Which of the following maintains a copy of that database?

    A. Master Browser

    B. BDC

    C. Member Server

    D. SAM

**38.** What is responsible for prioritizing print jobs?

    A. Print router

    B. Print spooler

    C. Print drivers

    D. Print Prioritizing Service

**39.** You have just installed a print device that uses TCP/IP to communicate with the network. What do you need to print to this device? (Choose all that apply.)

    A. IP address and the printer's name

    B. Name of the printer

    C. Media address

    D. IP address and subnet mask of the printer

**40.** You are running a mixed network of NetWare and Windows NT computers. You want to share a NetWare printer from Windows NT. Where will you do this?

    A. CSNW

    B. GSNW

    C. SYSCON

    D. Printers

**41.** You decide to enable auditing of a printer. What events can you audit?

A. Print, Delete, Purge Print Jobs, Change Permissions, Take Ownership

B. Print, Pause, Stop

C. Print, Delete, Change Permissions

D. Print, Full Control, Delete, Change Permissions, Take Ownership

**42.** What is responsible for managing and scheduling threads on Windows NT?

A. Processor

B. Executive Services

C. Kernel

D. Object Manager

**43.** You have a UNIX application that needs to be run on Windows NT. What environmental subsystem will allow this program to run?

A. UNIX subsystem

B. POSIX subsystem

C. OS/2 subsystem

D. VDM

**44.** Which of the following is not a component of WOW?

A. KRNL386.EXE

B. USER.EXE

C. GDI.EXE

D. NTVDM

**45.** You decide to use Performance Monitor to monitor memory on your Windows NT workstation. Will running this program affect the performance of the computer?

A. No, because it's run in its own address space.

B. No, because it takes its own performance into account.

C. No, because it runs from an area it's not monitoring.

D. Yes.

46. NTFS can use caching to improve performance. What kind of caching does NTFS provide?

    A. Write Ahead
    B. Write Back
    C. Write On
    D. Write Through

47. You want to check the counters for your hard disk, but when you use Performance Monitor, you can't see them. What must you do?

    A. Install the Service Pack for Windows NT.
    B. Run the command DISKPERF –Y from the command line.
    C. Run the command DISKPERF –N from the command line.
    D. Run the command DISKPERF –YE from the command line.

48. You are using Performance Monitor, and notice that the System: Processor Queue Length is greater than two. What does this mean?

    A. The processor is operating normally.
    B. The queue needs to be increased.
    C. More memory is needed.
    D. The processor may be causing a problem.

49. You are certain that some drivers aren't loading properly during the boot and load sequences. What can you use to find which drivers and services aren't loading?

    A. Drive Master
    B. Disk Administrator
    C. Performance Monitor
    D. Kernel Debugger

50. Of the following, which is the most damaging to a computer when it fails?

A. Hard disk
B. Memory
C. CPU
D. Motherboard

**51.** You want to obtain information about your computer, including what account is being used, statistics, and resources on your computer. What tool comes with Windows NT and provides inventory-style information about your system?

A. Windows NT Diagnostics
B. System Editor
C. Registry Editor
D. Performance Monitor

# Workstation Practice Exam I Answers

To pass the Workstation exam, you need to answer 36 questions correctly. We've provided explanations of the answers so you can review the questions you missed. How did you do?

1. **B.** The Windows NT Hardware Qualifier (Windows NTHQ) is a program that runs under DOS (on computers with Intel chips), and checks a computer for hardware incompatibilities. Before Windows NT 4.0, you would have to install the operating system and see if it failed—with little information given as to what the actual problem was. The Windows NTHQ verifies that your system and components are going to be supported under Windows NT. While the Hardware Compatibility List (HCL) is also given as a choice for this question, it is not software, as is specified by the question.

2. **C.** NetBEUI is a small, fast, and efficient protocol that is not routable. It was developed at a time when networks were small, and therefore didn't require routers.

3. **D.** The Security Reference Monitor is part of NT Executive and resides in Kernel mode. The choices given in this question outline what happens during logon. A password is given during the logon process. The security subsystem takes this information, builds, and then sends an authentication package. This package is sent from User mode into the Kernel mode of Windows NT, where the security reference monitor checks it against the security account database. If the correct password has been entered, the security reference monitor then builds and sends an access token back to the security subsystem.

4. **B.** All 16-bit Windows applications would lock up. This is because they share common memory space, as if they were in their native Windows 3.x environment. Because of this, one application can potentially bring down all other 16-bit Windows programs.

**5.** **A.** Using WINNT.EXE or WINNT32.EXE with the /B switch will force the setup program not to use the three setup floppies that come with Windows NT Workstation. Instead, the files that exist on the floppies will be copied from the CD-ROM and stored in a temporary directory. However, since the question requires an upgrade to be performed, and not a full installation, the WINNT32.EXE /B command would be used. Using this switch, the boot files are copied from the CD-ROM to the hard disk, saving users the trouble of loading and removing floppy disks.

**6.** **C.** The CONVERT *<drive letter>* /FS:NTFS command will convert an existing FAT partition to NTFS without deleting any files on that partition. Remember that this is a one-way conversion. There is no utility to convert the partition back to FAT.

**7.** **B.** The RDISK utility can be used to create an emergency repair disk (ERD) after installation is completed. The ERD is used to rescue your system if it is corrupted, such as by a power outage, or when there is a problem with Windows NT's boot or system files.

**8.** **C.** The recommended initial paging file size is the size of your physical RAM plus 12MB. In this case that would mean that the initial paging file should be 44MB (32+12). It is important that you remember this simple math equation. This type of question has a nasty way of appearing on Windows NT Workstation exams!

**9.** **D.** The maximum size of the Registry can be changed in the Virtual Memory Window. This is reached by clicking the Change button on the Performance tab of System Properties. Here you will see the current size of the Registry, and what its maximum size is set at. The maximum size can be increased or decreased one megabyte at a time.

**10.** **D.** The easiest method of making changes to the Registry is with Control Panel. Regedt32 and Regedit are complex and difficult to use. System

Editor is used to make changes to the system files, such as AUTOEXEC.BAT and SYSTEM.INI. Any changes made through the Control Panel are subsequently made to the Registry.

**11.** **A.** You can search the Registry with both Regedit and Regedt32, but only Regedit will allow you to search for values. Regedit permits searches by keys, subkeys, and values, but Regedt32 will only search for keys.

**12.** **A.** The Replicator group is a special group used by the Replicator service. It can automatically update files from a server to a workstation in a network, and is used for replicating such things as account information between PDCs and BDCs in a domain.

**13.** **B.** Renaming an account is the only way to keep all permissions and descriptions intact. Creating a new account by any of the other methods would mean losing this information. By far, the easiest method of removing one user from the system, and putting another user onto the system with the same permissions, is to rename the account.

**14.** **D.** Dial-In Permissions allow a user to connect to a Windows NT workstation using Remote Access Service (RAS). Even though RAS may be configured correctly, and the user has a valid user account, he or she will not be able to connect without this permission set.

**15.** **C.** A stripe set cannot be extended. Therefore, if you plan on increasing the capacity of your set, use a volume set.

**16.** **A.** For backward compatibility, VFAT creates a FAT file system directory entry that meets the 8.3 DOS naming convention. The first six letters appear the same, but a tilde and number (starting at one and ending at nine) is added. This means that a file called Michael Resume would become MICHAE~1.

**17. A.** Windows NT 4.0 does not recognize HPFS. You must convert the existing file system to NTFS, then do the upgrade. While previous versions could use HPFS, version 4.0 does not support it. Some might find it strange that while the operating system no longer supports this file system, it makes regular appearances on the Windows NT Workstation exam!

**18. A.** Changes to permissions won't take effect until the next time the user logs on. This is because he is still using the same access token. A new access token will be created the next time he logs on.

**19. C.** The Local Security Authority (LSA) is responsible for managing local security policies, and authenticating users. (It may help you to remember the LSA's functions by thinking of it as the Local *Subway* Authority: It issues tokens; its turnstiles validate subway users; and it manages the subway security.)

**20. B.** When a user who is a member of the Administrators group owns a file, that file is not owned by the user. It is owned by the Administrators group.

**21. B.** The file system used determines the level of file security you can use on Windows NT. For example, FAT doesn't support folder and file permissions, while NTFS does.

**22. A, D.** TCP/IP and NWLink are routable protocols.

**23. A.** The binding order of protocols can be changed by using the Bindings tab in the Network applet (shown in the next illustration), which is found in the Control Panel. By raising the protocol in the binding order, the protocol can be accessed faster by the computer.

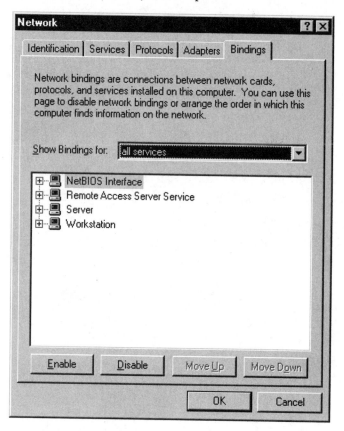

**24.** **D.** Windows NT Explorer is the program used to share folders.

**25.** **C.** Dynamic Host Configuration Protocol assigns an IP address to a computer on a TCP/IP network. It selects the IP address from a range of addresses defined on the DHCP server, and issues it to the computer requesting the address.

**26. D.** Peer Web Services comes with Windows NT Workstation 4.0, and can be used to publish electronic documents from your workstation. It allows you to publish HTML documents, allows file transfers, and has Gopher services.

**27. A.** Windows NT uses the LMHOSTS file to map IP addresses to NetBIOS names. The HOST file is used to map hostnames (hence its name) to IP addresses.

**28. A, B, C.** Peer Web Services includes FTP, Gopher services, and WWW browsing. It is not as robust as Internet Information Server, and thereby doesn't provide virtual servers.

**29. A.** Shares on NetWare servers can be accessed through Network Neighborhood on Windows NT Workstation 4.0. While the appearance in Network Neighborhood is a little different when connecting to NetWare, it is essentially the same as accessing a share on a Microsoft computer.

**30. A.** The Auto setting is best suited for most network adapter cards (NICs). This will enable automatic detection of the frame type. However, the first frame type that Windows NT is introduced to will be the frame type that's used.

**31. B.** For communications with NetWare, Windows NT uses the NWLink IPX/SPX-compatible transport protocol. This is because the standard protocol of NetWare is IPX/SPX. As with other services for interaction with NetWare, CSNW, GSNW and the Migration Tool all require that NWLink is running. NWLink must be running on the Windows NT workstation or server if you want these tools and services to work.

**32. B.** Point to Point Tunneling Protocol is a good choice when you need to keep costs down, but security is still an issue.

33. **D.** RAS can supply full access to a remote network because it functions as an IP and IPX router. No additional software is required.

34. **A.** RAS will use the first compatible protocol found. If both the RAS client and the RAS server are using NetBEUI, then that is what will be used for the session. Since Windows Sockets programs are only accessible through TCP/IP, RAS will not be able to support it under these conditions. The way to fix this problem is to raise TCP/IP in the binding order, which will then cause the RAS server and client to use that protocol.

35. **B.** By adding a domain account to the Local Administrators group, you can retain administrative control over a Windows NT workstation.

36. **A, B, C.** Network browsers keep a list of domains, workgroups, computers, and any shared resources it sees on the network. It does not store a listing of users on the network.

37. **D.** You must join either a domain or workgroup when installing Windows NT Workstation. The installation will not allow you to leave both blank, and will also not allow you to skip over that part of the installation. However, if you don't want to join either, you can specify a workgroup name that isn't in use.

38. **A.** When the Master Browser becomes unavailable, an election datagram (also called an election packet) is sent, calling for an election for a new Master Browser. The computer with the best qualifications will then become Master Browser. The election packet contains the qualifications of the computer that sent it. These qualifications include whether the computer is a PDC, what operating system it's running, and what the version type is. When a network computer receives this packet, it compares the sender's qualifications to its own. If the receiving computer has higher qualifications, then it will broadcast its own election packet. This continues until the best computer for the job becomes Master Browser.

**39. C.** NWLink is Microsoft's implementation of IPX/SPX. The IPX/SPX protocol is the standard protocol of NetWare, and NWLink is used by Windows NT to communicate with such networks. This is not to say that NetWare is limited to using this one protocol, but on Microsoft exams, unless it's stated otherwise, always assume the NetWare network is running IPX/SPX as its transport protocol. When required to print to a NetWare Print Server, the default protocol to use on your Windows NT workstation is NWLink.

**40. A.** When print jobs can't be deleted and aren't printing, it is a good indication that the print spooler has stalled. It is remedied by simply stopping and then restarting the spooler service. This can be done from Printers in Control Panel, or by using the command line NET START SPOOLER or NET STOP SPOOLER from the command line.

**41. A, B, C.** There are three ways to start and stop the spooler service. The first is by using Printers in Control Panel. The second method is by using the command line NET START SPOOLER or NET STOP SPOOLER. The third is by using the Services applet in Control Panel.

**42. B.** Object Manager is, as its name suggests, responsible for the management of objects. It is responsible for naming, security, and use of objects. It creates and manages objects in Windows NT.

**43. A, B.** AUTOEXEC.NT and CONFIG.NT aid in allowing 16-bit applications to run as they would in their natural environment, Windows 3.*x*. AUTOEXEC.NT is used by 16-bit programs to load TSRs and to set environment variables. CONFIG.NT is used to load system files that are required by these programs to run.

**44. B.** Windows NT relieves users from the need to run a PIF editing program to edit a DOS program's behavior. You can edit a PIF, and configure its environment, through the Properties dialog box for that program. By right-clicking an executable file in Windows NT Explorer, you can bring up the properties sheet for that program. Here, you will be able to make changes to how that program will run under Windows NT Workstation. However, while it seems you're directly changing the program's behavior, you really aren't. In actuality, you are changing the environment of the VDM that it will be using.

**45. A.** To keep a 16-bit program from interfering with other 16-bit programs, you must run it in its own separate memory space. Doing so is simple in Windows NT. From the RUN command, simply type in the program you wish to run, and check the Run in Separate Memory Space check box. This will run the program in its own VDM.

**46. D.** Performance Monitor is a tool provided with Windows NT for optimizing performance. The other tools mentioned here give inventories of your system, and provide other information and services, but do nothing for optimization.

**47. A.** When the Page Fault/sec are high, it means that memory is swapping to the paging file at a high rate. This is not good. The term for it is "disk thrashing", and it can slow down a system considerably. This is because significant time is wasted by the system for the purpose of swapping memory to and from the disk. Installing new memory is the best choice for solving this problem.

**48. A.** Windows NT divides memory into 4KB pages. These are the slices of memory that the Intel processor works with. In other words, the processor can allocate 4KB slices of memory to an application. If the process needs 7KB, then it gets two 4KB pages. If it requires 3KB, then it gets one 4KB page. Because the pages are so small, memory is managed more efficiently.

**49. C.** If the Timeout entry in the BOOT.INI file is set to 0, the computer will automatically boot into the default operating system. Changing this entry to a higher number will fix the problem. To do this, simply open the BOOT.INI file with a text editor (such as dear old DOS's EDIT.EXE). In the BOOT.INI file, you'll find a line that says TIMEOUT=0. If you want the timeout to be 30, change the value so that the entry reads TIMEOUT=30. The next time you reboot, you'll now have the chance to choose which operating system to enter.

**50. A, B.** The LastKnownGood configuration is loaded when the user selects it. When booting, there is always the option of hitting your spacebar to use this configuration. It is also loaded when the system experiences, and is recovering from a critical device loading error. If making changes to your system causes problems with Windows NT, this allows you to use the configurations that enabled Windows NT to last load properly. Basically, it reverts to the way it was before you muddled up the system.

**51. B.** NTLDR is a hidden, read-only file that loads the Windows NT operating system on *x*86-based operating systems like Intel. After being loaded by the boot sector routine, it finds and loads the Windows NT operating system.

# Workstation Practice Exam 2 Answers

To pass the Workstation exam, you need to answer 36 questions correctly. We've provided explanations of the answers so you can review the questions you missed. How did you do?

1. **D.** Windows NT supports cooperative and preemptive multitasking. Preemptive multitasking means that the operating system is able to take control of the processor without the consent of the application currently using the processor. The OS can take control when a time slice for a task runs out or when a task with a higher priority needs the processor. Cooperative multitasking means that a task currently using the processor must relinquish its control before any other tasks can use it. This was the kind of multitasking used in older Windows programs, and would cause the entire system to lock up because of one program failing to relinquish its control of the processor.
While there are only two kinds of multitasking, many people confuse them. One way to keep them straight is to use the playground analogy. Remember that preemptive multitasking is like a teacher who needs to takes control of things, and cooperative multitasking is like children who don't always cooperate that well with each other!

2. **C.** The Domain model has Windows NT servers acting as Primary Domain Controllers (PDCs) and Backup Domain Controllers (BDCs), which authenticate users before they can access domain resources. The Domain model is recommended for networks with more than ten computers, or where a centralized control of user accounts and resources is required.

3. **A.** The Virtual Memory Manager (VMM) is responsible for using the hard disk to simulate RAM. It uses a system called demand paging to swap unused portions of memory to the hard disk and retrieve the pages of data, when needed, back into memory. The VMM is responsible for swapping this memory to a paging file on the hard disk, and makes sure that this virtual memory is being used efficiently.

**4. D.** You cannot install Windows NT Workstation 4.0 on a 386 processor. Workstation requires a minimum of a 486/33Mhz processor.

**5. B, D.** Windows NT supports both the FAT and NTFS file systems. Unlike previous versions of Windows NT, you cannot install it on a hard disk formatted with HPFS. If your current system is formatted to use HPFS, Windows NT gives you an option during installation to convert the existing HPFS partition to NTFS.

**6. A.** The SYSDIFF utility is used to preinstall applications during setup. It is used to take snapshots of the Registry and other files on your system and/or network drives before and after installations. It creates an $OMF$ directory that can be used as part of installations.

**7. A.** The BOOT.INI file contains a Timeout entry that controls the delay time before booting into the default operating system. The entry in this file can be modified either by editing it directly with a text editor, or by using the Startup/Shutdown tab in the System applet found in the Control Panel of Windows NT. If the setting is set to 0, it will automatically start the default operating system, giving the user no time to choose another.

**8. D.** There are options that, when changed, will only affect a user's settings, and other changes that will affect everyone who uses a workstation. Because of this, to change system settings (such as display drivers) a user must be a member of the Administrator group. If he or she is not, then the user will be unable to make such changes.

**9. C.** The Windows NT boot loader installs two selections for Windows NT: the normal Windows NT we usually use, and the Windows NT 4.0 VGA mode. The VGA mode allows you to boot into a safe video mode (VGA) so that you can fix any incorrect configurations. This allows you to change display drivers back to the way they were without having to reinstall Windows NT.

10. **A.** The UPS applet is used to configure an uninterruptible power supply. A UPS is a device that keeps power flowing to the computer through batteries. Higher-end UPSs can also provide power conditioning, which keeps a steady flow of electricity going to the machine, protecting it from power spikes. If your area suffers a blackout or brownout, the UPS will continue providing your computer with power. This allows you to safely shut down the computer.

11. **A.** The Guest account is disabled by default when you install Windows NT. If users without an account of their own wish to gain limited access to your machine, you must enable this account.

12. **D.** Passwords in Windows NT are case sensitive. What this means is that smudge, SMUDGE, Smudge, and sMuDgE are all viewed as different passwords. This is a common problem with users who choose a password that uses proper capitalization of a name or word, then lazily slam in the password the next time they log on without capitalizing anything. The result is the same as if they had used a completely different password.

13. **C.** Audited events are recorded to the Security log, and can be viewed with Event Viewer. This allows users with proper access (members of the administrators group) to view various successful and unsuccessful events at any time. The log can be filtered through Event Viewer, so that only specific types of audited events, or those that occurred during a set time period, are seen.

14. **A.** User Rights apply to an entire computer, while Permissions apply to specific objects such as directories and printers.

15. **C.** When a disk fails in a volume set, all information on the set is lost. The only way to recover the information is to replace the disk, recreate the volume set, and restore the information from a backup. Of course, this is

assuming you were prepared and followed the cardinal rule of backing up your hard disks!

**16. D.** DOS uses an 8.3 naming convention. It will only allow eight characters followed by a period and an optional three-letter extension. BLANK.TXT would be an example of a valid DOS filename. Certain characters (/ \ ^ = ? [ ] ; : *) are not allowed, as these are used for other purposes. In addition, names like LPT1, COM2, NUL, CON, PRN aren't allowed, as they are reserved.

**17. D.** NTFS supports long filenames, compression, and security attributes. Windows NT Workstation does not support HPFS. While VFAT supports long filenames, it does not provide security attributes. In addition, Windows NT workstations and servers cannot view a drive compressed with DriveSpace 3.

**18. B.** The Security Account Manager (SAM) maintains a secure database that holds user, group, and computer accounts. During logon, the Local Security Authority compares logon information to this database to ensure it is a valid account.

**19. C.** The Restricted User Mode prevents programs from running until after a valid logon occurs. Until you have logged in, you can't run a program.

**20. A.** By setting the value ShutdownWithoutLogon to 0 in the Registry key HKEY_LOCAL_MACHINE\SOFTWARE\Microsoft\WindowsWindows NT\CurrentVersion\Winlogon, a user will not be able to shut down the system by pressing CTRL-ALT-DEL.

**21. D.** The seven layers of the OSI model are listed correctly in D. The OSI model is a theoretical model that shows how various components of a network work together. The Windows NT networking model corresponds to it. An easy way to remember the seven layers is with a nonsense phrase using the first letter of each layer, such as, "All People Seem To Need Data Processing".

| OSI Model |
| --- |
| Application |
| Presentation |
| Session |
| Transport |
| Network |
| Data Link |
| Physical |

22. **A.** DLC is used to communicate with mainframes and HP printers, but it is not routable. If you need to communicate with an HP printer through a routed network, you will have to set up a gateway. On one side of the gateway, you will have the protocol your network normally uses (such as TCP/IP), while the other side of the gateway retransmits your data using DLC.

23. **A, D.** You can access a hidden share, even though you can't see it when browsing the computer it is on. To access it, you need the proper permissions, the name of the share, and the name of the computer that this share is on. Since it can't be seen via browsing, you can't simply click to open it. You must know the name.

24. **B.** Browser elections can cause increased traffic on a network. To remedy this, configure one computer per subnet to be a preferred browser.

25. **B.** File Transfer Protocol (FTP) is part of the TCP/IP suite, and is used for exchanging files from one computer to another. When you download a file

on a TCP/IP network (like the Internet) from a server, FTP is used to perform the file transfer.

26. **B.** Internet Services Manager is a tool that comes with Windows NT Workstation 4.0. It is used to stop and start the Internet services you've implemented on your workstation. It is also used for configuring various operations of these Internet services.

27. **C.** The Network applet allows configuration of protocols and their binding order. Regardless of what device you're using with the protocol (modem or NIC), TCP/IP IP addresses are configured through this applet.

28. **A.** Client Services for NetWare (CSNW) gives Windows NT Workstation users the ability to access NetWare resources. With CSNW, they can connect and use files, print queues, and other resources on NetWare 2.*x*, 3.*x*, and 4.*x* servers.

29. **A.** Gateway (and Client) Services for NetWare (GSNW) is the easiest way for large groups of users to use a NetWare server. You only have to install this service on one Windows NT server, rather than having to install CSNW on multiple machines.
    It is important not to confuse GSNW with CSNW. GSNW can only be installed on Windows NT Server, while CSNW is used on Workstation. The "Client" portion of GSNW's full name reflects how CSNW is automatically installed on Server with the Gateway portion. GSNW's main purpose is to provide a gateway for Workstations to interact with NetWare servers.

30. **B.** By typing IPXROUTE CONFIG from the command prompt, you will be able to view the frame type information you are using for NWLink. This is of particular importance when communicating with NetWare networks. If the frame types between two computers are different, they won't be able to communicate.

**31. B.** File and Print Services for NetWare (FPNW) allows NetWare clients the ability to use Windows NT printers and files. It is an add-on utility that must be purchased separately. It is sold as part of the Services for NetWare package.

**32. A, C.** RAS can dial out using either PPP or SLIP. However, it cannot answer calls with SLIP. It can only make inbound connections with PPP.

**33. A, C.** Dial Up Networking Monitor provides information about how long you were connected, usernames of who was connected, protocols and devices used to make the connection, and the connection speed. When DEVICE.LOG is enabled, information that is more detailed than that provided by Dial Up Networking Monitor is recorded.

**34. D.** MS-CHAP is Microsoft encrypted authentication that encrypts all data, including passwords. It is the best of all authentication methods. CHAP stands for Challenge Handshake Authentication Protocol. PAP stands for Password Authentication Protocol. PAP just sends clear text over the wire.

**35. A.** A member server is the best choice to be an application server. Programs like SQL server can use considerable memory, hard disk space, and processor time. PDCs and BDCs are used to validate computer logons, and have duties that can be bogged down when applications are running. Always choose a member server to be an application server, unless you have no other choice.

**36. A.** A Windows NT Server or workstation will always win a browser election. This is, of course, if there are no other conditions to take into consideration. The reason is that Windows NT operating systems work better as master browsers. In this situation, when the server goes down, there are no other Windows NT servers in this network. Therefore, a Windows NT workstation will win the election.

**37. B.** The BDC maintains a replicated copy of the PDC's database. This allows the BDC to authenticate users with up-to-date information. This information is replicated between the PDC and BDC at regular intervals.

**38. B.** The print spooler is responsible for prioritizing print jobs, and for routing print jobs to the proper port. It also tracks which print jobs are going to which printer, and which ports are connected to which printer.

**39. A.** When printing to a TCP/IP print device, you require the name and IP address of the printer. Without it, your computer would not be able to find the printer on the network.

**40. D.** In Windows NT, printers are always shared through the Printers applet in Control Panel. Except for this applet, there is no other way to share printers.

**41. D.** You can audit the following events through a Print Audit: Print, Delete, Take Ownership, Full Control, and Change Permissions. You can set as many or as few of these events as you like in a print audit. The audited events are recorded to a log, which can be viewed through Event Viewer.

**42. C.** The Kernel is the core process of Windows NT. It is responsible for scheduling and managing threads, handling exceptions and interrupts. It is basically the heart of this preemptive multitasking operating system.

**43. B.** The POSIX subsystem is used for running UNIX programs on Windows NT. The POSIX subsystem is one of the environment subsystems shown in the next illustration. Other subsystems include OS/2, obviously for running OS/2 applications, Win32 for 32-bit Windows applications, and Windows NTVDM for providing a DOS environment for DOS and Windows 3.*x* programs.

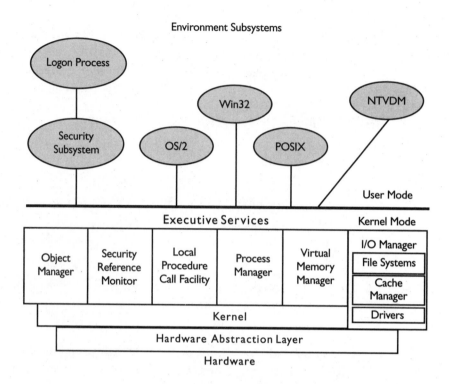

**44. D.** The components of WOW are as follows: WOWEXEC is used for emulating Windows 3.*x*, USER is used to translate user requests, GDI translates graphic functions, and KRNL386 translates Kernel operations.

**45. D.** Because Performance Monitor is running in memory, or using other system resources to monitor, it does affect the performance of your system. This can be seen by displaying memory counters in Performance Monitor, when it is the only program running on the system. By simply resizing this application, memory changes appear in the display. Since it is using the system, it affects the system.

**46. B.** NTFS uses Write Back caching to improve performance.

**47. B.** Running the command DISKPERF –Y enables the counters for your hard disk, so that Performance Monitor can monitor your drive. DISKPERF –N turns off these same counters. Before DISKPERF –Y is run, Performance Monitor will show no counters. These counters are activated as shown in the next illustration. It is important to remember that running DISKPERF won't allow you to view the counters right away. As the warning will tell you, the counters will become active after you reboot your computer.

```
Command Prompt                                              _ □ ✕
Microsoft(R) Windows NT(TM)
(C) Copyright 1985-1996 Microsoft Corp.

C:\>E:

E:\>diskperf -y

Disk Performance counters on this system are now set to start at boot.
This change will take effect after the system is restarted.

E:\>_
```

**48. D.** The System: Processor Queue Length is a counter that shows the number of threads waiting to be processed. If the queue length is consistently greater than two, you may have a processor problem.

**49. D.** Kernel Debugger is useful for finding which services and drivers aren't loading during the boot and load sequences. It logs events leading up to STOP, STATUS or messages caused by malfunctioning hardware. Here's how it works: Two computers are connected to each other, with Kernel Debugger running on one of them. Information is passed back and forth between the two, allowing Kernel Debugger to log the events taking place on the other computer.

**50.** **A.** The most damaging failure is a hard disk. When it goes, all your data (and quite possibly Windows NT itself) is gone. This is why making backups of data on hard disks is stressed so hard! An additional reason that it's so damaging is that hard disks aren't cheap. While memory, processor, motherboard, or even network failures aren't pretty, they generally won't destroy every piece of data on a server or workstation.

**51.** **A.** Windows NT Diagnostics provides inventory-style information about your system, and allows you to check a wide variety of facts about your workstation. As the next illustration shows, Windows NT Diagnostics allows you to view which account is being used, which services and devices are running, and much more. While the other programs do offer considerable information, they do not offer it in an inventory style.

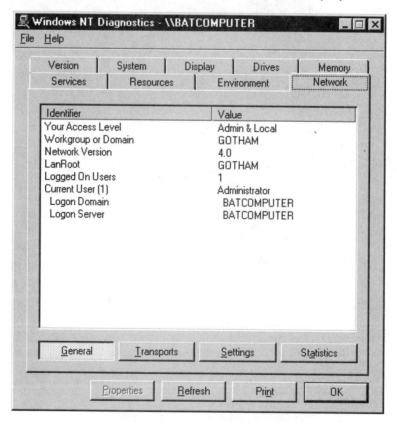

MCSE
MICROSOFT CERTIFIED SYSTEMS ENGINEER

# Test Yourself: Windows NT Server 4.0

*Q & A*

# Server Practice Exam 1

Before you call to register for the actual exam, take the following test and see how you make out. Set a timer for 90 minutes—the time you'll have to take the live Server exam—and answer the following 50 questions in the time allotted. Once you're through, turn to the end of the module and check your score to see if you passed! Good luck!

1. You've noticed several errors on files located on your Windows NT Server, which is on an EIDE drive and formatted with an NTFS partition. The errors state that the file is corrupt. Since NT performs hot fixing, you don't worry about it. You recover the damaged files from a tape backup to restore the data. Five hours later you get another corrupted file. Once again, you restore the data from tape. Then again, two hours later you get corrupted files. Why is this happening?

   A. NT supports hot fixing, but only on SCSI devices formatted with NTFS. The drive that has the errors is an EIDE drive; therefore the damaged sector is never marked unusable.

   B. The hard disk must be failing in more than one sector, or it has a bad read/write head.

   C. You must run CHKDSK in order for NT to hot-fix a failing sector.

2. You want to use hot fixing on your hard disk. Your hard disk specs are as follows:

   ■ Formatted with FAT

   ■ 8GB

   ■ SCSI-II

   ■ 10MB/sec transfer rate

   What must be changed before you can use hot fixing?

   A. Convert the drive to NTFS.

   B. Only use 2GB partitions.

   C. You must get a standard SCSI drive.

   D. The transfer rate must not exceed 5MB/sec.

   E. Turn hot fixing on under the System Control Panel.

**3.** When your computer is thrashing, what should you do? (Choose two.)

    A. Add memory.
    B. Add hard disk(s).
    C. Replace the CPU.
    D. Increase the paging file.
    E. Switch to 16-bit addressing.

**4.** You are editing your Registry using the REGEDIT.EXE program, and you want to set the security on a Registry key. How do you do this?

    A. On the menu bar click Security | Permissions and set the appropriate permissions level.
    B. Run CACL from the command prompt.
    C. You can't set permissions using the REGEDIT.EXE program. You must use the REGEDT32.EXE program instead.
    D. Right-click the Registry key and choose Permissions. Then set the appropriate permissions level.

**5.** Your manager has directed you to take several security measures to help protect your systems from intrusion. One of the directions he gives you is to format all your NT Server hard disks with NTFS. How should you do this? Currently all your hard disks are using FAT.

    A. Back up the data and format the hard disk using NTFS, then restore the data from the backup tape. This is the most secure way of changing the file system. If you use a utility to convert the data, there will be security holes in NTFS allowing intruders to easily break into your server.
    B. Use the CONVERT.EXE command on each partition.
    C. Use a third-party utility that changes partition types.
    D. You can't change a FAT partition to an NTFS partition without voiding the licensing, so you'll need to buy another NTFS license.

**6.** You really like the Windows 95 Registry editor. You think the interface is much easier to use and navigate than the old Windows NT 3.51 Registry editor. You want to change the value of one of the Registry subkeys. Which command should you run?

    A. REGEDT32.EXE

    B. REGEDIT.EXE

    C. REG95.EXE

    D. REGNT.EXE

**7.** You created a file called JESSE'S HOMEWORK.DOC on a FAT partition. You later move this file to the Homework directory, which is compressed. What will occur?

    A. The file will be compressed.

    B. The file will be uncompressed.

    C. You'll be prompted if you want to compress the file.

    D. It depends on how you've configured compression.

**8.** What's wrong in the following configuration scenario for the "Dias and Sons" organization? You are planning to install ten servers, using TCP/IP to connect them via routers. Each server will be on its own subnet. You plan to name all computers by your company name followed by _# (where # is the server number 1-10). You'll place an underscore (_) where there are spaces between words. So the first server's name is DIAS_AND_SONS_1.

    A. TCP/IP doesn't allow underscores.

    B. NetBIOS names can't exceed 15 characters.

    C. TCP/IP isn't the best protocol to use, NetBEUI is the fasted protocol for ten or fewer servers.

    D. The naming convention should be more descriptive.

**9.** What is the first step the upgrade wizard performs when upgrading from Windows NT 3.51 to Windows NT 4.0?

    A. Verifies information about your computer hardware

    B. Gathers information about your computer hardware

    C. Upgrades the device drivers

    D. Verifies you have the proper SCSI drivers

**10.** You're attempting to install Windows NT 4.0 on a computer that has around 125MB of free disk space. You know this is cutting it close, but you figure NT will calculate the actual size required, and tell you how much space you need. As you run Setup it reports that there is enough disk space to install. As you proceed with the install you run out of disk space. What is happening?

    A. Setup may detect there is enough free disk space but, to make your life miserable, it purposely states the opposite.

    B. Setup does not check for free disk space. It always assumes there is enough for an installation.

    C. Setup may detect there is not enough free disk space but there is a known bug in it that makes it report the opposite.

    D. Setup does not take into account sector size. Hence, it may think there is enough free disk space when in reality there may not be.

**11.** You have ten NT servers and 1,000 clients. The clients need access to all the servers 24 hours per day. What type of licensing should you use on the servers?

    A. Per Seat

    B. Per Server

    C. Site metering

    D. 1,000 pack per server

**12.** You don't have enough IP addresses to meet all your network needs. Your network has 300 computers and only 255 IP addresses. Luckily, there are never more than 200 computers on the network at a time. In order to ensure all computers can get an IP address, you've configured DHCP with a lease for three hours. Since you set the lease period for only three hours, you're worried about the added network traffic, so you extend your WINS renewal interval to eight days. Everything runs fine for the first half of the day. However, when the second shift of workers comes in, their computers can't connect to each other for peer-to-peer file sharing. How do you fix this problem?

A. You need to get more IP addresses. You must have at least the same number of IP addresses as computers.

B. Set the WINS renewal period to one and a half hours.

C. Set the WINS renewal period to six hours.

D. Set the DHCP lease duration to four days.

**13.** You have six disk drives with the following free space available: 100MB, 100MB, 200MB, 400MB, 500MB, and 600MB. What is the largest stripe set with parity you can create?

A. 600MB

B. 800MB

C. 1100MB

D. 1200MB

E. 1900MB

**14.** You are configuring two new disk drives using Disk administrator. You need to get maximum performance from the two drives. How should you configure the disks?

A. Mirror

B. Stripe set

C. Stripe set with parity

D. Volume set

**15.** You're installing a DHCP server to automatically assign IP addresses to your Windows 95 clients. What are the other options it can supply? (Choose all that apply.)

A. WINS server addresses

B. DNS server addresses

C. FTP addresses

D. Default Gateway

E. Subnet mask

**16.** Every summer your company hires interns. How should you manage accounts for these temporary workers?

 A. Create one account and allow all the interns to log on using the same ID and password.

 B. Create individual accounts for each intern and delete them when they leave the company.

 C. Create individual accounts for each intern and disable them when they leave the company.

 D. Create individual accounts for each intern and use the account information property page to automatically disable the accounts on the date that the interns leave the company.

**17.** You want to allow a user to create user accounts, but you don't want the user to assign or change user rights. What group should you add the user to?

 A. Administrator

 B. Server Operator

 C. Account Operator

 D. Domain User

**18.** You are too busy to manage your entire network, so you decide to let one trusted user create shares on your domain controllers. What group should the user belong to?

 A. Domains Admin

 B. Power User

 C. Domain User

 D. Server Operator

**19.** Which of the following groups have the right to log on locally to a domain controller? (Choose all that apply.)

 A. Server Operators

 B. Administrators

 C. Backup Operators

 D. Power Users

20. What will be the effect if you change the Lockout Duration from 30 minutes to Forever in the next illustration, when a normal user enters his password incorrectly five times?

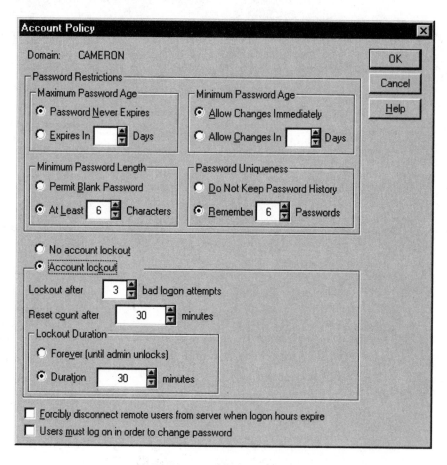

A. It will disable the account permanently until the account is recreated.

B. When a user enters three bad logons, it will lock the account until the administrator or account operator unlocks the account.

C. When a user enters three bad logons, it will lock the account until the administrator unlocks the account.

D. The administrator will be notified to unlock the account after three bad attempts.

**21.** The folder MANAGEMENT has the following NTFS permissions:

- RESEARCH group: Change
- SALES group: Read
- MARKETING group: No Access
- MANAGERS group: Full Control

User MaryS belongs to the RESEARCH group, MARKETING group, and MANAGERS group. What permissions will she have to the folder?

A. Full Control
B. Read
C. Change
D. No Access

**22.** User BigAl is one of your most trusted users. In fact, you made him an account operator last week. Evidently, one of the other administrators doesn't trust BigAl, so he removed his name from the account operators group. It's been one week, but BigAl is still able to add users and reset passwords. Why?

A. Another administrator must have placed his username back into the account operators group.
B. He must also be in the administrators group.
C. He hasn't ever logged off, so his access token still has him as part of the account operators group.
D. No one likes to mess with BigAl, not even Windows NT. NT will allow him to do whatever he wants.

**23.** You've just been hacked by someone using your administrator account. While he was in your system, he deleted all your users and administrators. He then changed the password to the administrator account. What should you do to get all your accounts back?

A. Recreate all the accounts.

B. After cracking back into the administrator account, you can run the utility RECOVER to recover all accounts that haven't been permanently deleted.

C. You can't do anything, because he has changed the administrator password, so there is no way to recover. If you can't log on, you can't even do a tape backup recovery.

D. First recover the SAM using the Emergency Repair Disk process. Next, recover from backup tape on your PDC. As long as you backed up the Registry you should be able to recover most the data.

24. On your network you have one PDC and three BDCs. You want to use the PDC as an application server. What should you do?

A. Promote a BDC to PDC and demote the PDC to member server.

B. Shut down the PDC and the BDC you want to promote, and start the BDC up again. It will automatic become PDC..

C. Shut down the PDC and promote a BDC to PDC.

D. Promote a BDC to PDC and the PDC will automatically be demoted to member server.

25. You have 25,000 users. The MIS department wants to control user accounts and account security. Local department managers need to manage local resources. Which domain model should you use?

A. Single Domain

B. Master Domain

C. Multiple Master Domain

D. Complete Trust Domain

26. You're the lead network project manager who needs to merge at least 16 separate Windows NT domains. The first phase of the project is going to interconnect all the domains using the Complete Trust model. How much memory should you have installed on your PDCs to create at least 250 trusts?

A. 16MB

B. 32MB

C. 48MB

D. 64MB

E. It doesn't matter, because the number of trusts is unlimited with NT 4.0.

**27.** What type of domain model does the next illustration represent?

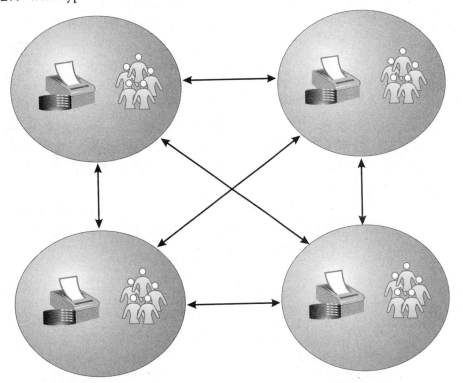

A. Single Domain

B. Master Domain

C. Multiple Master Domain

D. Complete Trust Domain

28. You want to replicate files to other servers in your domain. What is the default path that you put the files in on the export server?

   A. In the root of C:\WINNT\SYSTEM32\REPL\EXPORT
   B. In the root of C:\WINNT\SYSTEM32\REPL\IMPORT
   C. In any subdirectory of C:\WINNT\SYSTEM32\REPL\EXPORT
   D. In any subdirectory of C:\WINNT\SYSTEM32\REPL\IMPORT

29. You are setting up your files and directories that need to be replicated. For ease of management you create 33 subdirectories under your export directory. You test the replication process, but not all the files are replicated. Why?

   A. You need to add the service account to all import servers.
   B. You need to configure all the import servers for directory replication.
   C. You placed the subdirectories in the wrong directory. They should be placed in the import directory.
   D. You can only create up to 32 subdirectories under the export directory.

30. You have 25 BDCs. Every time the PDC updates the BDCs the PDC slows to a crawl. What should you do help alleviate the problem?

   A. Reduce the value of the PulseConcurrency.
   B. Increase the value of the PulseConcurrency.
   C. Increase the value of the Pulse.
   D. Increase the PulseTimeout1.

31. You're installing an HP printer equipped with a JetDirect card. You try to access it, but you can't see it. What's wrong?

   A. The printer is already installed.
   B. You're using the incorrect driver.
   C. You need to use the LPD print function.
   D. You need to install DLC.

**32.** You need to send a print job to a local UNIX server. The UNIX server's name is WEAKLING and the printer's name is Dotty. You've already installed TCP/IP on your Windows NT Server. What else must you do? (Choose all that apply.)

    A. Install Microsoft TCP/IP Printing service.

    B. Install the DLC protocol.

    C. Install the LPD print service.

    D. Type lpr –S WEAKLING –P Dotty *filename* at the command shell.

    E. Type NET START LPDSVC at the command shell.

**33.** You have a shared printer that the engineering department and the sales department print to. The engineers need to print documents immediately and can't afford to wait for anyone else, especially large print jobs. The only people that ever cause a problem are the sales team. The sales team only prints 500-page sales proposals, typically during heavy printing hours, even if they don't need the report until two days later. What should you do to alleviate this problem?

    A. Create two printers printing to the same printing device. Give engineers permissions to print to one of the printers, and everyone else can print to the other printer. Assign the engineers' printer a priority of 99 and assign the other printer a priority of 1.

    B. Create two printers printing to the same printing device. Give the engineers permissions to print to one of the printers and give the sales team permissions to print to the other printer. Schedule the engineers' printer to allow printing always and schedule the sales team's printer to allow printing from 8:00 P.M. to 6:00 A.M.

    C. Buy another printer and allow the sales people to print to it.

    D. Select to print documents after the last page is spooled.

**34.** You have over 70 Windows NT Workstation clients that use a shared printer on your NT server. The vendor recently released an updated driver that fixes several problems with your current driver. What is the best way to install this driver on all your workstations?

A. Manually install the driver on the server.

B. Manually install the driver on the clients.

C. Create a logon script that will automatically install the driver on all the clients.

D. Use SMS to distribute the driver.

**35.** In the next illustration, which printer tab would you select to print directly to the printer and bypass the spooler?

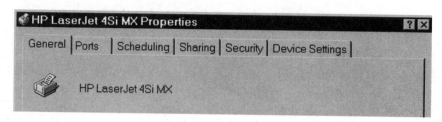

A. General

B. Ports

C. Scheduling

D. Sharing

E. Security

F. Device Settings

**36.** You have 30 MS-DOS clients and 15 WFW 3.11 clients, and you want to allow them to connect to two Novell servers for simple file and print sharing. You install NWLink on your server and create an NTGATEWAY group on the NetWare server. You attempt to connect to the Novell server from a DOS machine, but it fails. What happened?

A. You need to install GSNW.

B. The DOS client must use the Netware redirector, the NT server can only serve as a gateway for Windows clients.

C. You need to install NWLink on all the clients so they can communicate with the NT server and the Novell servers.

D. You must install RIP so the IPX traffic will be sent between the two networks.

**37.** When using the Migration Tool for NetWare, what are you allowed to migrate? (Choose all that apply.)

    A. User Accounts

    B. Groups

    C. Passwords

    D. Data

**38.** You're installing a modem in your RAS server that isn't on the hardware compatibility list. You check with the vendor, and he tells you that the modem is supported for Windows NT 4.0. What do you do?

    A. Use null port for modem.

    B. Use an unsupported modem from the list of modems.

    C. Add modem calls to the MODM.INF file.

    D. Change the SWITCH.INF file.

**39.** You're a network administrator who wants to establish a dialup connection for yourself. Your only concern is that you want to minimize system overhead. Which modem protocol should you use?

    A. PPP

    B. RAS

    C. SLIP

    D. MS-CHAP

**40.** You want to back up a Windows NT server's Registry without taking the server offline. How can you do this?

    A. Network Control Panel

    B. Disk Administrator

    C. Explorer

    D. NTBACKUP

**41.** You need to back up files every night as quickly as possible. Which type of backup should you do?

A. Differential

B. Normal

C. Incremental

D. Daily

42. You've recently been hired as a network administrator for an insurance company. You suspect that the paging file on one of the servers is not being utilized correctly and is running slower than should be expected. The server has four disks configured in the following way: one disk for the system/boot partition, and three disks in a stripe set. The page file resides on the boot/system partition. What should you do to improve the efficiency of the page file?

A. Increase the size of the page file.

B. Decrease the size of the page file.

C. Delete the page file.

D. Move the page file to the stripe set.

43. You are running Performance Monitor on a Windows NT workstation. You are monitoring memory and disk performance on ten NT servers. Performance on the NT workstation is poor, and you want to increase performance. How do you do so?

A. System Properties. Decrease time for foreground application.

B. Run Performance Monitor from a Command line using /START.

C. Start DISKPERF to build up a big cache.

D. Increase the time interval in which you collect data.

44. You have a Windows NT server with two 2GB disks formatted with NTFS. Both system files and the paging file are located on the first disk. What should you do to improve the performance of your disks?

A. Buy a faster hard disk.

B. Increase the page file size.

C. Optimize the page file by moving it to the second disk.

D. Add RAM.

**45.** What is a bottleneck?

   A. When one resource has a high rate of use while other resources have a low rate of use.

   B. When one resource hits 100 percent utilization.

   C. The point at which no other process can work.

   D. The fastest part of a computer system. By increasing the length of a bottleneck you can increase the overall performance of your system.

**46.** You suspect a disk drive is creating a bottleneck within your system. You use the LogicalDisk:%Disk Time counter to take measurements, but it only reports zero. What should you do?

   A. Replace the disk drive, because it no longer functions properly.

   B. Enable disk drive performance counters.

   C. Use a different counter. The counter currently being used is supposed to report zero.

   D. You can't check disk drive bottlenecks.

**47.** A user on your network calls you complaining that his computer slows down every time someone sends large print jobs over the network. His computer is a Windows NT server serving as a print server. What should you do?

   A. Have Stace run Task Manager and increase the priority of the programs he is running.

   B. Increase the application performance boost to maximum foreground processing.

   C. Edit the Registry to allow only small print jobs.

   D. Move the spooler from his hard disk to a network share.

**48.** You have two SCSI drives mirrored, with your boot and system partitions located on them. Your SCSI drives don't have the SCIS BIOS enabled. The drive that you boot from fails. What should you do? (Choose only one.)

A. Create a boot floppy with NTLDR, NTDETECT, BOOT.INI, and NTBOOTDD.SYS. Reboot using the boot floppy.

B. Create a boot floppy with NTLDR, NTDETECT, and BOOT.INI. Reboot using the boot floppy.

C. Break the mirror set, removed the failed drive and reboot.

D. You don't need to do anything. A mirror set will automatically fail over to the proper disk when booting.

**49.** You're trying to install an HP printer that has a JetDirect card. You can't find the proper printer port on your server. What is the problem?

A. You need to install the DLC protocol.

B. You need to load Service Pack 2.

C. You need to install the HP JetAdmin utility provided by HP.

D. You can't attach a JetDirect card on two separate network segments.

**50.** Which tab would you select in the next illustration to configure your server to reboot when a STOP error is encountered?

A. General

B. Performance

C. Environment

D. Startup/Shutdown

E. Hardware Profiles

F. User Profiles

# Server Practice Exam 2

Before you call to register for the actual exam, take the following test and see how you make out. Set a timer for 90 minutes—the time you'll have to take the live Server exam—and answer the following 50 questions in the time allotted. Once you're through, turn to the end of the module and check your score to see if you passed! Good luck!

1. Which of the following features are examples of NT's fault tolerance? (Choose all that apply.)

   A. Directory replication
   B. NTFS
   C. RAID 5
   D. RAID 1
   E. RAID 0
   F. BDC

2. Which of the following is NOT a Windows NT subsystem?

   A. MDM
   B. Win32
   C. OS/2
   D. POSIX

3. What is the maximum number of processors Windows NT Server can support?

   A. 2
   B. 4
   C. 8
   D. 16
   E. 32

4. Your hard disk is formatted with the following partitions and sizes: two FAT-16 partitions of 100MB, one NTFS partition of 600MB, one FAT-32 partition of 100MB, and one HPFS partition of 200MB. How much hard disk space can Windows NT 4.0 access?

   A. 1100MB

   B. 1000MB

   C. 900MB

   D. 800MB

5. You're installing a LAN consisting of five computers. This is an internal network and will never need to connect to the Internet or remote sites. It is one subnet and will never need to have more than one subnet. Which protocol should you use?

   A. TCP/IP

   B. NWLink (IPX/SPX)

   C. DLC

   D. Apple Talk

6. Your computer is set up to dual boot between Windows NT Server and MS-DOS. You've formatted your hard disks with FAT partitions. While you're in NT, you name a file MY SPREADSHEET FOR MANAGING MY MONEY.XLS. When you're in MS-DOS will you be able to access this file? If so, how?

   A. No, MS-DOS doesn't support long file names.

   B. No, MS-DOS can't read files created by NT.

   C. Yes, NT will save the file with two names. When in MS-DOS the name will appear in the 8.3 format.

   D. Yes, MS-DOS can read anything on a FAT partition. If the partition was NTFS, you couldn't access it.

7. Mary uses a laptop computer to carry her work between her office and home. While she is at the office she uses a docking station to add a monitor and network card. When she gets home she receives the following message after booting Windows NT: One or more services failed to start. See Event Viewer for details. What should Mary do to stop the error messages?

   A. Create two user profiles: one for the office and one for home.
   B. Stop the event logging service.
   C. Create two hardware profiles: one for the office and one for home.
   D. Create two startup batch files: one for the office and one for home.

8. What's wrong in the following configuration? You're installing Windows NT on an Alpha box that is on the HCL. All components you're using are listed in the HCL, so you feel confident everything should go smoothly. For security reasons you delete all FAT partitions and format the hard disks with NTFS. The machine has 512MB RAM and eight 4GB hard disks. The computer name is ALPHA1, and there are no other computers named ALPHA1 on the network. You're using DHCP to assign an IP address to this computer.

   A. The system partition must be FAT.
   B. The computer name, ALPHA1, is an illegal name, since NT uses it to detect Alpha servers on the network.
   C. Alpha computers are no longer supported, so this must be an Windows NT 3.51 HCL.
   D. You can't use DHCP to assign an address to a server.

9. You are upgrading all your servers and workstations from NT 3.51 to NT 4.0. Which upgrade scenarios are allowed? (Choose all that apply.)

   A. Upgrade a 3.51 workstation to NT 4.0 member server.
   B. Upgrade a 3.51 PDC to an NT 4.0 member server.
   C. Upgrade a 3.51 PDC to an NT 4.0 PDC.
   D. Upgrade a 3.51 member server to an NT 4.0 PDC.

10. You're planning to install Windows NT Server on five computers. These computers all have at least four 4GB SCSI hard disks and 512MB RAM. Each one is going to be a dedicated file server. Which file systems would you choose?

    A. FAT

    B. HPFS

    C. NTFS

    D. CDFS

11. You're planning to roll out an entire NT domain over the weekend. You've done much planning and preparation for this project. You're going to use an unattended installation to install over 20 servers. Your domain will cross two separate geographic areas. One is in Atlanta, the other is in Orlando. The Orlando site is your Headquarters and will house the PDC. You figure that since the remote site only has two servers (one member server and one BDC) you should go ahead and fly out to Atlanta on Friday and return later that night. This way if anything goes wrong in Orlando you won't have a scheduled trip hanging over your head. When you try to install the BDC you get an error. What should you do to overcome this error?

    A. Fly back to Orlando and install the PDC.

    B. Ignore it and tell it to synchronize later.

    C. Increase the bandwidth of the link between the two sites.

    D. Install WINS on the BDC.

    E. Install the BDC as a PDC.

12. Your network is currently configured as two separate subnets, Subnet A and Subnet B. Your main objective is to enable communication between the two subnets. As a side objective, you want to minimize broadcast traffic between the two subnets.
    Your solution: You put two NICs in an NT Server and attach one NIC to Subnet A and the other NIC to Subnet B.
    What is the result?

A. You meet both your main objective and your side objective.

B. You meet only your main objective.

C. You don't accomplish either objective.

**13.** You have three 1GB drives. Your main objective is to provide a fault-tolerant disk set using all the available disks. One side objective is to allow for the most available disk space. A second side objective is to have at least three logical drives.

Your solution: Create a stripe set across all three drives. Then create an extended partition and create three logical drives.

What is the result?

A. Meets your main objective and both side objectives

B. Meets your main objective and one side objective

C. Meets only your main objective

D. Doesn't meet your main objective

**14.** You want to maximize fault tolerance and performance on your disk drives. You are considering using disk duplexing, but instead you want to use a stripe set with parity since you have seven hard disks for which you need to provide fault tolerance. You also have three hard disk controllers. What is the minimum number of disk drives and controllers NT requires for software RAID 5?

A. Five hard disks and two controllers

B. Two hard disks and two controllers

C. Three hard disks and one controller

D. Three hard disks and two controllers

**15.** You have one Windows NT server with two LAN segments. Each segment has 50 client PCs. The client PCs and the NT server use TCP/IP as their sole protocol. You want the NT server to be able to route traffic between the two segments and use DHCP. What do you do? (Choose all that apply.)

A. Install a second network card in the NT server.
B. Connect one LAN segment to the first network card and the second LAN segment to the other network card.
C. Install DHCP Server and create two scopes.
D. Enable DHCP forwarding.
E. Enable IP routing.

16. You have four hard disks with the following amounts of free space: 500MB, 400MB, 400MB, and 200MB. The system and boot partition will be on one of the 400MB partitions. You implement the largest possible stripe set with parity. How much useable disk space is available on the stripe set with parity?

A. 200MB
B. 400MB
C. 500MB
D. 600MB
E. 1000MB
F. 12000MB

17. You want to make it easier to create user accounts. Toward that end, you make a template called USER_TEMPLATE and assign permissions and groups to the template. How do you use the template when you make new accounts?

A. You create new accounts and highlight them, and copy USER_TEMPLATE into them.
B. You have to create a global group called USER_TEMPLATE and put new accounts in it.
C. You simply copy USER_TEMPLATE to a new account.
D. New accounts automatically get the permissions and groups specified in the template.

18. After you installed client-based administrative tools on your Windows 95 computer, which tool would you use to change the file-level permissions on an NTFS volume on NT Server?

    A. Server Manager
    B. Explorer
    C. User Manager for Domains
    D. File Manager

19. Jason just gave his two-week's notice. Two days later, your boss identifies Ruby as his replacement. How should you configure Ruby's account to give her the same level of network access as Jason? Ruby won't be replacing Jason for three weeks.

    A. From Server Manager, copy all of Jason's permissions and rights to Ruby's account.
    B. From Server Manager, rename Jason's account to an account name that Ruby will use.
    C. From User Manager, copy all of Jason's permissions and rights to Ruby's account.
    D. From User Manager, rename Jason's account to an account name that Ruby will use.

20. Thomas is working late on a special project. He needs to access network resources while he's working to complete the project. His account has been set up to not allow him to log on from 8:00 P.M. until 5:00 A.M. Thomas is logged on at 9:00 A.M. and works past 10:00 P.M. What happens to his ability to use the network at 8:00 P.M.? (Choose all that apply.)

    A. Thomas will be automatically disconnected from the network.
    B. Thomas will remain connected on the network but can't establish any new network connections until 5:00A.M.
    C. Thomas will be allowed to use the network as long as he doesn't log off.
    D. He will be asked to log on again to verify that he wants to remain on the network.

**21.** Jane works in the marketing department and is a member of the MARKETING group. Jane gets promoted and is subsequently added to the MANAGERS group. She tries to connect to the MGRS share that the managers have access to, but she sees no files. What else is required before Jane can access the files?

A. Add the Domain Users group to the share and assign it Change permissions.

B. Use User Manager for Domains and remove Jane from the MARKETING group.

C. Use Server Manager and remove the MARKETING group from the permissions on the MGRS share.

D. Create two accounts for Jane. Add one to the MARKETING group and the other to the MANAGERS group.

**22.** Your server has an NTFS partition with a folder called PUBLIC. You want to make this folder available to everyone on the network so they can read, write, and execute files within the directory. You don't want anyone to be able to delete files. How should you set the permissions? (Choose all that apply.)

A. Give everyone Read share permissions.

B. Give everyone Change share permissions.

C. Give everyone Add share permissions.

D. Give everyone Change NTFS file/folder permissions.

E. Give everyone Read, Write, and Execute Special File/folder permissions.

**23.** You manage two domains as shown in the next illustration. Which of the following statements is true?

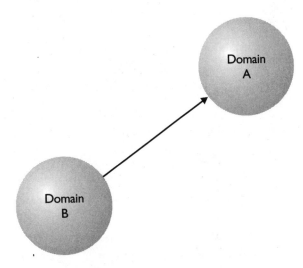

A. Users in Domain A can access Resources in Domain B.

B. Local Groups in Domain A can be assigned permissions to resources in Domain B.

C. Users in Domain B can access Resources in Domain A.

D. Local Groups in Domain B can be assigned permissions to resources in Domain A.

**24.** A coworker who helps you manage the domain asks you to adjust the replication governor. What will this do? (Choose all that apply.)

A. Decrease buffer size calls from PDC to BDC.

B. Decrease buffer size calls from BDC to PDC.

C. Decrease frequency calls from PDC to BDC.

D. Decrease frequency calls from BDC to PDC.

25. The SALES domain trusts the ENGINEERING domain. You create a local group in the SALES domain. What accounts and groups can this local group contain? (Choose all that apply.)

   A. Users from ENGINEERING

   B. Global groups from ENGINEERING

   C. Global groups from SALES

   D. Local groups from SALES

26. Your network consists of one PDC and three BDCs. One of the BDCs is located across a WAN link. The WAN link is capable of 1.54 Mbps, so bandwidth isn't a big issue. The link was down for two days. The ISP who provides your WAN link has finally fixed the problem, and you're back in business. You need to synchronize the BDC with the PDC as soon as possible. What should you do?

   A. Do nothing. The BDC will automatically synchronize with the PDC.

   B. Use Server Manager and manually synchronize the entire domain.

   C. Use Server Manager and manually synchronize the BDC with the PDC.

   D. Use User Manager and manually synchronize the accounts from the PDC with the BDC.

27. What type of domain model does the next illustration represent?

A. Single Domain

B. Master Domain

C. Multiple Master Domain

D. Complete Trust Domain

**28.** You need to change all your logon scripts to map a drive for all your users. This process should take at least 25 minutes to complete. What should you do to minimize the replication traffic while you update the scripts?

A. Place a lock on the script directory on the export server.

B. Place a lock on the script directory on the import server.

C. Stop the directory replication service on all computers.

D. Stop the directory replication service on the import server.

E. Stop the directory replication service on the export server.

**29.** You have an automated script that updates all your logon scripts to give a new quote of the day. This process runs every night at 6:00. Since it changes over 60 logon scripts, there is a possibility that replication will occur before all the scripts are changed. You don't want to replicate any data until all scripts are updated. What should you do?

A. Place a lock on the directory.

B. Select Wait Until Stabilized.

C. Choose to export the entire subtree.

D. Remove all locks on the directory.

**30.** The next illustration shows the screen that is required to configure the Replicator service account. Why do you need to select This Account instead of the System Account?

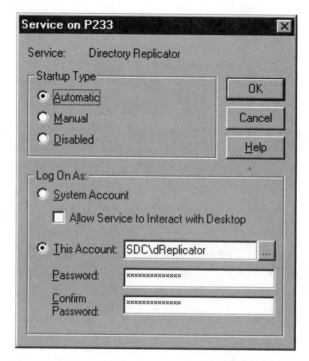

A. The Replicator account can't interact with the desktop.

B. The Replicator account works faster when you have it log on as a service account.

C. The Replicator service account needs to access resources on different computers, so it needs to log onto the external computer with this account information.

D. The System account is only for service accounts that the user interacts with.

**31.** You are establishing a printer pool. What must be the same for all printers?

A. They all must use the same printer driver.

B. They all must use a UNC.

C. They all must be the same model.

D. They must handle EMF data.

**32.** A member server that manages 50 printers locks up whenever large print jobs are sent to the printer. The server has one hard disk with two partitions. The boot partition (C:) has 50MB of free space and the (D:) has 500MB of free space. The server is a 486/33 with 128MB RAM. What should you do to resolve the problem?

   A. Edit the Registry, moving the default spool location from C: to D:.

   B. Use the Printers applet to move the default spool location from C: to D:.

   C. A 486/33 can't support 50 printers reliably. Either move some of the printers off this server or upgrade the hardware.

   D. Stop and restart the spooler service.

**33.** What's the difference between a print spooler and router?

   A. They both route documents, but one is internal and the other is external routing.

   B. The way they handle print jobs.

   C. The print spooler is an NT 4.0 function and the print router is used in NT 3.51.

   D. They are the same thing.

**34.** What determines if a printing device is local or shared?

   A. If the printing device is physically connected to your computer, it is local. Otherwise it is a shared network printer.

   B. If your computer's spooler can send print jobs directly to the printing device, it is considered local. If your computer's spooler sends a print job to a different computer's spooler, and then the remote spooler sends the print job to the printing device, it is considered shared.

   C. If the printing device is within 100 feet, it is local. Otherwise it is a shared printer.

   D. Nothing, they are the same thing.

**35.** You shared an HP LaserJet 5 on a Windows NT server for everyone in your department to use. When users try to connect to the printer using Windows 95 they get the following error message: "The server on which the printer resides does not have a suitable driver installed. Click on OK if you wish to select a driver to use on your local machine." What should you do to prevent users from receiving this error message?

A. Install the Client for NetWare Services.

B. Give them the proper access permissions.

C. Install an appropriate Windows 95 print driver on the server.

D. Change the default data type to RAW.

**36.** You have a printer pool created with six printing devices. You want to add a seventh printing device to the pool. How can you do this?

A. Create the printer and share it with the same sharename.

B. Create the printer using the same print port as the other printing devices.

C. Enter the port for the new printing device on the already established printer.

D. Add the appropriate driver to the already established printer.

**37.** How does Gateway Services for NetWare do what it does between a Windows NT workstation and a NetWare server?

A. The NT gateway translates SMB calls into an NCP packet over IPX for computers talking to the Novell server. When a Novell server sends IPX traffic to the NT clients, the gateway translates the NCP packet to an SMB call.

B. It bridges the traffic between the client and the NetWare server, allowing them to communicate directly.

C. It routes the traffic between the client and the NetWare server, allowing them to communicate directly.

D. The NT gateway translates NetBEUI protocol to IPX and IPX to NetBEUI.

**38.** When using the NetWare Migration Utility, what does selecting Use Mappings in File do? Use the next illustration to help answer the question.

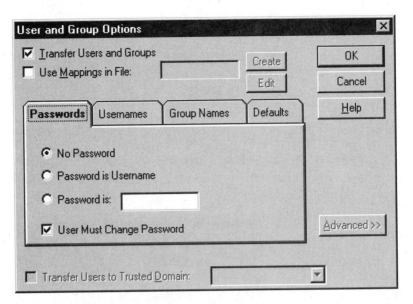

A. It allows you to change group names when you migrate the groups from NetWare to NT.

B. It allows you to assign drive mappings to the NTGATEWAY account.

C. It prevents passwords from migrating to NT.

D. It only migrates files and folders that are currently mapped for the user.

**39.** You have 25 DOS clients and 45 Windows 95 clients that will use RAS to connect to your network. The DOS clients only support DES encryption. You must maximize the authentication security. How should you set the RAS authentication requirements?

A. Require Microsoft Encryption.

B. Require any encryption.

C. Allow anything including plain text.

D. Text only.

**40.** Where do you enable the DEVICE.LOG file?

A. Modem applet in Control Panel

B. Network applet in Control Panel

C. System applet in Control Panel

D. Registry HKEY_LOCAL_MACHINE

**41.** What protocols are supported by a RAS client dialing in when the network configuration on the server is set as shown in the next illustration? (Choose all that apply.)

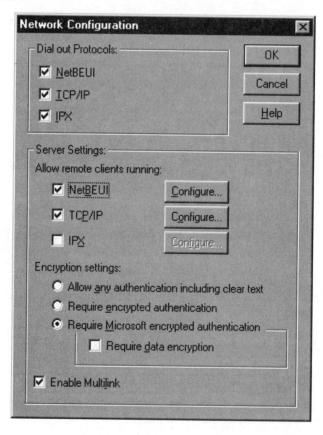

A. NetBEUI
B. TCP/IP
C. IPX
D. None of the above

42. You need to have a complete backup of your server every night. You only have one 4GB tape and the server has 3.8GB of data that needs backing up. How should you schedule your backup?

A. Perform a normal backup on Sunday, overwriting the existing data. Then every night do a differential on the same tape. Do not overwrite the existing data.

B. Perform a normal backup on Sunday, overwriting the existing data. Then every night do an incremental on the same tape. Do not overwrite the existing data.

C. Perform a normal backup on Sunday, overwriting the existing data. Then every night do a daily backup on the same tape. Do not overwrite the existing data.

D. Perform a normal backup every day overwriting the existing data.

43. You need to back up the Registry of ten Windows NT workstations. Your server has a 4mm DAT drive and you are in the Backup Operators group. How can you do this?

A. Select the workstations' C$ and choose to back up the Registry.
B. Select the workstations' Registry within NTBACKUP.
C. Select the SAM using REGEDT32.
D. You can't back up a remote Registry.

44. You have 40 Windows NT Workstation clients on your network and one Windows NT server. Most of the time the clients are doing peer-to-peer file sharing using the NetBEUI protocol. Most of the clients also have TCP/IP installed to access the Internet. Which of the following changes will result in the most improved performance?

A. Move NetBEUI up on the server binding order.

B. Move NetBEUI up on the clients binding order.

C. Move TCP/IP up on the clients binding order.

D. Move TCP/IP up on the server binding order.

E. Remove TCP/IP from all the clients.

45. When viewing the System Log you see several red stop signs. What does this mean?

A. The log file wasn't able to record the event.

B. It's an error message that means a significant problem has occurred.

C. It's a warning message that indicates something bad has occurred, but it isn't preventing NT from running.

D. You need to purge the log file.

46. You've installed a Windows NT server to allow clients to run Office97 from it. What should you do to optimize the server?

A. Configure the Server service to Minimize Memory Used.

B. Configure the Server service to Balance.

C. Configure the Server service to Maximize Throughput for File Sharing.

D. Configure the Server service to Maximize Throughput for Applications.

47. You want to upgrade all your servers, because you feel they are impacting your customers. Your department manager wants to see numeric statistics on how the current servers are performing. Which type of view would you use in Performance Monitor to capture the data?

A. Alert

B. Chart

C. Log

D. Report

**48.** How do you change the computer you're monitoring in the next illustration?

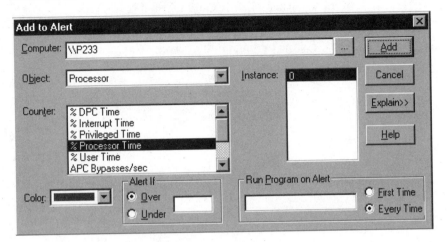

A. Click the Add button.

B. Click Cancel and select a different computer.

C. Click the ellipses (...).

D. You can't monitor a different computer using performance monitor.

**49.** You have installed a monitor on your Windows NT server, but when you test a resolution, it fails, so you install another video card. What must you do? (Choose all that apply.)

A. Start in VGA mode.

B. Change the drivers.

C. Reinstall NT Server.

D. Use LastKnownGood Configuration.

**50.** Your network consists of five servers and 50 clients on a 10base2 bus network. All computers use NWLink or IPX/SPX protocol as the only protocol. One of the servers isn't able to communicate with any of the clients or servers. What should you do to fix this server?

A. Change the frame type to match the frame type used by the other computers.

B. Uninstall NWLink and reinstall NWLink.

C. Add more RAM.

D. Fix the cabling on that server.

# Server Practice Exam I Answers

To pass the Server exam, you need to answer 40 questions correctly. We've provided explanations of the answers so you can review the questions you missed. How did you do?

1. **A.** NT requires NTFS and a SCSI device in order to hot fix bad sectors of a hard disk. Even though NT hot fixes damaged sectors of the hard disk, you may still lose data. Hot fixing attempts to write the data to a good sector, but if it can't recover the data is remains corrupted. Even though your data isn't recovered, the bad area of the hard disk is marked as unusable so it can't cause this problem again. However, if your hard disk is failing it may have more than one area of damaged disk space, in which case you'd need to replace your hard disk to ensure you don't lose any more data.

2. **A.** Hot fixing is only supported on SCSI drives formatted with NTFS. You'll need to convert the drive to NTFS before hot fixing will work. Once you have it formatted with NTFS hot fixing occurs automatically.

3. **A, D.** Typically, when your hard disk is thrashing it's because your paging file is swapping memory in and out of the hard disk. To help reduce the thrashing you need to add more RAM.

4. **C.** The REGEDIT.EXE program doesn't allow you to view or set the security permissions of Registry keys. This tool has enhanced search capabilities compared to REGEDT32.EXE, and allows you to view all hives in a single window. Which key you use should be determined by what you need to do. If you want to search for Registry key values you'll need to use REGEDIT.EXE.

5. **B.** Use the CONVERT.EXE command to change FAT file systems to NTFS. However, you can NOT use the CONVERT.EXE command to convert NTFS to FAT. To convert the C: drive from FAT to NTFS, type the following command at the command prompt: CONVERT. EXE C: /FS:NTFS

6. **B.** REGEDIT.EXE is the Windows 95 style Registry editor. However, this editor doesn't allow you to set security permission on the Registry keys.

7. **A.** The question doesn't specify whether you move the file on the same partition or a separate partition, but it should be obvious that it is a different partition. FAT doesn't support compression with NT; therefore, the file must have been moved to a partition with NTFS. When you move the file it actually copies the file to the new partition then deletes the old file. When you copy a file, it inherits compression attributes of the parent directory.

8. **B.** NetBIOS names can not exceed 15 characters. The last name required would be 16 characters: DIAS_AND_SONS_10. When taking the exam be sure to look at the NetBIOS names of the computers. NetBIOS names can contain spaces and special characters, whereas DNS names can only contain the letters A – Z, numbers 0 – 9, and the dash (-).

9. **A.** The upgrade wizard verifies the information about your computer hardware. It doesn't need to gather the information, since NT 3.51 has already performed this function.

10. **D.** The way that NT looks at available disk space doesn't take into account the sector size; it is only a close estimate of the amount of space available. In order to install NT on this system you'll need to free up more space.

11. **A.** Per Seat allows you to buy one license per client. The clients are then allowed to access any server on the network. This means you'll need to buy 1,000 licenses. If you used per server licensing you'd need to buy 10,000 (1,000 per server) licenses to ensure that the clients could connect to all the servers at any given time.

**12. B.** You need to make sure your WINS renewal interval is at least one half the DHCP lease. This ensures the IP addresses have valid computer names assigned. If the DHCP lease expires and the address is given to another computer WINS needs to be able to reflect that change. Setting the renewal interval to one half the DHCP lease ensures WINS has the correct IP mappings.

**13. D.** The largest stripe set with parity you can create is 1200MB. Combine three drives using 400MB, and you create a 1200MB stripe set with parity. Be very careful on the test not to just take all the available disks and calculate the stripe set size.

**14. B.** A stripe set provides the best performance out of the available answers. When you need high performance but not fault tolerance, you should use a stripe set. A stripe set maximizes performance by writing to each disk in 64KB blocks. The more disks you add to a stripe set, the better the performance gains. A volume set provides no fault tolerance, nor does it provide performance gains. A volume set is written to one partition at a time. After one partition is filled with data it will write to the next partition.

**15. A, B, D, E.** DHCP is used to assign IP addresses and configure other TCP/IP properties. This enables administrators to easily change TCP/IP properties without visiting all the client machines. Be careful if you use a lease that never expires, because the client will never update its TCP/IP values without manually renewing its lease.

**16. D.** You should set the account to automatically disable after their end hire date. This ensures their accounts are unusable the day after they leave the company.

**17. C.** You need to add the user to the Account Operators group. Account Operators have permissions to add, modify, and delete most user and group accounts in User Manager for Domains. They do not have the ability to modify any of the default groups mentioned in the question, nor can they modify any member that belongs to any of these groups.

**18. D.** The Server Operator group is intended to relieve the burden on the Administrator. Members of this group can shut down servers, format server hard disks, create and modify shares, lock and unlock the server, back up and restore files, and change the system time. Although its purpose is to decrease the administrator's workload, it may increase his paranoia. Members of this group should be well trained in Windows NT, because they have rights that can be very damaging to the network. The Server Operator group only exists on a Domain Controller.

**19. A, B, C.** Be sure to know which accounts can log on locally to a domain controller and which accounts can log on locally to a member server. A Power User can log on locally to a member server, but not a domain controller.

**20. B.** You may have chosen C because it says that it needs to be unlocked by an administrator, but remember that an account operator can also manage user accounts. Therefore, B is the best answer.

**21. D.** No Access always takes precedence. The No Access permission is processed first in the ACL. Once a No Access ACE is encountered, processing stops, and Access Denied is returned to the user.

**22. C.** BigAl needs to log off, then log back on for the new access rights to take effect. If BigAl doesn't log off, he'll keep the permissions he had when he logged on.

**23.** **D.** You'll need to recover from tape backup, but first you'll need to be able to log on. In order to log on you need to use the ERD to restore the SAM. If you're backing up your server regularly you shouldn't lose too much data.

**24.** **D.** Promote a BDC server to become the PDC. Since you want to use the PDC as an application server, you'll have to promote one of the other BDCs to the role of PDC. If you're smart, you'll do this before taking the PDC offline, although you don't need to.

**25.** **B.** The Master Domain is suitable for organizations of up to 30,000 users, in which you want to manage user accounts and security from a central office, but you want to manage resources through the local departments.

**26.** **D.** Before version 4.0, Windows NT had a recommended limit of 128 trusts per domain. NT 4.0 has increased the number of possible trusts to unlimited. It also increased the number of LSA secrets to an amount significantly higher than the previous limit of 256. (You use one LSA secret for each trust you establish.) Another limiting factor was the nonpaged pool size of the domain controllers on which the resource domains are stored. Whenever a domain controller starts, it sends a message to each domain, in an attempt to discover domain controllers in all trusted domains. Each domain controller in every trusted domain responds with a message to the starting domain controller. The response is temporarily stored in the nonpaged pool until NetLogon can read it. The default nonpaged pool size depends on the amount of physical RAM on your server.

**27.** **D.** This is the Complete Trust Domain model. Each domain has a two-way trust with every other domain. Resources and account management are managed locally by each domain adminstrator.

**28.** **C.** The key to answering the question (other than knowing the path) is that the files must go in a subdirectory of the export directory. Files placed directly into the export directory won't be replicated.

**29.** **D.** The export directory is only capable of exporting up to 32 subdirectories. You'll need to reduce the number of subdirectories in order to replicate all your files.

**30.** **A.** Reducing the PulseConcurrency value will reduce the number of BDCs receiving updates from the PDC at one time. By default the PDC will update 20 BDCs.

**31.** **D.** To operate a printer with an HP JetDirect card you must have the DLC protocol loaded. Of course you can use a different protocol if the JetDirect card supports it, but the HP network port print monitor that ships with Windows NT only supports DLC.

**32.** **A, D.** There are two steps you must take to print to the UNIX server. First, you need to install Microsoft TCP/IP Printing. Second, you need to give the print command at an NT command shell.

**33.** **B.** Allowing the sales team to print only after 8:00 P.M. prevents them from printing their 500-page report during peak printing hours. They can still send the print jobs to the printer, but they will remain in the queue until 8:00P.M.

**34.** **A.** Windows NT is point-and-print aware, so the driver only needs to be updated on the server. When NT clients attach to the server to send a print job, the server checks the version of the print drivers and updates the clients if necessary.

**35.** **C.** The Scheduling tab is where you select the type of spooling you want to use. You can select to start printing immediately (default), start printing after the last page is spooled, or print directly to the printer. The latter doesn't use the spool file at all.

**36.** **A.** On the NT server, you'll need to install GSNW. You can install NWLink without installing GSNW. However, when you install GSNW, NWLink is automatically installed.

**37.** **A, B, D.** The one thing you can't migrate using the NetWare Migration utility is the users' passwords. You can migrate the data, groups, user accounts, and permissions, but you can't migrate the passwords. You'll need to have the users log on with a password you give them, then they'll need to change it.

**38.** **C.** You'll need to know what commands are required to set up you modem, but that should be provided with the documentation that comes with your modem.

**39.** **C.** SLIP has many shortcomings compared to PPP, but it does require less overhead than PPP does.

**40.** **D.** Using NTBACKUP you can backup the Registry as long as you choose to back up at least one file that is on the same drive as the Registry.

**41.** **C.** An incremental backup will back up only those files created or changed since you performed the last normal or incremental backup. The incremental backup will mark files as having been backed up. Since an incremental backup only backs up files that have changed, it is the fastest way to back up your data.

**42.** **D.** Moving the paging file off the boot and system partition will help its performance. Also, moving it to a stripe set will help its performance.

**43.** **D.** Increasing the interval in which you collect data should help alleviate the performance hit while monitoring. Remember that any process you run on a computer consumes resources, as does performance monitoring. Normally, the impact isn't very noticeable, but when you monitor ten systems you'll probably notice an impact.

44. **C.** By moving your paging file off the boot partition, you'll improve disk I/O, because when the operating system runs, it generally accesses the system files and the paging file. When they are on separate drives, each drive can access the data independently from the other, especially if you have two disk controllers.

45. **A.** A bottleneck is some element of your system that prohibits it from operating at peak efficiency. The three main areas to target in looking for a bottleneck are processor performance, disk drive performance, and memory performance.

46. **B.** To monitor either LogicalDisk or PhysicalDisk performance, you must enable the disk drive performance counters by running the Diskperf utility. These counters are disabled by default because they degrade overall system performance by interrupting the processor during I/O. The counters should only be enabled when you want to monitor disk performance and should be disabled immediately when monitoring is complete. When you enable the counters, Diskperf installs the Disk Drive Performance Statistics Driver that actually collects the data for Performance Monitor, as well as a high precision timer that times each disk drive transfer. The driver and timer have been measured to take between 1 – 2 percent of overhead on Intel-based processor systems.

47. **B.** You should use the system Control Panel applet | Performance tab to increase the foreground boost to maximum. This will give his applications a higher priority. You could edit the Registry and lower the default priority of the spooler, but it is not recommended.

**48.** **A.** The key to this question is that you need to have the NTBOOTDD.SYS file on the boot floppy when your SCSI BIOS is not enabled. If you have SCSI BIOS enabled or are using IDE drives, you don't need to include this file.

**49.** **A.** DLC is required before you can use the HP Network Print Port Monitor. When you install DLC you can then access the HP port monitor that comes with Windows NT.

**50.** **D.** The Startup/Shutdown tab allows you to configure how your server responds to a STOP error. You can choose to write an event to the system log, send an administrative alert, write debugging information to a file, and automatically reboot the system.

# Server Practice Exam 2 Answers

To pass the Server exam, you need to answer 40 questions correctly. We've provided explanations of the answers so you can review the questions you missed. How did you do?

1. **A, B, C, D, F.** NT has many fault-tolerant features. The BDC serves as a backup in case the PDC fails. NTFS is a fault-tolerant file system that supports hot fixing. RAID1 and RAID5 are fault-tolerant disk drive configurations.

2. **A.** The MDM isn't a subsystem to NT. However, the VDM is a subsystem that consists of the WIN16 and DOS components.

3. **B, E.** This is a tricky question. NT Server supports four processors when you buy it off the shelf, but it can support up to 32 processors in OEM versions. If you see this question on the test, pay attention to whether it says off the shelf or OEM.

4. **D.** NT 4.0 supports NTFS, FAT-16, and CDFS file systems. HPFS is no longer supported and FAT-32 is not supported yet.

5. **B.** NWLink is the correct choice since NetBEUI isn't an option. TCP/IP requires too much configuration for this small network. Therefore, NWLink is the best answer.

6. **C.** NT truncates the long file name into an 8.3-recognizable name. Of course the file will no longer be called MY SPREADSHEET FOR MANAGING MY MONEY.XLS, but rather MYSPRE~1.XLS. You'll need to look for a file that begins with the same eight characters and ends in .XLS.

7. **C.** NT supports hardware profiles, but you must set them up manually. It isn't plug and play-capable like Windows 95. You must define the hardware profile for both configurations. When you boot your system you need to manually choose which hardware configuration you want to use.

8. **A.** RISC systems must use a FAT partition to boot; therefore the system partition can't be formatted with NTFS. You also need to use the disk formatting tool that ships with your RISC computer because NT cannot configure the partitions of a RISC computer.

9. **A, C.** You can't change the roles of a domain controller or a member server, even when upgrading. You can upgrade a workstation, because it's domain security role is basically the same as a member server: neither one authenticates users. In order to change the security role of an NT server, you must reinstall the operating system.

10. **C.** NTFS is the file system of choice here, because it performs better than FAT on larger drives, and it allows you to assign file- and folder-level permissions. Since the servers will be file servers, it is very likely you'll need to assign file- and folder-level permissions.

11. **E.** You should install the computer as a PDC. When you get back to Orlando, install a BDC, then promote it to the role of PDC. This will automatically demote the computer in Atlanta to a BDC.

12. **C.** Neither objective is met. In order to allow the two segments to communicate using NT as a router, you must enable IP Forwarding on the TCP/IP Properties page.

13. **D.** A stripe set doesn't provide fault tolerance. A stripe set is used for performance gains. It combines 2 – 32 equal areas of free space on separate disks. The drives are written to in 64KB blocks between the disks, going round robin.

**14.** **C.** A stripe set with parity (RAID 5) only requires one controller and three hard disks. You can use more controllers to increase the throughput to the hard disks. Also, more hard disks can be used in the set—up to 32. The more hard disks and disk controllers, the better the performance.

**15.** **A, B, C, E.** The red herring in this question is the DHCP forwarding. This step isn't necessary, since each segment has access to the DHCP server. Installing DHCP on the server will provide each segment with IP addresses. The other thing you must do is enable IP routing. If you don't enable IP routing, neither segment will be able to communicate with each other.

**16.** **B.** There are a couple things to pay attention to in this question. First of all, the system partition can't be part of the stripe set with parity, so you need to remove one of the 400MB partitions from your calculations. Now you've got a 500, 400, and 200MB partition to create a stripe set with parity. The largest partition you can use per disk is 200MB. 200 X 3 = 600. Is 600MB the answer, then? No. The question asked for available disk space. Subtract one drive for parity and you get 400MB of available disk space.

**17.** **C.** Using a template is easy. You simply create the template; then, when you need to use it, highlight the template file and copy it to a new account. You'll have to supply a username, full name, and password. All other information is supplied from the template.

**18.** **B.** Windows Explorer enables you to map to remote drivers to add, modify, or create files and directories. When you install Remote Administration Utilities, it allows you to edit file permissions on NTFS volumes.

**19.** **D.** It is easier to rename an account than it is to recreate an account with the same permissions. Based on the answers provided, it could only be C or D because Server Manager doesn't manage user accounts. Next, you can narrow the choice to D, because you can't copy permissions and rights from one account to another.

**20.** **A, B.** It depends on whether you have the domain set up to forcibly log off users. If so, the user will be logged off. If you didn't select this option, the user can continue to use the existing connections, but cannot create new connections until 5:00 A.M.

**21.** **B.** You need to remove Jane from the MARKETING group, so the No Access ACE won't be applied against her. If you chose option C, this would work, but it may cause other problems. You must assume there is a reason to have MARKETING with No Access permissions, so you can't simply remove this group from the share.

**22.** **B, E.** You'll need to understand how to mix file/folder-level permissions and share-level permissions on the test. The permissions that apply are the more restrictive of the two. Since share permissions aren't very granular, oftentimes you need to add NTFS permissions to set the security as required.

**23.** **A.** An arrow represents a trust relationship. Domain B trusts Domain A. Domain A is the trusted domain and Domain B is the trusting domain. (Think of the arrow as B handing his car keys to A. B is trusting A with his resource, the car.)

**24.** **B, D.** The replication governor is used to reduce the load on the network when BDCs are connected via slow WAN links. By lowering the replication governor, you reduce the amount of data sent to the BDC from the PDC each time it synchronizes.

**25.** **A, B, C.** The local group can contain users and global groups from the ENGINEERING domain because the trust allows them to pass through. It can also contain global groups from the SALES domain. Although it isn't a choice, it can also contain user accounts from the SALES domain.

**26.** C. Select the server in Server Manager, then click Computer | Synchronize With Primary Domain Controller. This will update the BDC with changes from the PDC.

**27.** A. The Single Domain is the simplest model, because all users and resources are in the same domain. A single domain is typically managed by a central MIS department.

**28.** A. Placing a lock on the server prevents the data from being replicated until it is removed. You could stop the service, but this would fill your servers up with errors, so this isn't the *best* choice.

**29.** B. By selecting the Wait Until Stabilized option, the export server will wait two minutes before sending an update notification while changes are being made. Therefore, if you change a file, you'll need to wait at least two minutes before NT will send out an update notification to the import servers.

**30.** C. You can't use the System Account to set up the directory replicator service. This service needs to logon to other computers to copy files from an export server to its import directory. In order to gain resources on any NT machine, you need to be logged on. This user account and password allow a computer to log onto another computer.

**31.** A. From the answers provided, the only correct answer is that they must all use the same driver. This doesn't mean you need to use the same printing device. You can use two different printing devices as long as they have a common driver.

**32.** A. You need to move the spooler for the printers. Edit the following Registry key:

HKEY_LOCAL_MACHINE\System\CurrentControlset\Control\Print\Printers.

**33. A.** The print spooler manages the entire printing process, including the routing of documents internal to the computer. Once it is determined that a document needs to be sent outside the computer to be printed (to a shared printer), the print spooler gives it to the print router. The print router then delivers the print job to the shared printer.

**34. B.** Often a network printing device is confused with a shared network printer. If your computer has a port that prints directly to the printer (like LPR1 or HP network port print monitor), it is considered a local printer. If your computer sends the print job to another printer to be spooled then printed, it is considered a shared printer.

**35. C.** Windows 95 supports point-and-print printing. All you need to do is add the appropriate Windows 95 driver on the printer. When clients connect to it they will automatically download the new driver.

**36. C.** Since a printer pool uses the same printer, all you need to do is add the new printer port for the printing device to the printer object. Make sure the new printing device uses the same print driver.

**37. A.** The answer is pretty much as stated. The gateway translates SMB calls from Windows clients to NCP calls to the NetWare server.

**38. A.** Not only does it allow you to change the group names, it also allows you to change the username and file/directory names that you migrate. In order to use this utility, you need to map the current names to the new names and save them in a file.

**39. B.** Requiring any encryption is necessary, because the DOS clients don't support MS-CHAP. In order to use DES you need to lower your logon authentication requirements to just requiring any encryption.

**40. D.** The DEVICE.LOG file is often used to help determine common RAS problems by maintaining a record of the conversations between RAS and your modems. Setting the value of Logging to 1 in the system Registry in the following subtree enables the DEVICE.LOG file:

HKEY_LOCAL_MACHINE\System\CurrentControlSet\Services\RasMan\Parameters

**41. A, B.** Notice that the Dial Out Protocols have IPX/SPX selected, but the Allow Remote Clients Running options are only set to NetBEUI and TCP/IP. If you didn't look at the screen carefully you may have missed this. Be very careful when taking the actual test.

**42. D.** Since you only have one tape, and it will be nearly full after backing up, you'll need to do a normal backup every night to ensure you have all the data on the server backed up.

**43. D.** NTBACKUP cannot backup the Registry on a remote machine. In order to back up the Registry, you'll need to run RDISK on the local machine or use a tape backup device on the local machine.

**44. B.** You don't need to change the binding order of the server, since the server will respond to the clients with the protocol the clients originally sent to the server. If NetBEUI is moved higher in the clients binding order it will be the first protocol chosen when clients try to communicate with each other.

**45. B.** Whenever you see a stop sign in your log files you should investigate it. This means that an error with a significant impact has occurred. It may be that something is expected. For instance, you have a scanner hooked up to your system, but you leave it turned off most of the time. When you boot your computer NT fails to initialize it; therefore, it gives a red stop sign. This isn't a very important error, but you can also receive a stop sign message when TCP/IP fails to bind to your network card. Now *that* will have you scrambling to fix it.

46. **D.** You should configure the Server service to Maximize Throughput for Applications. Note that SQL server is also an application. So if you see a similar question but with SQL, SNA, or Exchange, the answer is still to Maximize Throughput for Applications.

47. **D.** The Report view lets you display constantly changing counter and instance values for selected objects. Values appear in columns for each instance. You can adjust report intervals, print snapshots, and export data. For example, you could create a report on all the counters for a given object, then watch how they change under various loads.

48. **C.** If you click the ellipses (…), a Select Computer dialog box will appear. Use this dialog box to select a computer that you want to monitor. Monitoring a computer remotely will impact both computers and the overall network traffic, so you may want to set a longer interval for collecting data.

49. **A, B.** Start the computer in VGA mode so you can see the screen, then change the driver to use the new video card. LastKnownGood Configuration won't help here, since you changed the video card.

50. **A.** From the choices available, the only one that makes sense is to change the frame type. You may have considered a bad cable, but with 10base2, if one segment is down, they all are down.

MICROSOFT CERTIFIED SYSTEMS ENGINEER

# Test Yourself: Networking Essentials

*Q & A*

# Networking Essentials Practice Exam 1

Before you call to register for the actual exam, take the following test and see how you make out. Set a timer for 75 minutes—the time you'll have to take the live Networking Essentials exam—and answer the following 58 questions in the time allotted. Once you're through, turn to the end of the module and check your score to see if you passed! Good luck!

1. Current Situation: Your network currently consists of 250 client computers and eight server computers. The server computers use Windows NT server 4.0, and the client computers use Windows 95 and Windows NT Workstation 4.0. There is a very large relational database on one of the Windows NT servers.

   Required Result: Access to the corporate database must be sped up.

   Optional Desired Results: All client computers should be able to access the same database; the client computers should not have to use a different operating system.

   Proposed Solution: Install SQL Server.

   Which results does the proposed solution produce?

   A. The proposed solution produces the required result and produces both of the optional desired results.

   B. The proposed solution produces the required result and produces only one of the optional desired results.

   C. The proposed solution produces the required result but does not produce any of the optional desired results.

   D. The proposed solution does not produce the required result.

2. A _____ connects network cables by regenerating signals so they can travel on additional cable lengths.

3. _____ are used by both bridges and routers to store address information.

**4.** What is the cheapest method of allowing data to pass from Network #1 to Network #2 as shown in the next illustration?

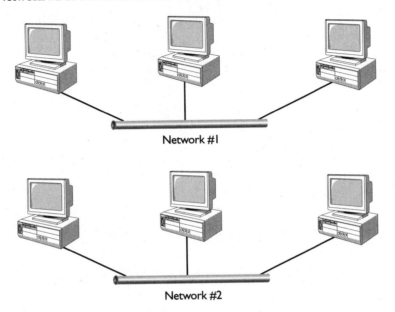

Network #1

Network #2

A. Use a fiber optic micro transceiver.

B. Use a router.

C. Use a repeater.

D. Use a bridge.

**5.** You have just joined a company that wants to connect all of its networks together so that data can be shared among all the machines. The networks consist of a mixture of 10BaseT Ethernet, 10Base2 Ethernet, and token ring. How are you going to join the networks so that information can be shared?

A. Add bridges to the network.

B. Add hubs to the network.

C. Add repeaters to the network.

D. Add routers to the network.

**6.** The OSI model consists of seven layers. What layer is missing in the next illustration?

A. Static

B. Simple

C. Session

D. Selective

**7.** What OSI layer is responsible for advertising available services to the network?

A. Data Link layer

B. Session layer

C. Presentation layer

D. Application layer

**8.** You have noticed that your network of six Windows NT servers and 240 Windows 95 clients has become remarkably sluggish over the last several weeks. You have decided to switch network topologies so that you can switch from the CSMA/CD access method to the CSMA/CA access method. What will be the result of your change?

A. Your network will speed up significantly.

B. Your network will speed up slightly.

C. Your network will slow down.

D. You cannot use the CSMA/CA access method.

**9.** The Server Message Block and NetWare Core Protocol reside at what OSI layer?

A. Application

B. Presentation

C. Session

D. Network

**10.** Your company has just merged with another company, and it is your job to link the two networks. One network consists of all Windows NT systems, and the other network consists of all Apple systems. What is the easiest way for you to allow the Apple systems access to the Windows NT systems?

A. Install AppleTalk on the Windows NT servers.

B. Install DLC on the Apple systems.

C. Install DLC on the Windows NT systems.

D. Install AppleTalk on the UNIX systems.

**11.** What is the purpose of binding?

A. Binding is the process of connecting the protocol stack to the network interface card.

B. Binding is the process of connecting the protocol stack to another protocol stack.

C. Binding is the process of connecting the protocol stack to the Presentation layer of the OSI model.

D. Binding is the process of connecting the protocol stack to the Data Link layer of the OSI model.

**12.** The next illustration shows an Ethernet network. What type of media does it use?

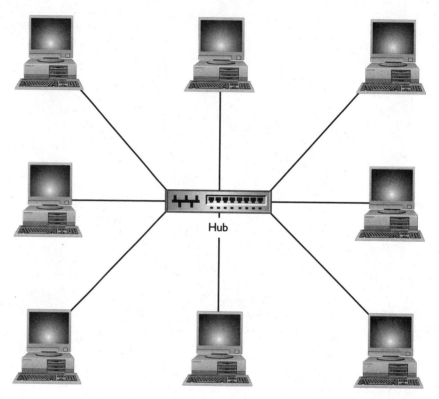

A. Thin coaxial

B. Thick coaxial

C. Unshielded untwisted pair

D. Unshielded twisted pair

**13.** What is the maximum transmission speed for ArcNet?

A. 2.5 Kbps

B. 2.5 Mbps

C. 16 bps

D. 16 Mbps

**14.** Current Situation: 17 standalone computers in an administrative office.
Required Result: Network the computers so that files can be shared.
Optional Desired Results: Minimal cost; fast speed.
Proposed Solution: Install a token ring network.
Which results does the proposed solution produce?

A. The proposed solution produces the required result and produces both of the optional desired results.

B. The proposed solution produces the required result and produces only one of the optional desired results.

C. The proposed solution produces the required result but does not produce any of the optional desired results.

D. The proposed solution does not produce the required result.

**15.** What IEEE standard defines 100VG-AnyLAN?

A. 802.21

B. 802.13

C. 802.12

D. 802.31

**16.** Kevin, a co-worker in the IS department, says that he lost the set of setup disks for Windows NT Server, and he would like to have a replacement set. What do you tell him?

A. Tell him to call Microsoft and order another set.

B. Tell him to use WINNT.EXE /OX to create a new set.

C. Tell him to create a new set by copying the %SYSTEMROOT%\ SYSTEM32 DIRECTORY structure.

D. Tell him to use WINNT.EXE /XO to create a new set.

**17.** You are the administrator of a Windows NT network, and you have noticed that your users never change their passwords. What can you do to increase the security of the network?

    A. Modify the age that passwords expire in the Account Policy dialog box from Server Manager.

    B. Modify the password length in the Account Policy dialog box from User Manager for Domains.

    C. Modify the password length in the Account Policy dialog box from Server Manager.

    D. Modify the age that passwords expire in the Account Policy dialog box from User Manager for Domains.

**18.** You have installed a Windows NT network that uses the TCP/IP protocol in the training department and you are receiving complaints that the network is operating sluggishly and the MS-DOS Network Client 3.0 systems are having trouble finding other systems in the domain. All Windows 95 systems are working properly. What is wrong with the MS-DOS Network Client 3.0 systems?

    A. The MS-DOS Network Client 3.0 systems do not know the correct WINS server address.

    B. The MS-DOS Network Client 3.0 systems do not know the correct DNS server address.

    C. The MS-DOS Network Client 3.0 systems do not have an LMHOSTS file.

    D. The MS-DOS Network Client 3.0 systems do not have a HOSTS file.

**19.** You have been hired as the new network administrator for a doctor's office, and you are reviewing the account policy for the domain. The next illustration shows the current account policy. What can you do to increase security for the domain?

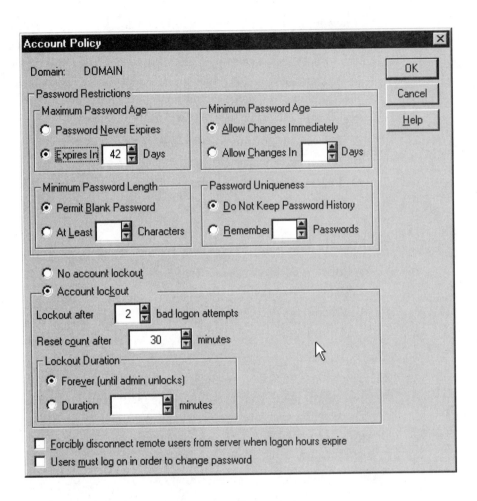

A. Require a minimum password length.

B. Increase the maximum password age.

C. Change the policy to no account lockout.

D. Reset the account lockout to 1 minute.

**20.** You work for an office supply company that has recently installed a network. The boss is mad because too many people are missing the meetings he holds at irregular times. The employees are mad because the boss decides to hold meetings when they have other commitments. How can you help make sure that the employees attend the meetings of the boss, and, in turn, see that the boss does not schedule meetings at inconvenient times?

    A. Implement individual scheduling.

    B. Implement a database server.

    C. Implement group scheduling.

    D. Implement a file server.

**21.** Which of the following products is not an example of groupware?

    A. Banyan VINES

    B. Novell Groupwise

    C. Microsoft Outlook

    D. Lotus Notes

**22.** You go into work one morning, and find that you and the boss are the only two people there. Your boss is hopping mad because someone sent out an e-mail telling everyone that they could have the day off (hmmm, you didn't get THAT message). Your boss demands that something be done about this situation immediately. What can you do?

    A. Implement LDAP on your mail system.

    B. Implement digital signatures on your mail system.

    C. Implement S/MIME on your mail system.

    D. Implement analog signatures on your mail system.

**23.** What type of application is shown in the next illustration?

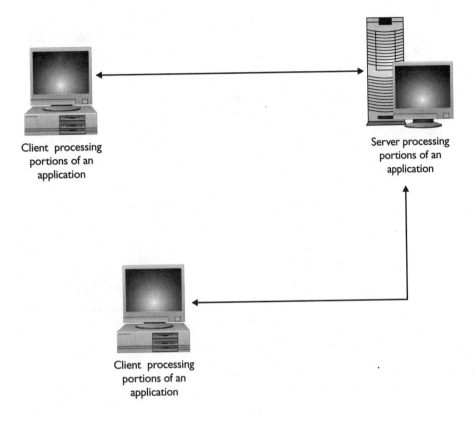

Client processing portions of an application

Server processing portions of an application

Client processing portions of an application

A. Client/Server

B. Mobilized

C. Centralized

D. Transitional

**24.** You work in the information systems department of a casino. The casino has expressed a need for the pit bosses to access data on the AS/400 located in your office. However, the pit bosses only have access to Windows NT workstations, which are located on the local area network. How can you provide access to the AS/400 to the pit bosses?

A. Install an SMA gateway

B. Install an NOS gateway

C. Install an MOS gateway

D. Install an SNA gateway

25. Joe needs a file located on the UNIX server. He tries to access the UNIX server from his Windows 95 client, but fails. He calls the help desk complaining that he needs the file immediately! Upon examining his system, you see that he does have the TCP/IP protocol installed. Why can't he access the UNIX server?

A. He does not have permission to access the SNA server.

B. He does not have an NFS client installed.

C. He does not have an FTP server installed.

D. He does not have permission to access the REQ server.

26. What is the name of the Apple file-sharing software?

A. AppleTalk

B. AppleShare

C. AppleCore

D. AppleSide

27. The next illustration shows the Network Properties for a Windows 95 system. What type of server(s) can it connect to?

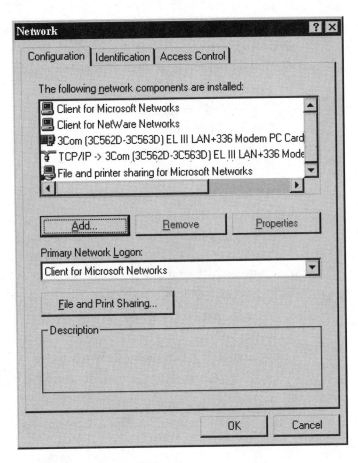

A. Windows NT and Novell NetWare

B. Windows NT

C. Novell NetWare

D. UNIX

**28.** Two secretaries need to share files, so a co-worker in their office decided to connect their two machines together in a "network". He plugged the cable into the wide "telephone" jack of each secretary's computer and set up the networking software. The arrangement doesn't work. One of the secretaries asks you for assistance. What determination do you come to after surveying the situation? (Choose all that apply.)

A. They need a crosscut cable installed.

B. They need a crossover cable installed.

C. They need a bridge installed.

D. They need a hub installed.

29. Mike and Mary work in the same office and would like to share data between them. Mike sees that both computers have BNC connectors, so he plugs a section of thinnet coaxial cable into both machines. He then configures both machines to use the NetBEUI protocol, but nothing happens. Why doesn't it work?

A. He needs to use RG-62 cable.

B. He needs to use RJ-45 cable.

C. He needs to use T connectors and terminators.

D. He needs to use solder-on connectors instead of the crimp-on connectors.

30. What is the maximum distance for 10Base2 media?

A. 2000 meters

B. 500 meters

C. 200 meters

D. 185 meters

31. What type of cabling is the least expensive?

A. Unshielded twisted pair

B. Fiber optic

C. Thicknet

D. Thinnet

**32.** Nina decided that she would install a network card in her system. Upon booting her machine after inserting the NIC, she received a message that her network interface card was conflicting with another device in her system and it could not be used. What could be causing the problem? (Choose all that apply.)

A. I/O base address conflict

B. AUI conflict

C. DMA conflict

D. IRQ conflict

**33.** Where is the Media Access Control address located?

A. It is located in the data bus structure.

B. It is located in the network adapter.

C. It is located in the network software.

D. It is located in the protocols.

**34.** A new network is being installed in your company, but your predecessor failed to order network cards already installed in the 14 new systems. After the new systems arrived, and he realized that he needed network cards, he told a purchasing agent to order him 14 network cards. Prior to the cards arriving, he quit and you were hired. Purchasing has just delivered the network cards to you, and you see that all 14 have an AUI connector. The network is wired for 10BaseT. Your boss has told you that you have to make those network cards work because they cost a lot of money. What is the best way to handle the situation since you cannot purchase correct network cards?

A. Replace the 10BaseT hubs and cable with 10Base5 cable.

B. Add a 10BaseT on-board transceiver to the AUI cards.

C. Replace the entire network with a wireless LAN.

D. Add a 10BaseT external transceiver to the AUI cards.

**35.** What type of data bus is needed for the network interface card shown in the next illustration?

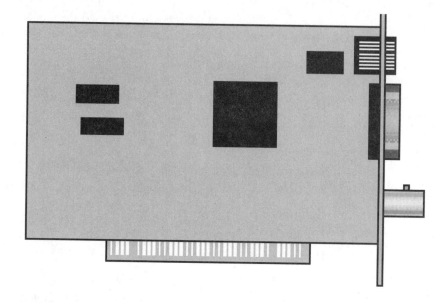

A. MCA

B. PCMCIA

C. PCI

D. EISA

**36.** What layer of the OSI model does a router function at?

A. Physical

B. Data Link

C. Network

D. Transport

**37.** Current Situation: Your 10BaseT network is located on the first floor of the administration building.

Required Result: Expand the network to the fifth floor of the administration building.

Optional Desired Results: Provide expandability for future bandwidth increases; monitor the router for routing table errors.

Proposed Solution: Add a passive hub to each floor until you reach the fifth floor.

Which results does the proposed solution produce?

A. The proposed solution produces the required result and produces both of the optional desired results.

B. The proposed solution produces the required result and produces only one of the optional desired results.

C. The proposed solution produces the required result but does not produce any of the optional desired results.

D. The proposed solution does not produce the required result.

**38.** How do switches know which port to send data packets to?

A. The switch examines each packet to find its sending MAC address.

B. The switch examines each packet to find its destination IP address.

C. The switch examines each packet to find its sending IP address.

D. The switch examines each packet to find its destination MAC address.

**39.** The network shown in the next illustration is suffering from 98 percent bandwidth utilization. What can you do to lower the bandwidth utilization for the network?

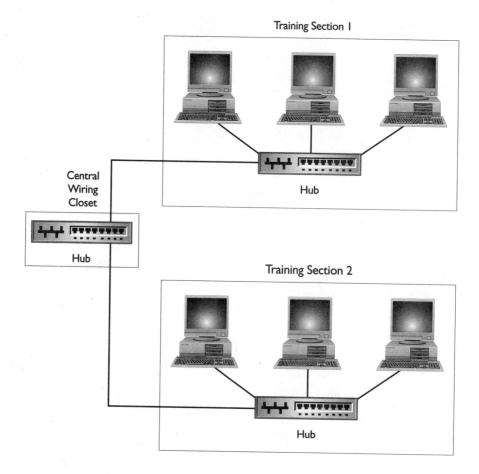

A. Change the protocol from NetBEUI to TCP/IP.

B. Add a repeater to the central wiring closet.

C. Replace the hub with a MSAU.

D. Split the network using a bridge.

**40.** Current Situation: LCD Chronometers Inc. has offices in Boston, Rapid City, and Lousiville. Each office has it own LAN. The users need to be able to access data in all three locations.

Required Result: Implement a WAN connection linking all three locations.

Optional Desired Results: The WAN connection must be able to work even if one of the links fails; the WAN connection must operate at the DS-3 level.

Proposed Solution: Install three separate T-1 connections. Install one from Boston to Louisville, another one from Louisville to Rapid City, and the last one from Rapid City to Boston.

Which results does the proposed solution produce?

A. The proposed solution produces the required result and produces both of the optional desired results.

B. The proposed solution produces the required result and produces only one of the optional desired results.

C. The proposed solution produces the required result but does not produce any of the optional desired results.

D. The proposed solution does not produce the required result.

41. Laptops R Handy Inc. has branch offices located in several cities. Currently, the branch offices send weekly sales statistics back to the main office using dialup synchronous communication. Future plans for the company are to implement a video conferencing link so that the CEO can communicate face to face with the branch managers in a daily executive meeting. What type of solution would you recommend for Laptops R Handy?

A. Install X.25 to connect the main office to all of the branch offices.

B. Install ATM to connect the main office to all of the branch offices.

C. Install PPP to connect the main office to all of the branch offices.

D. Install SLIP to connect the main office to all of the branch offices.

42. How do modems communicate?

A. They take digital signals from the wire and convert them to analog signals for the DTE.

B. They take digital signals from the DTE and convert them to analog signals to send over the wire.

C. They take digital signals from the wire and convert them to analog signals for the DCE.

D. They take digital signals from the DCE and convert them to analog signals to send over the wire.

**43.** What happens when the T1 link shown in the next illustration breaks?

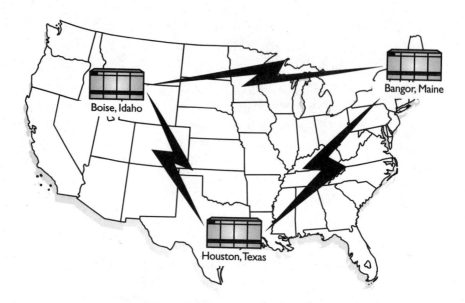

A. Boise cannot send any traffic to Houston until the T1 is fixed.

B. Houston cannot send any traffic to Boise until the T1 is fixed.

C. Bangor has to route all traffic destined for Houston through Boise.

D. Houston can send traffic destined for Boise through Bangor.

**44.** Hurricane Hovering Inc. needs to make sure that their network is able to work under extreme conditions, so they have designed a "constant uptime" plan. They have installed fault tolerance for their vital information, as well as having a sound backup plan. Is there anything that they have forgotten to add to their "constant uptime" plan?

A. No, the "constant uptime" plan has everything covered.

B. Yes, they forgot to add any levels of RAID protection.

C. Yes, they forgot to add any type of auditing capability.

D. Yes, they forgot to add uninterruptible power supplies.

**45.** What tool is used to implement fault tolerance for Windows NT Server?

A. User Manager for Domains

B. Disk Administrator

C. Server Manager

D. Network Disk Configuration Tool

**46.** Current Situation: Marigold Cleaning, a small, six-person company, has a small Windows 95-based network in their building, which they use to share various data.

Required Result: Implement security on the network.

Optional Desired Results: Audit all transfers into or out of the finance computer; minimize the administration of the network.

Proposed Solution: Implement user-level security.

Which results does the proposed solution produce?

A. The proposed solution produces the required result and produces both of the optional desired results.

B. The proposed solution produces the required result and produces only one of the optional desired results.

C. The proposed solution produces the required result but does not produce any of the optional desired results.

D. The proposed solution does not produce the required result.

**47.** Which RAID supported by Windows NT Server creates a disk stripe set but does not provide any redundancy?

A. RAID 5

B. RAID 4

C. RAID 1

D. RAID 0

**48.** Jerry in Sales says that he is having problems connecting to one of your Windows NT servers. You suspect that the server may be the cause of the problem. What can you do to verify your theory?

A. Use Network Monitor from the suspect server.

B. Use Server Manager from the suspect server.

C. Use Network Monitor from any server.

D. Use Server Manager from any server.

49. Network usage at your company has steadily declined over the last several weeks. The users of the network state that they don't feel comfortable using the network, because it is so complex. Some users have stated to you that they get very frustrated when they try to open documents that they should have access to, but instead they get an ACCESS DENIED! message. What part of the administrative plan has failed?

A. Security strategy

B. Backup strategy

C. Monitoring policies

D. Systems analysis policies

50. Daily, you review the event logs for all your servers. Over the last several days you have noticed a directory replication error that occurs sporadically at different times on Server 15. By the time you find out about the error it is too late to discover what else is happening on the system. How can you determine when the error occurs so that you can see what else is happening to the server?

A. Use Disk Administrator to configure the computer to send alerts.

B. Use Server Manager to configure the computer to send alerts.

C. Use Network Monitor to configure the computer to send alerts.

D. Use Performance Monitor to configure the computer to send alerts.

51. The custodian of the computer equipment for the building is looking for a computer that is on his inventory, but he has not been able to locate it. In desperation, he asks you if you can help him locate the asset. You figure it should not be that difficult or time consuming, so you agree to help. You ask him if he knows the computer name of the system he is looking for. He consults his inventory list and says that the computer is named MonkeyBoy.

Uh-oh, maybe this is going to be harder than you first thought, since you don't know the location of anyone named MonkeyBoy. What could have been a help in locating this computer system?

A. If the agent was turned on for the system.

B. If the custodian had a current list of systems.

C. If a standard naming convention had been used.

D. If the MIB was turned on for the system.

52. Clara from the accounts receivable department calls you because she can not log on the network from her Windows 95 computer. You use User Manager for Domains to check her user account, and it is not locked out. What do you do next? (Choose all that apply.)

A. Tell her to restart her computer.

B. Format her hard disk and reload Windows 95.

C. Delete her user account and create a new one for her.

D. Replace her network interface card.

53. How can you check your network cables for problems? (Choose all that apply.)

A. Use a cable tester.

B. Use a potentiometer.

C. Use a digital volt meter.

D. Use a time domain reflectometer.

54. ACME Mirror Breakers Inc. have a small network that consists of a single segment with one Windows NT server. The network administrator has a strict rule that they must keep network utilization to the server down to below 40 percent. What tool could he use to check the percent of network utilization for their network?

A. Performance Manager

B. Network Monitor

C. Oscilloscope

D. Network Statistics Manager

**55.** The network shown in the next illustration is having problems. What tool would provide the most help in troubleshooting the network?

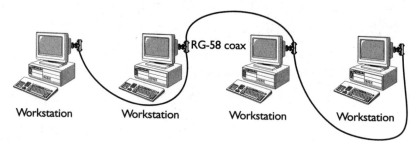

A. Digital volt meter

B. Time domain reflectometer

C. Network monitor

D. Protocol analyzer

**56.** You were able to convince the vice president of General Jalopy Inc. that they need to use the TCP/IP protocol in order to connect their network to the Internet. Now he is trying to convince you that they want their domain name to be www.genjalopy.mil. You try to explain to him that they cannot use that domain name, but once again he is insistent. He states that the CEO retired from the military so they are authorized to use the name. What is the correct top level domain for General Jalopy Inc.?

A. .EDU

B. .NET

C. .COM

D. .GOV

**57.** How does the name WWW.SYNGRESS.COM get translated to 146.115.28.75?

A. ARP

B. DNS

C. TCP

D. NBT

**58.** What is the application in the next illustration being used for?

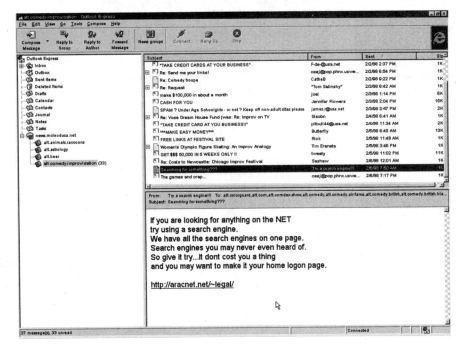

A. Electronic mail

B. Newsgroups

C. Internet Relay Chat

D. Telnet

# Test Yourself: Networking Essentials Practice Exam 2

Before you call to register for the actual exam, take the following test and see how you make out. Set a timer for 75 minutes—the time you'll have to take the live Networking Essentials exam—and answer the following 58 questions in the time allotted. Once you're through, turn to the end of the module and check your score to see if you passed! Good luck!

**1.** What type of topology is shown in the next illustration

    A. Star-bus topology

    B. Bus topology

    C. Star ring topology

    D. Ring topology

**2.** Why is network performance degraded when an extremely large number of broadcasts occurs?

    A. Broadcasts require each receiving computer to send an acknowledgment packet.

    B. Broadcasts are routed through every router on your network, causing a delay.

    C. Broadcasts are processed by every computer on the network segment.

    D. Broadcasts require special handling to ensure no packet fragmentation exists.

**3.** Melissa is a new employee in your company. She stops you as you're walking by her office and says that she cannot use the print server. What can be the problem?

A. She does not have a printer attached to her computer.

B. She has used up her quota of paper for the month.

C. She does not have the permissions necessary to use the print server.

D. She does not need to print the document, as another employee already printed it.

**4.** Which layer of the OSI model is responsible for taking raw data and placing it in frames?

A. The Session layer

B. The Data Link layer

C. The Presentation layer

D. The Application layer

**5.** You are reviewing the plans for expanding the 10BaseT network in your office building by adding four additional computers. The distance from each computer to the wiring closet is: (Choose all that apply.)

Computer 1: 418 feet
Computer 2: 541 feet
Computer 3: 320 feet
Computer 4: 624 feet

Which of the following statements is true?

A. The distance from Computer 1 to the wiring closet exceeds the 10BaseT specification.

B. The distance from Computer 2 to the wiring closet exceeds the 10BaseT specification.

C. The distance from Computer 3 to the wiring closet exceeds the 10BaseT specification.

D. The distance from Computer 4 to the wiring closet exceeds the 10BaseT specification.

**6.** Your company has two local area networks that cannot communicate directly with each other because they use different protocols. Users need to access data located on both networks. Which type of device allows communication between both of the networks?

A. Repeaters

B. Bridges

C. Routers

D. Gateways

**7.** What device operates at the Data Link layer of the OSI model?

A. Gateway

B. Router

C. Bridge

D. Repeater

**8.** What is located in place of the question mark for the packet shown in the next illustration?

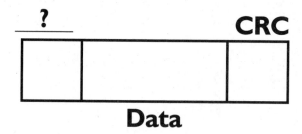

A. Header

B. Footer

C. Trailer

D. Checksum

**9.** Current Situation: There are five standalone Windows 95 computers in an office.
Required Result: Network the computers so they can share files with each other.

Optional Desired Results: No additional software must be purchased; it should take a minimal amount of configuration.
Proposed Solution: Use NetBEUI as the transport protocol.
Which results does the proposed solution produce?

A. The proposed solution produces the required result and produces both of the optional desired results.
B. The proposed solution produces the required result and produces only one of the optional desired results.
C. The proposed solution produces the required result but does not produce any of the optional desired results.
D. The proposed solution does not produce the required result.

10. What protocol must be installed for the computers in the next illustration?

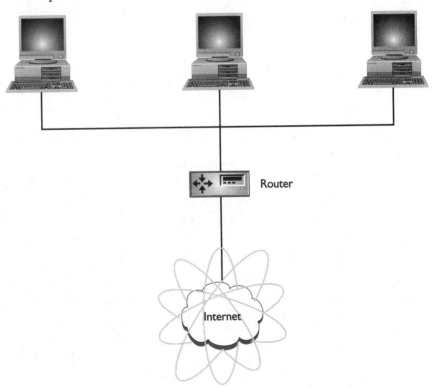

    A. DLC

    B. TCP/IP

    C. IPX/SPX

    D. NetBEUI

**11.** You have a Windows NT-based network at your location. Several disk drives have been shared out for use by all of the users. What protocol allows file sharing to be accomplished?

    A. NFS

    B. SMB

    C. FTP

    D. SMTP

**12.** What is another name for thicknet networks?

    A. 10BaseT

    B. 10Base5

    C. 10Base2

    D. 10BaseFL

**13.** You are hired as the system administrator for a company whose network is a token ring using unshielded twisted pair. Currently there are 69 workstations hooked to the network but the company may expand in the future. At the weekly staff meeting you are asked how much expansion the current ring is capable of handling. What do you tell them?

    A. The current ring can handle the addition of another three workstations.

    B. The current ring can handle the addition of another 191 workstations.

    C. The current ring can handle the addition of another 260 workstations.

    D. The current ring can handle the addition of another 72 workstations.

**14.** The next illustration shows a token ring network. The network has problems, and the beaconing frame stops at system 3. Which computer is causing the network problem?

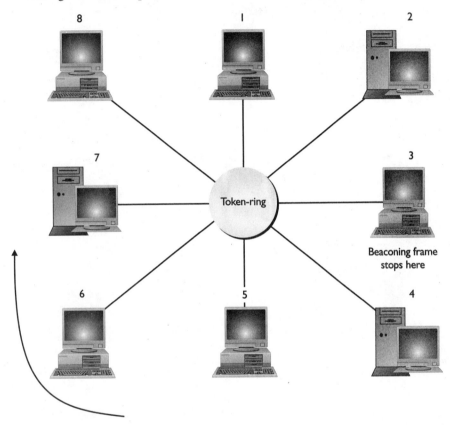

A. 1

B. 2

C. 3

D. 4

E. 5

15. You're called out to troubleshoot a thinnet network that has quit functioning. Arriving at the scene, you see 12 computers in an office all hooked to the same thinnet cable. None of the computers is working. What can be causing the network outage?

    A. The thinnet cable is terminated with a 50 ohm terminator.
    B. The T-connector is not hooked to a computer, but the cable is on each end of the T.
    C. The thinnet cable is not terminated.
    D. One of the computers is not turned on.

16. What is the maximum number of characters there can be in a NetBIOS computer name?

    A. 12
    B. 13
    C. 14
    D. 15

17. Your Windows NT network uses the TCP/IP protocol suite, and you have decided to set up a WINS server to resolve computer names to IP addresses. Your network has no other method of name resolution. What limitation is present on your network?

    A. All client computers must have a HOSTS file.
    B. All client computers must know the address of the WINS server.
    C. All client computers must have an LMHOSTS file.
    D. All client computers must know the address of the DNS server.

18. What are the default user rights for the Server Operators group? (Choose all that apply.)

    A. Back up files and directories.
    B. Log on locally.
    C. Restore files and directories.
    D. Shut down the system.

**19.** What protocol is installed by default in Windows NT Server 4.0?

A. TCP/IP

B. IPX/SPX

C. NetBEUI

D. DLC

**20.** Randy has been using a shared application located on his D: drive. All of a sudden the application does not work for him any longer. You recall that you dispatched a technician to his machine yesterday to install a CD-ROM drive into his system. What could be causing Randy's problem?

A. Randy is using the wrong password to access the application.

B. The Registry has references to a drive letter for the application.

C. Randy does not have write permission to the application.

D. The Registry has references to a UNC for the application.

**21.** You have been hired by a startup telemarketing firm to install a database for them to use. The firm employs 132 telemarketers who need to access data from the same database simultaneously while they are taking orders for merchandise. What type of database should they use?

A. An application database

B. A standalone database

C. A virtual database

D. A client/server database

**22.** What is the primary advantage of a client/server architecture?

A. The capability to distribute processing to both the server and client.

B. The capability for the server to perform all the processing.

C. The capability for the client to perform all the processing.

D. The capability to concentrate the auditing to both the server and client.

**23.** You work for a company that has just installed a network. There are 32 client machines and seven of them have minimal free hard disk space. Management has standardized the company on Microsoft Office 97 and is requiring that all users use the office suite to complete all of their work. This creates a dilemma for you, since management refuses to give you any money for equipment upgrades, and Office 97 does not fit on seven of your systems. How are you going to meet the requirement management has stipulated?

A. Install Office 97 on the clients' D: drives.
B. Do not install Office 97 on the seven systems until management upgrades the equipment.
C. Install Office 97 on your server.
D. Do not install Office 97 on any of the systems until all of them are capable of using it.

**24.** How does the client computer communicate with the servers shown in the next illustration?

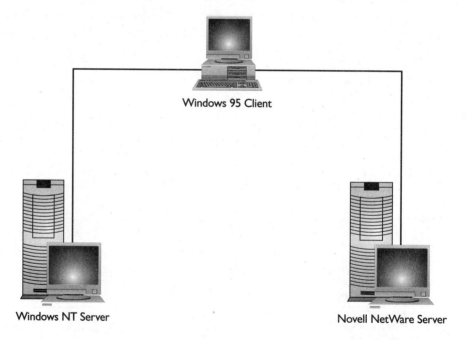

Windows 95 Client

Windows NT Server

Novell NetWare Server

A. It uses multiple redirectors.

B. It uses multiple resenders.

C. It uses a single redirector.

D. It uses a single resender.

**25.** Rob calls the help desk and states that he cannot access the NetWare server that houses an important database. You go to his cubicle and see that his machine has the Client for Microsoft Networks installed, as well as the NetBEUI protocol. Why can't he access the NetWare server? (Choose all that apply.)

A. His machine does not have the correct network interface card installed.

B. His machine does not have the correct client installed.

C. His machine does not have the correct protocol installed.

D. His machine does not have Novell Client64 installed.

**26.** ABC General Services has a network that consists of both Windows NT servers and Novell NetWare 4.*x* servers. They want their Windows NT 4.0 workstations to use NDS for browsing the network. What do you recommend they use to accomplish this?

A. GSNW

B. CSNW

C. GSNT

D. CSNT

**27.** What type of terminal is a standalone device?

A. Dumb terminal

B. Intelligent terminal

C. Smart terminal

D. Super smart terminal

**28.** ACME Butter Churners has contacted your consulting company with a concern about their token ring network. It seems that the company that installed the network ran the majority of the cable under the carpets in all of the offices. The lawyers for the company fear a lawsuit, because the cable presents a tripping hazard for the employees and visitors. How do you recommend they resolve the issue?

A. Replace the cable with Type 1 cable.

B. Replace the cable with Type 8 cable.

C. Replace the cable with Type 2 cable.

D. Replace the cable with Type 9 cable.

29. What type of transmission uses digital signaling?

A. Baseband

B. Narrowband

C. Broadband

D. Wideband

30. What type of connector is on the transceiver that connects directly to thicknet cable?

A. Piercing tap

B. RJ-45

C. AUI tap

D. RJ-11

31. ACME Clay Studios has been growing at a phenomenal rate in recent years, and they have to keep expanding their 10Base2 network. They are experiencing problems with the network since their last expansion. They give you the wiring layout of the network to examine, as they don't see anything wrong. As you look over the wiring layout you see that it uses four repeaters on the five segments, and that each segment has 30 computers on it. What is wrong with their network layout?

A. They have too many computers on each segment.

B. They don't have enough repeaters on the network.

C. They have too many segments populated.

D. They have not kept the wiring layout updated correctly.

**32.** How does a network interface card function?

    A. It takes the serial data from the computer and translates it to parallel data before putting it on the network media.

    B. It takes the network layer data and converts it to physical data before putting it on the network media.

    C. It takes the parallel data from the computer and translates it to serial data before putting it on the network media.

    D. It takes the physical layer data and converts it to network layer data before putting it on the network media.

**33.** You are going to put new network cards in several Windows 95 systems. Before taking out the old cards, you would like to know what IRQ and I/O base address they are using. How can you determine these statistics?

    A. Open up the Diagnostics window and choose the Resources tab.

    B. Use the MSD diagnostic tool in Windows 95.

    C. Open up the Device Manager and select the network card.

    D. Use a serial port diagnostics program, since the network card sends out serial data.

**34.** What type of connector is used for fiber optic network adapters?

    A. AB

    B. BA

    C. ST

    D. TS

**35.** ACME Turtle Racing Inc. purchased several diskless workstations that it now wants to put on their 10BaseT local area network. They have hired you to accomplish this, because their network administrator told them that it was not possible. How are you going to add the diskless workstations to the LAN?

    A. Use wireless network interface cards.

    B. Use 10BaseT network interface cards.

    C. Use network adapters that have remote boot PROMs.

    D. The network administrator is correct, they cannot be added to the LAN.

**36.** What type of device can send data directly from one port to another port as shown in the next illustration?

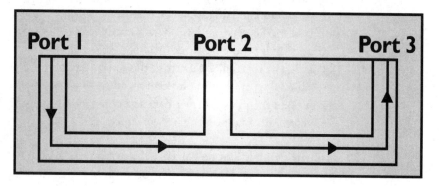

A. A router

B. A switch

C. A repeater

D. A gateway

**37.** Turntables R Us was very happy when you cleared up their slow network, but ever since you made the changes they have had another problem. All of the client computers on the second floor cannot get logged onto the network. All of the Windows NT servers are on the first floor, and no one on the first floor is having a problem logging on. What is causing the problem for Turntables R Us this time?

A. The users on the second floor forgot their passwords.

B. The router is not set up to pass DHCP broadcast messages.

C. The hard disks on the servers are corrupt.

D. The hub is not set up to pass BOOTP broadcast messages.

**38.** At what layer of the OSI model does a switch function?

A. Physical

B. Data Link

C. Network

D. Transport

**39.** What is the main advantage that thickwire has over thinwire?

   A. Thickwire is easier to work with than thinwire.

   B. Thickwire can be used with hubs and thinwire cannot.

   C. Thickwire can be used for longer distances than thinwire.

   D. Thickwire does not require the use of multi-port repeaters, and thinwire does.

**40.** Michael is a new employee who will be doing a lot of telecommuting, so he needs access to RAS. How can you give Michael the access that he needs? (Choose all that apply.)

   A. Use the User Manager for Domains.

   B. Use the Server Manager.

   C. Use Remote Access Admin.

   D. Use the Network Client Administrator.

**41.** Basic Rate ISDN is defined as _____

   A. two 64 Kbps D channels and one 16 Kbps B channel

   B. one 64 Kbps B channel and two 16 Kbps D channels

   C. two 64 Kbps B channels and one 16 Kbps D channel

   D. one 64 Kbps D channel and two 16 Kbps B channels

**42.** What type of network transfers data in small and fixed-length portions?

   A. Cell switched

   B. Packet switched

   C. Circuit switched

   D. Trunk switched

**43.** Jerry is trying to set up RAS on the company's Windows NT server, but he is encountering problems. He has inserted the CD-ROM and tried to go to Add/Remove programs, but he cannot find it. In desperation, he asks you to help him install RAS. How do you help Jerry get RAS installed?

   A. You run WINNT.EXE with the /RAS switch from a command prompt.

   B. You click the Modems icon in Control Panel.

   C. You run WINNT32.EXE with the /RAS switch from a command prompt.

   D. You click the Network icon in Control Panel.

**44.** What type of security is shown in the next illustration?

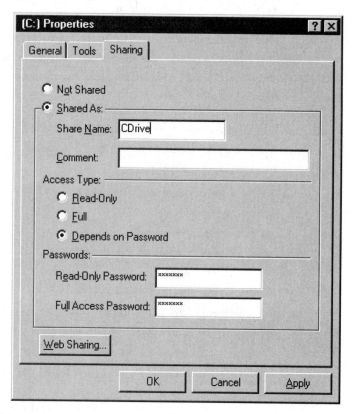

A. File-Level

B. User-Level

C. Share-Level

D. Drive-Level

**45.** Magic Monuments Inc. has suffered a loss of their entire database in the past. They lost an enormous amount of information, as they had not performed any backups. They hire you to implement software fault tolerance on their Windows NT database server to include the boot partition. What level of RAID are you going to use?

A. RAID 0

B. RAID 1

C. RAID 5

D. RAID 6

**46.** How can you determine who was the last person to open a file on your Windows NT server?

A. Enable auditing on the file.

B. Check the System Log on Event Viewer.

C. Enable properties on the file.

D. Check the Application Log on Event Viewer.

**47.** What type of tape backup backs up only files that have been created or changed since the last full backup and marks them as being backed up?

A. Differential

B. Incremental

C. Normal

D. Daily

**48.** The 10BaseT TCP/IP network at Plastic Flower Garden Industries consists of 14 routers and 23 hubs, which are located throughout the ten-story headquarters building. Looking over the Helpdesk log for the last several days, you see that users on the third floor have twice as many trouble calls as users on all the other floors combined. The majority of the calls are from users hooked to hub 12. Suspicious, you decide to monitor that hub for unusual activity. What tool do you use to monitor the hub?

A. MIPS

B. SMTP

C. MARS

D. SNMP

**49.** What program provides an interface to management information bases?

    A. SNMP

    B. Agent

    C. MIBS

    D. Probe

**50.** Last week you received a new dual-CPU server for use on the company network. You have been using Performance Monitor on it so that you can establish a baseline. However, you only have statistics for one of the processors. What do you need to do to get statistics for the other processor?

    A. Add another processor object to the chart.

    B. Add another processor counter to the chart.

    C. Add another processor report to the chart.

    D. Add another processor instance to the chart.

**51.** You have been having problems with one of your database servers locking up, because the processor usage is extremely high. You want to know when the server is starting to have problems. How can you do it?

    A. Set an alert threshold from Server Manager.

    B. Set an alert threshold from Disk Administrator.

    C. Set an alert threshold from Network Monitor.

    D. Set an alert threshold from Performance Monitor.

**52.** What method should you use when troubleshooting network problems?

    A. Logical

    B. Random

    C. Illogical

    D. Haphazard

**53.** You work for the Network Gurus Consulting Firm and are on location troubleshooting the network of a client. Their connection to the Internet seems to be working properly for all of the Windows NT servers, with the exception of one. You have isolated the symptoms of the problem to that one Windows NT server, but you are not sure how to fix the problem. What can you do?

A. Search the Knowledge Base at the Microsoft web site.

B. Format the server and reload the software.

C. Add more physical memory.

D. Change the size of the pagefile.

**54.** Why should you label the cables used on your network?

A. To help with troubleshooting.

B. To justify the budget for additional cables.

C. To help in monitoring the data that passes through them.

D. To help segment the network.

**55.** Your have noticed that the performance on the network has become very poor for the last two weeks. What could cause the network to perform so poorly? (Choose all that apply.)

A. Excessive collisions

B. Incorrectly operating hub

C. Excessive network traffic

D. Incorrectly configured UPS

**56.** General Jalopy Inc. has been very happy having their network connected to the Internet.... until last night. It seems as though someone accessed their network via the Internet and sabotaged one of their servers. The vice president has been fired, and they are considering firing you, since you put the network in place. What actions can you take to prevent this from happening in the future?

A. Implement a firewall.

B. Implement a backbone.

C. Implement a smokescreen.

D. Implement a securitybone.

**57.** What tool was used prior to the arrival of the web browser for accessing documents on the Internet?

A. Archie

B. Squirrel

C. Jughead

D. Gopher

**58.** Jane is a graphics designer who runs a home-based business. She is constantly using e-mail to send graphics designs to her clients for their review. Lately she has become very frustrated because it seems as though her business phone line is constantly in use sending the multi-megabyte graphics files. What can she use to transfer the information faster?

A. FTP

B. WWW

C. SMTP

D. ISDN

# Test Yourself: Networking Essentials Practice Exam I Answers

To pass the Networking Essentials exam, you need to answer 45 questions correctly. We've provided explanations of the answers so you can review the questions you missed. How did you do?

1. **A.** The proposed solution produces the required result, and produces both of the optional desired results. The best way to improve access to a large database such as those found in companies is to implement a client/server solution such as SQL Server.

2. **repeater.** A repeater is used to regenerate the signal. Computers on either side of the repeater can communicate with each other as long as they use the same protocol and transmission method.

3. **Routing tables.** Routing tables are used by both bridges and routers to store address information. More address information is stored in the routing table of a router than that of a bridge, such as the address of routers on other networks and the possible paths to those routers.

4. **C.** Using a repeater is the cheapest method of allowing data to pass from Network #1 to Network #2 as shown in the next illustration. Other methods of connecting the two networks (such as using a bridge or router) are available but they are more expensive options.

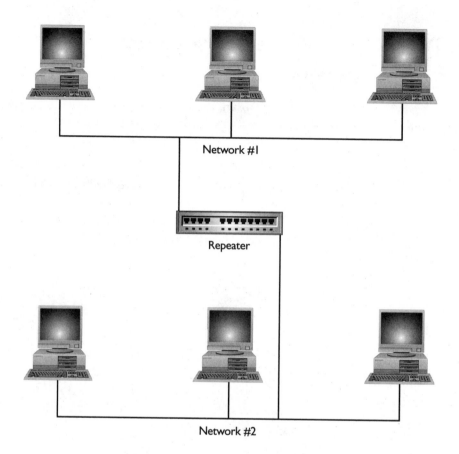

Network #1

Repeater

Network #2

**5. D.** Adding routers would allow the Ethernet and token ring networks to share data. They use the addressing information provided at the network level to join the many networks together to form an internetwork.

**6. C.** The Session layer is the layer missing from the illustration. The Session layer manages dialogs between computers. It does this by establishing, managing, and terminating communications between the two computers. There are three types of dialogs that the Session layer uses: Simplex, Half-Duplex, and Full Duplex.

**7. D.** The Application layer is responsible for advertising available services to the network. The Application layer also provides services on network, such as file/print sharing and e-mail.

8. **C.** Your network will slow down if you switch to the CSMA/CA access method. This is because CSMA/CA is a slower access method than CSMA/CD. It is slower because it broadcasts the intent to transmit data, which in turn increases the amount of traffic on the cable.

9. **B.** The SMB and NCP protocol reside at the Presentation layer of the OSI model. SMB and NCP are protocols that are implemented in redirectors (software that intercepts requests, formats them according to the protocol in use, and passes the message to a lower-level protocol for delivery). Redirectors also intercept incoming messages, process the instructions, and pass them to the correct upper-level application for additional processing.

10. **A.** Installing AppleTalk on the Windows NT servers will allow the two networks to communicate. Services for Macintosh allows the Windows NT server to become available to Macintosh clients.

11. **A.** Binding is the process of connecting the protocol stack to the network interface card. If the protocol stack is not bound to the network interface card, the protocol cannot be used. More than one protocol can be bound to the network interface card. The binding order is the order in which protocols are bound to the network interface card.

12. **D.** The illustration shows an Ethernet network that uses unshielded twisted pair. The three types of cable normally used for Ethernet networks are thin coaxial, thick coaxial, and unshielded twisted pair. Thin and thick coaxial are used for bus topologies, and unshielded twisted pair is used for the star topology.

13. **B.** The maximum speed for ArcNet is 2.5 Mbps. Not only is ArcNet slow by today's standards, but ArcNet uses a rare concept of manually configuring the network cards to act as node addresses (1–255) that are traveled in numerical order. The next node number may be at the farthest reaches of the network, and the frame has to travel to this station because it is the next numerical node number.

**14. B.** Installing a token ring network meets the required result of networking the 17 computers in the administrative office. The token ring network also provides the optional result of fast access, since it operates at 16 Mbps. However, the other optional result is not met, since it costs more to install a token ring network than it does to install an Ethernet network.

**15. C.** 100VG-AnyLAN is defined by IEEE standard 802.12. It differs from Fast Ethernet because it uses a different access method. The access method is called Demand Priority, and it uses the hubs to control the access to the stations. The hub acts as a traffic signal to determine who has access to the network.

**16. B.** A set of setup floppy disks for Windows NT Server can be created by using the /OX switch with WINNT.EXE. This may be necessary if the disks are lost or if a floppy disk goes bad. Using the /OX switch will only create the floppy disks and not actually install Windows NT Server.

**17. D.** To enhance the security of your network, you can set an age limit for passwords from within the Account Policy dialog box located in the User Manager for Domains. Some of the other items you can control in the Account Policy dialog box include minimum password length, and whether or not an account will be locked out after a number of bad logon attempts.

**18. C.** The network is sluggish because all the MS-DOS Network Client 3.0 systems have to send broadcasts to locate the systems they need to communicate with. This is because the MS-DOS Network Client 3.0 systems cannot use WINS, and they have no LMHOSTS file. Placing a correct LMHOSTS file on the MS-DOS Network Client 3.0 system will improve network performance.

**19. A.** Requiring a minimum password length would increase security for the domain. Currently, users are allowed to have blank passwords, which means that anyone walking by could log on and possibly have access to confidential patient records.

**20.** **C.** Implementing group scheduling would allow each user to keep his or her own schedule and store it on a server. Any other user on the server who has the appropriate permissions can then view that schedule. The boss then has the ability to suggest ideal times to schedule meetings with groups of people, because he can see when they have other commitments.

**21.** **A.** Banyan VINES is not an example of a groupware product. Banyan VINES is a Network Operating System. Groupware is a suite of software products that usually includes an e-mail client, a scheduling product, and a document collaboration system.

**22.** **B.** Implement digital signatures on your mail system so that the employees will know for sure that the e-mail that gives them the day off actually comes from the boss, and not from somebody that just wants to take off from work for a day.

**23.** **A.** The computers shown in the illustration are using a client/server application. The greatest advantage of using a client/server architecture is that many clients can access the data on the server at the same time, whereas in a more traditional architecture, only one user can work on the data at one time.

**24.** **D.** SNA (Systems Network Architecture) is a set of network protocols developed by IBM. Servers running SNA gateway software, such as Microsoft SNA Server, can act as the gateway between the local area network and the AS/400 midrange computer. The Microsoft SNA Server software only runs on Windows NT Servers.

**25.** **B.** To access the UNIX system he needs to have a Network File System (NFS) client installed. NFS provides access to shared files through an interface called the Virtual File System (VFS) that runs on top of TCP/IP. Users can manipulate shared files as if they are stored locally on their own hard disk.

26. **B.** AppleShare is the Apple file server software that provides file sharing. The client-side software is included with every copy of Finder and System Software, version 6.0 or greater. There is also an AppleShare Print Server, which is a server-based print spooler.

27. **B.** The Windows 95 client shown in the illustration can only connect to Windows NT servers. The client software is only one of the items necessary for connecting to a server. There has to be an appropriate protocol available for the client software to utilize. The TCP/IP protocol is available for the Client for Microsoft Networks to use but there is no protocol available for the Client for NetWare Networks to use. The Client for NetWare Networks uses an IPX/SPX compatible protocol to connect to Novell NetWare servers.

28. **B, D.** The problem in the scenario can be solved by one of two methods. You can connect the two secretaries' computers together using one wire, but it must be a crossover cable. A crossover cable is different from a normal cable, as the transmit and receive pairs are reversed. This would allow the two machines to communicate with each other. Another solution would be to buy a small hub and plug each secretary's computer into it.

29. **C.** Mike needs to use T connectors and terminators. Even when connecting two computers using thinnet, T-connectors and terminators are required to eliminate signal bounce from the cable.

30. **D.** The maximum distance for thinnet cable media is approximately 185 meters, or 607 feet. The signal starts to suffer from attenuation when this distance is reached.

31. **A.** Unshielded twisted pair cabling is the least expensive medium, but it requires an additional component that coaxial cable does not need: a hub. Each pair of wires contained in the cable is twisted together. The typical twisted-pair cable for network use contains three or four pairs of wires. The twists in the wires help shield against electromagnetic interference.

**32.** **A, C, D.** A hardware conflict occurs when two devices in a computer have been assigned the same resource settings. The I/O base address, DMA, or IRQ are causing a hardware conflict with another device in Nina's system. Before installing the network interface card, Nina should have checked the resource allocations, and chosen settings that were not already in use.

**33.** **B.** The Media Access Control address is located in the network adapter. It is built into the card by the manufacturer and includes portions that identify the brand, as well as uniquely identifying the card itself.

**34.** **D.** Since the cards cannot be replaced, you can add a 10BaseT external transceiver to the AUI port so they can be utilized. An AUI connector allows a network card to be used with multiple types of media. A common implementation is to use this configuration for an Ethernet card that can be attached to twisted pair, thickwire, or thinwire coax by changing the external transceiver type.

**35.** **C.** The card shown in the illustration is a 32-bit card that fits in a PCI data bus. The Peripheral Component Interconnect was first used for video adapter cards to increase their speed in graphics rendering. It has since been adopted for use by devices that need high throughput, such as disk controllers and network interface cards. This is the data bus preferred for network interface cards in high-capacity servers today.

**36.** **C.** Routers operate by using the IP address to calculate if the packet should be routed. Since the IP address is needed, routers function from the Network layer of the OSI model. Brouters also function from this level of the OSI model.

**37.** **D.** The proposed solution does not meet the required result, because passive hubs only pass data through, they do not repeat the data. An active hub provides the same functionality as a passive hub, except that it does repeat the data. By using active hubs, you can increase the length of your network.

It is important to remember that UTP cable can be run a maximum of 100 meters. With an active hub, you can run UTP cable 100 meters on each side of the hub. Using active hubs you could reach the fifth floor and successfully expand the network.

**38.** D. Switches automatically determine the MAC addresses of the devices connected to each port of the switch. The switch then examines each packet it receives to find its destination MAC address. The switch then determines which port the packet is destined for, and sends it out to that port only.

**39.** D. Split the network into two networks by replacing the hub in the central wiring closet with a bridge. Traffic will be reduced, because the bridge will filter local traffic between the two networks, and copies all other traffic to the other side of the bridge.

**40.** B. The proposed solution meets the required result because it implements a WAN connection between all three locations. It also meets one of the desired results: If any one of the links fails, communication can still continue because of the redundancy in the T-1 links. For example, if the link between Boston and Louisville fails, then the connection can be made by going through Rapid City. The other desired result is not met, because T-1 operates at DS-1 and not DS-3.

**41.** B. ATM should be used, since the CEO plans on using it daily for meetings with the branch managers. ATM uses much less overhead than other available technologies, and can transmit voice, video, or data easily over the higher speeds available to it.

**42.** B. Modems are data communications equipment (DCE) that takes a digital signal from a data terminal equipment (DTE), such as a computer, and converts it into a analog signal so that it can be sent over the wire. Modems also take the analog signal from the wire and convert it back into a digital signal to be sent to the DTE.

**43. D.** The network was designed for redundancy, since there is a T1 link going to each site. Houston and Boise can route traffic to each other by going through the T1 connections that they have to Bangor.

**44. D.** Hurricane Hovering has most of the items necessary to have "constant uptime" but they forgot to add any UPS to their plan. If the power goes out, the other steps they have in their "constant uptime" plan will be for nothing. They need to add enough uninterruptible power supplies of sufficient size to keep their network running for a period of time they deem necessary.

**45. B.** The implementation and administration of Windows NT server disk fault tolerance is done using the Disk Administrator tool. The Disk Administrator tool can also be used to change drive letters, format drives, and other disk related items.

**46. D.** The proposed solution does not meet the required result. While user-level security does provide security for a Windows NT-based network, it is not available for Windows 95-only networks. The only security that Marigold Cleaners could implement is share-level security.

**47. D.** RAID 0, also referred to as disk striping, is a technique by which data is written in stripes across a volume that has been created from areas of free space. These areas are all the same size and are spread over an array of 3 to 32 disks. The strip size for Windows NT is 64KB. A stripe set does not provide any fault tolerance, because there is no redundancy. Therefore, if a disk fails, there can be no recovery.

**48. A.** Use Network Monitor from the suspect server to watch the traffic between it and Jerry's computer. After starting the Network Monitor, have Jerry try the function that he says is not working correctly. Analyze the data applicable to his machine and the server to see if any abnormalities exist.

**49.** **A.** Care must be taken in developing your security strategy, because if your administrative plan goes to the extreme on security, then your users may be discouraged from using the network as they become frustrated trying to access their own files. That is exactly what happened in this situation. The users got extremely frustrated trying to access files that they should have been able to open, so they starting shying away from using the network.

**50.** **B.** You configure the computer to send alerts from the Server Manager. Alerts are generated by Windows NT, and relate to server and resource use. They are used to notify you of problems such as security, access, and directory replication problems. The list of alerts is predetermined by Windows NT.

**51.** **C.** If a standard naming convention was in use, then it might be easier to track down the missing computer system. It would at least give a good point to start looking. For example, if you used a building-room number convention, and the missing computer was named 4116-229B, then you would know to go to building 4116 and look in room 229B. If the computer isn't there, then maybe someone in that office would know where it was moved to.

**52.** **A.** You should tell Clara to restart her computer. Restarting affected hardware is probably the most common solution to network outages. Speaking from experience, I have encountered numerous "network outages" can be fixed simply by rebooting Windows 95 clients.

**53.** **A, C, D.** Cable testers, digital volt meters, and time domain reflectometers can all be used to check the status of your network cables. Normally your situation dictates which tool you will use.

**54.** **B.** To see the percent of network utilization to the Windows NT server, the administrator should run Network Monitor. It will show the percent of network utilization in real time. Network Monitor also shows other statistics that may be valuable to the system administrator, such as the frames per second and the bytes per second that are on the network.

55. **B**. The time domain reflectometer would provide the most help in troubleshooting the network problem. The TDR would let you know how far from your location a break in the cable occurs. Knowing the location of the break helps to speed up repair of the network.

56. **C**. The correct top level domain for General Jalopy Inc. is .COM. The .MIL domain is restricted to actual military installations such as KEESLER.AF.MIL, which is the domain for Keesler Air Force Base. The .COM domain is for commercial institutions.

57. **B**. The Domain Name Service (DNS) is used to resolve "friendly" names that are easily understood by humans, such as www.syngress.com, into the 32-bit IP address, such as 146.115.28.75, that computers on the Internet use to communicate with each other. Imagine trying to remember the IP addresses for several of the sites you regularly visit. It's much easier to remember www.microsoft.com and www.yahoo.com than 207.68.156.52 and 204.71.200.75!

58. **B**. The application in the illustration is being used to access the ALT. COMEDY.IMPROVISATION newsgroup. The application can also be used to access e-mail if the user so desires.

# Test Yourself: Networking Essentials Practice Exam 2 Answers

To pass the Networking Essentials exam, you need to answer 45 questions correctly. We've provided explanations of the answers so you can review the questions you missed. How did you do?

1. **B.** The topology shown in the illustration is the bus topology. It is easily identified by the single cable that connects all the computers to the network.

2. **C.** Every computer on the network segment has to process any broadcast message that it receives to see if the data is meant for it. If a high number of broadcasts are placed on the network, the machines spend a lot of time processing the broadcasts and not doing any other network-related functions.

3. **C.** Melissa cannot use the print server because she does not have the correct permissions. The print server checks the Access Control List (ACL) prior to allowing anyone to use the resource. If an individual is not in the ACL, they are not allowed to use the print server.

4. **B.** The Data Link layer is responsible for turning raw data into frames to send to higher layers. It also takes frames from the higher layers and breaks them down into raw data to be transmitted. The Data Link layer is also responsible for transmitting frames from computer to computer. Once it sends a frame, it waits for an acknowledgement that the frame was received.

5. **A, B, D.** The distance from computers 1,2, and 4 exceed the maximum distance allowed by 10BaseT of 328 feet or 100 meters. Since 10Base5 supports distances up to 1640 feet or 500 meters, it should be considered for hooking the three computers to the network.

**6.** D. Gateways are used to connect networks using different protocols so that information can be passed from one network to another network. Gateways function at the Network layer of the OSI model and are usually servers.

**7.** C. The bridge operates at the Data Link layer of the OSI model. Bridges join two or more network segments together, forming a larger individual network. They function similarly to a repeater, except a bridge looks to see whether data it receives is destined for the same segment or another connected segment. If the data is destined for a computer on the same segment, the bridge does not pass it along. If that data is going to a computer on another segment, the bridge sends it along.

**8.** A. The header is at the beginning of a packet. The header section of a packet contains the routing information. This information includes the source and destination of the packet. The header also contains the number of the packet, which is generated when the packet is created.

**9.** A. By using NetBEUI as the transport protocol, each user will be able to share files with the other users. The optional results are met because NetBEUI is already available from within Windows 95, and it requires minimal configuration.

**10.** B. TCP/IP must be installed on the computers so that they can communicate with the Internet. TCP/IP is the protocol that the Internet is built upon. The computers cannot communicate on the Internet unless they are running the protocol.

**11.** B. Server Message Block (SMB) is used for sharing files on Windows NT-based networks. Network File System (NFS) was created by Sun Microsystems for use on SOLARIS, Sun's version of UNIX. NFS is frequently used in the UNIX world for file sharing.

**12.  B.** Thicknet networks are also known as 10Base5. This signifies that thicknet uses a 10 Mbps transmission rate over baseband, and can be used for a maximum cable length of 500 meters.

**13.  A.** The current ring can handle the expansion of an additional three computers, because it uses unshielded twisted pair. Normally, shielded twisted-pair (STP) cabling is used with token ring networks, although unshielded twisted-pair (UTP) can be used. STP allows 260 computers on the same ring, whereas UTP allows 72 computers on the same ring.

**14.  D.** Beaconing refers to a frame that is sent around the network when a serious network problem occurs. This frame is sent to the nearest active upstream neighbor until the frame stops. When the frame stops, beaconing determines that the next upstream neighbor has a problem. In the illustration, the beaconing frame stopped at system 3 and the nearest upstream neighbor is system 4, so system 4 is causing the network problem.

**15.  C.** The network will not work if each end of the cable is not terminated with a 50 ohm terminator. The network would still function if the T-connector were not installed to a network interface card, as long as the coaxial cable was still connected to each end of the T-connector so that the path is not broken.

**16.  D.** The maximum number of characters there can be in a NetBIOS computer name is 15. It is also a good idea to limit computer names to alphanumeric characters. Using letters and numbers keeps the naming scheme simple and doesn't cause potential problems using miscellaneous symbols.

**17.  B.** All client computers need to know the address of the WINS server so that they can have it resolve computer names to IP addresses. If they cannot contact the WINS server, they will not be able to resolve the computer name to an IP address, which means they cannot communicate with another computer except for sending broadcasts trying to find the computer.

**18.** **A, B, C, D.** The default user rights for the Server Operators group are: back up files and directories, log on locally, restore files and directories, and shut down the system. If you have a single Server Operator who needs different user rights, you will need to add that person to his account manually, or you can add different user rights to all members of your Server Operator group, if needed.

**19.** **A.** With Windows NT Server 4.0, TCP/IP is installed by default. Other options include NetBEUI and the IPX/SPX-compatible transport. Your network design will dictate which protocol it is necessary to install on Windows NT Server 4.0.

**20.** **B.** The Registry has references to a drive letter for the application that no longer exists because of the CD-ROM installation. It is extremely important that you use universal naming conventions (UNC) to point to your application. A UNC, so long as the share is not deleted, is not dependent on a drive letter, and is much more stable.

**21.** **D.** Since the telemarketers need to access the same database of products simultaneously, they should use a client/server database such as Microsoft SQL Server, Oracle, or Sybase.

**22.** **A.** The primary advantage of a client/server architecture is its capability to distribute processing to both the server and client. One server can service many clients (even thousands). A well-designed client/server system is much more efficient than a more traditional architecture.

**23.** **C.** Install Office 97 on your server. Office 97 is a network-aware application that only installs the operating system shared components that are required by the application, plus per-user information and preferences on the client system. The advantage of this type of network application is that, instead of having to store 100+MB of files on their systems, users only have to store a few megabytes. There is no distributed processing like a client/server application, but when they load the application, they load it into their local computer's memory.

**24.** **A.** The Windows 95 computer must use multiple redirectors in order to access both the Windows NT server and the Novell NetWare server. Often, the network environment is such that multiple redirectors are required to fully utilize all of the resources available to users.

**25.** **B, C.** Rob's machine does not have the Client for NetWare Networks installed nor does he have the correct protocol installed to communicate with the Novell NetWare server. The Novell NetWare server cannot communicate with any system that has the NetBEUI protocol, because the NetBEUI protocol is proprietary to Microsoft networks. The Client for Microsoft Networks does not work with Novell NetWare servers, only Microsoft based servers.

**26.** **B.** Windows NT 4.0 workstations with Client Services for NetWare (CSNW) installed can authenticate to NDS trees and take advantage of NDS for browsing and managing NetWare networks. The NDS tree and context for authentication can be specified in the CSNW dialog box.

**27.** **B.** An intelligent terminal is a standalone device that contains main memory and a CPU. Other types of terminals are smart terminals and dumb terminals. A smart terminal contains some processing power, but not as much as an intelligent terminal. A dumb terminal has no processing capabilities. It relies entirely on the main computer's processor.

**28.** **B.** Replace the existing cable with Type 8 cable. Type 8 cable is housed in a flat jacket for use under carpets. Using Type 8 cable should alleviate the lawyers' concern.

**29.** A. Baseband transmission uses digital signaling. A baseband network uses only one channel on the cable to support digital transmission. Signals flow in the form of discrete pulses of electricity or light. With baseband transmission, the entire capacity of the communication channel is used to transmit a single data signal.

**30.** A. The diameter of a thicknet cable is about ½ inch and is harder to work with than a thinnet cable. A transceiver is often connected directly to thicknet cable by a connector known as a piercing tap.

**31.** C. They have too many segments populated. 10Base2 networks are subject to the 3-4-5 rule of repeater placement: The network can only have five segments connected; it can only use four repeaters; and of the five segments, only three segments can be populated with users (the other two must be inter-repeater links).

**32.** C. The network adapter is attached to the computer via a parallel data bus, such as an ISA or PCI bus. These parallel buses move data quickly between devices internal to the system. Network transmission, on the other hand, relies on a serial data stream in order to transmit messages. Therefore, all data sent from the network interface card must be transformed into a serial data stream before transmission.

**33.** C. To see the statistics for the network interface cards in the Windows 95 systems, use Device Manager. To get to the Device Manager, open Control Panel, select the System applet and select the Device Manager. All the devices on the system are displayed by category when expanded. Double-clicking any device opens property pages that show any resource conflicts and the current resource settings.

**34.** C. The mechanical connectors that join the cable are called ST connectors and are designed to pass light seamlessly across the joined fiber segments.

Fiber optic adapters have two connectors, one for each incoming and outgoing fiber cable.

**35. C.** A remote boot PROM can be added to a network adapter to allow the diskless workstations to boot using files stored on the network. An adapter capable of doing remote boot has an empty socket that can be populated with a boot PROM. Once installed and configured, this boot PROM directs the system to the network location of the boot files.

**36. B.** Switches automatically determine the MAC addresses of the devices connected to each port of the switch. The switch then examines each packet it receives to find its destination MAC address. The switch then determines which port the packet is destined for and sends it out to that port only. The other ports are oblivious to the data transfer.

**37. B.** The router is not set up to pass Dynamic Host Configuration Protocol broadcast messages. The network is set up to use DHCP, and the clients on the second floor cannot get an IP address, so they cannot log onto the network. The clients on the first floor don't have a problem because they are on the same side of the router as the Windows NT server that is the DHCP server. To resolve the situation, configure the router to pass DHCP messages. If the router is not able to pass DHCP messages, place a Windows NT computer on the second floor to act as a DHCP relay agent.

**38. B.** A switch resides within the Data Link layer of the OSI model, because it operates using the MAC address in the data packets. Switches know the destination MAC address, allowing the packet to use the direct route within the switch from the source port to the port that the device with the destination MAC address is connected to.

**39. C.** Thickwire can be used for longer distances than thinwire can. Thickwire has a maximum range of 500 meters. Thinwire has a maximum range of 185 meters.

**40.** **A, C.** You can give Michael the access he needs using either the User Manager for Domains or the Remote Access Admin tool. If you use the User Manager for Domains, then you would double-click his user account and then use the Dialin button to give him access to RAS.

**41.** **C.** Basic rate ISDN is defined as two 64 Kbps B channels and one 16 Kbps D channel. The Basic Rate is the most common configuration for end users connecting to a RAS or Internet connection.

**42.** **A.** Cell switched networks transfer data in small, fixed-length portions called cells. Due to the small size, cells do not need to be transferred to buffers or hard disks between the incoming port of a router and the outgoing port. Instead they remain in memory, which has much faster access.

**43.** **D.** Jerry was almost in the right area. At least he had opened the Control Panel. He just selected the wrong applet. Because Windows NT RAS provides network services, adding or configuring RAS must be done from the Network icon in Control Panel.

**44.** **C.** The illustration is an example of Share-Level security. Depending on the password used to access the CDrive share, the user will either have Read-Only or Full Access to the share.

**45.** **B.** Since Magic Monuments wants to provide fault tolerance for the boot partition, you have to use RAID 1, disk mirroring. RAID 0 does not provide fault tolerance, RAID 5 does provide fault tolerance but it cannot be used with system or boot partitions, and RAID 6 is not available from the Windows NT software.

**46.** **A.** To see who was the last person to open a file, you need to enable auditing on the file. An audit trail enhances security by letting administrators keep track of selected server resources. Any network resource, such as a directory, individual file, or print queue can be designated for auditing.

47. **B.** An incremental backup backs up only files that have been created or changed since the last full or incremental backup, and marks them as being backed up. To restore files when both full and incremental methods were used, start with the last full backup and then work through all the incremental tapes.

48. **D.** Simple Network Management Protocol (SNMP) is a tool that can be used to monitor several network components, including hubs, routers, bridges, and network interface cards. Depending on the MIB, devices can report back statistics such as packet errors and the total number of packets the device has processed.

49. **B.** An agent is an SNMP program that is installed on each managed device in a network. The agent program provides an interface to the management information bases (MIBs) installed on the device. SNMP management programs send requests to the devices on the network. The agent program on the device processes the request by retrieving information from the MIBs on the device. The agent then sends the information that was requested back to the SNMP management program that originated the request.

50. **D.** You need to add another processor instance to the chart. An instance is a single occurrence of a counter activity. For example, if you were using the %Processor Time counter of the processor object, you would need to have two instances of it to measure both processors that are in the system.

51. **D.** You can use Performance Monitor to trigger an alert when a threshold has been reached. In this case, you would want to set a threshold on the %Processor Time counter so you could be notified whenever the CPU usage started going high.

**52.** **A.** When troubleshooting network problems, it is important to follow a logical troubleshooting methodology. Look at the "big picture" and don't try to fix more than one problem at a time. All that will do is confuse an already confusing situation.

**53.** **A.** Since the client's connection to the Internet was working you should go out to the Microsoft web site and search the Knowledge Base to see if anyone else has had a similar problem. Even if the problem is really strange, it pays to check the Knowledge Base. In one case, Computer X had SCSI card Y in it. Computer X had all sorts of strange lockups, so the Knowledge Base was searched for the brand of computer as well as the name of the SCSI card. Lo and behold, there was a KB article on that very problem. It told me exactly what was needed to fix the problem.

**54.** **A.** Network cables need to be labeled to help with troubleshooting. If you don't know the destination of the cables leaving your hub, it can become very difficult trying to fix a problem. Imagine having to track a UTP cable that is 60 meters long through the ceilings of your building to see if it is the one you're looking for.

**55.** **A, B, C.** Poor network performance can be the result of many different things, including excessive collisions on the network, an incorrectly operating hub, or excessive network traffic.

**56.** **A.** To protect the network of General Jalopy Inc. you need to implement a firewall. Firewalls provide protection against users trying to access information on the local network from the Internet. Firewalls can be implemented in hardware or software. Hardware firewalls tend to be more expensive than software firewalls. Hardware firewalls are dedicated to that specific purpose, whereas software firewalls can be part of a Windows NT server, for example.

**57.** **D.** Before the technology of the Web browser, Gopher was the way to access documents on the Internet. Gopher provides the user a menu of item numbers that are selected by scrolling with arrow keys and pressing RETURN or ENTER to select an option. There are still Gopher sites on the Internet, but they are few and far between.

**58.** **D.** Jane should consider getting an ISDN line for her business. ISDN stands for Integrated Services Digital Network. ISDN takes the common analog phone line and upgrades it to a digital service. ISDN can operate at speeds up to 128 Kbps. This is nearly five times faster than today's analog connections.

# Test
# Yourself:
# Server in the
# Enterprise

*Q&A*

# Test Yourself: Server in the Enterprise Practice Exam 1

Before you call to register for the actual exam, take the following test and see how you make out. Set a timer for 90 minutes—the time you'll have to take the live Server in the Enterprise exam—and answer the following 50 questions in the time allotted. Once you're through, turn to the end of the module and check your score to see if you passed! Good luck!

1. You have two disk drives with one partition each on one disk controller. What can you use to increase the availability via software in Windows NT Server?

   A. Mirroring (RAID 1)
   B. Duplexing (RAID 1)
   C. Striping (RAID 0)
   D. Striping with parity (RAID 5)

2. Domain FARGO just set up a trust to domain UBETCHA. On a system in domain FARGO, a local group UPRINTSURE has been set up to control access to a certain printer. The user had added Domain Users to UPRINTSURE for print access (which has been working), but users from UBETCHA are unable to print to the printer. What still needs to be done to allow all users from UBETCHA to print?

   A. The UBETCHA\Domain Users group needs to be added to the FARGO\Domain Users group.
   B. The UBETCHA\Domain Users group needs to be added to the FARGO\UPRINTSURE group.
   C. The UBETCHA\Domain Users group needs to be added to the local UPRINTSURE group.
   D. UBETCHA needs to trust FARGO to be able to set up such access.

**3.** Which of the following are true about PDCs and BDCs?

   A. You should have two BDCs for every PDC in a domain.

   B. You must have a BDC for every domain.

   C. The number of PDCs in any domain model is equal to the total number of domains.

   D. You must have an active PDC in any domain.

**4.** Which of the following give you the ability to recover a file that was deleted accidentally? (Choose all that apply.)

   A. Disk mirroring

   B. Recycle Bin

   C. Tape backup

   D. NTFS UNDELETE utility

**5.** You are installing Windows NT Server, and reach the screen shown in the next illustration. It offers two licensing options. Which one will allow you to switch to the other option, should you decide to do so later?

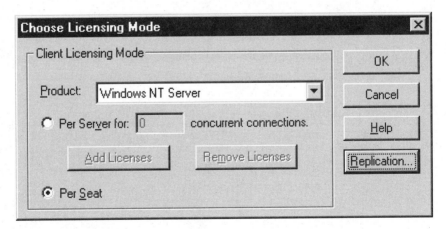

   A. Per Seat

   B. Per Server

   C. Both Per Seat and Per Server

   D. Neither Per Seat or Per Server

**6.** Which of the following are true about any replication export server?

A. It must be a PDC.

B. It must have a REPL$ share.

C. It's usually used to replicate logon scripts to domain controllers.

D. It's good for distributing copies of your databases for higher availability.

**7.** Stephen is using the master domain model on a LAN, and has 24 BDCs. Since these servers are only used for authentication, what parameters might he change to make sure the accounts database is as current as possible on all domain controllers? (Choose all that apply.)

A. Reduce Pulse

B. Increase PulseConcurrency

C. Increase Pulse

D. Increase Randomize

**8.** Peter knows a system crashed 30 minutes ago, but it still shows up in the Network Neighborhood. What is the problem, and how can he solve it?

A. This is normal; no action is required.

B. The domain isn't in synch; he must resynchronize the domain.

C. The Master Browser is hung; he must force an election.

D. The Master Browser is hung; he must reboot it.

**9.** In Windows NT terminology, what does the printing process look like?

A. Application to print queue to printer

B. Application to print device to print queue to printer

C. Application to printer to print device

D. Application to printer port to print queue to printer

**10.** Local groups in a domain may do which of the following? (Choose all that apply.)

A. Have local workstation users from another system in the domain as members.

B. Have domain users as members.

C. Belong to global groups.

D. Be used as a distribution list for mail.

E. Have global groups as members.

11. You are an account operator. Your company has hired ten people to help with a two-month project. These ten people will only be working for your company for two months, and they only need Read access to certain resources. Maximum security is your goal. Your best plan of action is to:

A. Rename a user account of any employee on leave and give the temps the password. When the employee comes back, the temps will no longer be working there, so security is not an issue.

B. Enable the Guest account and have the temps use that

C. Create a user account for each temp, setting each account to expire in two months. Then assign the accounts to the project's group, giving them full access to all resources.

D. Create a user account for each temp, setting each account to expire in two months. Then assign the accounts to a new group, Temps, granting this group the appropriate permissions to the resources they need.

12. ORT, Inc. has a marketing domain and a sales domain. Sales needs access to the Marketing printers, and Marketing needs access to Sales figures and forecasts, which are held in a shared directory on the Sales domain. Currently, no one trusts anyone. Which of the following needs to be done? (Choose all correct answers.)

A. Sales needs to trust the Marketing domain.

B. Marketing needs to trust the Sales domain.

C. Domain Admins in the Marketing domain must be added to the Administrators group on the Sales domain controller.

D. Sales\Domain Users needs to be added to the groups for printer access in the marketing domain.

E. Marketing\Domain Users needs to be added to the group allowed to access the share holding the sales figures and forecasts in the Sales domain.

13. Domain PETER trusts domain PAUL. Domain PAUL trusts domain MARY and domain PETER. Which of the following statements are true?

    A. Since PETER trusts PAUL, and PAUL trusts MARY, PETER trusts MARY.

    B. Users in domains PETER and MARY may log onto a system in domain PAUL.

    C. Users in domain PAUL may log onto a system in domain PETER.

    D. Users in domain MARY may log onto a system in domain PETER.

14. You have decided to set up a one-way trust between two domains. Which program will you use to define the relationship between these two domains?

    A. User Manager for Domains

    B. Server Manager

    C. Disk Administrator

    D. Services

15. Pete is running a network using NetBEUI. Which of the following can he use on his network?

    A. Router

    B. Bridge

    C. Switch

    D. Hub

16. You have configured your network to have IP addresses automatically assigned to host computers. You have decided that you would also like to have the Default Gateway, WINS Server, and DNS Server automatically assigned. Where must you go to configure these settings?

    A. DNS Server

    B. WINS Server

    C. Default Gateway

    D. DHCP Server

**17.** A recent merger with another company has added a number of Macintosh client computers to your Windows NT network. These new clients need to access and store files on a Windows NT server. Which file system must you use for this to happen?

    A. NTFS

    B. FAT

    C. FAT32

    D. HPFS

**18.** You have just connected your server to the Internet. Which of the following will you need to configure, if your ISP offers DHCP, and you haven't manually configured TCP/IP?

    A. IP address

    B. DNS tab

    C. Subnet Mask

    D. WINS

**19.** The subnet mask for a system you're looking at is 255.255.255.0. What is the maximum number of nodes on this subnet?

    A. 16

    B. 254

    C. 256

    D. 65536

**20.** Which utilities should you use to determine if a node is reachable? (Choose all that apply.)

    A. TELNET

    B. PING

    C. NETSTAT

    D. TRACERT

**21.** TCP/IP uses which protocol for logon, browsing, WINS name resolution, and DNS name resolution?

A. TCP

B. IP

C. UDP

D. NDP

**22.** You want to see which DNS servers are part of a particular domain. Which utility will you use to do this?

A. TRACERT

B. IPConfig

C. NSLOOKUP

D. DNSLOOKUP

**23.** Your network has obtained a pool of registered IP addresses, and you decide to give your PDC the lowest address of 199.128.244.0. What is the problem with this?

A. It is the broadcast address.

B. It is a reserved address for multicasting.

C. It is reserved for loopback operations.

D. It defines the entire network.

**24.** Pete is having problems setting up GSNW. He has installed the service on the Windows NT server, and the client side works fine. He can't set up any of the gateway services. What else does Pete need to do? (Choose all that apply.)

A. Create a group called NTGATEWAY on the NetWare server.

B. Create a user belonging to the NTGATEWAY group with Supervisor access.

C. Create a group called NWGATEWAY on the Windows NT server.

D. Create a user belonging to the NWGATEWAY group with Administrator access.

**25.** Which of the following cannot be migrated with Migration Tool for NetWare?

   A. Passwords

   B. Logon scripts

   C. Groups

   D. Files and Directories

**26.** Your network consists of 50 Windows NT workstations and three Windows NT servers. You are in the process of connecting this network to another that runs Novell NetWare. You have tried using the server as a gateway to the NetWare network, but it has been bogged down. What can you install on your workstations to connect to the NetWare network?

   A. GSNW

   B. CSNW

   C. FSNW

   D. DSNW

**27.** You are setting up a Windows NT server to use NWLink. You want to configure it to use the default frame type for a NetWare 4.*x* server. Which frame type will you choose?

   A. 802.2

   B. 802.3

   C. 802.5

   D. 802.3 SNAP

**28.** What best describes the difference between a bridge and a router?

   A. Routers can choose between different paths.

   B. Bridges can choose between different paths.

   C. Routers can only store information statically.

   D. Bridges only appear in Madison County.

**29.** You are connecting two segments that use different protocols. Which of the following would you use?

A. Router

B. Bridge

C. BOOTP Relay Agent

D. Gateway

**30.** You are using RIP on your network. A router goes down. How will the other routers handle this event?

A. They will attempt to deliver the packets using a protocol other than RIP.

B. They will attempt to deliver the packets using alternative routes.

C. They will return errors that the packets are undeliverable. Each segment will become isolated.

D. RIP will send a signal to the downed router to restart.

**31.** You have decided to use dynamic routing on a Windows NT Server 4.0 computer that is being used as a router. What must you do to add dynamic routing to your Windows NT server?

A. Nothing. Dynamic routing isn't available on Windows NT Server 4.0.

B. Install RIP. Dynamic routing is added when this is installed.

C. Use the ROUTE ADD command.

D. Use the ROUTE CONFIG command.

**32.** You have decided to install TCP/IP on a routed network. Which of the following must you supply?

A. IP address

B. Dynamic Router

C. Subnet mask

D. Default gateway

E. Bridge

**33.** You want to connect your laptop to a Windows NT server and transfer information between them. Unfortunately, the laptop isn't equipped with either a modem or a network adapter card. Which of the following will you need to complete this task? (Choose all that apply.)

   A. Null modem cable

   B. Nether modem cable

   C. RAS

   D. Notebook Monitor

**34.** You are having problems with RAS, and want to view communication information (initialization and response strings) between RAS and the modem. Which log contains this information?

   A. SYSTEM.LOG

   B. DEVICE.LOG

   C. SECURITY.LOG

   D. RAS.LOG

**35.** You decide to use Internet Explorer to access the Internet. The computer you are using is running RAS, which is set to receive incoming sessions. What will happen when you attempt to surf the Web?

   A. You won't be able to, because RAS can't dial out using SLIP.

   B. You won't be able to, because RAS can't dial out using PPP.

   C. You won't be able to, because RAS has locked the COM port.

   D. RAS will shut down and allow you to access the Internet.

**36.** You are having problems with RAS, and decide to view the DEVICE.LOG as part of your troubleshooting. Where is this log located on Windows NT Server?

   A. In the WINNT directory

   B. In the WINNT/SYSTEM directory

   C. In the WINNT/SYSTEM32 directory

   D. In the WINNT/SYSTEM32/RAS directory

37. You wish to allow users on the Internet to access files on your server with IIS. Which protocols can you use to allow users to transfer files from your system? (Choose all that apply.)

    A. FTP

    B. HTTP

    C. UUCP

    D. Gopher

38. DNS maps fully qualified domain names to what?

    A. MAC addresses

    B. IP addresses

    C. NIC addresses

    D. NDIS addresses

    E. IPX addresses

39. You have added two virtual servers to your original installation of IIS. How many IP addresses must you bind to the network adapter card?

    A. One

    B. Two

    C. Three

    D. One for each instance of IIS

40. When IIS is installed, it makes the guest account a member of which group?

    A. IUSER Guest

    B. User

    C. Domain User

    D. Domain Guest

41. You have installed IIS on your Windows NT server, and are now ready to start creating HTML documents that you will publish to your intranet. Where must you place these documents if they are to appear to browsers?

A. The WWW directory you specified during installation.

B. IIS root directory.

C. Your server's root directory.

D. The HTML root directory you specified during installation.

42. You want to view the current connections and the share names that are in use on the PDC. What application will allow you to do this? (Choose all that apply.)

A. Server Manager

B. Performance Monitor

C. Task Manager

D. NT Diagnostics

43. Your server is optimized as shown in the next illustration. This Windows NT server acts as a SQL server for numerous users across a WAN. What will you do to optimize this server?

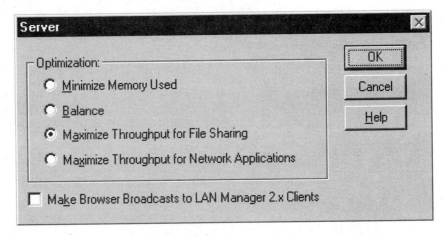

A. Change it to Minimize Memory used.

B. Change it to Balance.

C. Change it to Maximize Throughput for Network Applications.

D. Nothing. The server has the proper optimization settings.

44. You want to change the foreground application's performance boost to a value of 10 using the System Properties tab, shown in the next illustration.

Currently, its value is normal. What will you do to make the foreground application have this thread priority level?

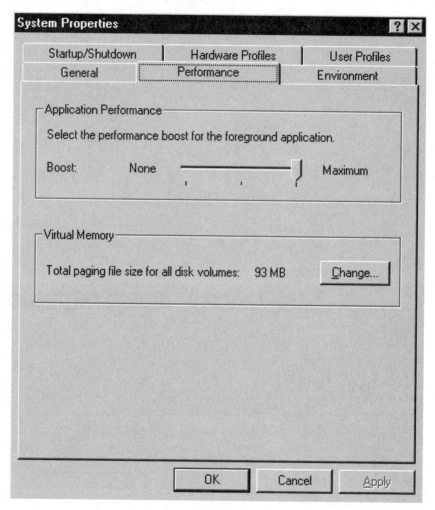

A. Move the slider bar to None.

B. Move the slider bar to the middle.

C. Leave the slider bar where it is, at Maximum.

D. Thread priority levels cannot be changed this way.

**45.** Your PDC has 50MB of RAM. What size pagefile should be created?

A. 50MB

B. 62MB

C. 32MB

D. 16MB

46. You are using disk duplexing, and one of two disks in the set fails. You check the disks and find that they are functional. What will you do?

A. Break the mirrored set, and then create a new mirrored set.

B. Replace the failed controller, break the mirrored set, and create a new mirrored set.

C. Replace the failed disk, break the mirrored set, and then create a new mirrored set.

D. Replace the failed controller.

47. You have just booted up Windows NT Server. What are the four phases of a successful boot process?

A. Initial, load, kernel, and logon

B. Initial, kernel, logon, and load

C. Boot, initial, kernel, and load

D. Initial, boot, kernel, and logon

48. You want to create a Windows NT boot disk. After formatting a floppy disk, which files should you copy onto the disk? (Choose all that apply.)

A. NTLDR, BOOT.INI

B. NTLDR, NTDETECT.COM, IO.SYS, , BOOT.INI, and (if it exists) NTBOOTY.SYS

C. NTLDR, NTDETECT.COM, BOOT.INI, and (if it exists) BOOTSEC.DOS or NTBOOTDD.SYS

D. NTLDR, NTDETECT.COM, COMMAND.COM, and (if it exists) BOOTSEC.DOS

**49.** You are having difficulty booting, and suspect a driver is causing problems during the boot process. What can you do to view the names of the drivers as they are being loaded?

A. Add the /SOS switch to the Windows NT entry in the BOOT.INI file.

B. Add the /S switch to the Windows NT entry in the BOOT.INI file.

C. Delete the BOOT.INI. This will cause a step-by-step load, which will display the driver names.

D. Create a batch file that loads the BOOT.INI file, and will list each driver as it loads.

**50.** Which of the following logs can Event Viewer display? (Choose all that apply.)

A. SYSTEM.LOG

B. SECURITY.LOG

C. APPLICATION.LOG

D. PERSONAL.LOG

# Test Yourself: Server in the Enterprise Practice Exam 2

Before you call to register for the actual exam, take the following test and see how you make out. Set a timer for 90 minutes—the time you'll have to take the live Server in the Enterprise exam—and answer the following 50 questions in the time allotted. Once you're through, turn to the end of the module and check your score to see if you passed! Good luck!

1. Stan wants to create the biggest RAID 5 partition that he can. He has six disks with the following contiguous free space on each: 100MB, 120MB, 200MB, 240MB, 280MB, and 350MB. What will the size of the partition be?

   A. 600MB with 500MB usable space

   B. 600MB with 480MB usable space

   C. 800MB with 600MB usable space

   D. 720MB with 480MB usable space

2. Jeremy is installing Windows NT Server to an unformatted hard disk on an Intel-based system using the three setup disks. Which of the following are true about the file systems available? (Choose all that apply.)

   A. He can choose to use FAT or NTFS.

   B. The setup will initially format the partition as FAT.

   C. He can choose FAT32, NTFS, or HPFS.

   D. Only NTFS partitions are supported.

3. You have a user with Windows 95 who wishes to upgrade to Windows NT Workstation 4.0. What can they do to avoid reinstalling all their Windows applications?

   A. Install Windows NT Workstation on a different partition.

   B. Install Windows NT Workstation in a different directory on the same partition.

   C. Install Windows NT Workstation in the original Windows 95 directory.

   D. There's nothing they can do; they must reinstall their applications.

4. Your company has just merged with another local company of the same size, and their employees are moving to your site. You both have about 20,000 employees, and you've been using the Master Domain model. What do you need to do to add them to your company's domain infrastructure?

   A. Double the number of BDCs in your master domain.

   B. Create another master domain with their employees similar to the one you have, adding trust relationships to create the Multiple Master Domain model.

   C. Promote a BDC in your master domain to be the PDC in a new master domain, split the user accounts alphabetically (A – M and N – Z) between the master domains (deleting the accounts that don't belong in that domain), and add the new users according to this Multiple Master Domain model.

   D. Hope that enough employees will be laid off during the merger so that you can fit the remaining ones in your current domain model.

5. A Windows NT member server with Preferred Master Browser set is booted. The domain it belongs to is located on a LAN (no subnets), and the PDC is operating normally. What will happen? (Choose all that apply.)

   A. The system will force a browser election.

   B. The system will become the master browser.

   C. The system will not become the master browser.

   D. By default, the system will be a browser.

6. Jill changed the logon script on the PDC in the export directory yesterday, but sometimes when she logs on, she's still using the old logon script. She checked, and replication to every BDC is working correctly, and their import directories show the new script. What has she forgotten?

   A. It takes time for the cached logon scripts on workstations to expire.

   B. She must set up replication from the PDC back to itself.

   C. The domain controllers must be rebooted for the change to take effect.

   D. She must set up the REPL$ share on the export directory.

7. When you open Network Neighborhood on a domain workstation that is not a browser, where does your computer get the information about workgroups and domains to display?

   A. It searches the network for all workgroups and domains.

   B. It gets the information from the PDC or Master Browser.

   C. It gets the information from a Backup Browser, which received it from a Master Browser.

   D. You can't use Network Neighborhood if your computer isn't a browser.

8. Daniel has been receiving complaints that computers in his domain can't see some other computers in the domain, and has determined that the various subnets aren't visible to each other. Which of the following probably apply to his situation?

   A. There is not a Master Browser for each subnet.

   B. Some Backup Browsers are not functioning.

   C. The PDC is offline and needs to be rebooted, or a BDC promoted.

   D. All computers have MaintainServerList set to No.

9. Your network uses the Single Domain model, with three Windows NT servers and 50 Windows NT workstations. Darren is a member of the Graphics group, while John is a member of the CAD group. Darren needs access to John's designs, while John needs access to Darren's graphics. It is your job to make this possible. How many trusts will you need to implement?

   A. A single one-way trust

   B. Two one-way trusts

   C. A two-way trust

   D. No trusts are needed

10. Which of the following file types is valid for a user profile? (Choose all that apply.)

A. .PRO

B. .POL

C. .MAN

D. .DAT

E. ROAM

11. You have an employee who is leaving the company. You don't want him to be able to log onto the domain any longer, and you want to prevent anyone else from using this account. Your best course of action is to:

A. Delete the account.

B. Disable the account.

C. Change the password for the account.

D. Change the account security ID.

12. Which of the following statements are true about the check box Users Must Log On In Order To Change Password in Account Policies in a domain? (Choose all that apply.)

A. When not checked, a user can change his password from any Windows NT workstation, whether it's in the domain or not, and without logging onto the domain.

B. When checked, administrators or account operators must change their passwords.

C. When checked, users must log onto the domain to change their password.

D. When not checked, it means users don't get the option to change their password (when it's expired) as they log on.

13. You have started a new domain, so that the only groups and users on the PDC are the ones set up by Windows NT during the installation. These groups and users have the default settings. A user attempts to use the Guest account, but the logon attempt fails. What is the most likely reason?

A. The Everyone group is disabled by default.

B. All of the accounts set up by Windows NT are disabled by default.

C. Only the accounts used by the server are set up by Windows NT, so no one has access but the administrator.

D. The Guest account is disabled by default.

14. Terri is setting up a temporary site with 50 Windows NT Workstation computers, which will only be networked with each other. The site will be used for a two-month project, but she must get it running as quickly as possible. Which protocol should she choose?

    A. TCP/IP
    B. IPX/SPX
    C. NetBEUI
    D. DLC

15. Norma has set up a Macintosh volume with access permissions for a particular group. She finds that some group members can access the volume and some cannot. What could be the problem?

    A. The Windows NT server is a seed router, and has not planted access seeds for some systems yet.
    B. Access to Microsoft networks has been blocked on some systems.
    C. The users having problems are trying to use their domain username and password to access the volume.
    D. The users having problems don't have the group in question set as their primary group.

16. You have decided to install Internet Information Server on your Windows NT server. Which services does IIS support? (Choose all that apply.)

    A. World Wide Web
    B. Gopher
    C. VRML Chat
    D. FTP
    E. News Services

17. What specification allows you to bind several protocols to a single network adapter, or a single protocol to multiple network adapters?

    A. PPTP
    B. PGP
    C. ISO
    D. NDIS

18. Your network uses NWLink as its protocol. You have just installed a new Windows NT server on the network, and it has trouble communicating with the network. You check the other computers, and find that they have no problem interacting with the network. What must you do to fix this problem?

    A. Change the IPX address.

    B. Change the packet type to that used by the network.

    C. Change the frame type to that used by the network.

    D. Change the subnet mask.

19. Brenda's system is unable to resolve the name www.microsoft.com. What could be the problem? (Choose all that apply.)

    A. Her system can't find the DNS server.

    B. Microsoft's network is currently unreachable from there.

    C. There's no WINS entry.

    D. There's no entry in her DNS server for www.microsoft.com.

20. Your network uses TCP/IP as its transport protocol. You have manually entered the IP address into your host machine. What other information is required?

    A. Computer name

    B. Subnet mask

    C. Subnet address

    D. MAC address

21. What protocol does PING use to test connectivity to a target system?

    A. ICMP

    B. RCMP

    C. TCP

    D. IP

22. You decide to download the latest service pack for Windows NT Server 4.0 from Microsoft. You access their web site and start the download. Which protocol is being used to download the service pack?

    A. TCP
    B. IP
    C. FTP
    D. HTTP

23. Which of the following are included with Windows NT Server? (Choose all that apply.)

    A. Client Services for NetWare (CSNW)
    B. Gateway Services for NetWare (GSNW)
    C. File and Print Services for NetWare (FPNW)
    D. Directory Service Manager for NetWare (DSMN)
    E. Migration Tool for NetWare

24. Ted just purchased Microsoft Services for NetWare to run on his Windows NT server. Which of the following can he now use there? (Choose all that apply.)

    A. NWLink
    B. CSNW
    C. GSNW
    D. FPNW
    E. DSMN

25. You are setting up a Windows NT server to use NWLink. You want to configure it to use the default frame type for a NetWare 2.x server. Which frame type will you choose?

    A. 802.2
    B. 802.3
    C. 802.5
    D. 802.3 SNAP

26. You have installed GSNW on a Windows NT server. Some users on the network need to use a printer located on a NetWare print server. Which application should you use to set up this printer so users on the Microsoft network can access it?

    A. GSNW

    B. FPNW

    C. Printers in Control Panel

    D. Nothing. You have to do all the work from the NetWare side of the network.

27. Julie is performing a migration from NetWare to Windows NT Server, but is concerned as to what the Migration Tool will preserve. Which of the following will Migration Tool preserve during a migration? (Choose all that apply.)

    A. User account information

    B. Effective rights on directories and files

    C. Passwords

    D. Logon scripts

28. Expansions to your network require you to connect two separate LAN segments. Which of the following would you use?

    A. Router

    B. Bridge

    C. BOOTP Relay Agent

    D. Gateway

29. You want to have dynamic routing on your TCP/IP network. You decide to install the RIP for IP service, but find that it doesn't work after the service has started. What is the problem?

A. You need to check Enable IP Forwarding from the Routing tab of TCP/IP Properties.
B. You need to use the ROUTE ADD command to add a routing table.
C. You need to check Enable Routing from the Routing tab of RIP For IP Properties.
D. You need to stop the service, then specify that routing is enabled when you restart it.

**30.** Users of your network want to access its resources through the Internet, but security remains a concern. What can you do to provide Internet access, yet still maintain security?

A. Use PPP
B. Use SLIP
C. Use RIP
D. Use PPTP

**31.** Which of the following is a benefit of static routing?

A. Changes to the network are reflected in the routing table automatically
B. Reduced network traffic
C. Decreased administration
D. Increased broadcasts

**32.** Bob has two systems running Windows NT Workstation in his office. How many incoming RAS connections could he support with both of them?

A. 2
B. 20
C. 256
D. 512

**33.** Barbara has borrowed Bill's laptop to dial in to the RAS server over the weekend. It works fine for Bill, and Barbara could use the laptop with the NIC at work, but Barbara discovers she can't log on when dialing in. What's
the problem?

  A. Barbara is not using the modem correctly.

  B. Barbara's account isn't in the Domain Users group.

  C. Barbara's account hasn't been granted dial-in permission.

  D. Only Bill may dial in using that computer.

**34.** Which media is supported by RAS for WAN connections? (Choose all that apply.)

  A. X.25

  B. ISDN

  C. PSTN

  D. X.12

  E. RX-232

**35.** Your office has several phone lines running into it. You've heard there is a way to increase the bandwidth by using multiple phone lines with RAS. What else will you need to do to accomplish this? (Choose all that apply.)

  A. Install the modems

  B. Use PPP

  C. Use PPP-MP

  D. Use Sonet

**36.** You are using RAS to connect to an ISP that uses older UNIX servers. Which of the following must be installed on your computer to connect with the ISP? (Choose all that apply.)

  A. TCP/IP

  B. PPP

  C. SLIP

  D. Client Services for UNIX

**37.** Ann is using her web browser to get files at an anonymous FTP site. What protocol is her web browser using to do this?

A. HTTP

B. HTML

C. Gopher

D. FTP

**38.** The World Wide Web is based on which of the following protocols?

A. HTTP

B. HTML

C. FTP

D. TCP/IP

**39.** You are at home, and want to administer your web site. Which application can you use to manage IIS from a remote location, through an Internet connection?

A. Internet Service Manager

B. Internet Service Manager (HTML)

C. Server Manager

D. FTP Service

**40.** Which of the following is text based, and can provide links to other sites? (Choose all that apply.)

A. HTML

B. FTP

C. CGI

D. Gopher

**41.** Your Windows NT server is showing slower performance since you installed a new protocol that has high overhead, and is rarely used. What can be done to improve performance?

A. The new protocol needs to be raised in the binding order.

B. The new protocol needs to be reinstalled.

C. The new protocol hasn't been broken in yet.

D. The new protocol needs to be lowered in the binding order.

**42.** You notice that the application server in your domain is sluggish. You want to view the information on memory and CPU utilization. Which application will supply this information, and is the fastest to access?

A. Server Manager

B. Performance Monitor

C. Task Manager

D. Network Monitor

**43.** Which is the most common bottleneck you will encounter on Windows NT Server?

A. Memory

B. Hard disk

C. Network

D. CPU

**44.** You want to view the %Network Utilization counters in Performance Monitor, but you can't see them. What must you do?

A. Install Network Monitor Agent.

B. Install Network Agent.

C. Run NETPERF.

D. Install NetBEUI.

**45.** Out of the box, how many processors does Windows NT Server 4.0 support?

    A. 2

    B. 4

    C. 16

    D. 32

**46.** Your PDC goes down, and cannot be used on the network. You still need to make account changes that can only be done on a PDC. What can you do?

    A. Promote a workstation to a PDC.

    B. Promote a member server to a PDC.

    C. Promote a BDC to a PDC.

    D. Demote the PDC.

**47.** Which utility would you use to create an emergency repair disk?

    A. Disk Administrator

    B. RDISK

    C. ERD

    D. Disk Manager

**48.** You want to use RDISK to back up user accounts and file security. How will you do this?

    A. Run RDISK, and press U from the menu.

    B. Run RDISK /S.

    C. Run RDISK /U.

    D. Run RDISK /SOS.

**49.** One of two disks in a mirror set fails. What will you do?

    A. Break the mirrored set, and then create a new mirrored set.

    B. Replace the failed disk. The information will regenerate automatically.

    C. Break the mirrored set, replace the failed disk, and then create a new mirrored set.

    D. Create a new mirrored set.

**50.** You have decided to set up a computer on your network as an export server. This server will replicate files from its %SYSTEMROOT%SYSTEM32\ REPL\EXPORT directory to an import server. Which of the following can be set up as this kind of server? (Choose all that apply.)

    A. PDC

    B. BDC

    C. Member server

    D. NT workstation

    E. NetWare server

# Test Yourself: Server in the Enterprise Practice Exam I Answers

To pass the Server in the Enterprise exam, you need to answer 40 questions correctly. We've provided explanations of the answers so you can review the questions you missed. How did you do?

1. **A.** Windows NT Server can mirror two drives on the same controller for greater availability. While striping with parity also provides availability, it requires at least three partitions. Duplexing is mirroring across two controllers, but the question stipulated only one. Striping without parity not only doesn't provide higher availability, it decreases it by providing another point of failure.

2. **C.** The user added the global FARGO\Domain Users group, but still needs to add the global UBETCHA\Domain Users group, which should now be visible because of the trust relationship. Global groups can't belong to other global groups, so answer A is impossible. There was no global group FARGO\UPRINTSURE, and local groups are used to control access to resources, so answer B is out. The trust relationship is correct; the trust would only need to be made two-way to allow access to resources in UBETCHA by FARGO users as well.

3. **C.** There is one and only one PDC for every domain. However, a domain can survive without an active PDC; logon requests will be serviced by a BDC, if one is present. Logons are still possible without a domain controller, if the username and password are still in the cache of the workstation to which you're logging on.

4. **B, C.** Backups are your primary protection against losing a file due to accidental deletion. The mirror volume will dutifully delete the file at the same time as the primary, and the stripe set with parity will also keep a coherent picture of the partition with the file deleted. No UNDELETE utility is available with Windows NT, though some third-party companies may have implemented something along these lines. Basically, the only thing mirroring would protect you from is a single disk failure.

You may have some protection with the Recycle Bin, depending on your settings and how the file was deleted. As long as the "Do not move files to the Recycle Bin. Remove files immediately when deleted" check box is not checked, deleted files will be stored until certain events occur. You can configure the maximum size of the Recycle Bin from its Properties dialog box, shown in the next illustration. When the maximum size of the Recycle Bin is reached, the oldest files stored here are purged. You can also delete the files manually. If neither of these actions or events occurs, then you can restore the deleted files.

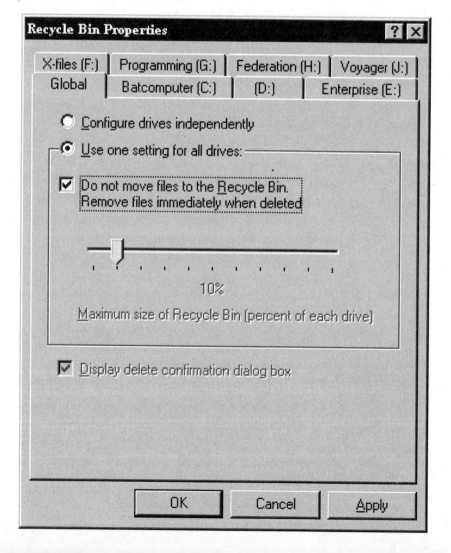

5. **B.** Per server will allow you to switch over later to the per seat option. You are allowed a one-time-only switch from per server to per seat licensing. You cannot switch from per seat licensing to per server.

6. **B, C.** Any Windows NT server can export, although it's usually a PDC replicating logon scripts to BDCs. Since an export server is mainly for distributing seldom-modified files, it's not a good candidate for distributing database files. The REPL$ share is created so that the import computers can access the area to be exported. (Note: share names ending in a "$" aren't browsable, so don't expect to see them in your network neighborhood.)

7. **A, B.** The Pulse parameter is how many seconds between pulses sent when there have been updates. Reducing the pulse time from five minutes to one minute would keep the BDCs in synchronization more often. The default for PulseConcurrency is 20, so increasing it to 24 would allow all 24 BDCs to synchronize at the same time, instead of possibly four of them having to wait. The Randomize setting controls the maximum BDC back-off time that a BDC will wait after it gets a pulse. Increasing it from its default of one second would make some BDCs wait longer to request synchronization. It probably wouldn't be a good idea to reduce it to zero with 24 BDCs, though, because the instantaneous load on the PDC would be greater. If Stephen found that his PDC was having trouble handling the load when synchronizing the domain, he might increase Randomize without adding any real delay to the process. Also, remember that these systems were all on the same LAN, so network bandwidth should not be an issue.

8. **A.** This behavior is normal. Once a system has been up for a while, it only announces what it's sharing every twelve minutes. The Master Browser won't remove it from the Browse List until it has missed three consecutive announcements. So, about half the time (depending on how close it was to its next announcement before it went down) it would still be in the Master Browser's browse list half an hour later. Add to this the delay of Backup Browsers only getting updates every 15 minutes, and you can see that the system would more often than not still be shown in the Network Neighborhood 30 minutes after it crashed.

9. **C.** In Microsoft terminology, the printer is the software configuration and drivers, and the print device is the physical printer. So you send print jobs to a printer, not a print queue, and they print out on a print device, not a printer. In Microsoft terminology, a printer is software. This distinction will help when reading Help files or on the exam, but you shouldn't expect others to adhere to these definitions, since the generic terms and meanings were in common usage years before Microsoft sold its first operating system.

10. **B, E.** Local groups may contain local users, domain users, and global groups. Global groups cannot contain local groups. Local groups also cannot contain local users from another system (they aren't visible to this system). Neither local nor global groups can be used as e-mail distribution lists.

11. **D.** Assigning the temp workers their own usernames allows better auditing, and you certainly don't want to give them full access if they only need Read access. You should not depend on their absence after their employment ends as equivalent to disabling or removing their accounts.

12. **A, B, D, E.** The domains must trust each other to have their respective Domain Users global groups visible to the other domain. Then permissions must be set allowing the resources to be shared with those users. Answer C would effectively make it possible for administrators in the Marketing domain to administer the Sales domain, which was not a goal.

13. **B, C.** PETER and PAUL have a two-way trust, so their users may log onto a system in either domain. However, trusts are not transitive, so PETER trusting PAUL trusting MARY doesn't mean PETER trusts MARY. Since PAUL trusts MARY, users in domain MARY may also log onto a system in domain PETER. Notice in the next illustration that each domain has one arrow pointing at it, and its users may log onto exactly one other domain.

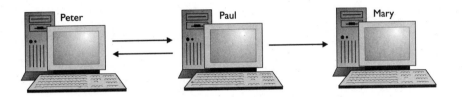

**14. A.** User Manager for Domains is used to set up trust relationships. You do this by choosing Trust Relationships from the Policies menu. No other program offers the options for setting up such a relationship between domains.

**15. B, C, D.** NetBEUI isn't routable, so he can't use a router. A bridge will forward all packets with a destination address not on the same segment as the sender. A hub just connects multiple segments, and a switch is similar in function to a hub with a bridge on every port.

**16. D.** Dynamic Host Configuration Protocol (DHCP) servers aren't merely limited to assigning IP addresses. You can also use them to configure settings like the default gateway, DNS server, and WINS server that a host computer will use (based on the IP address they receive).

**17. A.** NTFS is the only file system supported by Windows NT that can store Macintosh files.

**18. B.** If your ISP offers DHCP, and you plan to have your IP address and subnet mask issued this way, the only thing you need to configure is the DNS tab. This will enable you to resolve fully qualified domain names to IP addresses off the Internet.

**19. B.** The subnet mask of 255.255.255.0 equates to an entire Class C network (though it could be a subnet of a larger network). Since the x.y.z.0 address is reserved for the network, and x.y.z.255 is reserved for the broadcast address, that leaves x.y.z.1-254, or 254 possible valid node addresses. In fact, the number of valid nodes for any subnet will always be a power of two minus two. The other answers are obviously wrong simply because they're powers of 2.

**20. B, D.** While a successful telnet connection would tell you the node is reachable, not all nodes run telnet daemons or servers (Microsoft Windows systems, for example). PING will send back packets, and TRACERT will trace the route packets take to their destination. Both will serve to see if a node is reachable, and TRACERT will also tell you where the failure is if the node isn't reachable. It's always possible that a firewall or router filtering may foil these methods, so sometimes the best test is the application itself. Netstat only shows connections to the current system.

**21. C.** UDP is a connectionless, lightweight protocol. It does not guarantee delivery of a packet, but is useful in cases where the data being sent isn't vital – such as browsing, WINS and DNS name resolution, and logons. TCP is a connection-oriented protocol that would be overkill for the things UDP is used for, and IP is used for packet deliveries.

**22. C.** NSLOOKUP is used to display information about DNS servers. If you want to see the DNS servers on a particular domain, you can do that with this utility by typing **NSLOOKUP type=ns** *<domain name>*.

**23. D.** While 256 numbers are available, two of these are reserved. Addresses ending in a zero (for example, 223.128.115.0) define the entire network. An address containing 255 (for example, 223.128.115.255) is used for broadcasting messages to the entire network. Numbers that fall in between 0 and 254 can be issued to a host, so long as you're registered to use them, or not interacting with the Internet.

**24.** **A, B.** An NTGATEWAY group must be created on any NetWare servers that will be used, and a user account must be created that is a member of this group. This account must have Supervisor access. Then, Pete can configure the gateway services from any account with Administrator access on the Windows NT server. He'll need to specify the account created on the NetWare server and the password used, when he configures the gateway.

**25.** **A.** Migration Tool for NetWare cannot migrate passwords unless a mapping file is used. This is because passwords are encrypted in NetWare.

**26.** **B.** Client Services for NetWare is included with Windows NT Workstation. It doesn't pass requests through the server, as is done with Windows NT servers running GSNW. Workstations can connect to the NetWare network, keeping the Windows NT server from being bogged down.

**27.** **A.** The 802.2 frame type is an industry standard, and the default frame type for all versions of NetWare, including version 3.12 and after.

**28.** **A.** Routers can choose from multiple paths. If a route is inactive, it can choose from alternative paths (if they're available) to deliver the packets.

**29.** **D.** Gateways are used to connect two different segments that use different protocols. The gateway receives a packet from one side of the network, translates it into the protocol used by the other side of the network, and then delivers it through a second modem in the multihomed computer. Windows NT Server can act as a gateway on networks.

**30.** **B.** Because RIP dynamically exchanges routing information, the other routers have relatively up-to-date information on what paths are available to deliver a packet. If one path becomes unavailable, the router will attempt delivering the packets via an alternative route.

**31. B.** Dynamic routing is added when RIP is installed on your server. RIP dynamically shares information about routes and changes to the network with other routers that use dynamic routing. Windows NT Server 4.0 is the first release to offer dynamic routing.

**32. A, C, D.** To install TCP/IP on a routed network, you must supply the IP address, subnet mask and default gateway. If TCP/IP were to be installed on a non-routed network, you wouldn't need to specify the default gateway. This is true because all packets would be sent to the same network, and so would never need to go to a default gateway for delivery to another network address.

**33. A,C.** By using a null modem cable and RAS, you can connect a laptop computer to your Windows NT server, and transfer information between the two. The laptop can not only access information on the server, but also participate as if it were actually part of the network.

**34. B.** The DEVICE.LOG contains dialog information between the RAS server and the modem. Information such as initialization strings and response strings are recorded to this file.

**35. C.** When RAS has been set to receive incoming calls, it locks the COM port, making it impossible to use any other communication devices.

**36. D.** The device log is stored in the WINNT/SYSTEM32/RAS directory, and contains information on dialogs between RAS and the modem.

**37. A, B, D.** Historically, the File Transfer Protocol was used to transfer files on the Internet. When Gopher was developed, it could also transfer text or binary files. Now, HTTP servers can transfer text or binary files as well. With the advent of HTTP, Gopher is seldom used, although FTP is still popular, primarily due to its bi-directional nature (both sending and receiving files). UUCP (UNIX to UNIX Copy Protocol) isn't an Internet protocol, and isn't supported by IIS.

**38.** **B.** DNS maps fully qualified domain names (FQDN) to the four-octet IP address, usually written in dotted-decimal notation (for example, 141.225.1.24). An example of a MAC address is a six-byte Ethernet address, usually written in dashed-hexadecimal notation (for example, 02-A9-2B-96-4C-D0), and has nothing to do with TCP/IP, except as a data-link layer for its network layer protocol.

**39.** **C.** Since you now have your original web server, and two virtual servers, you must have three IP addresses associated with you network adapter card. This way, no matter which server a user attempts to access, he or she will connect to the adapter card on Windows NT Server.

**40.** **B.** When IIS is installed it creates the IUSER_COMPUTERNAME account, and automatically makes it a member of the Domain User group.

**41.** **A.** Any HTML documents you plan to publish to your intranet or on the Internet through IIS must be placed in the WWW directory that you specify during installation of IIS.

**42.** **A.** Server Manager allows you to view current connections, the idle time on connections, and share names in use.

**43.** **C.** By changing the server optimization to Maximize Throughput For Network Applications, the server is better able to support distributed applications. This setting supports 64 or more users, and is best for applications that use memory caching.

**44.** **C.** The normal value for priority level, starting in Windows NT 4.0, is 8. Before Windows NT 4.0, the normal level was 7. To change the foreground application's priority boost to 10, you would move the slider bar to the Maximum setting.

**45.** **A.** The default size of PAGEFILE.SYS is the amount of physical RAM, which in this case is 50MB. If Windows NT Server has less than 22MB of physical RAM, the PAGEFILE.SYS is 22MB or the amount of available space, whichever is less. (This is different from Windows NT Workstation, where the optimum size of PAGEFILE.SYS is the amount of available space plus 12MB. Do not get these two confused on the Enterprise exam.)

**46.** **D.** Disk duplexing is the same as disk mirroring, except that two disk controllers are used. If one of these controllers fails, you just need to replace the controller. Nothing has happened to the disks; it was the controller that failed.

**47.** **D.** The four phases of the Windows NT Server boot process are: initial, boot, kernel, and logon.

**48.** **C.** A boot disk allows you to boot into Windows NT. It is not the same as an ERD. After formatting a floppy in Windows NT 4.0, just copy NTLDR, NTDETECT.COM, BOOT.INI, and (if it exists) BOOTSEC.DOS or NTBOOTDD.SYS onto the disk. You can now use it to boot into NT.

**49.** **A.** The /SOS switch, when added to the entry for Windows NT in the BOOT.INI file, will cause the name of each driver to display on the screen as it is loaded.

**50.** **A, B, C.** Event Viewer can view the SYSTEM.LOG, SECURITY.LOG, and the APPLICATION.LOG to view logged information regarding system events.

# Test Yourself: Server in the Enterprise Practice Exam 2 Answers

To pass the Server in the Enterprise exam, you need to answer 40 questions correctly. We've provided explanations of the answers so you can review the questions you missed. How did you do?

**1.** **C.** All of the answers represent valid RAID 5 sets formed from the disks in question. Answer A uses all six, answer B uses the five with the most free space, answer C the four with the most free space, and answer D the three with the most free space.

Stripe sets must be formed with equal-sized areas. So the maximum partition space for all disks included in the set is the amount of free space on the disk with the least free space available. With RAID 5, the usable region is reduced by the size of the parity data, which is equivalent to the space contributed by one drive in the set. The next table shows the calculations.

| | Disk 1 | Disk 2 | Disk 3 | Disk 4 | Disk 5 | Disk 6 | Total | Usable |
|---|---|---|---|---|---|---|---|---|
| **All Six** | 100MB | 100MB | 100MB | 100MB | 100MB | 100MB | 600MB | 500MB |
| **Top Five** | | 120MB | 120MB | 120MB | 120MB | 120MB | 600MB | 480MB |
| **Top Four** | | | 200MB | 200MB | 200MB | 200MB | 800MB | 600MB |
| **Top Three** | | | | 240MB | 240MB | 240MB | 720MB | 480MB |

**2.** **A, B.** While Jeremy has a choice of FAT or NTFS, the setup will always format the partition as FAT. If NTFS is selected, the FAT partition is automatically converted to NTFS during the reboot. Windows NT 4.0 doesn't support HPFS (though it was supported in earlier versions), and there is currently no support for FAT32, either. If Jeremy were installing Windows NT on a Digital Alpha, the system partition would have to be FAT.

3. **D.** You can't upgrade Windows 95 to Windows NT 4.0. You might as well be installing it over DOS, and all Wndows applications must be reinstalled. There is an upgrade path from earlier versions of Windows and Windows NT 3.51.

4. **B.** Increasing the number of BDCs doesn't allow the accounts database to grow beyond 40MB. About the best you can hope for is to create a Multiple Master model by adding another master domain with the other employees. While answer C might seem to be easier to maintain later, it's just not possible to perform the first step, promoting a BDC in one domain to be PDC of another. If you're holding out for answer D, chances are yours will be one of the jobs eliminated.

5. **A, C, D.** Anytime a system with Preferred Master Browser is started, it starts an election. Since the PDC always wins such an election if it's available, the system will not become the master browser. Since Windows NT servers have MaintainServerList set to Yes by default, it will browse by default. You'd expect this setting anyway if someone went to the trouble of setting IsDomainMaster to True.

6. **B.** Jill probably manually copied the script files from the export area to the import area when she set them up. Since the logon script that executes is in the import directory, replication on the PDC itself must be configured to automatically copy the files from the export directory to the import directory. To get things corrected quickly, she should do the manual copy again, and then set up the PDC import replication. As for the other options, workstations don't cache logon scripts, domain controllers don't need to be rebooted to serve new scripts, and the REPL$ share is created by the service when it's started.

7. **C.** A computer gets the browse list from a Backup Browser, which periodically receives it from the Master Browser, which may, in turn, get information from a Domain Master Browser about other Master Browsers, if the domain spans subnets. In a technical sense, browsing is something computers do, not what you do when you open Network Neighborhood to

see the results of browsing. Browsing isn't so much a process of finding computers with shared resources as it is of listening to the announcements broadcast by those computers advertising those resources.

**8.** **C.** The PDC is always the Domain Master Browser, which makes information from Master Browsers in each subnet available to the others. Because broadcasts don't go through routers, LMHOST files are used to make the transfer of this information possible. While browser elections will quickly make sure that there is a Master Browser in each subnet, there is no such mechanism for Domain Master Browser. To make the entire domain browsable again, there must be an active PDC. Preferably, the current PDC should be brought online. If that's not possible, a BDC should be promoted.

**9.** **D.** Since these users are both part of the Single Domain model, no trusts are needed. Trusts are used when a domain needs to access resources in another domain, but aren't required when only one domain exists.

**10.** **C, D.** NTUSER.DAT is the default name. You can make it a mandatory profile by renaming it to NTUSER.MAN.

**11.** **B.** By disabling the account you can still audit attempts to use the account, so that's better than deleting it. Just changing the password might lead another administrator to change it as a forgotten password, unaware that the account should no longer be used. You can't change the Security ID, and wouldn't want to even if you could.

**12.** **A, C.** It's surprising how many people don't know that answer A is not only possible, but is, in fact, what this check box is all about. If you give the "three-finger salute" (CTRL+ALT+DEL) on a Windows NT system, one of the options available is "Change Password". After selecting that, you can type in the name of a domain instead of just using the names available in the drop box. You still need to know the current password to the account, so all you gain by checking the box is that the computer in question has to be set up to log onto the domain, and then log on before changing the password. If you wanted answer B, you'd use the "User Cannot Change Password" check box on the user's individual account.

13. **D.** The Guest account is disabled by default when Windows NT is installed. The only other user account created during installation is the Administrator account. It is up to the Administrator to enable the Guest account, or set up accounts for individual users.

14. **C.** Terri can't beat NetBEUI for its easy setup. There's really nothing to configure apart from the computer name, and it works just fine in this situation. IPX is only slightly more difficult to set up, but why bother with the frame type and network ID issues unless you have to? TCP/IP would require the most work, assigning and configuring addresses and subnet masks on each computer manually. DLC isn't an option for connecting Windows computers with each other.

15. **D.** Only the user's primary group may be used for access to Macintosh volumes. So if the users are members of a group, but it's not set as their primary group, they still won't be able to access the volume. Providing services for Macintosh is the whole reason setting a primary group, as it doesn't matter for anything else in a Windows NT domain. As for answer C, users *do* use their domain credentials to access the Macintosh shares. Answer A and answer B are nonsense.

16. **A, B, D.** Internet Information Server supports World Wide Web, FTP and Gopher services. It is a World Wide Web server that can be used on the Internet or on an intranet.

17. **D.** NDIS (Network Device Interface Specification) allows multiple protocols to be bound to a single Network Interface Card (NIC), or a single protocol to be bound to multiple NICs. This allows you to use such protocols as NWLink, TCP/IP and NetBEUI on a computer with a single network adapter.

**18. C.** If a new computer is the only one on a NWLink network having trouble interacting with the network, then the problem is probably the frame type. On the new computer, the frame type is set wrong, or may be set to Auto. Auto does not mean that it will use all frame types. If it is set to Auto, it will configure itself to use the first frame type it encounters.

**19. A, B.** If her system can't reach the DNS server, or her DNS server can't reach Microsoft's, then the translation won't happen. WINS is not used, and her DNS server shouldn't list nodes outside her domain other than by referral to an authoritative server.

**20. B.** The IP address and subnet mask are required when manually configuring TCP/IP. The IP address identifies the computer on the network, while the subnet mask allows the computer to determine if a packet is for the subnet this computer is on, or a different subnet. If the packet is for a different subnet, the computer sends it to the default gateway (which is the third piece of information required for the TCP/IP configuration).

**21. A.** PING uses ICMP to send echo request packets to a destination host. After these packets are sent out, the system waits up to one second for a reply. Using this utility, you can test the connectivity to another host computer.

**22. C.** When you transfer a file with TCP/IP from one computer to another, you use the File Transfer Protocol (FTP). Even though you're accessing the web site using HTTP, the transfer itself is taking place with FTP.

**23. B, E.** Client Services for NetWare is included with Windows NT Workstation, not Server. The Gateway Services for NetWare acts as both client and gateway, and is included. Both FPNW and DSMN are add-on products for Windows NT Server. The Migration Tool for NetWare, which helps in migrating from NetWare to Windows NT, is also included in Windows NT Server.

**24.** **A, C, D, E.** NWLink provides the IPX/SPX protocol, and is a prerequisite for Gateway Services for NetWare. GSNW is also a prerequisite for either of the Microsoft Services for NetWare products: FPNW and DSMN. Client Services for NetWare is only on Windows NT Workstation.

**25.** **B.** Versions of NetWare previous to 3.12 used the 802.3 frame type. It was developed by NetWare, and is often called Raw 802.3. Because NetWare chose to break from the emerging standard of 802.2, it has resulted in frame type conflicts with networks.

**26.** **C.** Printers in Control Panel is used to manage printers from the Microsoft side of the network. This is because Printers is using GSNW to pass through all requests to access the printer. Using Printers on a Windows NT server to set up and manage a printer located on a NetWare print server is the same as setting up a printer located on a Microsoft network.

**27.** **A, B, D.** Because NetWare passwords are encrypted, you can't migrate them. The Migration Tool does, however, preserve the effective rights on directories and files, logon scripts, and user account information.

**28.** **B.** A bridge is used to connect two separate LAN segments, such as Ethernet or Token Ring. Windows NT Server can act as a bridge to connect these two different segments.

**29.** **A.** RIP for IP isn't enabled until you check the Enable IP Forwarding check box on the Routing tab of TCP/IP Properties.

**30.** **D.** The Point to Point Tunneling Protocol (PPTP) can be used on the Internet, but is a highly secure protocol.

**31.** **B.** Static routing requires changes to be made by hand to the routing table. While this is a disadvantage in that you must do the work (rather than the router doing it for you), it does reduce network traffic, since the routers don't need to communicate changes with each other. Because static routers don't broadcast changes, it results in reduced network traffic.

**32.** **A.** Windows NT Workstation allows only one RAS connection, while Windows NT Server allows up to 256. With two Workstation systems, he could have two RAS connections. If those same systems were running Server, he could have up to 512!

**33.** **C.** Every account that's allowed to dial in must be granted dial-in permission through either User Manager for Domains or the Remote Access Admin program.

**34.** **A, B, C.** RAS supports Public Switched Telephone Network (PSTN), ISDN and X.25 (an old protocol that uses packet switching) for WAN connections. It also supports PPTP. RS-232 is supported as well, but isn't actually a modem or a protocol. It is a cable for connecting two computers together, allowing them to communicate via RAS.

**35.** **A, C.** PPP-MP (Multilink) aggregates multiple data streams into a single bundle. It combines the bandwidth of ISDN channels or modems on separate phone lines into one bundle, thereby increasing the overall throughput and bandwidth.

**36.** **A, C.** Since you're connecting to the Internet, you need TCP/IP installed on your computer. This is the protocol of the Internet, and the default transport protocol of UNIX computers. Since this is an older UNIX computer, you must use SLIP. PPP is newer, and not supported by older UNIX computers.

**37.** **D.** Most web browsers, like Internet Explorer, can use several protocols. They use the Gopher protocol to talk to Gopher servers, HTTP to talk to web servers, and FTP to talk to FTP servers. Don't confuse the multi-client capabilities of browsers with the protocols or servers. Each server program speaks one protocol, although a single system can run servers of each type, as is available in IIS. The clients tend to support the protocols that preceded them. FTP was first, and FTP clients generally only use FTP. Gopher was next, so Gopher clients support both FTP and Gopher protocols. Web browsers are the new kids on the block, so they were designed to support FTP, Gopher, and HTTP.

**38.** **A.** The World Wide Web is based on the Hypertext Transfer Protocol (HTTP). It allows the transfer of documents created with the Hypertext Markup Language (HTML). File Transfer Protocol (FTP) is used to transfer programs from one computer to another, while TCP/IP is the protocol suite that HTTP is a part of.

**39.** **B.** The Internet Service Manager (HTML) allows you to administer IIS through an HTML version of Internet Service Manager.

**40.** **A, D.** Gopher is an Internet service that is older than HTML. It is text based, and can provide links to other Gopher sites. When HTTP came out, and was able to serve HTML documents, it replaced Gopher. Gopher sites still exist on the Internet.

**41.** **D.** Protocols that have high overhead, or that are rarely used, should be lowered in the binding order. Windows NT Server starts with protocols at the top of the list, and works its way down. If you lower the protocol in the binding order, Windows NT will attempt to connect with other protocols first.

42. **C.** Pressing CTRL-ALT-DEL accesses the Task Manager. It supplies information on memory and CPU utilization, and allows you to start, stop, and view applications.

43. **A.** Memory is the most common bottleneck. When memory becomes a bottleneck, this generally means that you should add more memory to your server.

44. **A.** To view the %Network Utilization counters in Performance Monitor, you must install Network Monitor Agent. These will activate the counters.

45. **B.** Out of the box, Windows NT Server 4.0 supports 4 processors. It can be upgraded to support up to 32 processors.

46. **C.** You can promote a BDC to a PDC, if your original PDC becomes unavailable. You cannot promote a member server or workstation to a PDC, however. If you did want to make a computer that was a member server into a PDC or BDC, it would require reinstalling NT.

47. **B.** RDISK is a utility that can be used to create an emergency repair disk.

48. **B.** To back up user accounts and file security with RDISK, use the /S switch.

49. **C.** If one disk in a mirrored set fails, use Disk Administrator to break the existing mirrored set, then replace the failed disk. After you've done that, go back into Disk Administrator, and create a new mirrored set.

**50.** A, B, C. Windows NT servers are the only computers that can be configured as export servers. These can be PDCs, BDCs, or Member servers.

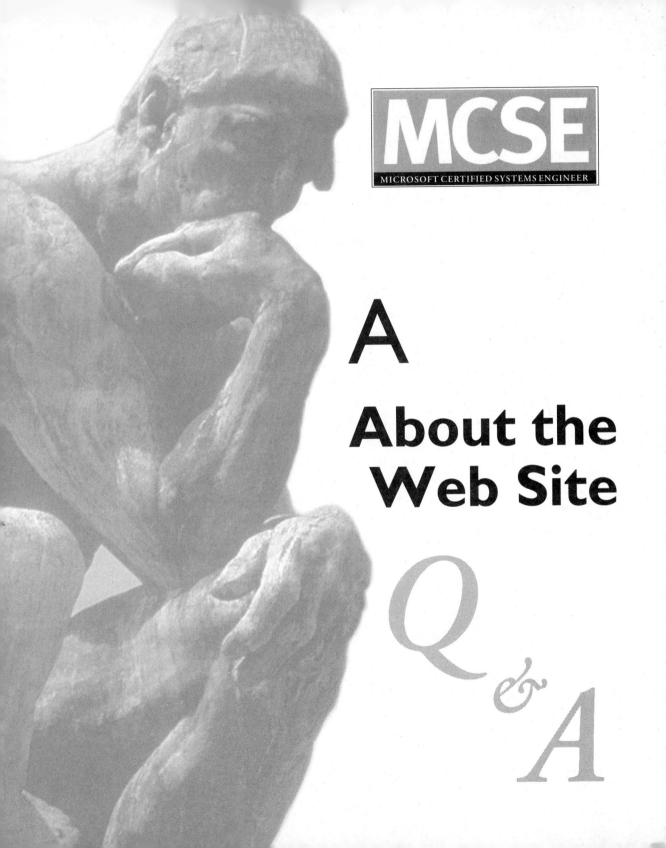

**MCSE**
MICROSOFT CERTIFIED SYSTEMS ENGINEER

# A

# About the Web Site

*Q & A*

# Access Global Knowledge Network

As you know by now, Global Knowledge Network is the largest independent IT training company in the world. Just by purchasing this book, you have also secured a free subscription to the Access Global web site and its many resources. You can find it at:

http://access.globalknowledge.com

You can log in directly at the Access Global site. You will be e-mailed a new, secure password immediately upon registering.

## What You'll Find There. . .

You will find a lot of information at the Global Knowledge site, most of which can be broken down into three categories:

### Skills Gap Analysis

Global Knowledge offers several ways for you to analyze your networking skills and discover where they may be lacking. Using Global Knowledge Network's trademarked Competence Key Tool, you can do a skills gap analysis and get recommendations for where you may need to do some more studying. (Sorry, it just may not end with this book!)

### Networking

You'll also gain valuable access to another asset: people. At the Access Global site, you'll find threaded discussions as well as live discussions. Talk to other MCSE candidates, get advice from folks who have already taken exams, and get access to instructors and MCTs.

### Product Offerings

Of course, Global Knowledge also offers its products here—and you may find some valuable items for purchase: CBTs, books, courses. Browse freely and see if there's something that could help you.

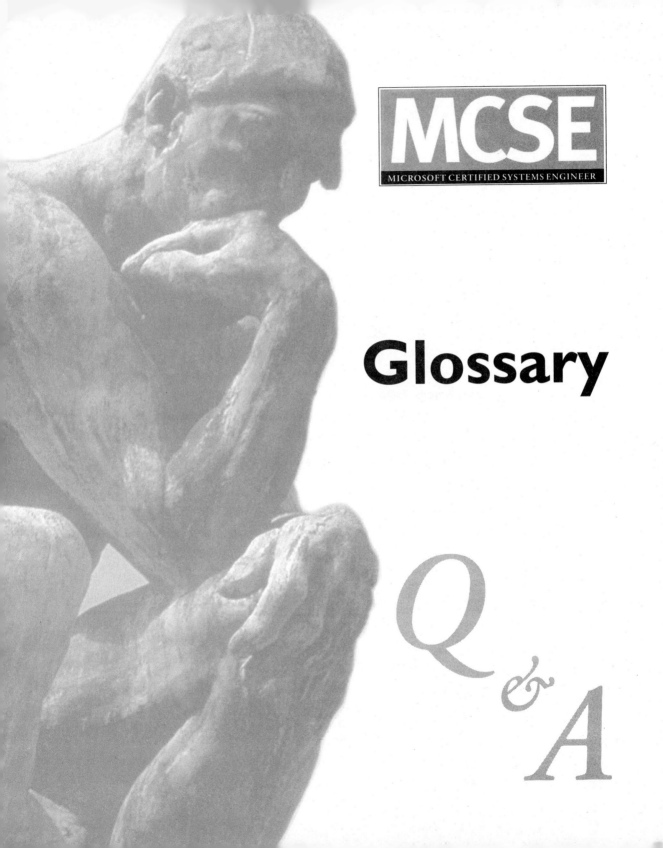

# MCSE
MICROSOFT CERTIFIED SYSTEMS ENGINEER

# Glossary

Q&A

**10Base-2**   An Ethernet topology using thin Ethernet coaxial cable, also known as Thin Ethernet or thinnet.

**10Base-5**   Also called thicknet, this form of cable was once commonly used for backbones in Ethernet networks. It is now being replaced by 10Base-T.

**10Base-T**   An Ethernet topology that uses unshielded twisted pair cable. 10Base-T has become the most popular Ethernet cable because many buildings are already wired for 10Base-T, it is inexpensive and easy to work with, and if the cable specifications are CAT5, it can transmit data at 100Mbps.

**access permissions**   Access permissions set your rights and privileges to manipulate files and directories. Depending on your permissions, you may or may not be able to copy, delete, or otherwise manipulate files and directories on the network.

**account**   An account or user account provides access to the network. It contains the information allowing a person to use the network, including username and logon specifications, password, and rights to directories and resources.

**account restrictions**   Restrictions on an account determine when and how a user gains access to the network.

**acknowledgment (ACK)**   A packet of information sent from the recipient computer to the sending computer for the purpose of verifying that a transmission has been received and confirming that it was or was not a successful transmission. Similar to a return receipt.

**active hub**  A hub device used in a star topology to regenerate and redistribute data across the LAN. Unlike a passive hub, the active hub requires electricity. See also hub, and passive hub.

**adapter**  A network adapter card, also called a network interface card, transmits data from the workstation to the cable that connects the machine to the LAN. It provides the communication link between the computer and the network. See also Network Interface Card.

**administrator account**  The account used to administer the settings on an NT Server and network. This account is created during install and has unlimited access to the server. Care must be taken when logged into a server as an administrator, because administrator access rights include the ability to shut down the server or erase critical data.

**alias**  A name used to reference a person or group on a computer system. Mail aliases are a common use of the alias feature. When an alias is used, the computer system still recognizes a person by a username, but an alias can be set so that people can send mail or other information using the alias name instead of the username.

**analog**  A continuous, non-digital data transmission usually associated with telephone communications.

**AppleTalk**  The set of network protocols used by Macintosh computers.

**archiving**  A process that allows you to move old files off the file server to preserve disk space for new files. If the old files are later needed, they can be unarchived and retrieved. Archived data can be saved to CD-ROM, WORM, or tape.

**ArcNet (Attached Resource Computer Network)**  A bus network topology that is similar to token ring, in that it uses a token to transmit data across the network. ArcNet transmits data at 2.5 Mbps and can run on coaxial, twisted pair, and fiber optic cable.

**ASCII (American Standard Code for Information Interchange)**
A representation of standard alphabetic and other keyboard characters in a computer-readable, binary format.

**Asynchronous Transfer Mode (ATM)**   A packet-switching network technology for LANs and WANs that can handle voice, video, and data transmissions simultaneously.

**ATM**   See Asynchronous Transfer Mode (ATM).

**Attachment Unit Interface**   A connector on a NIC used to connect a cable to the card. Frequently used with coaxial cable.

**attributes**   The characteristics of files and directories. On networks such as Windows NT, attributes are set by the administrator and define the rights for users and groups to manipulate files. On a stand-alone system, the main user can set file attributes. Attributes affect whether a file can be opened, copied, deleted, executed, modified, or otherwise manipulated.

**AUI**   See Attachment Unit Interface.

**back door**   Used by system administrators to access the network at an administrator's level if something happens to the network administrator's home account. This provides a means to rebuild the administrator's account or otherwise fix the network.

**back up**   The process of saving files to a separate location, usually an offline storage location, such as tape.

**backbone**   The main cable that connects file servers, routers, and bridges to the network.

**backup**   Copies all of the files on a network to some form of offline storage. Backups should be performed nightly, and full copies of the backup should be stored off-site.

**Backup Domain Controller (BDC)**   A computer that contains a backup of a domain's security policy and domain database, maintained by the NT server. Serves as a backup to the primary domain controller. A BDC is not required but is recommended.

**bad sector**   A damaged or non-working area of a hard disk. If data has been saved to that area, it cannot be accessed.

**bandwidth**   The capacity to transmit data across a communications link. Bandwidth is usually measured in bits per second (bps).

**base I/O address**   The address that identifies a hardware device to the computer.

**baseline**   The baseline captures the activity on the network on a normal day. This can be used to compare future readings for diagnostic purposes.

**BNC (British Naval Connector)**   Also known as a barrel connector, the connector type used in 10Base2 (thin Ethernet) networks to connect two cable segments, creating a longer segment.

**bootup**   The process a computer executes when powered up is known as bootup. This includes the files that initialize the hardware, and the starting of the operating system.

**bridge**   A hardware device that connects two LAN segments of either the same or different topologies.

**buffer space**   A reserved portion of RAM that provides room for the storage of incoming and outgoing data.

**bus**   A network topology that connects all computers to a single, shared cable. In a bus topology, if one computer fails, the network fails.

**cache**   An area in memory that duplicates information to provide faster access.

**CD-ROM**   A device, similar to a musical compact disc, that stores data.

**client**   A machine used to access the network.

**client/server network**   A network architecture, based on distributed processing, in which a client performs functions by requesting services from a server.

**coaxial cable**   A cable used in networks, consisting of a conductive center surrounded by a layer of insulation and a non-conductive outer layer.

**command line**   A character mode interface for computer applications that relies on commands instead of a graphical interface to process information.

**compression**   A mathematical technique that analyzes computer files in order to compress them to a smaller size. Most backup systems, and many file servers, compress files to provide increased storage capacity.

**computer virus**   A computer program built to sabotage or destroy a computer or network.

**concentrator**   A device that connects workstations to the path of the file server. Concentrators typically have 8 – 12 ports into which workstations attach.

**conventional memory**   The memory below 640K. If you have room, your LAN drivers are loaded in conventional memory.

**CSU/DSU (Channel Service Unit/Data Service Unit)**   A piece of hardware that sits between a network and a digital telephone line, to translate data between the two formats. CSU/DSUs are most commonly used to attach a network router to a T1 or other digital telephone line.

**DAT (Digital Audio Tape)**   A hardware option for tape backup. Some are 4mm while others are 8mm.

**Database Management System**   A software application that manages a database, including the organization, storage, security, retrieval, and integrity of data in a database.

**DBMS**   See Database Management System (DBMS).

**differential backup**   Backing up only the files that have changed since the last backup, this differs from a full backup, in that a full backup saves all files regardless of when they changed. A differential backup differs from an incremental backup in that archive attributes are not reset.

**directory path**   The path to a directory on a file system, including the server, volume, and other names leading to the directory.

**directory tree**   The file structure, including directory and subdirectory layout below the root directory.

**disk mirroring**   Provides redundancy by mirroring data from one hard drive to another. If a crash or other problem occurs on the active drive, Windows NT automatically begins to use the backup drive and notifies you of the switch.

**distributed-star**   A combination of a bus and star topology used by ArcNet.

**DLC (Data Link Control)**   A method that allows token ring-based workstations to connect to IBM mainframes and minicomputers. It has also been adopted by printer manufacturers to connect remote printers to print servers, which is how Windows NT uses DLC.

**DLL**   See Dynamic Link Library (DLL).

**DLT (Digital Linear Tape)**   A hardware solution for tape backup and storage that allows multiple tapes to be loaded into the system, providing unattended backups and easy access for keeping data in online storage.

**DMA (Direct Memory Addressing)**   Matches an area in memory with an area on the NIC, so that when information is written to memory, it is copied to the NIC and vice versa.

**DNS**   See Domain Name Service (DNS).

**Domain Name Service**   DNS is a hierarchical name service that translates host names to IP addresses. It is used with TCP/IP hosts.

**domain**   A set of workstations and servers, on a network, that are administered as a group.

**driver**   Coordinates the communications between hardware and the computer. For example, it is a driver that allows a LAN adapter or other card to work.

**Dynamic Host Configuration Protocol (DHCP)**   Designed by Microsoft to handle IP address ranges through temporary assignments of addresses, DHCP provides automatic IP address allocation to specific workstations.

**Dynamic Link Library (DLL)**   A module of executable code that is loaded on demand. Used in Microsoft Windows products.

**edge connector**   The portion of an expansion board inserted into an expansion slot when the card is seated in the computer. The number of pins and the width and depth of the lines differ depending on the various types of interfaces (i.e., ISA, EISA, PCI, Micro Channel).

**EIDE (Enhanced IDE)**   EIDE is a disk drive interface that can support up to four 8.4GB drives.

**EISA (Extended Industry Standard Architecture)**   A standard for the PC bus that extends the 16-bit ISA bus (AT bus) to 32 bits EISA; also provides bus mastering.

**electronic mail (e-mail)**   Mail messages transmitted electronically from one network user to another, or across the Internet.

**emergency startup disk**   Provides a bootup option for Windows NT if the server will not boot from its hard disk.

**encryption**   An algorithm that hides the contents of a message, or other file or communication, by deliberately scrambling the elements that compose the item. The item must then be decrypted to its original form before it can be read.

**Ethernet**   The most popular LAN network topology.

**event logs**   Log files containing the system events, including security and application events.

**Explorer**   The file system navigation tool for Microsoft's Windows 95 and NT 4.0 operating systems.

**FAQ (Frequently Asked Questions)**   Appear in specific areas of bulletin boards and web sites and contain answers to questions about a product or service that are frequently asked. These are used in newsgroups to cover questions that have appeared often.

**Fast Ethernet**    Ethernet provides 100 Mbps data transmission.

**FAT (File Allocation Table)**    Originally the layout of a DOS disk storage system. In Windows NT, a FAT is a NT Server volume that is accessible by DOS and that is using the DOS file storage system instead of NTFS.

**fault tolerance**    A computer system that is resistant to hardware problems and software errors is said to be fault tolerant.

**FDDI (Fiber Distributed Data Interface)**    A very fast and expensive fiber-based network access method. FDDI provides 100 Mbps network access.

**fiber-optic cable**    Instead of electrical impulses, fiber-optic cables move light. This type of cable is built around conductive elements that move light, not electricity. For most fiber-optic cables, the conductive element is most likely a form of special glass fiber, rather than copper or some other conductive metal. The beauty of fiber-optic cable is that it is immune to electronic and magnetic interference and has much more bandwidth than most electrical cable types.

**file server**    A network computer that runs the network operating system and services requests from the workstations.

**file system**    The network operating system's rules for handling and storing files.

**firewall**    A hardware or software solution that protects a computer system from external intrusion. Firewalls have become more instrumental on computer systems as access to the Internet has grown more popular.

**full backup**   A complete copy of all the data on the network. These should be run frequently, and at least one current copy should be stored off-site.

**gateway**   A device that connects two or more dissimilar computer systems. Gateways can be electronic or software devices and are becoming more common as the need for cross-platform communications increases.

**GB**   The abbreviation for gigabyte, which is treated as equivalent to a billion bytes.

**Hardware Abstraction Layer (HAL)**   A translation layer between the NT kernel and I/O system, and the actual hardware.

**HCL (Hardware Compatibility List)**   Lists all the hardware tested by Microsoft that works with NT. Check this before purchasing hardware.

**host**   A server that is accessed by clients. In a TCP/IP network, any computer connected to the network is considered a host.

**hot-swappable parts**   Parts that can be replaced without shutting down the system.

**hub**   The device used in a star topology that connects the computers to the LAN. Hubs can be passive or active. See also passive hub, active hub.

**incremental backup**   Backs up all the files that have been changed since the last backup. The file is not replaced on the backup, it is appended to the backup medium.

**interference**   Noise that disturbs the electrical signals sent across network cables.

**intruder**   Any person trying to break into a network.

**IP (Internet Protocol)**   A common protocol that sets up the mechanism for transferring data across the network. Usually seen in TCP/IP.

**IPX**   The native transport protocol for Novell's NetWare. It is also available in the Windows NT environment.

**ISA (Industry Standard Architecture)**   The bus used in most PCs since it was introduced in 1985.

**Kbps**   See kilobits per second.

**kilobits per second (Kbps)**   A data transfer speed of 1,024 bits per second.

**lag**   The slowing of network performance usually caused by increased demand for available bandwidth.

**LAN (Local Area Network)**   Consists of any two or more computers joined together to communicate within a small area, usually not larger than a single building.

**LAN driver**   Provides the information to allow the NIC to communicate with the network.

**legacy system**   An existing system that either needs updating or is no longer capable of maintaining required performance.

**load**   The amount of data present on the network. Also known as network traffic.

**log off (or log out)**   The procedure for exiting the network.

**logical printers**   Created by NT, logical printer capability allows you to set a single print definition that can be serviced by multiple physical printers.

**log on (or log in)**   The procedure for checking on to the network so that you can access files and other network information. When you have access to the network, you are said to be logged on. When you exit the network, you log out.

**loopback test**   A test that allows a NIC to talk to itself to see if it is working.

**MB**   megabyte

**Mbps (megabits per second)**   Used to measure throughput or communication speed. A communications rate of 1,048,576 bits per second.

**media filter**   Used on token ring networks to change the type of media from Type 1 (shielded twisted pair) to Type 3 (unshielded twisted pair) or vice versa.

**mirroring**   The process of duplicating data so that if one system fails, another can take its place.

**modem**   A device used to translate digital signals from the computer into analog signals that can travel across a telephone line.

**multi-disk volume**   A storage system that uses multiple hard disks connected with the OS, so that they act as a single entity with a single drive name/letter.

**multistation access units (MAUs)**   MAUs are the central hubs in a token ring LAN.

**multithreading**   The process that allows a multitasking operating system, such as Windows NT, to multitask the threads of an application.

**NDIS (Network Driver Interface Specification)**   A network device driver specification, NDIS provides hardware and protocol independence for network drivers. A benefit of NDIS is that it offers protocol multiplexing, which allows multiple protocol stacks to coexist in the same host.

**near-line backups**   These backups differ from offline backups in that they are kept on devices connected to the network for faster restoration of files. They require more effort to restore than accessing a file from a hard disk, but less effort than restoring a file from an offline backup.

**NetBEUI (NetBIOS Extended User Interface)**   A transport layer driver that is the Extended User Interface to NetBIOS. It is used by Windows NT and other operating systems to deliver information across a network. NetBEUI cannot be routed.

**NetBIOS (Networked Basic Input-Output System)**   A networked extension to PC BIOS. NetBIOS allows I/O requests to be sent and received from a remote computer.

**NetWare**   Novell's network operating system.

**network**   Two or more computers linked together so that they can communicate.

**network adapter**   See network interface card.

**network infrastructure**   The physical equipment that hooks computers into a network. This includes the cables, hubs, routers, and software used to control a network.

**Network Interface Card (NIC)**   The card that allows the computer to communicate across the network. The network cable attaches to the NIC.

**network map**   A detailed map of information about what's on the network. Includes an inventory of machines and other hardware, a map of cable layout, and other information to document the network.

**Network Operating System**   An operating system that permits and facilitates the networking of computers. Windows NT is one.

**NIC**   See network interface card (NIC).

**node**   Each device on a network is an individual node. It can be a workstation, a printer, or the file server.

**NOS**   See Network Operating System.

**NT File System (NTFS)**   The file system used by Windows NT. It supports large storage media, and file system recovery, in addition to other advantages.

**NTDETECT**   The hardware recognition program used by Windows NT.

**offline backups**   Backups that are kept offline. They are removed from the operation of the server and require the medium, usually tape, to be loaded in order to restore.

**off-site storage**   A place in a separate location from the file server, used to store backup tapes. A complete backup should always be kept off-site.

**online backups**   Backups that are stored online so that they are immediately available.

**overhead**   The control attached to packets transmitted across a network. Overhead data includes routing and error-checking information. Overhead also refers to the bandwidth used to sustain network communications.

**packet**   A unit of data transmitted across a network as a whole.

**packet burst**   Used in IPX when a packet burst-enabled source sends multiple packets across a network without waiting for an acknowledgment for each packet. Instead, one acknowledgment is sent for the group of packets.

**partition**   A logical division on a physical hard disk that is treated as though it were a separate hard disk.

**passive hub**   A hub device used in a star topology that connects machines to the network and organizes the cables, but does not regenerate or redistribute data.

**password**   The key to access the network during logon.

**patch**   A program that edits the binary code of another program to insert new functionality, add more capability, or correct a bug in the earlier release. Patches provide software updates in between full releases of the program.

**PCI (Peripheral Component Interconnect)**   A PC local bus that provides high-speed data transmission between the CPU and a peripheral device.

**peer to peer network**   A network in which any machine can serve as the server or as a client. These networks are used to allow small groups to share files and resources, including CD-ROM drives, printers, and hard drives.

**Performance Monitor**   A utility that provides performance information about your network to help you locate bottlenecks, determine which resources are too taxed, and plan upgrades to the system's capacity.

**permissions**   Sometimes called rights, permissions regulate the ability of users to access objects such as files and directories. Depending on the permissions, a user can have full access, limited access, or no access to an object.

**platform**   A type of computer system (e.g., Intel x86, or UNIX).

**Point-to-Point Protocol (PPP)**   A communications protocol that provides dial-up access to a network. It's commonly used to connect to the Internet.

**PostScript**   Defined by Adobe Systems, PostScript is a page description language. A printer must be PostScript-compatible in order to print PostScript files; otherwise, reams of garbage code prints.

**POTS (Plain Old Telephone Service)**   The standard analog telephone system, like the one used in most houses.

**PPP**   See Point-to-Point Protocol.

**preemptive multitasking**   A method of multitasking that has the capability to prioritize the order of process execution, and preempt one process with another.

**Primary Domain Controller (PDC)**   The NT Server running the master copy of the WINS service for an NT domain. It contains the domain's security policy and domain database. It handles synchronization with the Backup Domain Controller.

**print queue**   The line that handles printing requests and supplies files to the printer in their proper order. From the British word queue meaning line.

**print server**   Controls network printing and services printing requests. Print servers can be hardware devices or a software solution.

**properties**   Object descriptors set in the Windows NT naming system or Registry, depending on the type of object.

**protocol**    A set of rules of formatting and interaction, used to permit machines to communicate across a network. Networking software usually supports multiple levels of protocols. Windows NT supports several protocols, including TCP/IP and DLS.

**QIC (Quarter Inch Cartridge)**    A tape cartridge format common for backup tapes.

**RAID (Redundant Array of Inexpensive Disks)**    A disk mirroring scheme that duplicates data across several disks, creating a fault-tolerant storage system. A RAID system can maintain data integrity as long as one disk has not failed.

**RAM (Random Access Memory)**    Short-term storage memory, physically residing in the computer on memory chips. Since computer applications use RAM in their processing, the amount of RAM in a computer is a major determinant of how well the computer works.

**RAS (Remote Access Server)**    A Windows NT server configured to use the dial-up service to provide remote access.

**redirector**    Also called a requester, a redirector is software that accepts I/O requests for remote files, and then sends the files to a network service on another computer.

**Registry**    The Windows NT database that stores all information about the configuration of the network.

**Remote Access Server**    See RAS.

**Remote Access Service**    The dial-up service in Windows NT that allows users to access the network remotely by telephone lines.

**rights**   Authorizes users to perform specific actions on a network. Similar to permissions.

**ring**   A network topology that connects the computers in a circular fashion. If one computer fails, the complete network fails, so this topology is rarely used.

**root**   The top level of a directory structure, above which no references can be made.

**router**   A device that connects more than one physical network, or segments of a network, using IP routing software. As packets reach the router, the router reads them and forwards them to their destination, or to another router.

**RPC (Remote Procedure Call)**   A request sent to a computer on the network by a program, requesting the computer to perform a task.

**scaleable**   The capacity to change with the network. As requirements change, a scaleable network can grow or shrink to fit the requirements.

**script**   Used to describe programs, usually those written in an interpreted language, as opposed to a compiled language, because the instructions are formatted similar to a script for actors.

**SCSI (Small Computer System Interface)**   A high-speed interface used to connect peripherals such as hard disks, scanners, and CD-ROM drives. SCSI allows up to seven devices to be lined in a single chain.

**Security Accounts Manager (SAM)**   The application that handles the assignment of rights and permissions to users, groups, resources, and other objects in Windows NT.

**Serial Line Interface Protocol (SLIP)** A TCP/IP protocol that provides the ability to transmit IP packets over a serial link, such as a dial-up connection over a phone line.

**server** The computer running the network server software that controls access to the network.

**server mirroring** Duplicating a complete server to reduce the demand on the main server.

**services** Options loaded on computers allowing them to help each other. Services include the capability to send and receive files or messages, talk to printers, manage remote access, and look up information.

**share** A setting to make resources such as printers, CD-ROM drives, or directories available to users on the network.

**shell** A program that provides communication between a server and a client, or a user and an operating system.

**shielded twisted pair** A twisted pair cable that has foil wrap shielding between the conducting strands and the outer insulation.

**SLIP** See Serial Line Interface Protocol.

**SNA (Systems Network Architecture)** The basic protocol suite for IBM's AS/400 and mainframe computers.

**SNMP (Simple Network Management Protocol)** Used to report activity on network devices, SNMP is a popular network monitoring and control protocol.

**star** A network topology, in which separate cables connect from a central hub to individual devices.

**stateless**   The most efficient type of network communication, a protocol that needs no information about communications between sender and receiver.

**subnet masking**   Used in TCP/IP communications, the subnet mask allows the recipient of IP packets to distinguish the Network ID portion of the IP address from the Host ID portion of the address.

**swap file**   An area on a disk that allows you to temporarily save a program, or part of a program, that is running in memory.

**Switched Multimegabit Data Service (SMDS)**   SMDS is a 1.544 Mbps data service that supports many common LAN architectures.

**Synchronous Optical Network (SONET)**   A fiber-optic network communications link, SONET supports rates up to 13.22 Gbps.

**system administrator**   Manages the network. It is this person's responsibility to ensure that network functions are running smoothly—for example, that backups are complete, network traffic is running smoothly, and drive space is available when needed.

**T-1**   A widely-used digital transmission link that uses a point-to-point transmission technology with two-wire pairs. One pair is used to send, and one to receive. T-1, also written as T1, can transmit digital, voice, data, and video signals at 1.544 Mbps.

**T-3**   Designed for transporting large amounts of data at high speeds, T-3, also written as T3, is a leased line that can transmit data at 45154 Mbps.

**T-connector**   A device used in Thin Ethernet cabling to connect the cable to the NIC.

**TCP/IP (Transmission Control Protocol/Internet Protocol)**
An industry standard set of protocols used to connect computers within a network, as well as to external networks such as WANs and the Internet. TCP/IP is the most widely-used networking protocol and can be used to connect many different types of computers for cross-platform communication.

**TechNet**   The technical support CD-ROM published by Microsoft. It includes thorough information about Windows NT and other Microsoft products.

**Telnet**   A TCP/IP network service that allows a computer to connect to a host computer over the network and run a terminal session.

**template**   A template is a partially completed object, designed to help you start a task. Windows NT Server provides templates to help the new administrator configure objects and complete other tasks.

**Thick Ethernet**   See 10Base-5.

**Thin Ethernet**   See 10Base-2.

**throughput**   A measure of the rate at which data is transferred across a network measured in bits per second (bps).

**token**   An electronic marker packet, used in ArcNet and FDDI networks, that indicates which workstation is able to send data on a token ring topology.

**token ring**   A networking topology that is configured in a circular pattern and circulates an electronic token on the ring to pass data.

**topology**   The physical configuration of a network, including the types of cable used. Common topologies include bus, ring, and star.

**transceiver**    A device that allows you to connect a NIC for one medium (cable) to another medium. Most commonly used to translate thin or thick Ethernet to unshielded twisted pair.

**Transmission Control Protocol/Internet Protocol**    See TCP/IP.

**trust relationship**    Used on NT networks with multiple domains, trust relationships occur when users from one domain are given permission to access resources from another domain without having to log onto that domain explicitly.

**twisted pair**    A cable type in which conductive wires are twisted to help reduce interference. There are two types of twisted pair: shielded and unshielded.

**Uninterruptible Power Supply**    See UPS.

**unshielded twisted pair**    A twisted pair cable that does not have any shielding between the conducting strands and the outer insulation.

**UPS (Uninterruptible Power Supply)**    A battery backup system commonly used on file servers to protect them in times of power outages.

**URL (Uniform Resource Locator)**    The URL provides the address to a document on the World Wide Web.

**user account**    An account on a network designed for a particular user. Based on user account options, a person has access to specific files and services. See account.

**User Manager**    What you use to create users and groups, assign passwords, and control access rights to files, directories, and printers.

**User Profile Editor**    What you use to set several user options.

**user**   Any person who accesses the network.

**username**   A name used by a user to log on to a computer system.

**volume**   A logical division of a disk on a Windows NT file server.

**WAN (wide area network)**   While a LAN is a network where all machines are in close proximity to each other—usually in the same building—a WAN is extended over longer distances, ranging from a few miles to across the world. TCP/IP is the primary WAN protocol and was developed to provide reliable, secure data transmissions over long distances.

**Windows Internet Name Service**   See WINS.

**WINS (Windows Internet Name Service)**   The Windows NT service that provides a map between NetBIOS computer names and IP addresses. This permits NT networks to use either computer names or IP addresses to request access to network resources.

**wireless networking**   A network configured to use communication techniques such as infrared, cellular, or microwave, so that cable connections are not required.

**workgroup**   A group of users who share files and resources on a network. Members of a workgroup usually have related job functions. For example, they may be in the same department.

**workstation**   The client machine used to access a network.

**WORM (Write Once, Read Many)**   An optical storage medium that only permits you to write to it once, but allows you to read from it many times. CD-ROM drives are basically WORM devices.